CALVIN

and

CULTURE

EXPLORING A WORLDVIEW

EDITED BY

DAVID W. HALL

and

MARVIN PADGETT

P U B L I S H I N G

P.O. BOX 817 • PHILLIPSBURG • NEW JERSEY 08865-0817

Printed in the United States of America

Library of Congress Cataloging-in-Publication Data

Calvin and culture : exploring a worldview / edited by David W. Hall, Marvin Padgett.
    p. cm. -- (The Calvin 500 series)
 Includes bibliographical references and index.
 ISBN 978-1-59638-098-1 (pbk.)
 1. Calvin, Jean, 1509-1564. 2. Christianity--Philosophy. 3. Christianity and culture.
I. Hall, David W., 1955- II. Padgett, Marvin, 1944-
 BX9418.C3645 2010
 261--dc22
                        2010014257

This final volume of the Calvin 500 series is affectionately dedicated
to the next generation of worldview Christians,
especially our own children, whom we love dearly:
Megan Hall, Devon Hall, Andrew and Amanda Hall,
Steve Padgett, Heather Kennedy, and Tim Padgett

CONTENTS

FOREWORD

John Calvin was not only a theologian. He was trained as a legal scholar and formulated laws for the city of Geneva. He reflected much on the role of the state. He was active in the development of worship music for the church. He founded an academy that taught subjects in many fields of culture. But theology, teaching Scripture, was always the main thing for him. His other activities were, for all their general importance, side interests for him personally. Those side interests, in themselves, would not have justified a book titled *Calvin and Culture*.

The reason for such a book is found in the nature of Calvin's theology. That theology describes not only God's way of saving sinful people, but a worldview significantly different from any human philosophy or other religion.

As a worldview, Calvin's theology is comprehensive. It affects all fields of human study and activity. So although Calvin is not as famous for other accomplishments as for his theology, he has inspired a large number of followers to apply his thought to every form of human endeavor. The chapter titles for this volume list many of these: history, law, the arts, economics, literature, philosophy, politics, science, business, music, medicine, and journalism.

In his *Institutes*, Calvin begins by telling us that without a knowledge of God, we have no knowledge of ourselves, and vice versa. So from the very first page of Calvin's most famous writing, it is clear that the knowledge of God, the subject of theology, is tied to everything human. God is not only Lord of the "sacred" realm, not only Lord of salvation. He is Lord over every area of human life. We cannot understand the point of any human activity, whether preaching, music, or journalism, until we see how that activity is related to God.

In his essay in this volume, Leland Ryken writes, citing Georgia Harkness, "whereas Luther had asserted the possibility that one can 'serve God *within* one's calling,' Calvin took the bolder step of claiming that one can 'serve God *by* one's calling.'" For Calvin, God is interested in everything in his creation. He wants human beings to fill and subdue the earth.

The sad truth, of course, is that in Adam we all sinned, so that our labors fail to glorify God as they ought. But in Christ, redemption restores us to his service. Apart from redemption, we cannot know God rightly. Although God is clearly revealed to us in ourselves and in creation (Rom. 1:18–21), we suppress this knowledge. For as Calvin says, we cannot know God rightly without piety, trust, and worship (*Institutes*, 1.2.). But it follows that without Christ we cannot know ourselves either, or any legitimate human undertaking.

The gospel of Christ in Scripture redeems us from all sin, including the sin of rebellious thinking. The Scriptures, which proclaim that gospel, bring the true knowledge of ourselves. Calvin says, "God bestows the actual knowledge of himself upon us only in the Scriptures" (*Institutes*, 1.6.1). He continues:

> For as the aged, or those whose sight is defective, when any book however fair, is set before them, though they perceive that there is something written are scarcely able to make out two consecutive words, but, when aided by glasses, begin to read distinctly, so Scripture, gathering together the impressions of Deity, which, till then, lay confused in our minds, dissipates the darkness, and shows us the true God clearly.

And with this "actual knowledge of God" comes knowledge of ourselves and all of human life, clarified through the "glasses" of Scripture.

So for Calvin, theology is not just one subject among many. It is the key to everything human, and therefore to culture. Culture is what human beings do with God's creation. The marks of the fall permeate it. We see cruelty in human government, nihilism in human art, lies in human journalism. But redemption changes people comprehensively, so that they carry God's wisdom into their workplaces: compassion and justice into government, meaning into art, truth into journalism.

So the worldview of Calvin, which is the worldview of Scripture, necessarily energizes God's people to serve God by their callings, and thereby to change everything. Redeemed people renew and ennoble everything human. Sin does continue to tempt them, and they do fall. But from a wide historical perspective, we can see that through their Spirit-motivated efforts, culture does change for the better. The gospel has in fact motivated God's people to care for widows and orphans, to build hospitals, to paint and sculpt, to oppose tyranny, to take God's Word to the ends of the world.

The writers in this volume are well chosen to describe this renewal. They are careful and intelligent scholars who know the Scriptures, who understand Calvin, and who are themselves inspired by the gospel. I am very pleased to see these essays available. I have learned much from them myself, and I hope they will have a wide circulation so as to excite many in the church with the challenges of this world-shaking worldview.

JOHN M. FRAME

ACKNOWLEDGMENTS

s this final volume of the Calvin500 series is going to print, we wish to express our deepest gratitude to all the authors of this volume and especially to the fantastic team of publishers at P&R. Without them, and the fine editorial work of John Hughes (on many volumes) and Brian Kinney (on this volume), our efforts would have fallen short. Thank you!!

INTRODUCTION

This final volume of the Calvin 500 series seeks to explore the worldview spawned by John Calvin and his disciples. With the fourteen contributing authors for this volume, added to several other monographs in the series—which features 62 other contributors' voices—the Calvin 500 project provides a current sampling of Calvin and his influence. The series would be incomplete without this volume, which seeks to exhibit how Calvinism has been extended and promulgated through a wide variety of academic and cultural endeavors.

While many contemporaries owe their awareness of the "worldviewishness" of Christianity to modern thinkers such as Francis Schaeffer, R. C. Sproul, or Harry Blamires, those exemplars sat perched on the shoulders of the likes of Cornelius van Til, Herman Dooyweerd, Abraham Kuyper, James Orr, and Guillaume Groen van Prinsterer. Not only is Calvinism diffused throughout various disciplines, but it also appears to have a type of succession—ideological, not institutional or hierarchical—that carries it into the next generations. Few other offshoots of Christianity in general, or the Protestant Reformation in particular, have blossomed as widely or as tenaciously as Calvinism in its worldview extensions.

Still, some doubt that Calvinism is a coherent system of life; others doubt that Calvin, the churchman, intended to provide a platform for such an expansive cultural impact.

Should one inquire, however, "Did Calvin's work, in fact, generate much activity outside the ecclesiastical realm?" That query is easily answered. Critics and fans alike note that, for whatever reasons, during and shortly after Calvin's time, business flourished, inventiveness and technological innovation seemed to multiply, the arts did well and were patronized by numerous Calvinists, music (first in the church but then in an ever-widening circle) was cultivated and nourished by Reformational thinking, political presuppositions changed radically, the poor were cared for, education leapt forward—beginning in Calvin's Geneva—and modern science began. Publishing, writing, constitutionalism, and open markets seemed to discover a clear "before and after" with the establishment of Calvinism in each geographic locale. Thus in practice, his thought seems to have infused, if not inspired, a worldview that filtered into all sectors of life. This volume, written from the observational distance of nearly five centuries, draws on professionals from various fields to assess how Calvinism makes a difference in their areas of expertise. With one voice and many different timbres, this faculty (even though they may not agree on all particulars) asserts that Calvinism, rightly understood, fuels a distinctive, living, and salutary worldview.

If, however, one asks another question—"Did Calvin himself explicitly refer to these disciplines, largely what we call the liberal arts in most educational curricula?"—that inquiry is also answered, at least as early as in his *Institutes*.

While addressing the topic of what knowledge humans may possess about God, and specifically under the topic of the truth and authority of God's revelation, even with the highest regard for a *sola Scriptura* epistemology, Calvin saw no conflict in Christians being involved with and knowing certain other, extrabiblical areas. He spoke of "the innumerable evidences both in heaven and on earth that declare [God's] wonderful wisdom," including:

> not only those more recondite matters for the closer observation of which astronomy, medicine, and all natural science are intended, but also those which thrust themselves upon the sight of even the most untutored and ignorant persons, so that they cannot open their eyes without being compelled to witness them. Indeed, men who have either quaffed or even tasted the liberal arts penetrate with their aid far more deeply into the secrets of the divine wisdom.[1]

What may be surprising to some is to see Calvin's overt reference to disciplines such as medicine and astronomy—"To be sure, there is need of art and of more exacting toil in order to investigate the motion of the

---

1. *Institutes*, 1.5.2

stars to determine their assigned stations, to measure their intervals, to note their properties"[2]—and the cornucopia of scientific endeavors. He even commends those who sample these various humanistic disciplines. Of course, if one but recalls Calvin's education in the Renaissance humanism, one will remember that Calvin was steeped in these liberal arts and knew their value. In addition, his legal training would serve him and his callings well for decades. Remember also that it was Calvin's Academy that sought to spawn a medical school and was filled with legal scholars (Hotman and Godefroy), erstwhile poets (Beza, Marot), linguistic experts, political experts, and historians. Moreover, some of the earliest journalism—not in theory only but with the grave threat of decapitation—was practiced by a host of printers, editors, authors, and publishers who were attracted to Calvin's Geneva during his lifetime.

His combination of appreciation for the scientific basis of medicine, while affirming God as Creator, is seen in that same context, as he noted:

> Likewise in regard to the structure of the human body, one must have the greatest keenness in order to weigh, with Galen's skill, its articulation, symmetry, beauty, and use. But yet, as all acknowledge, the human body shows itself to be a composition so ingenious that its Artificer is rightly judged a wonder-worker.[3]

Calvin spoke of history as "the teacher of life" (while commenting on Rom. 4:23–24) and as the "mistress of life" (from the preface to his commentary on Acts), implying both that believers and unbelievers alike were capable of benefiting from the pedagogy of the past, and that history was a subject of true importance and value.

Elsewhere in his writings, Calvin spoke about economic matters, the arts, the role of history (his reliance on earlier authors is not only a luminous part of his writing but also an indication of how he valued past research, if well founded), the role of law in society, and the right place for music and beauty in the Christian life. Furthermore, his emphasis on vocation itself is surely a subsidiary argument that Calvin intended for his theology to overflow into a worldview emporium.

2. *Institutes*, 1.5.2
3. Ibid.

Whether Calvin *consciously* strove to birth a worldview or create a movement, one may not be able to tell; it is entirely possible that the extent of his success in inspiring and facilitating a life system that contained a robust worldview may have been a surprise that Calvin is still observing while he waits in the great cloud of witnesses (Heb. 12:1). What this volume documents and explores is the result of Calvin's work that, in fact, gave rise to Calvinism as a powerful and enduring intellectual torrent in the streams of life's thought and practice. If that assigns us a place among the witnesses, we shall be thankful merely to be in the crowd.

As we explore the cultural impact of Calvinism through this world-view, we intend, as with each volume in this series, to give a sincere tribute, although appreciative criticism will be included as well. We think the father of Calvinism would appreciate the healthy balance of tribute and analysis contained herein.

With that editorial *adieu*, we dedicate this book to the organizers of all future Calvin centenaries and celebrations, with our thanks and best wishes, as we hope to enjoy the next ones ourselves from more elevated stadium seating, with a great company of other witnesses.

DAVID HALL AND MARVIN PADGETT

ABBREVIATIONS

AP   Associated Press

CO   John Calvin, *Ioannis Calvini opera quae supersunt omnia*, ed. Guilielmus Baum, Eduardus Cunitz, and Eduardus Reuss, 59 vols., *Corpus Reformatorum* series, vols. 29–87 (Brunswick: C. A. Schwetschke and Son, 1863–1900)

Comm.   *Commentary*, from CO

CR   W. Baum, E. Cunitz, and E. Reuss, eds., *Corpus Reformandum: Joannis Calvini opera quae supersunt omnia* (Brunswick: Schwetschke, 1863–80)

CSR   *Christian Scholar's Review*

ID   Intelligent Design

Institutes   John Calvin, *Institutes of the Christian Religion*, various editions. Unless noted otherwise, this is the edition from the Library of Christian Classics, John T. McNeill, ed., Ford Lewis Battles, trans. (Philadelphia: Westminster Press, 1960). This edition is translated from Calvin's 1559 Latin Text, collated with his other editions.

JCR   *The Journal of Christian Reconstruction*

KJV   King James Version

Lect.   *Lecture*, from CO

NASB   New American Standard Bible

NIV   New International Version

PCA	Presbyterian Church in America
R. Consist.	Robert M. Kingdon et al., eds., *Registres du Consistoire de Genève au temps de Calvin*, 21 vols. (Geneva: Droz, 1996–)
RMJ	*Reformed Music Journal*
Serm.	*Sermon*, from CO
WSC	Westminster Shorter Catechism
WTJ	*Westminster Theological Journal*

1929 and All That, or What Does Calvinism Say to Historians Searching for Meaning?

Darryl G. Hart

The year 1929 was a significant one in the lives of many Americans. That year, as most people know, was the time of the Great Crash on Wall Street that escalated into the Great Depression. Most historians of the United States recognize this as one of the most profound crises in the life of the nation. The most recent economic downturn has generated even greater awareness of the nation's economic history as policy makers and citizens alike look for lessons from the Depression.

In 1929 another event transpired, one usually omitted from survey textbooks on United States history, but with arguably even more significance than the decline in stock prices that hit Wall Street on October 29, 1929. This was the reorganization of Princeton Seminary and the subsequent start of Westminster Seminary to carry on Princeton's original mission. The larger events surrounding Princeton's administrative adjustment are part of the fundamentalist controversy that engaged liberal and conservative Presbyterians for most of the 1920s. Although Princeton did not experience directly a liberal takeover, its new administrative structure after 1929 meant that conservatives were a minority on the board that oversaw academic and theological standards. J. Gresham Machen's decision, with support from many Presbyterian conservatives, to found a successor seminary to Princeton was arguably one of the major developments in the Presbyterian controversy. Even if the founding of Westminster did not affect as many Americans as did the crash of the stock market, the stakes for the new seminary were higher since they reflected not the price of temporal assets but the value of eternal realities—ones pertaining to the redemption purchased by Christ. From the perspective of eternity, the downfall of old Princeton and the creation of Westminster were more important than the fall of stock prices at the New York Stock Exchange.[1]

If this comparison is not adequate to start mental gears turning on the subject of doing history from a Calvinistic outlook, then perhaps what will do so is Machen's perspective on the meaning of 1929 for conservative Presbyterians. At his convocation address for Westminster, delivered before faculty, students, and well-wishers in center city Philadelphia, Machen admitted that he was at a loss in trying to make sense of Princeton Seminary's demise. He said:

> At first it might seem to be a great calamity, and sad are the hearts of those Christian men and women throughout the world who love the gospel that the old Princeton proclaimed. We cannot fully understand the ways of God in permitting so great a wrong. Yet good may come even out of a thing so evil as that.[2]

As a student of Scripture, Machen knew that many times throughout redemptive history God had accomplished his purposes through events

---

1. On events that led to the reorganization of Princeton and the creation of Westminster, see Bradley J. Longfield, *The Presbyterian Controversy: Fundamentalists, Modernists, and Moderates*, Religion in America (New York: Oxford University Press, 1991).

2. J. Gresham Machen, "Westminster Theological Seminary: Its Purpose and Plan," in D. G. Hart, ed., *J. Gresham Machen: Selected Shorter Writings* (Phillipsburg, NJ: P&R Publishing, 2004), 194.

that looked as if God's people were experiencing defeat. The story of Joseph and his brothers, the selection of the diminutive David as king of Israel, and above all Christ's death on the cross all made plausible Machen's sense that good might spring from evil in the course of redemptive history. Even so, he was unsure about Princeton. And if uncertain how to interpret developments in the church, how much more reluctant would Machen have been to try to interpret the significance of the Great Depression?

As disquieting as historical uncertainty may be, Machen's Calvinistic instincts were exactly on target. Although many historians and theologians have claimed that the Reformed faith specifically and Christianity more generally equip historians with insights about the meaning of historical developments, a deeper reality exists: that the Reformed faith may hinder attempts to derive the ultimate meaning of historical events. As Machen's own example suggests, the Reformed faith encourages epistemological humility when trying to tell what God is doing in history. Instead of adding up to a complete narrative, with beginning, middle, transitions between chapters, and an upbeat ending, history from a Calvinist outlook is actually filled with mystery. No one knew this better than John Calvin, whose doctrine of providence and instruction on how to view the world represents one of the best starting points for Reformed Protestants who study the past and want to make sense of it.

Providence According to Calvin

Reformed Protestants generally have raised few objections to the doctrine of providence. Because many come to the Reformed faith precisely *because* of the tradition's understanding of God's sovereignty, the belief—according to the Westminster Shorter Catechism—that providence involves God's "most holy, wise, and powerful preserving and governing his creatures and all their actions" makes perfect sense. Providence implies a created order where God is in charge and humans need not worry whether his purposes will be accomplished (WSC, Q. 11).

Calvin was no more comfortable with providence than other Reformed Protestants when he developed the doctrine in book one of the *Institutes*. This was the section of his systematic exposition of the Christian religion in which he discussed man's knowledge of God the Creator. At the end of this section of the *Institutes*, Calvin duly discussed first God's work of creation and then his works of providence, two divine acts closely connected because of the relationship between creating out of nothing and the subsequent preservation needed to maintain the original stuff of creation. Calvin's basic definition of providence was this: God governs heaven and earth such that he "regulates all things that nothing takes place without his deliberation".[3] The French Reformer explained that this regulation was not simply an extension of nature, as if God had simply created the world and let it run without direct and ongoing support and government. Calvin wrote, "Those as much defraud God of his glory as themselves of a most profitable doctrine who confine God's providence to such narrow limits as though he allowed all things by a free course to be borne along according to a universal law of nature".[4] In other words, providence is not passive, as if God merely sits "idly" observing the universe, but "as the keeper of the keys, he governs all events".[5]

Under the general category of God's regulation of creation, Calvin distinguished four layers of providence. The first was the natural world, such as "the alternation of days and nights, of winter and summer." This aspect of providence included the animal world where God "gives food to the young of the ravens" and governs the flight of birds by a "definite plan".[6] These were works of God because the days and seasons followed according to a "certain law" established by God himself.[7] A second layer concerned God's providential care for man. Calvin insisted that "we know that the universe was established for the sake of mankind".[8] Here Calvin quoted Jeremiah (Jer. 10:23) and Solomon (Prov. 16:9) to show that God directs man's steps even to the point of Calvin's denying man control of his own affairs within the bounds of a natural order given by God. "The prophet and Solomon," Calvin wrote, "ascribe to God not only might but also choice and determination." He added that it is "an absurd folly that miserable men take it upon themselves to act without God, when they cannot even speak except as he

---

3. *Institutes*, 1.16.3.
4. Ibid.
5. *Institutes* 1.16.4.
6. *Institutes*, 1.16.5.
7. Ibid.
8. *Institutes*, 1.16.6.

wills." This meant that nothing happens to man by chance because nothing in the world is "undertaken without [God's] determination".[9]

The third level of providence extended to natural occurrences. The examples Calvin used here were the weather and human procreation. "Whenever the sea boils up with the blast of winds," these forces testify to the presence of God's power and confirm Scripture's teaching that God "commanded and raised the stormy wind, which lifted up the waves of the sea" (Ps. 107:25). Human fertility was also an indication of God's control of all things. As much as all men and women (with few exceptions) possessed the power to procreate, some marriages were more barren or fertile than others. The reason for the difference was God's "special favor".[10]

The fourth and final dimension of providence outlined by Calvin is the one most relevant for considering God's control of history and what a Reformed perspective on historical scholarship might involve. Calvin rejected adamantly the Stoic doctrine of fate, although he knew his teaching on providence might sound as if he were saying God's activity in controlling all things left man in a passive state, only to be acted upon rather than acting in space and time with purpose. Calvin could deny Stoicism because of his rejection of the necessity of causes. The created order did not unfold in a mechanical way, but according to God's eternal decree and attributes. Accordingly, God ruled and governed all things according to his being, wisdom, power, holiness, goodness, and truth. Rather than an abstract law or a distant force being at the center of all things, creation developed according to a personal God, and providence embodied that personality. This meant for Calvin that "not only heaven and earth and the inanimate creatures, but also the plans and intentions of men, are so governed by his providence that they are borne by it straight to their appointed end".[11] Such an execution of God's decree eliminated any room for fortune or chance. "Nothing is more absurd," Calvin wrote, "than that anything should happen without God's ordaining it, because it would then happen without any cause".[12]

A number of questions naturally follow from Calvin's discussion of providence. What is the relationship between divine sovereignty and

9. Ibid.
10. *Institutes*, 1.16.7.
11. *Institutes*, 1.16.8.
12. Ibid.

human freedom? Does man have a free will? What is the difference between secondary causes—those ways in which God carries out his purposes through the actions of man or circumstances of the created order (such as the rising of the sun or gravitational pull)—and God's primary causes, such as his powerful and direct intervention with the created order in the form of miracles, special revelation, and the incarnation? As important as these questions are for understanding the Reformed doctrine of providence, they are somewhat beside the point in assessing a Calvinistic outlook on history that stems from Calvin's teaching on providence.

Calvin did not stop to entertain such questions but moved directly in the *Institutes* from an exposition of providence to an aspect of God's control that bears directly on historical inquiry and is crucial for its work. He said that no matter how much God was in control of all events, and no matter how much Christians believed in divine sovereignty so that nothing occurs in history by chance or fortune, to us the unfoldings of providence "are fortuitous".[13] Christians know that everything is "ordained by God's plan" and unfolds according to "a sure dispensation," yet in his experience of human existence, natural circumstances, and social development, man cannot discern meaning or direction sufficient to counter the impression that life is marked by accidents or fortunes. Calvin insisted he was not arguing that fortune "rules the world and men, tumbling all things at random up and down." Such was a foolish outlook and had no place in "the Christian's breast." Even so, because "the order, reason, end, and necessity" of everyday life "for the most part lie hidden in God's purpose, and are not apprehended by human opinion," those things that happen according to God's will and sovereign plan "are in a sense fortuitous".[14]

Calvin used the following example to make his point:

> Let us imagine, for example, a merchant who, entering a wood with a company of faithful men, unwisely wanders away from his companions, and in his wandering comes upon a robber's den, falls among thieves and is slain. His death was not only foreseen by God's eye, but also determined by his decree. For it is not said that he foresaw how long the life of each

13. *Institutes*, 1.16.9.
14. Ibid.

man would extend, but that he determined and fixed the bounds that men cannot pass. (Job 14:5) Yet as far as the capacity of our mind is concerned, all things therein seem fortuitous.[15]

Most human occurrences, whether considered "in their own nature or weighted according to our knowledge and judgment," on the surface appear to have no intrinsic meaning other than occurring according to God's eternal purpose. In the case of the merchant's death, a Christian will regard it "as fortuitous by nature" but will not doubt "that God's providence exercised authority over fortune in directing its end".[16]

Finding some proximate meanings in the world's affairs was not, however, impossible for Calvin. He cautioned against thinking that God made "sport of men by throwing them around like balls." He also counseled that if man had a "quiet and composed" mind he would always see that God had the best reasons for the way events turn out, such as to encourage patience, correct "wicked affections," encourage self-denial, or arouse from "sluggishness".[17] At the same time, Calvin taught that although God revealed the meaning of certain mysteries, not all parts of history are transparent. Here he appealed to Moses' instruction in Deuteronomy 29:29, i.e., that the secret things belong to God but the revealed things could be seen and understood. In this way Calvin was recognizing that Scripture unlocked the ultimate meaning of history by revealing God, his plan of redemption, and his will for believers.[18] Man could take encouragement from the revealed truth that God took "especial care" of his people.[19] But beyond the general disclosure found in Scripture Calvin was unprepared to go. Man had to be content with a general sense of divine providence—that God worked all things according to his plan and for the good of his children. Since that ultimately good plan also involved hardships and sufferings, interpreting events according to whether they pleased or comforted man was folly. Because the most revealing moment in history involved the death of God's only

15. Ibid.
16. Ibid.
17. *Institutes*, 1.17.1.
18. *Institutes*, 1.17.2.
19. *Institutes*, 1.17.6.

begotten Son, Christians need to remember that adversity or suffering was "sent by God's just dispensation".[20]

The lesson that Calvin's understanding of providence would seem to hold for historians is the rather sobering one that history is generally indecipherable apart from Christ. History lacks meaning unless Scripture is true in declaring the glory of God as revealed in the life and work of the incarnate Son of God. But the truth of God's revelation in Christ does not lead where many Reformed scholars think it does. The gospel explains why people exist and where history is going. But beyond the Sunday-school-like answer to every historical question— "Christ"—historians have no real access to interpreting the ultimate meaning of historical events and actors. For instance, to the question, "Why did Andrew Jackson win the 1828 election for president of the United States?" the answer, "Christ" or "the gospel" or "the glory of God" hardly satisfies. Historians are much more likely to talk about changes in the demographics of the United States, Jackson's reputation as a war hero, granting voting rights to citizens previously excluded from the electoral process. Any number of these proximate or temporal explanations make sense of what changed with Jackson's victory. But these are not exactly Christian answers. They are not at odds with the Christian truth that God controls all things, including secondary causes such as those that explain Jackson's success. They simply have no direct relationship to Christ's work on behalf of God's people.[21]

Efforts to connect events in history to the person and work of Christ can be downright disastrous, not only by historical standards but according to Christian orthodoxy. If someone argued that Jesus Christ accomplished salvation so that Andrew Jackson would be elected the seventh president of the United States, the case would be a difficult one if based solely on what Scripture reveals. Christ does rule over the nations and he did providentially govern the election of 1828, but saying that Christ was fulfilling his redemptive work through the Jackson administration does not do justice to any number

---

20. *Institutes*, 1.17.8

21. Recent books on Andrew Jackson include Sean Wilentz, *Andrew Jackson* (New York: Times Books, 2005), and Jon Meacham, *American Lion: Andrew Jackson in the White House* (New York: Random House, 2008).

of policies or initiatives that Jackson conducted that were contrary to God's revealed will.[22] Meanwhile, to say that Jackson was carrying out Christ's intentions is equally absurd and patently untrue. Reformed Christians may debate the proper function of the magistrate and the degree to which he may be responsible for true religion in his realm, but rare has been the Reformed historian who argued—as Eusebius did with Constantine—that a particular ruler was supplying meaning to history because he was carrying out Christ's redemptive work and purpose.

But just because historians—even Reformed ones—do not hold the interpretive key that unlocks the significance of events or actors that lack a direct bearing on the outcome of redemptive history, their work is not in vain. This is the place at which Calvin's teaching on providence is especially helpful. Because God governs all things and because everything happens according to his eternal purpose, historians do not study accidents even if the events they attempt to explain do not possess an inevitable quality. Historians not only study a meaningful order (and are created in such a way to perceive order as opposed to chaos in the movement of history), but they also can see the connections between secondary causes such that historians are capable of giving wise and learned explanations for why certain things happen, according to the host of circumstances in which man lives by virtue of God's creation and providence. In other words, historians can tell the difference that tyranny, justice, scarcity, creativity, virtue, and productivity make for the history of people, nations, and societies. But they cannot link these attributes and factors to the direction and meaning of history from an eternal perspective; that is, historians cannot definitively tell how such circumstances contribute to the advance of Christ's kingdom.

Calvin's doctrine of providence, then, was a reiteration of Augustine's thoughtful and biblical understanding of history and its meaning. In *The City of God*, the Bishop of Hippo wrote:

22. For instance, Jackson's treatment of Native Americans—removing them to the Western territories—and unresponsiveness to abolitionism, as well as his personal conduct, are generally regarded as blemishes on his character. For some perspective on Jackson the man, see Meacham, *American Lion*, 25–32.

We do not know by what judgment of God this good man is poor and that bad man right; why he who, in our opinion, ought to suffer acutely for his abandoned life enjoys himself, while sorrow pursues him whose praise-worthy life leads us to suppose he should be happy; why the innocent man is dismissed from the bar not only unavenged, but even condemned, being either wronged by the iniquity of the judge, or overwhelmed by false evidence, while his guilty adversary, on the other hand, is not only discharged with impunity, but even has his claims admitted; why the ungodly enjoys good health, while the godly pines in sickness. . . . But who can collect or enumerate all the contrasts of this kind? But if this anomalous state of things were uniform in this life, in which, as the sacred Psalmist says, "Man is like to vanity, his days as a shadow that pas-seth away" (Ps. 144:4)—so uniform that none but wicked men won the transitory prosperity of earth, while only the good suffered its ills—this could be referred to the just and even benign judgment of God. . . . But now, as it is, since we not only see good men involved in the ills of life, and bad men enjoying the good of it, which seem unjust, but also that evil often overtakes evil men, and good surprises the good, the rather on this account are God's judgments unsearchable, and His ways past finding out (Rom. 11:33). Although, therefore, we do not know by what judgment these things are done or permitted to be done by God, with whom is the highest virtue, the highest wisdom, the highest justice, no infirmity, no rashness, no unrighteousness, yet is salutary for us to learn to hold cheap such things, be they good or evil, as attach indifferently to good men and bad, and to covet those things which belong only to good men, and flee those evils which belong only to evil men. (20.2)[23]

Handicapped Historians?

As clear as Calvin was about the nature of providence, Christian historians have been reluctant to obey the stop sign that he placed on historical explanations of events lacking a scriptural interpretation. Since the rise of a self-consciously Christian association of scholars, not only in academic history, various evangelical and Reformed academics have advanced arguments about the value of Christian historians performing

---

23. Augustine, *The City of God against the Pagans*, trans. and ed. R. W. Dyson (New York: Cambridge University Press, 1998).

their scholarship with explicitly religious motivations or perspectives. These arguments have often included the idea that Christian historiography should be in some way noticeably different from the work of their secular peers. Of course, the difference between Christian and secular interpretations stems precisely from the different beliefs and convictions that believing academics possess by virtue of their faith. Nevertheless, appealing to Calvin on this point is anachronistic since a secular academy would have been inconceivable to him. But his teaching on providence is relevant to many of the recent arguments made on behalf of the difference that Christianity makes for historical scholarship.

C. Gregg Singer, professor of history at Catawba College, represented the outlook of an older set of Christian academics who were teaching and writing before American evangelicals started to go to graduate school in the normal course of training. He believed that secular historians rejected "the possibility of meaning and ultimate purpose in history." The task of Christian historians was consequently to "confront the unbelieving world with an interpretation of history which is both true to Scripture on the one hand, and relevant to the intellectual climate" of the times.[24] The doctrine of providence was key. For Singer, it ensured that "history has both meaning and purpose because it is real." He had a point when it came to a believer's sense of living in space and time and wondering where history is going. But when Singer applied this truth to historical judgments he sounded less certain. For instance, the decay of Western culture in the latter half of the twentieth century "was part of the sovereign purpose of God to bring to naught the pagan philosophies of the ancient world."[25] Singer took it a step further in calling the Christian historian to demonstrate that "the decline of Western culture itself is the direct result of the triumph of the Renaissance over the Reformation in Western life." He added that the French and American revolutions were the result of "resurgent paganism" in the eighteenth century. To make these judgments was the "historian's task," he said.[26]

24. C. Gregg Singer, *Christian Approaches: To Philosophy, To History* (Memphis: Craig Press, 1978), 35.
25. Ibid., 36.
26. Ibid., 37.

A younger group of historians has emerged to take over the case for a Christian approach to history. Their assessment of the West and its decline, perhaps reflecting the difference between America's "Greatest Generation" and the baby-boomer generation, was not as dire as Singer's. But like Singer they argued that religious convictions separated their understanding of history from secular scholars and enabled them to see the meaning or divine pattern in historical development. The most comprehensive and judicious assessment was that of David Bebbington, an English evangelical historian whose book *Patterns in History* (1979), contrasted Christian conceptions of history with the ancients, moderns, Marxists, and historicists. Bebbington's points about Christianity involving a linear view of history, an end or *telos*, and a God who intervened in space and time that distinguished Christianity from other intellectual outlooks, was clearly welcome. It even showed how much modern Western academic history—while often rejecting God—has borrowed heavily on Christianity's triumph over pagan philosophy.[27] But when Bebbington took the truth that God intervenes in history and gave Christian historians a measure of access to the meaning of history, thanks to their belief in a God who is active in the world, he seemed to go past where Calvin's doctrine of providence allowed. For instance, Bebbington wrote that "when good surprisingly emerges from evil, God is evidently at work."[28] He also suggested that, aided as they were with a divinely revealed morality, Christian scholars should be able to make moral judgments about the past. Bebbington did caution against Christians interpreting the past in a providential way when their readers or audiences were interested simply in "technical history." Yet, "the Christian historian can discern God at work in the past without necessarily writing of him."[29]

George M. Marsden argued in a fashion similar to Bebbington, although showing directly the influence of Kuyperian (or neo-Calvinist) arguments on his thinking. Christian faith influenced historical scholarship, according to Marsden, in three important ways. The first was the

27. David Bebbington, *Patterns in History: A Christian Perspective on Historical Thought* (Grand Rapids: Baker, 1990), chap. 3.
28. Ibid., 184.
29. Ibid., 186–87.

selection of a subject. Christians would invariably value some aspects of historical research as more worthwhile than others because of their beliefs. The second was the type of question a Christian historian would ask about a subject. "Christian scholars are likely to be interested in a different set of issues than are other scholars and to see different things."[30] The third influence on Christian historiography came in the selection of theories by which to approach a topic and set of questions. For instance, "scholars who accept the authority of ancient texts are unlikely to accept radical postmodern deconstruction of the authority of all texts or that humans are, in effect, the only creators of reality."[31] The particular contribution that Christian historians could make, Marsden added, was in displaying moral standards in their work, and resisting cultural and historical relativism.[32] Although Marsden interacted less directly with ideas of purpose or meaning in history, his argument did suggest that believing historians could make judgments about the past that were unavailable to their peers, by virtue of their understanding of God's revealed truth.

One last example of reflection on the nature of Christian history comes from Ronald A. Wells, who taught at Calvin College for much of his career and wrote the book devoted to history for the Christian College Coalition, *History Through the Eyes of Faith* (1989). Wells was writing with something of a different purpose from Singer, Bebbington, or Marsden, since his book was supposed to supplement textbook surveys of Western civilization. Even so, he argued that Christian college students need to understand their place in the coming of God's kingdom, and this will lead to certain evaluations of the West's history. It would, for instance, show that the "secular-scientific humanism of the Enlightenment" had led humankind down a "blind alley."[33] Wells argued that believers could see a pattern of moral and spiritual bleakness in the history of the West. He added that since "the rationalism of the Enlightenment is incompatible with Christian belief, and since America was to be a testing ground for

30. George M. Marsden, "What Difference Might Christian Perspectives Make," in Ronald A. Wells, ed., *History and the Christian Historian* (Grand Rapids: Eerdmans, 1998), 15.

31. Ibid., 16.

32. Ibid., 17–18.

33. Ronald A. Wells, *History Through the Eyes of Faith*, Christian College Coalition Series (San Francisco: Harper & Row, 1989), 234.

the progressive beliefs of the Enlightenment, it was always clear—on [the Christian's] terms—that such a test would be a failure."[34] Wells may have disagreed with Singer on the nature of the American experiment, but like him, Wells, along with Marsden and Bebbington (to a lesser extent), felt comfortable making moral evaluations of history. This moral outlook was both a gift and responsibility for the believing historian.

Undoubtedly, Calvin would not have denied the validity of divinely revealed moral standards and that all historical actors will be judged according to God's law. But whether this is properly the historian's task is another question. Nor does a moral perspective on history necessarily resonate with the doctrine of providence as Calvin explained it. Surely moral judgments are present in the work of secular historians, perhaps on the different side of an issue, but moral judgments are not the sole domain of believing professional historians. Subjects such as slavery, Nazism, patriarchy, and capitalism are especially revealing since historians even without faith have had little trouble condemning these features of the past. At the same time, appreciating the variety, complexity, and mystery of the past—whether from an appeal to providence or not—rarely results from the moral certainty that Christians and unbelieving historians have exhibited. Such certainty is at odds with the interpretive humility that Calvin encouraged in his doctrine of providence.

Accepting the Limits of Meaning

Calvinism has nurtured intellectual creativity, traditions of scholarly accomplishment, and strong institutions of higher learning. These attainments have not always cultivated intellectual modesty among Reformed Protestants. Because of a prowess for interpreting the Bible and reflecting on its truths in systematic ways, Calvinists have generally taken pride in their tradition as one of the most intellectually advanced among Protestants. Whether or not this pride is becoming, historians who work within a Reformed outlook may have the ingredients for supplying the intellectual modesty necessary to keep Reformed scholars from hubris.

34. Ibid., 230.

The doctrine of providence is a good place to start. Although this truth, especially as Calvin expounded it, would appear to encourage Christian scholars to find meaning everywhere—because God is in control of all things—it does precisely the opposite. Because God created and sustains all things according to his infinite wisdom, goodness, and justice, everything in the created order has meaning and purpose. Furthermore, because this meaning and purpose reside squarely in God's eternal decree, no ambiguity exists in creation's significance, at least in the mind of God. This comprehensive outlook on God's relationship to creation has tempted believing academics to think they can know the mind of God and hence the meaning and purpose of the objects they study.

The problem with which Christian scholars must wrestle is that God has revealed only part of his mind, will, and purpose. Reformed Protestants believe that God reveals himself in the two books, the book of nature and the book of Scripture. But only one of those books reveals Christ, whose life, ministry, and redemption constitute the meaning of creation. The other book, general revelation, does indeed reveal its author but only in a way sufficient to condemn unbelief and wickedness. The book of nature does not reveal Christ. For that reason, Christian efforts to find meaning in the pages of history, the natural world, social development, or human nature run into the wall of Scripture's limits. To go beyond that wall is to engage in speculation.

This is as true for history as it is for other spheres of human inquiry. Christian biologists have no better idea about the meaning of microbes than Christian mathematicians do about algebraic equations or English professors do about *Hamlet*. Believing historians may be tempted more than other Christian scholars to speculate about the significance of their studies because Christianity is bound up with history. The Bible itself begins with human origins and ends with a vision of the end of time. Scripture would seem to invite those who believe its truths to understand intervening human developments in the light of the Bible's narrative of creation, fall, redemption, and consummation. Although Scripture is clear about the meaning of several high points in the historical drama it reveals, it has next to nothing to say about the historical circumstances that made places such as Athens, Rome, London, and Philadelphia, for instance, such important sites in the history of the West.

Accepting the limits that Christianity places on finding meaning in history runs against the knowledge that Christians do know the ultimate meaning of history. The trick is to accept another truth, namely, that a difference exists between finding the ultimate meaning of human history (which is Christ) and the proximate meaning of wars, presidential elections, laws, and mass movements (which is uncertain). With this distinction in mind, Christian historians can assert with confidence that the meaning of redemptive history is clearly revealed, while in the realm of secular history they can work within an interpretive framework that stems from the people, institutions, and ideas they adopt and explore (such as the value of republicanism and liberty, or the advantages of constitutional monarchy, or the need for strong nation-states, or the worth of local institutions and culture). This is not a position of relativism or skepticism. It is the necessary result of not knowing all God's hidden purposes in the warp and woof of his creation. The distinction between God's hidden and revealed secrets is no less true for church history. With the closing of the canon of Scripture and the loss of access to divinely revealed interpretations of events in redemptive history, believing church historians are just as much at a loss in determining why the Reformation, for instance, started in Germany as Christian historians who study the history of politics are unable to explain ultimately the causes of the French Revolution.[35]

Although Machen had not trained as a historian, he certainly seemed to understand the limits that Christianity placed on his powers of discerning meaning in history. While more animated by the significance of developments in the Presbyterian world than by the declining fortunes of Wall Street, Machen was no more willing to identify the meaning of developments at Princeton Seminary than he was to attach divine significance to America's failing economy. That kind of interpretive restraint may be rare for Calvinists, but if Reformed historians can learn its discipline they may provide a crucial service as models of the kind of intellectual humility that should characterize Christian discernment.

---

35. These paragraphs summarize the argument made in D. G. Hart, "History in Search of Meaning: The Conference on Faith and History," in Wells, ed., *History and the Christian Historian*, 68–87.

2

LAW, AUTHORITY, AND LIBERTY IN EARLY CALVINISM

JOHN WITTE JR.

The Calvinist Reformation transformed not only theology and the church but also law and the state. John Calvin himself was a well-trained lawyer, and he crafted more than a hundred statutes for Geneva—including new constitutions for the local church and state, new civil and criminal laws and procedures, and many discrete ordinances on sexuality and sumptuousness, marriage and family life, morality and charity, education and poor relief, among many other topics.[1] Calvin also sat on the Genevan consistory bench for two decades, adjudicating thousands of cases, and he dealt with many intricate legal questions in his *Institutes*,

1. This chapter is drawn in part from my *The Reformation of Rights: Law, Religion, and Human Rights in Early Modern Calvinism* (Cambridge: Cambridge University Press, 2007), and *Sex, Marriage, and Family in John Calvin's Geneva*, 3 vols. (Grand Rapids: Eerdmans, 2005–), with Robert M. Kingdon; these volumes include detailed sources that are not duplicated here.

commentaries, sermons, consilia, and correspondence.[2] Calvin's attention
to legal detail would become a trademark of early Calvinist communities in
early modern France, the Netherlands, Scotland, England, Germany, and
their colonies overseas. Calvinists in each of these communities developed
elaborate new ordinances on all manner of public, private, and criminal law
topics. Their local consistories were often sophisticated legal tribunals, as
were their broader synods, councils, and presbyteries, which heard cases
on appeal and made new church laws. Their universities produced a great
number of jurists who led both church and state in the reformation of
law, politics, and society.[3]

This chapter samples some of the main legal teachings and contributions of Calvin and later Calvinist jurists before 1700. It focuses on the
unique models of law and liberty, authority and discipline, and church and
state that Calvinists developed on the strength of their cardinal theological
teachings. After analyzing Calvin's views in detail, the chapter focuses
on the distinctive contributions of selected French, Dutch, English, and
American Calvinists who wrote in response to major legal and political
crises. The aim is straightforward: to illustrate how Calvin and Calvinism
influenced the legal arena.

John Calvin and Geneva

Calvin's reformation of Geneva charted a deft course between Lutherans, who tended to subordinate the church to the state, and Anabaptists,
who tended to withdraw the church from the state and society altogether.
Like Lutherans, Calvin insisted that each local polity (such as Geneva) be

2. See Calvin's legal writings in CO 10/1; *Les sources du droit du canton de Genève*, ed.
Emile Rivoire and Victor van Berchem, 4 vols. (Aarau: H. R. Sauerländer, 1927–35); *Regis-
tres de la compagnie des pasteurs de Genève au temps de Calvin*, ed. Jean-Francois Bergier and
Robert M. Kingdon, 2 vols. (Geneva: Droz, 1964); *R. Consist.* See discussion in Josef Bohatec,
Calvin und das Recht (Graz: H. Boehlaus, 1934); Josef Bohatec, *Calvins Lehre von Staat und
Kirche mit besonderer Berücksichtigung des Organismusgedankens* (Breslau: M. & H. Marcus,
1937; repr., Aalen, 1961); Walter Köhler, *Zürcher Ehegericht und Genfer Konsistorium*, 2 vols.
(Leipzig: M. Heinsius Nachfolger, 1932–42); Robert M. Kingdon, *Adultery and Divorce in
Calvin's Geneva* (Cambridge, MA / London, 1995).

3. Christoph Strohm, *Calvinismus und Recht: Weltanschaulich-konfessionelle Aspekte im
Werke reformierter Juristen in der frühen Neuzeit* (Tübingen: Mohr Siebeck, 2008).

a uniform Christian commonwealth that adhered to the general principles of the Bible and natural law and translated them into detailed positive laws for public and private life. Like Anabaptists, Calvin insisted on the basic separation of the offices and operations of church and state, leaving the church to govern itself without state interference. But, unlike both groups, Calvin insisted that both church and state officials play complementary legal roles in the creation of the local Christian commonwealth and its laws, and in the cultivation of the rights and duties of citizens.

Calvin's Early Views

John Calvin developed some of his legal teachings as early as his 1536 *Institutes*. In this early masterwork, Calvin echoed the Protestant call for Christian liberty already made famous by Martin Luther and other Reformers a generation before—liberty of the individual conscience from Catholic canon laws and clerical controls, liberty of political officials from ecclesiastical power and privilege, liberty of the local clergy from central papal rule, liberty of the young Protestant churches from oppression by church and state alike in violation of the people's rights and liberties.

Calvin called for a basic separation of church and state. The church holds the spiritual power of the Word. Ministers are to preach the Word and administer the sacraments. Doctors are to catechize the young and educate the parishioners. Elders are to maintain discipline and order and adjudicate disputes. Deacons are to control the church's finances and coordinate its care for the poor and needy. Each of these church officials, Calvin elaborated in his *Ecclesiastical Ordinances* of 1541, is subject to the limitation of his own office and the supervision of his fellow officers.

The state holds the legal power of the sword. State officials are God's "vice-regents,""vicars," and "ministers" in this earthly life. They are vested with God's authority and majesty, and are "called" to an office that is "the most sacred and by far the most honorable of all callings in the whole life of mortal men." They are commanded to embrace and exemplify clemency, integrity, honesty, mercy, humanity, and other godly virtues. Political rulers must govern by written positive laws, not by personal fiat. Their laws must encompass the biblical principles of love for God and neighbor, but they must not embrace biblical laws per se—particularly not the ceremonial and juridical Jewish laws of the Old Testament. Instead, "equity alone must be the goal and rule and limit of all laws." Through such written, equitable laws, political rulers must promote peace and order in the earthly kingdom, punish crime and civil wrongdoing, and protect persons in their lives and properties, "to ensure that men may carry on blameless intercourse among themselves" in the spirit of "civil righteousness."[4]

These God-given duties and limits define not only the political office but also the political liberty of Christian believers. Political liberty and political authority "are constituted together," said Calvin. The political liberty of believers is not so much a subjective right as a function of the political office. When political officials respect the duties and limits of their offices, believers enjoy ample political liberty to give "public manifestation of their faith." When political officials betray their office, however, through negligence, injustice, overreaching, or outright tyranny, the political liberty of the believer is abridged or even destroyed. As a consequence, said Calvin, "those who desire that every individual should preserve his rights, and that all men may live free from injury, must defend the political order to the utmost of their ability."[5]

Calvin insisted that private individuals have a godly duty to obey tyrannical political officials up to the limits of Christian conscience. "The powers that be are ordained by God," and the Bible repeatedly enjoins our obedience to them (Rom. 13:1–7; Titus 3:1; 1 Peter 2:13–14). These obligations of obedience continue even when the authorities become abusive and arbitrary, Calvin insisted. This is particularly true in the political sphere, which provides order and stability for individuals as well as for families, churches, businesses, and other social structures to flourish. Some political order is better than no order at all, and private disobedience usually brings greater disorder. Some justice and equity prevail even in the worst tyrannies, and even that is jeopardized when individuals take the law into their own hands. Sometimes tyrannies are God's test of our faith or punishment for our sin, and we insult God further by resisting his instruments. Individuals must thus obey and

4. *Institutes* (1536), 1.33, 6.33–49.
5. Ibid., 6.54; *Comm.* Rom. 13:10.

endure patiently and prayerfully, and leave vengeance and retribution to God.

But honor for earthly authorities cannot be dishonor for God, Calvin continued. When earthly authorities command their subjects to disobey God, to disregard Scripture, or to violate conscience, their political citizens and subjects not only may disobey, they must disobey. Our "obedience is never to lead us away from obedience to Him, to whose will the desires of all kings ought to be subject, to whose decrees their commands ought to yield," Calvin wrote. "If they command anything against Him, let it go unesteemed." For to love and honor God is the first and greatest commandment. All authorities who betray their office to the detriment or defamation of God forfeit their office and are reduced to private persons. They are no longer authorities but mere "brigands" and "criminals." "Dictatorships and unjust authorities are not governments ordained by God," and, "Those who practice blasphemous tyranny" are no longer "God's ministers" of law.[6]

The question that remained for Calvin was how such abusive or tyrannical authorities should be disobeyed. Calvin urged a "moderate and equitable" solution. He knew enough about the insurrection and rioting triggered by the Anabaptist radicals of his day, and had read enough in classical history about the dangers of simply unleashing the crowd against tyrants. So, he sought a more structured and constructive response both by the state and church authorities, even while calling individuals quietly to disobey laws that violated Christian conscience and commands. No political regime is governed by "one person alone," Calvin argued. Even monarchs have a whole coterie of lower officials—counselors, judges, and chancellors—charged with implementation of the law. Moreover, many communities have "magistrates of the people, appointed to restrain the willfulness of kings," such as the ephors of ancient Greece or the elected parliamentarians of our day. These lower magistrates, especially elected officials, must protect the people through active resistance, even revolt, if higher magistrates become abusive or tyrannical in violation of God's authority and law.[7]

6. *Institutes* (1536), 6.56; *Comm*. Rom. 13:1–7; *Comm*. Acts 5:29; 7:17.
7. *Institutes* (1536), 6.55.

Church leaders, in turn, must preach and prophesy loudly against the injustice of tyranny and petition tyrannical magistrates to repent of their abuse, to return to their political duties, and to restore the political freedom of religious believers. Calvin opened his 1536 edition of the *Institutes* with such a petition to King Francis I, on behalf of the persecuted Protestants in France. In his dedicatory epistle to Francis, Calvin stated that, as a believer, he was compelled to "defend the church against [political] furies," and to "embrace the common cause of all believers." Against "overbearing tyranny," Calvin later put it, a Christian must "venture boldly to groan for freedom."[8]

Calvin's Later Views

In his mature writings, Calvin worked out a much fuller legal and political understanding, based on an expanded theory both of the uses of the moral law in this earthly life and of the role of the church in helping to realize these uses of the law.

Calvin described the moral law as a set of moral commandments, engraved on the conscience, repeated in the Scripture, and summarized in the Decalogue. He used widely varying terminology to describe this law: "the voice of nature," the "engraven law," "the law of nature," "the natural law," the "inner mind," the "rule of equity," the "natural sense," "the sense of divine judgment," "the testimony of the heart," and the "inner voice," among other terms.

God makes three uses of the moral law in governing humanity, said Calvin. *First*, God uses the moral law theologically—to condemn all persons in their consciences and compel them to seek God's liberating grace. By setting forth a model and mirror of perfect righteousness, the moral law "warns, informs, convicts, and lastly condemns every man of his own unrighteousness." The moral law thereby punctures his vanity, diminishes his pride, and drives him to despair. Such despair, Calvin believed, is a necessary precondition for the sinner to seek God's help and to have faith in God's grace. *Second*, God uses the moral law civilly—to restrain the sinfulness of nonbelievers. "[T]he law is like a halter," Calvin wrote, "to

8. Ibid., proemium; Letter to Melanchthon (June 28, 1545), CO, 12.98–100.

check the raging and otherwise limitlessly ranging lusts of the flesh. . . . Hindered by fright or shame, sinners dare neither execute what they have conceived in their minds, nor openly breathe forth the rage of their lust." The moral law imposes on them a "constrained and forced righteousness" or a "civil righteousness." *Third*, God uses the moral law educationally—to teach believers, those who have accepted his grace, the means and measures of sanctification, of spiritual development. Even the most devout saints, though free from the condemnation of the moral law, still need to follow the commandments "to learn more thoroughly . . . the LORD's will [and] to be aroused to obedience." The law teaches them not only the "civil righteousness" that is common to all persons, but also the "spiritual righteousness" that is becoming of sanctified Christians. As a teacher, the law not only coerces them against violence and violation, but also cultivates in them charity and love. It not only punishes harmful acts of murder, theft, and fornication, but also prohibits evil thoughts of hatred, covetousness, and lust.[9]

The moral law thus creates two tracks of norms: "civil norms" that are common to all persons, and "spiritual norms" that are distinctly Christian. These two sets of norms, in turn, give rise to two tracks of morality: a simple "morality of duty" demanded of all persons regardless of their faith, and a higher "morality of aspiration" demanded of believers in reflection of their faith.[10] This two-track system of morality corresponded roughly to the proper division of responsibility between church and state, as Calvin saw it in his later years. It was the church's responsibility to teach aspirational spiritual norms. It was the state's responsibility to enforce mandatory civil norms. This division of responsibility was reflected in the procedural divisions between the consistory and the city council in Calvin's Geneva. In most cases that did not involve serious crimes, the consistory would first call parties to their higher spiritual duties, backing their recommendations with (threats of) spiritual discipline. If such spiritual counsel failed, the parties were referred to the city council to compel them, using civil and criminal sanctions, to honor at least their basic civil duties.

9. *Institutes* (1559), 2.7.6–12; 2.8.6, 51; 3.3.9; 3.6.1; 3.17.5–6; 3.19.3–6; *Comm.* Gal. 3:19; 5:13; *Serm.* Deut. 5:4–27; *Comm.* 1 Peter 1:14.

10. These phrases are from Lon L. Fuller, *The Morality of Law*, rev. ed. (New Haven: Yale University Press, 1969).

Calvin based this division of legal labor on the assumption that the church was a distinct legal entity with its own legal responsibilities in the local Christian commonwealth. This was a new emphasis in his later writings. God has vested in this church polity three forms of power (*potestas*), Calvin argued in his 1559 *Institutes*. The church holds "doctrinal power" to set forth its own confessions, creeds, catechisms, and other authoritative distillations of the Christian faith, and to expound them freely from the pulpit and the lectern. The church holds "legislative power" to promulgate for itself "a well-ordered constitution" that ensures "proper order and organization," "safety and security" in the church's administration of its affairs and proper decency, and "becoming dignity" in worship, liturgy, and ritual. And, the church holds "jurisdictional power" to enforce positive ecclesiastical laws to maintain discipline and prevent scandal among its members.[11]

The church's jurisdictional power remains "wholly spiritual" in character, Calvin insisted. Its disciplinary rules must be "founded upon God's authority, drawn from Scripture, and, therefore, wholly divine." Its sanctions must be limited to admonition, instruction, and, in severe cases, the ban and excommunication—with civil and criminal penalties left for the magistrate to consider and deliver. Its administration must always be "moderate and mild," and left "not to the decision of one man" but to a consistory, with proper procedures and proper deference to the rule of law.[12] But the consistory had vast subject-matter jurisdiction over cases of sex, marriage and family life, charity and poor relief, education and child care, and "public morality," which included "idolatry and other kinds of superstition, disrespect towards God, heresy, defiance of father and mother, or of the magistrate, sedition, mutiny, assault, adultery, fornication, larceny, avarice, abduction, rape, fraud, perjury, false witness, tavern-going, gambling, disorderly feasting, gambling, and other scandalous vices."[13]

Calvin's mature theory of the church combined ingeniously the principles of rule of law, democracy, and liberty. First, Calvin urged respect for the rule of law within the church. He devised laws that defined the

11. *Institutes* (1559), 4.1.5; 4.8.1; 4.10.27–38; 4.11.1.
12. Ibid., 4.10.5, 30; 4.11.1–6; 4.12.1–4, 8–11.
13. *Les sources du droit du canton de Genève*, vol. 3, item no. 992.

church's doctrines and disciplinary standards, rights and duties of officers and parishioners, and procedures for legislation and adjudication. The church was thereby protected from the intrusions of state law and the sinful vicissitudes of members. Church officials were limited in their discretion. Parishioners understood their spiritual duties. When new rules were issued, they were discussed, promulgated, and well known. Issues that were ripe for review were resolved by proper tribunals. Parties that had cases to be heard exhausted their remedies at church law. To be sure, this principle of the rule of law within the church was an ideal that too often was breached, in Calvin's day and in succeeding generations. Yet this principle helped to guarantee order, organization, and orthodoxy within the Reformed church.

Second, Calvin urged respect for the democratic process within the church. Pastors, elders, teachers, and deacons were, eventually, in later Calvinist churches, elected by communicant members of the congregation. Congregations periodically held meetings to assess the performance of their church officers, to discuss new initiatives within their bodies, and to debate controversies that had arisen. Delegates to church synods and councils were elected by their peers. Council meetings were open to the public and gave standing to parishioners to press their claims. Implicit in this democratic process was a willingness to entertain changes in doctrine, liturgy, and polity; to accommodate new visions and insights; and to spurn ideas and institutions whose utility and veracity were no longer tenable. To be sure, this principle did not always insulate the church from a belligerent dogmatism in Calvin's day or in the generations to follow. Yet this principle helped to guarantee constant reflection, renewal, and reform within the church.

Third, Calvin urged respect for liberty within the church. Christian believers were to be free to enter and leave membership; partake of the church's offices and services without fear of bodily coercion and persecution; assemble, worship, pray, and partake of the sacraments without fear of political reprisal; elect their religious officers; debate and deliberate matters of faith and discipline; pursue discretionary matters of faith, the *adiaphora*, without undue laws and structures. This principle, too, was an ideal that Calvin and his followers compromised, particularly in their

25

execution of Michael Servetus for heresy and blasphemy. Yet this principle helped to guarantee constant action, adherence, and agitation for reform by individual members.

It was Calvin's genius to integrate these three cardinal principles into a new ecclesiology. Democratic processes prevented the rule-of-law principle from promoting an ossified and outmoded orthodoxy. The rule of law prevented the democratic principle from promoting a faith swayed by fleeting fashions and public opinions. Individual liberty kept both corporate rule and democratic principles from tyrannizing ecclesiastical minorities. Together, these principles allowed the church to strike a unique perpetual balance between law and liberty, structure and spirit, order and innovation, dogma and *adiaphora*. This delicate ecclesiastical machinery helped to render Calvinist churches remarkably adaptable and resilient over the centuries in numerous countries and cultures.

This integrated theory of the church had implications for the theory of the state. Calvin hinted broadly in his writings that a similar combination of rule of law, democratic process, and individual liberty might serve the state equally well. Such a combination, he believed, would provide the best protection for the liberty of the church and its members. What Calvin adumbrated, his followers elaborated. In the course of the next two centuries, European and American Calvinists wove Calvin's core insights for the nature of corporate rule into a robust constitutional theory of republican government that rested on the pillars of rule of law, democratic processes, and individual liberty.

Theodore Beza and French Calvinism

Shortly after Calvin's death in 1564, his teachings on law and liberty, and church and state faced their first major crisis. In the St. Bartholomew's Day Massacre of 1572, up to 100,000 French Calvinists were slaughtered in a month of barbarism instigated by French Catholic authorities. A mere decade before, Calvinism had seemed ready to contest Catholicism for the heart and soul of France. By 1562, some two million French souls had converted to Calvinism and gathered in more than two thousand new churches throughout France. The number of

Calvinist converts and churches was growing rapidly in all ranks of French society, but especially among the aristocracy. This growth was in no small part a result of the disciplined campaigns of missionary work, book publication, church planting, school building, and charity work offered by the Calvinists. It was also in part a result of the ready exportation of Geneva's sturdy system of local city-state rule and spiritual discipline that was ideally suited for many of the small French cities and towns that converted to Calvinism.

After 1560, French Calvinism spread because of the growing military prowess of French Calvinists. That year, despite strong protests from Geneva, a group of Calvinists attempted a *coup d'etat* against the young French King Henry II. This brought harsh reprisals on various Calvinist communities and the establishment of a French inquisitorial court targeting Calvinists. In 1562, French Catholic forces slaughtered a Calvinist congregation gathered for worship in the town of Vassy. That triggered a decade of massive feuds between Catholic and Calvinist forces in many parts of France. The St. Bartholomew's Day Massacre, which exploded after a lull in hostilities, placed French Calvinism in grave crisis.

Calvin's teachings provided little guidance for responding to a crisis of this magnitude. Calvin assumed that each local community would have a single faith. How could Calvinists countenance religious pluralism and demand toleration as a religious minority in a majority Catholic community? Calvin assumed that church and state would cooperate in the governance of a godly polity. What if church and state came into collision, or even worse into collusion against Calvinists? Calvin assumed that Christian subjects should obey political authorities up to the limits of Christian conscience, and bear persecution with penitence, patience, and prayer in hopes that a better magistrate would come. But what if the persecution escalated to outright pogrom? Were prayer, flight, and martyrdom the only options for conscientious Christians? Was there no place for resistance and revolt, even regicide and revolution in extreme cases? These challenges had faced Calvinists in various places throughout the 1540s to 1560s. They became stark life-and-death issues for French Calvinists after 1572.

It was Calvin's hand-picked successor in Geneva, Theodore Beza, who responded most decisively to this crisis—working alongside such Calvinist worthies as John Ponet, John Knox, and Christopher Goodman from England and Scotland; Frenchmen Lambert Daneau, François Hotman, Philippe DuPlessis Mornay, and Peter Martyr Vermigli; as well as Swiss Reformers Heinrich Bullinger and Pierre Viret. By reason of the originality of his ideas and his authority as Calvin's successor, Beza's formulations proved to be the most influential. His most important work was the 1574 tract *The Rights of Rulers Over Their Subjects and the Duty of Subjects Toward Their Rulers.*[14]

Every political government, Beza argued, is formed by a covenant or contract sworn between the rulers and their subjects before God, who serves as third party and judge. In this covenant, God agrees to protect and bless the community in return for obedience of the laws of God and nature, particularly as set out in the Decalogue. The rulers agree to exercise God's political authority in the community, and to honor these higher laws and protect the people's rights. The people agree to exercise God's political will for the community by electing and petitioning their rulers and by honoring and obeying them so long as they remain faithful to the political covenant. If the people violate the terms of this political covenant and become criminals, Beza argued, God empowers rulers to prosecute and punish them, and in extreme cases to sentence them to death. But if the rulers violate the terms of the political covenant and become tyrants, God empowers the people to resist and to remove them from office, and in extreme cases to sentence them to death. The power to remove tyrants, however, lies not directly with the people, but with their representatives, the lower magistrates, who are constitutionally called to organize and direct the people in orderly resistance—in all-out warfare and revolution if needed.

For Beza, tyrants were rulers who violated the terms of the political covenant, particularly its foundational requirement that all must honor the rights of God to be worshiped and the rights of God's people to discharge the duties of the faith in conformity with God's law. Beza made the rights of

14. See Théodore de Bèze, *Du Droit des Magistrats*, ed. Robert M. Kingdon (Geneva: Droz, 1970), and further materials in Bèze, *Tractationum Theologicarum*, 3 vols., 2nd ed. (Geneva, 1582).

the people the foundation and condition of good government. "The people are not made for rulers, but rulers for the people," he wrote. If the magistrate rules properly, the people must obey him. But if the magistrate abuses his authority in violation of the political covenant, the people, through their representatives, have the right and the duty to resist him as a tyrant.

The issue that remained for Beza was how to ground his doctrine of rights and to determine which rights were so fundamental that, if breached by a tyrant, they triggered the right to organized resistance. Here Beza cleverly reworked Calvin's main arguments, taking his cues from Calvin's own late-life statements about the "natural rights" or "common rights of mankind," and the "the equal rights and liberties" of all persons.[15] The first and most important rights, Beza reasoned, had to be religious rights—"liberty of conscience" and "free exercise of religion." Persons are, after all, first and foremost God's subjects and called to honor and worship God above all else. If the magistrate breaches these religious rights, then nothing can be sacred and secure any longer. What is essential to the protection of the liberty of conscience and free exercise of religion, Beza continued catechetically, is the ability to live in full conformity with the law of God. What is the law of God? First and foremost, it is the Decalogue, which sets out the core duties of right Christian living. What do these Ten Commandments entail? The rights to worship God, to obey the Sabbath, to avoid foreign idols and false oaths in accordance with the first table of the Decalogue, and the rights to marriage, parentage and a household, and to life, property, and reputation protected by the second table. Is the Decalogue the only law of God? No, the natural law that God has written on the hearts of all people teaches other rights that are essential to the protection of a person and a people. Beza touched on several of these broader natural rights: freedom of religious mission and education, freedom of church government and emigration, freedoms of speech, assembly, and petition, and freedom of marriage, divorce, and private contract. Beza did not do much to ground and systematize these natural rights, nor did he make clear which of them was so fundamental that their breach could trigger organized resistance. But he put in place

15. *Comm.* Gen. 4:13; ibid., Harm. Law Numb. 3:5–10, 18–22; Deut. 5:19; ibid., Ps. 7:6–8; *Lect.* Jer. 22:1–3; 22:13–14; *Lect.* Ezek. 8:17; *Comm.* 1 Cor. 7:37.

much of the logic of a fundamental rights calculus that later Calvinists would refine and expand.

Johannes Althusius and Dutch Calvinism

These types of arguments had immediate application in the revolt of Dutch Calvinists against the tyranny of their distant sovereign, Spanish Emperor Philip II. In the 1560s, Philip imposed a series of increasingly onerous restrictions on the Netherlands—heavy taxes, commercial regulations, military conscription, forced quartering of soldiers, and more—in breach of centuries-old charters of the rights and liberties of the Dutch provinces. Even worse, Philip set up the terrifying Spanish Inquisition in the Netherlands, slaughtering Calvinists and others by the thousands and confiscating massive amounts of private property in a determined effort to root out Protestantism and to impose the sweeping new decrees of the Catholic Council of Trent. In the late 1560s and 1570s, under the inspired leadership of William of Orange and others, the Dutch put into action Calvinist principles of resistance and revolution. Whipped up by thunderous preaching and thousands of pamphlets, Calvinists and other Dutchmen eventually threw off their Spanish oppressors. They issued a declaration of independence, justifying their revolt from Spain on the strength of "clear truths" about "the laws and liberties of nature." They established a confederate government featuring seven sovereign provinces and a national government, each with its own constitution and bill of rights. Some of these provincial constitutions embraced the most advanced rights protections of the day, rendering the Netherlands a haven for many, though not all, cultural and religious dissenters from throughout Europe.[16]

The Dutch Revolt and the founding of the Dutch Republic drew a number of powerful Calvinist jurists and political theorists, including C. P. Hooft; Peter Bertius; Paul Buis; Daniel Berckringer; Gisbertus, Paulus, and Johannes Voetius; William Apollonius; Jacob Triglandus; Antonius Walaeus; Martinus Schookius; R. H. Schele; Antonius Matthaeus I, II, and III; and Ulrich Huber.

16. E. H. Kossman and A. Mellink, eds., *Texts Concerning the Revolt of the Netherlands* (London, New York: Cambridge University Press, 1974).

The most original work came from the prolific pen of the German-born Calvinist jurist, Johannes Althusius, who served as both a city counselor and consistory member in the city of Emden in the early seventeenth century. Drawing on a vast array of biblical, classical, Catholic, and Protestant sources, Althusius systematized and greatly expanded many of the core political and legal teachings of Calvin, Beza, and other co-religionists. He held that the republic is formed by a covenant between the rulers and the people before God; that the foundation of this covenant is the law of God and nature; that the Decalogue is the best expression of this higher law; that church and state are separate in form but conjoined in function; that families, churches, and states alike must protect the rights and liberties of the people; and that violations of these rights and liberties, or of the divine and natural laws that inform and empower them, are instances of tyranny that must trigger organized constitutional resistance.

Althusius added a number of core ideas to this Calvinist inheritance in his two masterworks: *Politics* (1603/14) and *A Theory of Justice* (1617/18).[17] Althusius developed a natural law theory that still treated the Decalogue as the best source and summary of natural law but layered its commandments with all manner of new biblical, classical, and Christian teachings. He developed a theory of positive law that judged the contemporary validity and utility of any human law, including the positive laws of Moses and the canon laws of the church, against both the natural law of Scripture and tradition and the fundamental law of the state. He called for a detailed written constitution as the fundamental law of the community and called for perennial protection of the rule of law and rule of rights within church and state alike. He developed an expansive theory of popular sovereignty as an expression of the divine sovereignty that each person reflects as an image-bearer of God. He developed a detailed and refined theory of natural rights—religious and social, public and private, substantive and procedural, contractual and proprietary rights. He demonstrated at great length how each of these rights was predicated on the Decalogue and other forms of natural law, and how each

17. Carl J. Friedrich, ed., *Politica Methodice Digesta of Johannes Althusius* (Althaus) (Cambridge, MA: Harvard University Press, 1932); Carl J. Friedrich, ed., *Dicaeologicae libri tres, totum et universum Jus, quo utimur, methodice complectentes* (Herborn, 1617; Frankfurt, 1618).

was to be protected by public, private, and criminal laws and procedures promulgated by the state. Particularly striking was his call for religious toleration and absolute liberty of conscience for all as a natural corollary and consequence of the Calvinist teaching of the absolute sovereignty of God, whose relationship with his creatures could not be trespassed.

More striking still were Althusius's "symbiotic theory" of human nature and "covenantal theory" of society and politics. While acknowledging the traditional Calvinist teaching of the total depravity of persons, Althusius emphasized that God has created all persons as moral, loving, communicative, and social beings, whose lives are most completely fulfilled through symbiotic relationships with others in which they can appropriately share their bodies and souls, their lives and spirits, their belongings and rights. Thus, while persons are born free, equal, and individual, they are by nature and necessity inclined to form associations—marriages and families, clubs and corporations, cities and provinces, nation-states and empires. Each of these associations, from the tiniest household to the vastest empire, is formed by a mutually consensual covenant or contract sworn by all members of that association before each other and God. Each association is a locus of authority and liberty that binds both rulers and subjects to the terms of their founding contract and to the commands of the foundational laws of God and nature. Each association confirms and protects the sovereignty and identity of its constituent members as well as their natural rights and liberties.

Althusius applied this Christian social contract theory most fully in his description of the state. Using the political history of ancient Israel as his best example, he showed historically and philosophically how nation-states develop gradually from families to tribes to cities to provinces to nations to empires. Each new layer of political sovereignty is formed by covenants sworn before God by representatives of the smaller units, and these covenants eventually become the written constitutions of the polity. The constitutions define and divide the executive, legislative, and judicial offices within that polity, and govern the relations of its rulers and subjects, clerics and magistrates, associations and individuals. They determine the relations between and among nations, provinces, cities, and private and public associations—all of which Althusius called a form of federalism (from *foedus*, Latin for covenant). The constitutions also make clear the political acts and omissions that constitute tyranny and the procedures and remedies available to those who are abused. Althusius produced the most comprehensive Calvinist theory of law and politics in the early modern period, and many of his insights anticipated teachings that would become axiomatic for Western constitutionalism.

John Milton and English Calvinism

Such ideas found immediate application a generation later in England, and became part of what John Milton called "a new reformation of the Reformation" of law, authority, and liberty. The catalyst for this new English Reformation was, again, tyranny—this time by the English monarchy against the people of England, not least the swelling population of English Calvinists descended from the first Puritans who had settled in England a century before. In 1640, these Calvinists joined many others in armed rebellion against the excesses of the English Crown—the oppressive royal taxes and fees, the harsh new Anglican establishment laws, the abuses of the royal and ecclesiastical courts, and more. When Parliament was called into session in 1640, after an eleven-year hiatus, its leaders seized power by force of arms. Civil war erupted between the supporters of Parliament and the supporters of the king. The Parliamentary party, dominated by Calvinists, eventually prevailed and passed an act in 1649 "declaring and constituting the People of England to be a Commonwealth and Free State." Parliament abolished the kingship and, remarkably, King Charles was tried by a special tribunal, convicted of treason, and beheaded in public. Parliament also abolished the aristocratic House of Lords and declared that supreme authority resided in the people and their representatives. Anglicanism was formally disestablished, and episcopal structures were replaced with Calvinist church forms. "Equal and proportional representation" was guaranteed in the election of local representatives to Parliament. England was now to be under "the democratic rule" of Parliament and the Calvinist military leader, Oliver Cromwell.

After Cromwell died in 1658, however, the commonwealth government collapsed. King Charles II, son of Charles I, returned to England, reclaimed the throne in 1660, and restored traditional monarchical government, Anglican establishment, and pre-revolutionary law. This Restoration era was short-lived, however. When his successor King James II, the other son of Charles I, began to abuse his royal prerogatives as his father had done, Parliament forced him to abdicate in 1688 in favor of the new dynasty of William and Mary. This was the Glorious Revolution. It established government by the king and Parliament and introduced a host of new guarantees to English subjects, notably those set out in the Bill of Rights and the Toleration Act of 1689.

The English Revolution unleashed a torrent of writings and legislation calling for the reformation of English law and the enforcement of the rights and liberties of Englishmen. Part of the effort was to extend the traditional rights of life, liberty, and property in the *Magna Carta* (1215) to apply to all churches and citizens, not just Anglicans and aristocratic freemen. Another aspect of the effort was to build on the Petition of Right (1628), a Parliamentary document that had set out several public, private, and procedural rights for the people and their representatives in Parliament. But the most radical and memorable efforts of the English Revolution were the many petitions and platforms issued in the 1640s and 1650s calling for establishment of a democratic government dedicated to protection of a panoply of rights and liberties. These included freedom of religion, speech, press, and assembly; the right to conscientious objection to oaths, tithes, and military service; freedom from forced quartering of soldiers and sailors; freedom of private property and from unjust takings; freedom from excessive taxation and regulation; freedom of private contract, inheritance, marriage, and divorce; the right to civil and criminal jury trial; and all manner of criminal procedural protections. They also included prohibition for *ex post facto* legislation and bills of attainder, warrantless arrests, and illegal searches and seizures; the right to bail, to a fair and speedy trial, to face one's accusers, and to representation in court; the privilege against self-incrimination, freedom from cruel investigation and punishment, and the right to appeal. While most of these rights proposals were quashed—partly by Cromwell's Protectorate and altogether by the

Restoration government of 1660—they provided a normative totem for the later common law to make real. Already in the Glorious Revolution of 1689, freedoms of religion, speech, and assembly were partly realized, as were several criminal procedure protections. Many more of these rights proposals came to vivid expression and experimentation with the English colonists in North America.

Scores of sturdy English Calvinists emerged to lead this "reformation of the Reformation," including Henry Ireton, John Lilburne, Richard Overton, John Owen, Henry Parker, Isaac Pennington, William Prynne, John Pym, Henry Robinson, Samuel Rutherford, John Saltmarsh, Henry Vane, William Walwyn, Gerrard Winstanley, and many others. It was the great poet and political philosopher John Milton who provided the most interesting integrative political theory. While some of Milton's ideas strayed beyond Calvinist conventions, most of his political ideas remained within the Calvinist tradition and indeed extended it.[18] Using Calvin and an array of Continental Calvinists, Milton argued that each person is created in the image of God with "a perennial craving" to love God, neighbor, and self. Each person has the law of God written on his and her heart, mind, and conscience, and in Scripture, most notably in the Decalogue. Each person is a fallen and fallible creature in perpetual need of divine grace and forgiveness, which is given freely to all who ask for it. Each person is a communal creature, naturally inclined to form private, domestic, ecclesiastical, and political associations. Each such association is created by a consensual covenant or contract that defines its form and function and the rights and powers of its members, all subject to the limits of natural law. Each association is headed by an authority who rules for the sake of his subjects and who must be resisted if he becomes abusive or tyrannical. All such resistance must be as moderate, orderly, and peaceable as possible, but it may rise to revolt and regicide if necessary in the political sphere.

18. See Don M. Wolfe, ed., *Complete Prose Works of John Milton*, 7 vols. (New Haven: Yale University Press, 1953–80), with other writings in William Haller, *Tracts in the Puritan Revolution, 1638–1647*, 3 vols. (New York: Columbia University Press, 1934); Don M. Wolfe, ed., *Leveller Manifestoes of the Puritan Revolution* (New York, London: T. Nelson and Sons, 1944); A. S. P. Woodhouse, *Puritanism and Liberty, Being the Army Debates (1647–49)*, 2nd ed. (Chicago, 1951).

In devising his own reformation of rights, Milton seized on what he thought to be the Calvinist Reformers' most important lesson, that the Reformation must always go on, *semper reformanda*. England must not idolize or idealize any Protestant teachings, Milton insisted, even those of Calvin and the Genevan fathers. England must rather develop and deepen, apply and amend these teachings in a continuous effort to reform church, state, and society anew. Milton further seized on what he took as a cardinal teaching of Calvinism: God calls every person to be a prophet, priest, and king, and vests each person with natural rights and duties to speak, worship, and rule in church and state, family and society at once. For Milton, the driving forces of England's perpetual Reformation, therefore, were not only clerics or magistrates, scholars or aristocrats. The true Reformers were just as much the commoners and householders, craftsmen and farmers of every peaceable type. Every person was created by God with the freedom of conscience, reason, and will. Every person was called by God to discharge both private Christian vocations and public social responsibilities in expression of love of God, neighbor, and self. This was a form of Christian populism and popular sovereignty that the Calvinist tradition had not put quite so strongly before.

Milton went even further beyond traditional Calvinist teachings in defining the religious, domestic, and civil rights and liberties that each person must enjoy in discharging these offices of prophet, priest, and king. Among religious liberties, he defended liberty of conscience; freedom of religious exercise, worship, association, and publication; equality of multiple biblical faiths before the law; separation of church and state; and disestablishment of a national religion. Among domestic liberties, he stressed urgently the right to marry and divorce in accordance with the explicit teachings of Scripture alone as well as attendant rights to nurture, discipline, and educate one's children and to have one's private home free from unwanted searches and seizures of papers and possessions. Among civil liberties, he offered a brilliant defense of the freedoms of speech and press, and defended earnestly the rights to democratic election, representation, petition, and dissent, as well as to private contract and association and to jury trial. All these arguments were echoed in hundreds of Calvinist pamphlets, sermons, and learned treatises on both sides of the Atlantic,

and would become commonplace among Calvinist constitutional reformers in the eighteenth and nineteenth centuries.

Covenant Theology and Politics in Colonial New England

Some of the most vivid amplification and application of these English
legal and political ideas in action came in Puritan Massachusetts and
other New England colonies from 1620. The Puritan colonists were given
freedom in their founding charters to experiment locally with many of the
most radical proposals and ideals that the English Calvinist revolutionaries had propounded.[19] While adapting Geneva's congregational polity
and consistorial government within the church, the colonists adopted
English proposals for a democratic state government. In his *Body of Liberties* (1641), Calvinist jurist and theologian Nathaniel Ward set forth a
twenty-five-page bill of rights for the colony of Massachusetts Bay, which
captured every one of the rights and liberties proposed by Calvin, Beza,
Althusius, Milton, and the Puritan pamphleteers, and added many more
rights and liberties, particularly in protection of women, children, and
animals. The *Body of Liberties* was an anchor text for New England colonial
constitutionalism, and anticipated many of the rights provisions of the
later state constitutions. While these legal instruments were often breached
and ignored by autocratic and theocratic colonial leaders, they provided
an essential legal substratum of rights that has proved enduring.

A number of New England Puritans, most notably John Winthrop,
John Cotton, Thomas Hooker, Samuel Willard, and three members of
the Mather family—Richard, Increase, and Cotton—distilled prevailing
Calvinist views of the person into a basic theory of authority and liberty,
society and politics. On the one hand, they argued, every person is created
in the image of God and justified by faith in God. Every person is called
to a distinct vocation that stands equal in dignity and sanctity to all others. Every person is a prophet, priest, and king, and responsible to exhort,
minister, and rule in the community. Every person thus stands equal before
God and before his or her neighbor. Every person is vested with a natural

---

19. See representative documents in Edmund S. Morgan, ed., *Puritan Political Ideas
1558–1794* (repr., Indianapolis: Hackett Publishing, 2003).

liberty to live, to believe, and to love and serve God and neighbor. Every person is entitled to the vernacular Scripture, to education, to work in a vocation. On the other hand, every person is sinful and prone to evil and egoism. Every person needs the restraint of the law to deter him from evil, and to drive him to repentance. Every person needs the association of others to exhort, minister, and rule him with law and with love. Every person, therefore, is inherently a communal creature. Every person belongs to a family, a church, and a political community.

These social institutions of family, church, and state, Protestants believe, are divine in origin and human in organization. They are created by God and governed by godly ordinances. They stand equal before God and are called to discharge distinctive godly functions in the community. The family is called to rear and nurture children, to educate and discipline them, to exemplify love and cooperation. The church is called to preach the word, administer the sacraments, educate the young, aid the needy. The state is called to protect order, punish crime, promote community. Although divine in origin, these institutions are formed through human covenants. Such covenants confirm the divine functions, the created offices, of these institutions. Such covenants also organize these offices so they are protected from the sinful excesses of officials who occupy them. Family, church, and state are thus organized as public institutions, accessible and accountable to each other and to their members. The church is to be organized according to a democratic congregational polity, with a separation of ecclesiastical powers among pastors, elders, and deacons, election of officers to limited tenures of office, and ready participation of the congregation in the life and leadership of the church.

The New England Puritans, echoing some of their European co-religionists, cast these theological doctrines into democratic forms. On the one hand, they cast the doctrines of the person and society into democratic social forms. Since all persons stand equal before God, they must stand equal before God's political agents in the state. Since God has vested all persons with natural liberties of life and belief, the state must ensure them similar civil liberties. Since God has called all persons to be prophets, priests, and kings, the state must protect their freedoms to speak, to preach, and to rule in the community. Since God has created persons as social creatures, the state must promote and protect a plurality of social institutions, particularly the church and the family. On the other hand, the New England Puritans cast the doctrines of sin into democratic political forms. The political office must be protected against the sinfulness of the political official. Political power, like ecclesiastical power, must be distributed among self-checking executive, legislative, and judicial branches. Officials must be elected to limited terms. Laws must be clearly codified, and discretion closely guarded. If officials abuse their office, they must be disobeyed. If they persist in their abuse, they must be removed, even if by revolutionary force and regicide.

Conclusions

In his *Social Contract* of 1762, Jean-Jacques Rousseau offered this charitable assessment of his compatriot, John Calvin: "Those who consider Calvin only as a theologian fail to recognize the breadth of his genius. The editing of our wise laws, in which he had a large share, does him as much credit as his *Institutes*. . . . [S]o long as the love of country and liberty is not extinct among us, the memory of this great man will be held in reverence."[20] A similar assessment might be offered about much of early modern Calvinism. Calvinism was both a theological and a legal movement, a reformation both of church and state. Beginning with Calvin and Beza, who were trained in both fields, theologians and jurists together formed the leadership of the Reformed churches, and they made ample use of pulpits and printers alike. For every new Calvinist catechism in the early modern era there was a new Calvinist ordinance, for every fresh confession of faith an elaborate new bill of rights. Early modern Calvinists believed in natural and positive law as a deterrent for sin, an inducement to grace, a teacher of Christian virtue. They also believed in the rule of law, structuring their churches and states alike to minimize the sinful excesses of their rulers and to maximize the liberties of their subjects to live their lives in order to more promptly and more readily obey God in all things.

20. *Du contrat social* (1762), 2, 7n., in Jean-Jacques Rousseau, *The Social Contract and Discourse on the Origin of Inequality*, ed. Lester G. Crocker (New York: Pocket Books, 1967), 44n.

3

THE ARTS AND THE REFORMED
TRADITION

WILLIAM EDGAR

Why do so many assume that Protestants in the Reformed tradition are at best extremely cautious about the arts? Hans Rookmaaker, himself in the Reformed camp, considers that the Puritans slouched into a pietistic mysticism that denied the pleasures of the visual arts because of their priority on spiritual worship. He calls this a "secondary stream of mysticism," which looked for holiness in a subjectivist and legalistic manner that kept clear of the so-called worldliness of the fine arts.[1] Protestantism often fell into this fear of culture. Missions were such a priority that such pursuits as the arts seemed distracting at best. With the birth of modern missions, the evangelical revivals produced the popular view that enjoying the arts was akin to polishing the brass on the sinking Titanic. As evangelist Dwight L. Moody

---

1. Hans R. Rookmaaker, *Modern Art and the Death of a Culture* (Downers Grove, IL: Inter-Varsity Press, 1970), 30.

was reputed to have said, "I look upon this world as a wrecked vessel; God has given me a lifeboat and said to me, 'Moody, save all you can.'"[2]

But is there more to the story? Yes, lots more. In order to tell it properly, we must go back to the most frequently accused Philistine, John Calvin.

Against Calvin

Opinions abound that Calvin and Calvinism degrade the arts. Voltaire said Calvin was responsible for the city of Geneva being dour, hostile to the pleasures of theater and the arts.[3] Ferdinand Brunetière, literary critic in France's Third Republic, equated Calvinism with the horror of art. We can add Orentin Douen, who is unrelenting in his criticism of Calvin, whom he deems the "ennemi de tout plaisir et de toute distraction, même des arts et de la musique."[4] For the Roman Catholic historian Louis Réau, Calvinist iconoclasm belongs quite simply to the "history of vandalism."[5]

These critiques carry a certain plausibility. In a letter to a young student, written in 1540, Calvin encourages greater devotion to religion. He makes the following comparison: "Those who seek in scholarship more than an honored occupation with which to beguile the tedium of idleness I would compare to those who pass their lives looking at paintings."[6]

Rehabilitations

Does this settle the case? Hardly, although achieving clarity about Calvin and his legacy on the arts is fraught with pitfalls. At least two

2. For a brief history of this aspect of Protestantism and the arts, see Hilary Brand and Adrienne Chaplin: *Art and Soul: Signposts for Christians in the Arts* (Carlisle, UK: Piquant, 2001), chap. 3.

3. See also Graham Gartgett, "Goldsmith as Translator of Voltaire," *The Modern Language Review* 98 (2003): 842–56. In fairness, Voltaire would later be a defender of the Huguenots, and would praise Geneva for its industriousness.

4. This translates as "enemy of all pleasure and of all diversion, even of the arts and music" (Orentin Douen, *Clément Marot et le psautier Huguenot*, vol. 1 [Paris: Imprimerie Nationale, 1878], 377).

5. Louis Réau, *Histoire du vandalisme: Les monuments détruits de l'art français* (Paris: Robert Laffont, 1995 [orig. 1959]).

6. *CR*, 11.56.

major types of rehabilitation have been attempted. They are based on two historiographies. The first is represented by Abraham Kuyper (1837–1920) and Émile Doumergue (1844–1937) and their heirs. Kuyper's approach to Calvinism and the arts is best ascertained from the fifth lecture, "Calvinism and Art," in the 1898 *Lectures on Calvinism* sponsored by the L. P. Stone Foundation at Princeton University.[7] Not surprisingly, Kuyper's thoughts, while emanating from a Reformed heritage, carry a decidedly nineteenth-century ethos. His orientation is theological and apologetical. The arts exist, he said, to elevate "the Beautiful and the Sublime in its eternal significance." They are one of God's richest gifts to mankind. Kuyper believes they have a role to foster a "proper mysticism" that helps recognize the benefits of true religion, although he railed against the tendency to abandon such mysticism for an "art-intoxication."[8] One senses an affinity with Matthew Arnold here as well (whether or not Kuyper ever read him). According to that influential British thinker, culture is "the best that has been thought and said in the world." Furthermore, culture exists "to make reason and the will of God prevail."[9]

Kuyper here defended Calvinism's role in moving in an evolutionary way into a "multiformity of life-tendencies," as over against putting everything under the tutelage of the state or other established institutions. The effect of this is to free the arts from functioning merely in the context of worship. However closely they are aligned in the "lower stage of human development," it is now time to evolve away from such a congruence, and in effect send the arts out of the church.[10] He added that since art is "incapable of expressing the very essence of Religion," it must live in a sphere of its own. Calvinism, he said, released art from the guardianship of the church and so, even more than the Renaissance, was the first to recognize its maturity.[11]

7. Abraham Kuyper and Émile Doumergue, "Calvinism and Art," *Lectures on Calvinism* (Grand Rapids: Eerdmans, 1931), 142–70.

8. Ibid., 143.

9. Matthew Arnold, *Culture and Anarchy* (Cambridge: Cambridge University Press, 1960 [orig. 1882]), 6, 42.

10. Kuyper and Doumergue, "Calvinism and Art," 146–47.

11. Ibid., 157.

This does not mean religion cannot generate an art style. On the contrary, Kuyper argued that, unlike the rationalist Enlightenment, Calvinism has generated a rich heritage in the arts.[12] Calvinism did this not by reaching some higher stage that forbids the symbolical expression of religion in visual terms, but by setting forth a world and life view that inspires artists to interpret the world and represent it in a certain way.[13] To defend Calvin against the charge of Philistinism, Kuyper cited many passages in which the Reformer shows approval of the arts. But his central argument is that Calvinism promotes a good aesthetic principle, derived from Calvin's view of the creation. Accordingly, the artist's calling is "to discover in those natural forms the order of the beautiful, and, enriched by this higher knowledge, to produce a beautiful world that transcends the beautiful of nature." Thus, the arts should remind us of what was lost through the curse and what is to be hoped for in the creation's "perfect coming luster."[14]

So what does this all look like in the visual arts? Through Calvinism, and also by God's common grace, much fruit has been produced. Kuyper finds important examples in the Netherlands, where, he said, poetry, and more especially music and painting, flowed out of a "reformational" orientation. He cited Rembrandt and other painters, and argued that they began from the doctrine of election by free grace, which led to the implication of special importance for simpler people and ordinary events in the eyes of God. Consequently, he argued, the arts could focus far more on the seemingly small and insignificant, and elevate *real* people as opposed to high-placed people.[15] Using decidedly populist and romantic rhetoric, Kuyper declared that "ecclesiastical power no longer restrained the artist, and princely gold no longer chained him in fetters. If artist, he also was man, mingling freely among the people, and discovering in and behind their human life, something quite different from what palace and castle had hitherto afforded him."[16] In music, the same evolution occurred. No longer attached to the church, composers were free from

12. Ibid., 148, 151–52.
13. Ibid., 152.
14. Ibid., 154–55.
15. Ibid., 165–66.
16. Ibid., 167.

Gregory's chant, and now "selected their melodies from the free world of music."[17]

Émile Doumergue takes a similar approach. Although French, he too goes from Calvin to the golden age of Dutch art, and particularly Rembrandt.[18] The Calvinists not only freed the arts, but made them relevant to the people, and stressed the possibility of psychological and spiritual interiority. Among the heirs to these views we should include Léon Wencélius, whose classic work, *L'esthétique de Calvin*, similarly defends the Reformed worldview as a generator of the arts.[19]

Hans Rookmaaker would echo these views a generation later. Rookmaaker was an art historian, so that one would expect him to go into much more detail than Kuyper or Doumergue, which he most certainly did. His essays on individual artists such as Dürer, Bruegel, Rubens, and so many more, introduce us to the ways by which a world and life view informs paintings.[20] Rookmaaker's best-known work is a critique of the contemporary world through the lens of the arts. *Modern Art and the Death of a Culture* is a fascinating journey through art history with a historiography of decline, based on the epistemology of the artists within their different epochs.[21]

In addition to the brilliant appreciation of the way a worldview enlightens history and culture in these thinkers, one cannot miss the romantic and even Hegelian spirit that informs the approach of Kuyper and Doumergue, although the approach of Rookmaaker is more complex. We believe that the idea that culture and everything related to it emanates from a worldview, a religious consciousness that characterizes all of human activity in a given period, is a biblical idea, at least in part. But the broad periodization, the search for an ethos

17. Ibid., 168.

18. Émile Doumergue, *L'art et le sentiment dans l'oeuvre de Calvin* (Genève: Société Genevoise d'Edition, 1902; repr. Genève: Slatkine Reprints, 1970), 13–14, 36–34.

19. Léon Wencelius, *L'esthétique de Calvin* (Paris: Les Belles Lettres, 1937).

20. See, for example, his articles on Western art history, collected in Hans Rookmaaker, *Western Art and the Meanderings of a Culture*, vol. 4 of *Complete Works*, ed. Marleen Hengelaar-Rookmaaker (Carlisle, UK: Piquant, 2002), 1–187.

21. These generalists are not the only ones who connect Calvinism to, say, seventeenth-century Dutch landscapists. Maarten de Klijn and other contemporary art historians make such connections as well.

or a zeitgeist that characterizes a given era, can lead to anachronisms and oversimplifications when we are not careful to honor the details. At worst this approach can lead to an unhealthy endorsement of culture wars.

Nuance and Context

Reactions were to be expected, and they have been plentiful. But with them, a door has been opened for a second historiography of how Calvinism relates to the arts. One of the first to put into question the first historiography is Ernst Gombrich. His major contribution to the discussion is *In Search of Cultural History*.[22] He questions whether different epochs are really held together by a single zeitgeist. As he looks at the arts he notes the many rival schools and approaches within each period. Each of these has its own coherency, but also shares, unwittingly or not, with the others, making problematic the idea of a worldview governing a movement that affects the way artists work.

Besides Gombrich, all kinds of culture critiques have arisen, challenging the Hegelian model. One can think of schools such as culturalism, structuralism and post-structuralism, the Frankfurt School, feminism, Foucaultian views, and many others.[23] The extreme version of this new direction must be in the various approaches known as postmodernism. This elusive term can at least refer to several tendencies that oppose "meta-narrative" historiographies. Jean-François Lyotard famously called for "incredulity toward meta-narratives, the *grand récit*, particularly as proffered by science and education.[24] For him and many others, knowledge is not an end in itself, but cultural capital, power to arrive at a particular end.

22. Ernst Gombrich, *In Search of Cultural History* (New York: Oxford University Press, 1969). Rookmaaker reviews this book favorably in *Western Art*, 275–77. My guess is that Gombrich was moving in the direction of this second historiography.

23. See Jean-François Lyotard, *The Postmodern Condition: A Report on Knowledge* (Manchester: Manchester University Press, 1984), 46. For an excellent summary of these and other schools in relation with culture studies, see John Storey, *An Introduction to Culture Theory and Popular Culture*, 2nd ed. (Athens, GA: University of Georgia Press, 1998).

24. Jean-François Lyotard, *The Postmodern Condition: A Report on Knowledge* (Minneapolis: University of Minnesota Press, 1984), xxiii; *ad loc.*

These schools, decidedly anti-Hegelian, bring needed correctives and modesty to the enterprise of culture studies. Yet, they are not without their own agendas, some of which make almost any generalization difficult. For example, the very thoughtful culture analyst Pierre Bourdieu seeks to locate value and meaning in the world of everyday experience. Although he began as almost a pure relativist, he looked for universals in his more mature scholarly phase.[25] He helpfully guides us through various cultural tastes, to unveil the many layers of lifestyles and habits. Still, his purpose is to identify the relations of power and economic dominance of one group over another. The unintended result may be, in Storey's words, that, "The much heralded collapse of standards rehearsed (almost weekly) in the so-called 'quality' media of our postmodern new times, may be nothing more than a perceived sense that the opportunities to use culture and to make and mark social distinction are becoming more and more difficult to find."[26] What has happened here is that cultural impact and cultural differences are simply more complex to identify. The tools given us by the second historiographers are most useful, as long as one is able to discern the ideologies behind their not-so-innocent approaches.

Applied to the question of Calvinism and the arts, this second historiography brings helpful clarifications. It not only guides us in answering the larger question, Does Calvinism form a cultural sensibility that is coherent? but it also helps us be more empirically responsible. In the bargain, it reminds us how culture works. The question remains whether Calvin's aesthetic ideals could crystallize into a movement

25. See, for example, Pierre Bourdieu, *Distinction: A Social Critique of the Judgment of Taste*, trans. Richard Nice (Cambridge, MA: Harvard University Press, 1984). Note from *Rules of Art*: "For Bourdieu, artists and other agents possess certain capitals, of which there are four basic types: first, economic capital—stocks and shares but also the surplus present in very high salaries; second, social capital—the network of influential patrons that you can use to support your actions; third, cultural capital—including the knowledge of the artistic field and its history, which in turn serves to distinguish the naïve painter from the professional, and including also scholarly capital of a formal type (a postgraduate degree, the award of a Rome visiting scholarship, etc.); finally, symbolic capital—your reputation or honour, as an artist who is loyal to fellow-artists and so on." Bridget Fowler, *Pierre Bourdieu and Cultural Theory: Critical Investigations* (London: Sage Publications, 1997).

26. Storey, *Introduction to Culture Theory*, 198.

so deeply rooted that it could eventually give rise to such fruit as the Dutch landscapists of the seventeenth century, as was claimed by Kuyper and Doumergue.

In Search of a Middle Ground

Philip Benedict is also skeptical about the claims of the first historiography. He shares some of the doubts of the second. But he is unwilling to abandon the quest for some kind of connection between Calvinism and the arts.[27] Like Gombrich and his heirs, Benedict questions whether something as sweeping as Calvinism could successfully come to dominate an entire region, changing its culture one hundred percent. For example, he points out that careful studies of particular regions and epochs reveal that Calvinism could not quite achieve a total recasting of artistic or musical culture and remake it into a new image. The reality on the ground is more complex. Here is a case in point. Emmanuel LeRoy Ladurie's *The Peasants of Languedoc* affirms that the Cévennes were so steeped in Calvinist culture that even lullabies were taken from the Psalms and no local or traditional songs were used. Benedict notes, though, that Ladurie based his conclusions on the work of nineteenth-century folklorists. More modern studies show something different. Again, Benedict points out that in the Cévennes, the Huguenot minister Pierre Jurieu had wished to train the heart, "so that it conceives its thoughts and forms its meditations only in the terms of the Holy Spirit as expressed in the Psalms."[28] But Benedict argues that such an aspiration was quite impossible in reality because "the Bible always had to make its peace with beliefs, motifs, and genres derived from non-biblical sources, even in the greatest strongholds of Calvinist fidelity."[29] He cites an interesting example: the folk belief that May was an unlucky month in which to get married. He found that the Huguenots of the Cévennes abstained just as

27. Philip Benedict, "Calvinism as a Culture?" in Paul Corby Finney, ed., *Seeing Beyond the Word: Visual Arts and the Calvinist Tradition* (Grand Rapids: Eerdmans, 1999), 1–45.
28. Pierre Jurieu, *traité de la devotion* (Rouen, 1675), 184.
29. Benedict, "Calvinism as a Culture?" 25.

readily as Roman Catholics, despite their rhetoric against superstitious religion. Benedict further argues that the circles of those given to literary, artistic, scientific, or antiquarian interests were in locales where the confessional differences of the era were easily overcome. He states that Catholics and Huguenots gathered there in order to cultivate their common interests in ways where their religious views may not have been particularly inflected.[30] As E. W. Zeeden and others have shown, there was even overlap in popular devotional literature.[31]

My own observation confirms Benedict's approach. I recently traveled in Central Europe, where I witnessed the burgeoning democracies born since 1989. No one would deny the change. Yet the shadow of the older, oppressive regime still lurks. Whatever else one might want to say about the vestiges of communism, it is hard to deny the influence of such a bureaucratic system on communications, architecture, and religious life. The ethos still hanging over many of the newborn democracies. At the same time, communism itself partly depended on age-old authoritarian systems; while particularly brutal, it was not altogether different from previous models of tyranny.

So then, to take Benedict's point, we should not give up trying to find connections between Calvinism and the arts, but we must find them by giving attention to simpler, more concrete questions than the grand schemes of Kuyper and Doumergue seem to allow.

One of these questions is whether theological pronouncements had important implications for the place of the arts in church and in life. How much were artists affected with the religious beliefs, permissions, and prohibitions connected with Calvinism? Three subject matters will guide us. First, Calvin's views on the arts. We will need to know something of his approach to images, both his iconoclasm and his cautious approval of the arts in their place. Second, the development of a Reformed ontology for the arts. Here we will want to move from the worldview set forth by Calvin, to implications and applications probably not foreseen by the

---

30. Ibid., 26.

31. Ibid. See E. W. Zeeden, *Die Entstehung der Konfessionen* (Munich: Oldenbourg, 1965); and Quentin Skinner, "The Origins of the Calvinist Theory of Revolution," in Barbara C. Malament, ed., *After the Reformation: Essays in Honor of J. H. Hexter* (Philadelphia: University of Pennsylvania Press, 1980), 309–30.

Reformer. And third, a final word about cultural change. Here we will briefly look at the question of appropriations.

Iconoclasm, the Background

It is a given that John Calvin strongly preached and practiced the reformation of worship. One of his consistent polemics was against idolatry, and particularly the use of images as aids for the cult. Most often his invectives are labeled iconoclasm. His views were not developed in a vacuum. The cult of images was quite widespread in the Middle Ages, and became particularly strong in the fifteenth century. Practices included devotion to relics, pilgrimages to shrines and other symbolic places, the cult of the saints, and the externalization of the Mass, including bleeding hosts and the full development of the feast of Corpus Christi.[32] Already there were critiques of this popular piety well before the Reformation, even in the West, which had generally resisted the *iconodules* of the Byzantine Church. Although Pope Gregory I and even Thomas Aquinas had defended the use of imagery for the education of the illiterate, various preachers and movements warned against them. One may think of the Cistercians and the Franciscans, who cautioned against the use of symbols to adorn places of worship. One can also think of the precursors of the Reformation, men such as John Wycliffe and Jan Hus, who made moderate criticisms of images, particularly those used to elevate the Virgin Mary in near competition with Christ.

Erasmus

Certainly the most systematic of the critics in the late fifteenth and early sixteenth centuries was Erasmus of Rotterdam (ca. 1466–1536). His widely read *Enchiridion Militis Christiani* (1503) is a strong tract against the corruption of the church.[33] In it Erasmus lamented the formalism

32. See, for example, Hermann Heimpel, "Characteristics of the Late Middle Ages in Germany," in G. Strauss, ed., *Pre-Reformation Germany* (New York: MacMillan, 1972), 68.
33. W. Welzing, ed., *Erasmus von Rotterdam: Ausgewählte Schriften*, vol. 1 (Darmstadt, West Germany: Wissenschaftliche Buchgesellschaft, 1968). For an English edition, see

and materialism of current practice, and affirmed the inward, spiritual nature of worship. Clearly influenced by Plato, it nevertheless pleaded for an intimate relation between God and the human soul. Venerating images was accordingly condemned, with the exception of those who "from weakness of mind" can only worship according to the flesh.[34] Still, Erasmus argued, there could be nothing more "disgusting" than the cult of relics or other so-called blessed objects, since Christ himself eschewed all use of divine power and instructed his followers to go straight to him in heaven without intermediaries.[35] Erasmus' views were enormously influential on the Reformers, even those who thought his overall theology to lack consistency.

Switzerland in general and Geneva in particular were profoundly marked by the iconoclasm of the Reformation. Merle d'Aubigné's *Histoire de la Réformation au XVIème siècle* [*History of the Reformation in the Sixteenth Century*] tracks the story of the Protestant movement in Switzerland largely through the acts of iconoclasm.[36] His assessment is that, "in the times of the Reformation, the doctors attacked the Pope and the people the images."[37] He is not far off. According to Carlos M. N. Eire, while iconoclasm varied in place and intensity in the Reformation, it was prominent because it meant publicly testing whether or not Roman Catholic worship was legal, and set forth how the Mass could be replaced by a spiritual and Word-based religion.[38] Switzerland became a crucial place for this pattern to be displayed, he argues, for at least three reasons: (1) It is where Ulrich Zwingli was able to produce what is the most consistent and influential iconoclastic theology.[39] (2) Switzerland was the first area, far more than

---

Raymond Himelink, trans., *Enchiridion, or The Manual of the Christian Knight* (London: Kessinger, 2003).

34. Ibid., 90–91.

35. Ibid., 204.

36. Merle d'Aubigné, *Histoire de la Réformation au XVIème siècle*, (Paris: Firmin Didot Frères, 1938).

37. Ibid., 767.

38. Carlos M. N. Eire, *War against the Idols: The Reformation of Worship from Erasmus to Calvin* (Cambridge: Cambridge University Press, 1986), 107.

39. Ulrich Zwingli's *De vera et falsa religione* had a direct influence on Calvin. Compare S. M. Jackson, ed., *The Latin Works and the Correspondence of Huldreich Zwingli: Together with Selections from his German Works*, vol. 3 (New York: Putnam's Sons, 1912), 332, with Calvin's *Institutes*, 1.11.9.

Germany, where iconoclasm became a consistent policy, particularly in the patterns established whereby its cities became officially Protestant. (3) Because the towns had a republican structure, the people were better able to participate and use iconoclasm as a political tactic.

The City of Geneva

Geneva, in the years before Calvin arrived (particularly 1530–36), experienced this process intensely. Her alliance with Bern meant it had important encouragements to reform, particularly in the struggle to become independent from both the House of Savoy and the prince-bishop of Geneva.[40] The Bernese council had staged a disputation in 1527 in which the Protestant faith triumphed over Roman beliefs and practices such as the merits of Christ, tradition, transubstantiation, the Mass, and the cult of images. The Reformation triumphed from then on. Geneva fell under the sway of Bern at first through a military alliance with its armies against the Savoy. As the Bernese army marched down through the Southern territories it destroyed images, quartered its horses in churches, and generally imposed on the city its own services, including preachers. Although these armies left, they had begun to stir the people to anti-Catholic behavior. Then in 1532 Pope Clement VII proclaimed a general indulgence in Geneva. The Protestant sympathizers rose up and posted placards all over the city mocking the indulgence system and proclaiming forgiveness was available by praying directly to Christ.

After these incidents the Reformation began to take root in the city for theological reasons. Guillaume Farel, Pierre Olivetan, and others began to arrive in 1532, and preached clandestinely. When opposed, they said they were preaching "in God's authority," accusing the priests of foisting human traditions and inventions upon the people.[41] Although expelled, Farel and Olivetan would return in 1533 with their friend, Antoine Fromment, to

40. One can date this struggle from 1519, when Genevan patriots led by Besançon Hughes, the "oath-fellow," succeeded in their fight. He eventually garnered support from those who signed treaties with Bern and Fribourg, and may have given the Swiss Confederates the name *Eidgenossen*, from which we derive the term *Huguenot*.

41. See Provana di Collegno, "Rapports de Guillaume Farel avec les Vaudois du Piémont," *Bulletin de la Société d'Études des Hautes-Alpes* (1891): 257–78.

continue preaching Reformation principles. Preaching was followed by rioting, and many church ornaments and statues were destroyed. Disputations and revolts accumulated, and finally, after a message preached by Farel in the cathedral in August of 1535, a serious revolt occurred, destroying most of the icons, including the Foyseau altarpiece. Although there were laws forbidding or at least curtailing this activity, the sympathies of the Town Council were clearly with the iconoclasts.

On May 25, 1536, the Council voted unanimously to "Live according to the Holy Gospel Law and the Word of God, according as it is preached, wanting to abandon all Masses and other Papal ceremonies and abuses, images and idols."[42]

Iconoclasm in Geneva was both a revolutionary act and a theological statement. Obviously it carried mixed motives. But the central concern was truly a religious conviction.[43] As Oecolampadius put it, describing the religious conflicts in Basel, the hesitancy of the government had been a "hard knot" to untangle, but iconoclasm represents "the wedge of the LORD" that simply split the knot.[44] Here we have political action that concretizes theological conviction. Thus, iconoclasm was never pure vandalism, but intended as reform. Such was the case for Geneva.

Calvin and Icons

When Calvin arrived in Geneva he found a magistracy already committed to this approach. While he never advocated tyrannicide, he favored iconoclasm. As was the case of earlier Reformers, his views must be seen within the overall context of his theology. His own spiritual journey must have played a part in his convictions. Although we know little about his conversion, we do have the oft-quoted testimony in his *Commentary on the Psalms* where he spoke of God "by a sudden conversion" pulling him out from "so profound an abyss of mire" as the "superstitions of Popery."[45] In the *Institutes*, from the earliest edition until the final one, he devel-

42. *R. Consist.*, 13:576, my translation.
43. Carlos M. N. Eire, *War against the Idols*, 155.
44. Ibid., 156.
45. CR, 31.22.

ops extended arguments against images in worship. By the 1559 edition the discussion is robust, especially in the relevant section on the knowledge of God (1.11–12) and the portion on the second commandment (2.8.17–21).

The foundation for Calvin's theology of worship, hence his attacks on idolatry, is the doctrine of life's central purpose: the glory of God. In the powerful words of the Geneva Catechism:

1. Quelle est la principale fin de la vie humaine?
   C'est de connaître Dieu.
2. Pourquoi dis-tu cela?
   Parce qu'il nous a créés et mis au monde pour être glorifié en nous. Et c'est bienraison que nous rapportions notre vie à sa gloire puisqu'il en est lecommencement.
3. Quel est le souverain bien des hommes ?
   Cela même.[46]

Farther into the catechism, in the section regarding the Ten Commandments, the following reasons are given as an explication of the Second Commandment:

144. Veut-il du tout défendre de faire aucune image?
   Non, mais il défend de faire aucune image, ou pour figurer Dieu, ou pour adorer.
145. Pourquoi est-ce qu'il n'est point licite de représenter Dieu visiblement?
   Parce qu'il n'y a nulle convenance entre lui, qui est Esprit éternel, incompréhensible, et une matière corporelle, morte, corruptible et visible.[47]

46. 1. What is the chief end of human life? It is to know God. 2. Why do you say this? Because he created us and placed us in the world to be glorified in us. And this is surely the reason to connect our life to his glory, since he is its beginning. 3. And what is the supreme good of men? The same.

47. 144. Does it forbid any image at all? No, but it forbids making any image either to portray God, or to worship. 145. Why is it illicit to represent God visibly? Because there is no conformity between him, who is an eternal, incomprehensible Spirit, and a physical, dead, corruptible and visible object

We should note here what we will soon discover, that Calvin does not forbid any image whatsoever, but only images of God.

Throughout his preaching and his writing, Calvin insisted that only God was worthy of all glory. Any use of images leads to idolatry, he argues. In Book I of the *Institutes* he takes on a number of papal abuses by citing the fathers. For example, he rebuts the "papist" argument that images are to help the unlearned develop a better idea of theology by citing Augustine and others who say that statues are a way to "remove fear and add error."[48] Teachers in the church lapsed into the veneration of images because "they themselves were mute." Imagining there being some divinity in the image, "Therefore, when you prostrate yourself in veneration, representing to yourself in an image either a god or a creature, you are already ensnared in some superstition."[49] His frequent attacks on Roman Catholic "idolatry" center on robbing God of his due.

At the heart of Calvin's opposition to images in worship is a concern for the spiritual nature of truth. Indeed, because God is for him the endpoint of all human acts and aspirations, and because he is a pure spirit, one should never attempt to form any earthly replica of him. For Calvin, the worship of God must be spiritual, so that it may correspond to his nature. A further level that leads Calvin to banish images from worship is his understanding of the fulfillment of all the Old Testament figures that announced Christ. Calvin recognized the propriety of images in the age of preparation. But once Christ had come, and the church was founded, all images, except the representations in the two sacraments, are abolished.

Thus images were often destroyed. Sculpture was particularly targeted, paintings somewhat less; stained glass was often preserved. A constant call to vigilance was characteristic of the Reformers. Sometimes this could be quite extreme, as it was in Puritan England.[50] At the same time, it must not be forgotten that never did the magisterial Reformers issue blanket condemnation of images nor forbid the proper enjoyment of the arts.

48. *Institutes*, 1.11.6–7.
49. Ibid., 1.11.7.
50. See Patrick Collinson: *From Iconoclasm to Iconophobia* (Reading: The University of Reading, 1986).

Music

We should mention that Calvin's approach to music was the same. As Charles Garside has demonstrated, Calvin's preference for singing mostly the Psalms, unaccompanied, during worship, comes from the same conviction. When he came to Geneva, he found the people still "ignorant" because of the troubles the city had experienced. So, the singing of the Psalms was among the first actions for which Calvin pleaded, along with church discipline, including excommunication (to safeguard the Lord's Supper), catechism, and licensing of marriage. Without these, he did not how there could be a well-ordered or "regulated" church life according to the Word of God.[51] Why the Psalms? They are prayers given by God himself. Following Augustine, Calvin insisted that worshipers know what they were singing, so he had them sung in French.[52]

Less the musician than Martin Luther, Calvin nevertheless developed a theology of music that separated singing for inside the church and that for outside the church. Still, wherever it was practiced, music needed to be appropriately unassuming. He did believe strongly that music can lift the soul to heavenly joy. As such, music is the gift of God. At the same time (echoing Plato), he cautioned against immoderate music that could lead to "immodesty" (*impudicité*) and "effeminacy by disordered delights" (*de nous effeminer en délices désordonnées*).[53] He required the entire congregation to sing, and forbade the use of choirs. Accordingly, the Psalms should be rendered in music with both gravity and majesty. Here is not the place to develop Calvin's appropriation of Louis Bourgeois and Claude Goudimel, who wrote simple but elegant melodies for the sacred texts. He frowned on musical instruments in worship because he thought they belonged to the Old Testament times, when people were spiritually less mature, "while they were yet tender and like children, by such rudiments until the coming of Christ. But now, when the clear light of the gospel has dissipated the *shadows* of the law and taught us that God is to be served in a simpler

51. CR, 10.7.
52. Ibid., 2.17.
53. Ibid., 2.16.

form, it would be to act a foolish and mistaken part to imitate that which the prophet enjoined only upon those of his own time."[54]

Anti-Art?

Some give the impression that Calvin's strong views against images came from his opposition to the arts in general. Despite statements such as the one above to his student, it is unjust to cast him as being against the arts. While he strongly denounced images of sacred subjects because they would stand as open invitations to idolatry, he nevertheless acknowledged the place for artistic expression in life. In the *Institutes* we find several instances where he sees the legitimacy of the visual arts. For example, alongside the condemnation of altars and "votive pilgrimages to see images," he adds, "and yet I am not gripped by the superstition of thinking absolutely no image permissible." "But," he says, "because sculpture and painting are gifts of God, I seek a pure and legitimate use of each." Although it is wrong to represent God because he is invisible, it is fine to sculpt or paint things that the eye can see. This allowance is admittedly somewhat grudging.[55]

But there are others. His most comprehensive statement about the arts in general is found in the *Institutes* (2.2.12–16). The discussion is within the larger question of the vestiges of gifts and the freedom of the will. Calvin affirms that our natural gifts have been corrupted, including reason—the power of understanding—and the will. Still, there exists common grace. Calvin notes that we still may operate within the realms of government, household management, all mechanical skills, and the liberal arts. Despite the fall, we still know about the need for law to run human organizations. In the *Institutes* (2.2.14) he discusses both liberal and manual arts. He notes that hardly anyone is without talent in some art. He disagrees with Plato, who said the ability to perfect the arts is merely from memory. Rather, it is inborn, Calvin says. In the *Institutes* (2.2.15–16) he celebrates the gifts from God's Spirit to those who do not confess the name of Christ. These include discernment of

54. *Comm.* Ps. 81:3.
55. *Institutes*, 1.11.12.

civic order, equity, the art of disputation, physics, mathematics, poetry, and "the useful arts."[56]

Calvin had similarities and differences with the other Reformers. Zwingli, very much the iconoclast in matters of worship, wrote in 1525, "No one is a greater admirer than I of painting and statuary." He allowed freedom for imagery to adorn the home, even though he was careful to limit the visual arts in church.[57]

Where and What Kinds?

It is clear that Calvin is not set against the arts in general, nor does his kind of iconoclasm and restrictions on music in worship indicate an abhorrence of the arts, as Brunetière, Douen, Réau, and others maintain. To be sure, one cannot miss the power of the iconoclastic arguments from Calvin and the other Reformers. More than most polemics, it struck at the heart of medieval piety. Still, there was legitimate room for a reasonable appreciation for the arts.

So here is the question. Did Calvin's view generate something more than he may have envisaged? Did his successors, especially those who developed a positive view of the arts, rightly draw on the worldview that Calvin set forth, to give us such phenomena as Rembrandt's biblical paintings, the Dutch landscapes, and much more, into the Reformed worlds of the nineteenth and twentieth centuries and their flourishing aesthetic fields, not excluding music?

Here is how Christopher Richard Joby argues convincingly that there is a real evolution.[58] He says the way Calvin restricted musical practice to a cappella singing of (mostly) psalms in worship was counterbalanced by his call for imagination, and this characterized the evolution of Calvinism in the arts. Clément Marot needed to show exceptional creativity in order

---

56. No doubt he is mindful of Cicero, who cites Plato's *Timaeus* in his *Tusculan Disputations* (1.36.64). Leon Wencelius presents an extensive discussion of this and other passages in various parts of Calvin's writings. Wencelius, *L'esthétique de Calvin*, 97–126.

57. See S. M. Jackson and C. N. Heller, eds., *Commentary on True and False Religion* (Peabody: Labyrinth Press, 1981).

58. Christopher Richard Joby, *Calvinism and the Arts: A Reassessment* (Leeuven, Paris, Dudley: Peeters, 2007).

to metricize the poetry of the Psalms and set the rhythms to patterns in the music. Marot sometimes took liberties with the text in order to make a theological point, almost in the way of the Hebrew midrash.[59] This "ontology and epistemology" justified later modifications and reforms in the musical practice, such as the use of the organ in Holland and the extensive revisions by Isaac Watts. In a similar way, the visual arts found their way into the culture of Calvinism by exploring the nonpropositional visual motifs and turning them into didactic concepts.[60]

Put a little differently and in more contemporary terms, the worldview developed by Calvin included a deep respect for poetry and visual interpretation beyond simply a strong conservatism on the practice of worship. This worldview evolved into a fuller appreciation of the creation, and thus a greater comfort with the visual arts. So it should not surprise us to find, for example, that early in the seventeenth century, a polemic developed in Holland between Jacob Trigland and the Quakers. Trigland, a Reformed believer, defended the propriety of paintings (except nudes) against the Quakers, who prohibited the possession of any painting whatsoever.[61]

Specific Connections

Here are some specific examples of ways a Calvinist sensibility can be said to be represented in particular art forms. Let's begin with some very basic and obvious examples, and then move to more indirect examples. One connection is well known, though perhaps not much of a statement about larger aesthetic questions. Numerous illustrated Bibles were produced by Reformed artists. Interestingly, the biblical illustrations from Strasbourg and Zurich were richer and more original than those coming out of Wittenberg.[62] We might also think of the devotional works, with psalms to be used devotionally often printed in editions containing rich and varied woodcut vignettes. These would send the reader into the

---

59. Ibid., 86.
60. Ibid., 87.
61. Cited in Benedict, "Calvinism as a Culture?" 32.
62. Illustrated Bibles would be discouraged in Geneva after 1566 because artists were becoming too creative! Ibid., 33.

world of the New Testament, giving a Christological interpretation to many of the psalms. At the same time, images from the Old Testament could be sufficient. One edition features a priest with his burnt offering to illustrate Psalm 150.[63]

Important for the development of Reformation artistry were the polemics of the time. Often the illustrations were cartoon-like, making their point in a way appealing to the people. Graphic satire was particularly popular. Lucas Cranach (the Elder), famous for his portrait of Martin Luther, was a favorite cartoonist against the Roman Catholic Church. His *Antichristus* was so popular in Geneva that it saw nine editions published. Indeed, the visual arts were regularly used to foster all the Reformation ideas.

When we move up to Holland, later in the sixteenth century, we find that Jan Swart van Groningen (1500–ca. 1560) was a prolific engraver and illustrator whose works were often based on biblical passages and taught a Protestant view. His pair of drawings, "The Broad Way" and "The Narrow Way," based on Matthew 7:13–14, contrast the high and mighty on their way to destruction with the humbler folks, able to trust in simple faith, on their way to heaven.[64] Here von Groningen shows Potiphar's wife denouncing Joseph in the story that would eventually prove, "You meant evil against me, but God meant it for good."[65] One could also think of Dirck P. Crabeth (1501–77) from Gouda, whose drawings and stained-glass windows carried distinctively Reformed ideas.[66] Crabeth was often fascinated by the need for the new birth in the journey to heaven, rather than good works.

Connections between Calvinism and the arts, again, are obvious in certain art forms, particularly those directly connected with

---

63. *Les cent cinquante Psalmes du royal prophete Dauid* (Paris: Par Iean Ruelle demourant en la rue S/. Jacques a l'enseigne S. Nicolas, 1554?). This work is available online at http://www2.lib.virginia.edu/rmds/portfolio/gordon/religion/poictevin.html.

64. See Max J. Friedländer, "Zu Jan Swart van Groningen," *Oud Holland* 63, 1–6 (1948): 2–9.

65. J. Q. Van Regteren Altena, "Teekeningen van Dirck Crabeth," *Oud Holland* 55, 1–6 (1938): 107–14.

66. Here King Solomon is pictured. Philip II had recently married Mary Tudor, and fancied himself a second Catholic Solomon. Dirck Crabeth is saying, "Yes, but only if you follow in the Lord's ways."

worship. For example, communion tokens, known as *méreaux*, would bear designs such as a shepherd, an open Bible, a communion cup, or the like. The communion cups themselves could be ornate, carrying images of biblical themes.

Architecture

There is a clear connection between Calvinist principles and church architecture and furnishings. Architectural issues generated less controversy, since in many cases Protestants often simply took over existing Catholic churches and modified them in order to conform to Reformed principles of worship. Replacing the altar with a pulpit as a focal point was a typical statement of Word-centered worship.[67] Calvin did not write much about the configuration of churches, but allows that for the first 500 years of the church there was "purer doctrine thriving," and the "churches were commonly empty of images."[68] He uses Augustine for support. One can argue, as does Joby, that using Augustine proves there were images before the fifth century, and likely quite early.[69] Calvin is probably arguing against statues and ostentatious signs, not against any image whatsoever.

The primary way to know Calvin's intentions is to examine St. Pierre in Geneva under his ministry. By the time he assumed regular preaching there (certainly from 1541 on, and occasionally from 1536 till his exile), there was considerable iconoclasm. Both the rood screen and the choir were demolished. The pulpit was moved to the first pillar on the left, both symbolically and practically significant: the preaching of the Word was made the central element of Reformed worship. Moreover, the entire configuration of the space was changed, moving from the "receptacle" approach, whereby God meets his people on the altar at the Eucharist,

67. The *Second Helvetic Confession* required buildings that are chosen to be churches "to be purged of everything that is not fitting for the church," and to be banished are "luxurious attire, all pride, and everything unbecoming to Christian humility, discipline and modesty" (XXII).

68. *Institutes*, 1.11.13. The word Calvin uses, *imagines*, is somewhat broader than the English "images," and probably referred to symbolism in general.

69. Joby, *Calvinism and the Arts*, 91.

to the "relational" use of space whereby God meets with his people in the assembly.[70] This pattern was duplicated and developed in Scotland and the Netherlands.[71]

In France before revocation of the Edict of Nantes, a good number of churches accommodated these Word-centered principles of the Reformation. The disposition of the chairs around the pulpit signaled not only a listening assembly but also a closer fellowship.[72] When new buildings were constructed, often they were notable for their simplicity. Cévenols would build churches in the form of barns, similar to those used for their farming.[73] Touches such as a weather vane in the form of a rooster were often found, to signify the preaching of the Word.[74]

In all of this, the church as a building represents something about sanctification, and, of course, Christian identity. For all his stress on the invisibility of God and the impropriety of picturing him, Calvin nevertheless believes that the world and the human conscience testify to God's immanence. As Jérôme Cottin points out in his fascinating *Le regard et la parole*, Calvin practices "esthetics without images," whereas Luther has "images without esthetics." In any case, although God is unknowable in visible form, he gives us analogues of his presence so that, "One cannot then separate the beauty of God from the spectacle of the world. The universe is beautiful because it is the theater of the glory of God."[75] So, while the use of images in church is nearly absent in Calvin's own time, a sober imagery could and did develop in the worship space, but then especially in the private or "secular" realm. For

---

70. The terms are from Catharine Randall, *Building Codes: The Aesthetics of Calvinism in Early Modern Europe* (Philadelphia: University of Pennsylvania Press, 1999), 26.

71. See, for example, St. Giles' Cathedral, Edinburgh, and St. Bavokerk, Haarlem. Joby, *Calvinism and the Arts*, 95–101.

72. See André Biéler, *Liturgie et architecture: Le temple des chrétiens* (Geneva: Labor et Fides, 1961).

73. For example, the barn-like design using long beams was derived from rural structures in the Cévennes. See Hélène Guicharnaud, "An Introduction to the Architecture of Protestant Temples," in Finney, ed., *Seeing Beyond the Word*, 141.

74. Or, according to some, to remind Roman Catholic onlookers that Peter (whom they consider the first pope) betrayed Christ three times before the cock crowed.

75. Jérôme Cottin, *Le regard et la parole: Une théologie protestante de l'image* (Genève: Labor et Fides, 1994), 303–4.

Calvin, these could serve not only for pleasure, but also for memory and instruction in Christian truth.[76]

Developments in Holland

Now we move to the less-direct connections. How much carryover of such aesthetic principles was there to the rest of the arts, particularly those not meant for the churches? Here is where matters become interesting and complex. Again, Joby and others argue for an evolution from Calvin's worldview to a sensibility that grew in the visual arts. Let us focus on the issue of landscape art from the Dutch seventeenth century. Hans Rookmaaker argues that a problem arose with the Renaissance, namely that historical scenes (or for that matter natural scenes) require realism and interpretation.[77] Should you show what the eye could see (which might end up in what we now call positivism, or simply acknowledging raw data), or should you depict interpretation, which might require departing from the literal scene and highlighting interpretation? This problem was especially present in the portrayal of biblical narrative. If the picture is made to be historically exact, it will resemble a photograph, but will not be capable of theological interpretation. According to Rookmaaker, this dilemma led many seventeenth-century painters in Reformation countries simply to abandon the painting of biblical scenes.

Then, two possibilities arose. The first is represented in Rembrandt. According to Rookmaaker, Rembrandt alone overcame this problem, by using compositional and psychological means to render meaning. In his drawing *Christ on the Road to Emmaus*, we see three men walking down a path. It becomes clear that the one in the middle, who is Jesus, is the most important. Rembrandt achieves this by drawing a house on the right side of the canvas, thus "creating a rhythm, man-Christ-man-house, with the downbeat on Christ and the house."[78] No halo is needed because one of

76. Olivier Millet, *Calvin: Un home, une œuvre, un auteur* (Gollion, Switzerland: Infolio, 2008), 167.

77. The following discussion is taken from H. R. Rookmaaker, *Modern Art and the Death of a Culture*, 16–19. See also Joby, *Calvinism and the Arts*, chaps. 5–7.

78. H. R. Rookmaaker, *Modern Art and the Death of a Culture*, 18.

the trees silhouetted in the background is halo-like.[79] Other depictions of Christ at Emmaus tell us about Calvin's approach to the Eucharist: Christ is present—he is there in the *sursum corda*, whether we fully apprehend him rationally or not; the supper is for sinners; they are on earth, yet mystically transported to heaven (the interplay of light adds an unearthly tone); the bread and wine are means of the real presence; Christ is always present with his people.[80]

These observations are confirmed by art historian Christian Tümpel, who has argued convincingly that the Dutch tradition of biblical histories rendered in such a psychological or applicatory way represent "a fundamental Protestant contribution to art." Tümpel recognizes that Rembrandt had a Catholic teacher (Pieter Lastman), yet believes the entire genre was developed in a Calvinist culture.[81] Whether or not Rembrandt was alone in this achievement, as Rookmaaker maintained, the view that his Calvinism informed these kinds of choices does make sense.

Landscape Art

The second approach to landscape painting was to paint them in ways that celebrate the creation and God the Creator. Rookmaaker gives an interesting example. Jan Van Goyen's *Landscape* (1646) is a depiction of the world, not as it could be photographed as one thin slice, but as it is in all its beauty, its complexity, and its fragility. Such paintings are so real that we imagine we could see just such a sight or catch it on a photograph. That is impossible, since this is highly thought-out *composition*, not reproduction. In contrast, say, with Poussin's often nostalgic or idealist landscapes, Van Goyen "sings his song in praise of the beauty of the world here and now, the world God created, the fullness of reality in which we live—if we only open our eyes."[82] While these are landscapes, they are pregnant with theistic meaning, simply by the way each motif is displayed, their "musicality,"

79. See H.-M. Rotermund, "The Motif of Radiance in Rembrandt's Biblical Drawings," in *Journal of the Warburg and Courtauld Institutes* 15, 3–4 (1952): 101–21.

80. Joby, *Calvinism and the Arts*, 161–69.

81. Christian Tümpel: "Die reformation und die Kunst der Niederlande," in Werner Hoffman, ed., *Luther und die Folgen für die Kunst* (Munich: Prestel, 1983), 314–15.

82. H. R. Rookmaaker, *Modern Art and the Death of a Culture*, 23.

and the underlying assumption that we are living in God's world, one that is fallen, yet being redeemed. (Here, then, Kuyper and Doumergue had a point: Calvinism contributed to uncoupling the arts from the church alone and helped free them to depict all of life, including landscapes.)

Can this view be sustained today, particularly in light of the challenges of the second historiography? Here are the elements of the discussion. Along with a good number of art historians, Rookmaaker believes that from 1615 to 1630, in places such as Haarlem, a new style developed which is generally more realistic and "secular" than the traditional "mosaic-like" Flemish landscape art. This was nourished by several factors, including a reaction against mythology, leaning toward a sort of "art for art's sake," or simply an attention to personal feelings or moods. There was a strong Christian factor involved. Maarten de Klijn argues that, in keeping with Francis Bacon, Calvinism saw nature as God's "second book," the first being the Bible. Thus, depictions of the creation should show forth God's power and the loveliness of a divine order without recourse to keys, halos, or the like. This mentality also explains the move from a more mannerist to a more realistic kind of picture.[83]

Other art historians find similar connections between the enjoyment of the world and the Calvinist view of the creation. One of the finest studies on the connection between the Reformed worldview and the Dutch landscapists is by E. John Walford, *Jacob van Ruisdael and the Perception of Landscape*.[84] The book provides an overview of the artist's work and his critical reception. Walford discusses the way representation in painting communicates meaning. While the details are scrupulously observed, all is at the service of the larger worldview, including the glory of creation, but also the fall with its threat to original beauty. Walford discusses various aspects of the painter's artistry: his themes and motifs; his selection, combination, and representation of particular elements of the landscape; his scrupulous observation of the details of indigenous vegetation and of the massing of clouds; and his understanding of the conflicting forces of growth and inevitable dissolution in nature. The

---

83. Marten de Klijn, *De invloed van het Calvinisme op de Noord-Nederlandse landscap-schilderkunst, 1570–1630* (Apeldoorn: Willem de Zwijgerstichting, 1982).

84. E. John Walford, *Jacob van Ruisdael and the Perception of Landscape* (London: Yale University Press), 1991.

serene images of grandeur are contrasted with the ultimate transience of nature.

Boudewijn Bakker argues that the Reformed artist Claes Jansz Visscher (1587–1652) paints in songs of praise to God the Creator. Bakker examines an interesting print series called *Plaisante plaetsen* (ca. 1612). This series is an imaginary journey along Haarlem's historical landmarks and sites of industry. Some of the scenes allude to painful events, such as the siege of the city in 1573, but many allude to the markers of the new prosperity of the city and its industrial success.[85] In one of them is a woman paging through a travel book. There are messages in Latin and Dutch explaining that even if a viewer has no time to go to the "pleasant places" in the environs of Haarlem, the sights can be enjoyed through the pictures.[86] Bakker suggests the enjoyment of such scenes is motivated by the Christian worldview, whereby we understand nature to be a "proper song in praise of God."[87]

Not everyone agrees with this connection. Reindert L. Falkenburg asks that we take a closer look at the Visscher series.[88] He agrees that the sequence is meant to please the eyes of the viewer, particularly since it recalls a favorite pastime—taking walks outside the city walls and enjoying the stimuli of the senses. However, he questions whether there is a clear connection to a Calvinist worldview. He even questions whether these sensuous pleasures are in some important ways opposed to the Calvinist view. He wonders whether a Calvinist ethic might even associate these pleasures with the fall, not the "second book" of God.

Falkenburg is not completely opposed to finding any Calvinist element in the series. He simply asks us to weigh the complexity of such associations. He cites Huygen Leeflang, who argues that there is a multiplicity of semantic relations that viewers may have attached to landscape images,

85. See Mariët Westermann, *The Art of the Dutch Republic, 1585–1718* (London: Laurence King Publishing, 2004), 104.

86. One good website is www.oldmasterprint.com, especially the page "Early Flemish Landscape from the Sixteenth Century," http://www.oldmasterprint.com/xxd.htm.

87. Boudewijn Bakker, "Levenspelgrimage of vrome wandeling? Claes Janszoon Visscher en zijn serie 'Plaisante Plaetsen,'" *Oud Holland* 107, 1 (1993): 97-116.

88. See for example Reindert L. Falkenburg, "Landschapschilderkunst en doperse spiritualiteit in de zeventiende eeuw—een connectie?" *Doopsgezinde Bijdragen* 16 (1990): 129–53.

rather than setting forth a single, overarching meaning. These might include an Enlightenment secularism, pride in the new Republic, particularly because of its economic prosperity, or the praise of the Creator.[89] Nevertheless Falkenburg does argue that Calvinism was not likely in the purview. He thinks that "the development toward a realistic idiom and secular staffage in early seventeenth-century Dutch landscape is, as a general principle, not likely connected with a religious, and more specifically Calvinist, view of nature."[90]

My own view is that it could be both! A Reformed sensibility and an Enlightenment outlook are not always mutually exclusive. In some cases they complement one another fairly well.[91] In the end, I do side with Philip Benedict and others who have critiqued the sweeping associations of Kuyper, Doumergue, and the like, on the one hand, and opened doors for significant research into the connections between Calvinism and choices made by painters, on the other hand.

Appropriations and Cultural Change

If these arguments are valid it means we need to look a bit differently in order truly to identify a Reformed approach in the arts. How, then, does the worldview emanating from Calvin's Reformation affect cultures at the local level? In the realm of the arts this will mean at least three avenues of pursuit. (1) Comparative work should be done on the similarities and differences between art done in a primarily Protestant or Roman Catholic context. In the former case, for example, we know that it took time for the arts to return to full favor after the constrictions of iconoclasm. Often the very numbers of artists declined until a better balance could be restored.[92] Ecclesiastical patronage waned considerably in these countries.

89. H. Leefland, "Het landschap in boek en prent," in Boudewijn Bakker, *Nederland naar 't leven: Landschapsprenten uit de Gouden Eeuw* (Zwolle/Amsterdam: Waanders, 1993), 18–32.

90. Reindert L. Falkenburg, "Calvinism and the Emergence of Dutch Seventeenth-Century Landscape Art," in Paul Corby Finney, ed., *Seeing Beyond the Word: Visual Arts and the Calvinist Tradition* (Grand Rapids, 1999), 364.

91. This is true in America, where the Founding Fathers shared elements of both. Not every Enlightenment movement was as secular as the French case. Holland saw more of a congruence.

92. See Carl C. Christensen, "The Reformation and the Decline of German Art," in *Central European History* 6 (1973): 207–32.

Eventually, however, things went better. Individuals began to want to own paintings. In primarily Catholic areas, the arts continued to flourish, but were affected by factors such as the Catholic Counter-Reformation and the Enlightenment. The case was different again when Protestants and Catholics lived more or less side by side.

(2) Related to this, what choices of subject matter were made by Protestant and Catholic artists or patrons? In seventeenth-century Amsterdam, for example, although the contrast was not sharp, one can note that Catholics tended to own more paintings with directly religious subjects than did Protestants. When the subject was religious, Calvinists preferred stories from the Old Testament, then the New, then nativity scenes. Catholics preferred the crucifixion, the Virgin, and saints.[93] As Philip Benedict demonstrates, these choices reflect the differences in sensibilities of the two groups, particularly in that Protestant polemics required true, biblical histories, or landscapes that showed God's creation, rather deliberately rejecting crucifixions and other motifs associated with Catholic piety. At the same time there was common property, which meant that the different sensibilities were not always as manifest as we might think.

(3) Finally, the matter of cultural appropriations. There is also fruit to be found in the study of cultural appropriations. A pioneer in this research is Roger Chartier, who has extensively studied the numerous ways in which one group will appropriate materials found in the surrounding environment for its own purposes.[94] This brings us back to our discussions of local folk customs and larger worldviews. It makes decisions about choices apparently so modest as preferring a painting about an Old Testament story over a crucifixion. Or it might consider such large trends as the secularization of art, moving the arts out of the context of worship

93. John Michael Montias, "Works of Art in Seventeenth-Century Amsterdam: An Analysis of Subjects and Attributions," in David Freedberg and Jan de Vries, eds., *Art in History/History in Art: Studies in Seventeenth-Century Dutch Culture* (Santa Monica, CA: Oxford University Press, 1991), Table 5.

94. Roger Chartier and Lydia G. Cochrane, *On the Edge of the Cliff: History, Language and Practices*, Parallax: Re-visions of Culture and Society (Baltimore: Johns Hopkins University Press, 1996), 40–43. See also Roger Chartier, *Forms and Meanings: Texts, Performances, and Audiences from Codex to Computer*, New Cultural Studies (Philadelphia: University of Pennsylvania Press, 1995), 83–87.

and into the world outside, thus leaving the church in order to live more fully in God's world.

The Call Today

There is a good deal of work to be done. The good news is that in recent times Christians, in the Reformed tradition particularly, have moved from asking whether one may engage in the visual arts to how it is to be done. The task for artists must begin with the level of skill. Whatever else we may say about art in the Calvinist tradition, it must strive for excellence in the craft. Second, the subject matter will need to reflect the worldview that our Dutch forebears taught us. It is easy to say the words creation, fall, redemption, but if these are to be more than a mantra we will need to apply them diligently in our work. Third, to be an artist is not an easy calling. The church is not 100 percent behind the creative vocations. It is a high-risk endeavor to go into the world of the arts with one's Christian integrity uppermost. But the aesthetic world desperately needs artists who can reject both sentimentality and nihilism, and show a third way, one that articulates our misery but also our hope in the Lord.

· 4

CALVIN'S CONTRIBUTIONS TO ECONOMIC THEORY AND POLICY

TIMOTHY D. TERRELL

As a theologian and as a statute adviser to the city of Geneva, John Calvin made such vital contributions to the Protestant Reformation that we can hardly conceive of the Reformation without his work. Nor can we easily envision the development of Western market-oriented civilization without Calvin and his followers, if we properly appreciate his impact on economic theory and policy. Calvin's theological work was eminently practical, not only by its encouragement of personal piety, but also in the ways it informed the Christian's participation in public affairs. As Alister McGrath pointed out, Calvin's "vision of the Christian faith extended far beyond the piety of a privatized faith or the cerebral conundrums of an intellectualized theology. Theology for Calvin offered a framework for engaging with public life."[1] Although Calvin's ideas are frequently associated with a "tyranny of Puritanism"[2] (as Max Weber put it), or a dour, overbearing theocracy, Calvin's thought actually contributed to the suppression of tyranny. And although Calvin certainly retained some errors of his time, his work improved economic theory and policy and led to enduring moral defenses of liberty.

Calvin had a lifelong interest in political matters, as Douglas Kelly has pointed out.[3] The objective of this essay, however, is not to elucidate Calvin's ideas on the general purposes of civil government, or the framework by which a Christian government should operate. Rather, the goal here is to show how Calvin's thought changed economic thought and economic policy. Of course, there are likely to be substantial areas of overlap with political philosophy. In particular, Calvin's ideas on government included limitations on the authority of the civil magistrate, limitations that tended to enhance economic freedom. Discussion of other political issues, such as the relationship between civil and ecclesiastical authorities, will be left to others.[4]

There are several areas in which Calvin's work enhanced the case for economic freedom. First, the Calvinistic work ethic provided a defense of "secular" occupations, so that merchants and industrialists in societies influenced by Calvinism were less commonly viewed as second-class Christians. Second, Calvin's ideas about interest and usury marked an important advance in liberalism, as opposed to the inconsistent restrictions and generally confused thinking of the time. Third, Calvinist thought—perhaps because of conflict with Catholic rulers—began to assert limits on the civil magistrate that provided an ethical basis for a *laissez-faire* economic policy.

1. Alister McGrath, "Calvin and the Christian Calling," *First Things* 94 (June/July 1999): 31–35.

2. Max Weber, *The Protestant Ethic and the Spirit of Capitalism* (New York: Routledge, 2001), 37.

3. Douglas Kelly, *The Emergence of Liberty in the Modern World: The Influence of Calvin on Five Governments from the 16th through 18th Centuries* (Phillipsburg, NJ: P&R Publishing, 1992), 4–5.

4. An important resource on this issue is Calvin's 1541 *Ecclesiastical Ordinances*, in which Calvin discusses the necessity of the church's freedom from political interference. See David W. Hall, *The Legacy of John Calvin* (Phillipsburg, NJ: P&R Publishing, 2008), 20–21.

The Spirit of Capitalism and the Calvinistic Ethic

Max Weber observes the frequent correlation between Calvinism and business success:

> A glance at the occupational statistics of any country of mixed religious composition brings to light with remarkable frequency . . . the fact that the business leaders and owners of capital, as well as the higher grades of skilled labour, and even more the higher technically and commercially trained personnel of modern enterprises, are overwhelmingly Protestant.[5]
>
> [I]t is characteristic and in a certain sense typical that in French Huguenot Churches monks and business men (merchants, craftsmen) were particularly numerous among the proselytes, especially at the time of the persecution. Even the Spaniards knew that heresy (i.e., the Calvinism of the Dutch) promoted trade, and this coincides with the opinions which Sir William Petty expressed in his discussion of the reasons for the capitalistic development of the Netherlands. Gothein rightly calls the Calvinistic diaspora the seed-bed of capitalistic economy.[6]

A casual survey of economic history yields several anecdotal instances of relative success in nations with a Calvinistic background. Predominantly Calvinistic Britain has been economically successful, along with many former colonies (e.g., the United States, Australia, New Zealand, and Hong Kong). In contrast, Catholic Spain and Portugal have not only trailed Britain, but have left a generally less-than-stellar colonial legacy (e.g., Mexico and Central and South America, the Philippines, and Macao). The comparisons are difficult to resist, although critics have long attacked those empirical connections.

In essence, Weber's argument is that Protestantism led to capitalism by elevating ascetic stewardship to a virtue for all Christians in their callings, not just monks. The idea of the calling led Calvinists to be less otherworldly and more focused on this world than in other religions and sects. This, as Anthony Giddens has written, "projects religious behaviour

5. Weber, *Protestant Ethic*, 35.
6. Ibid., 43.

into the day-to-day world, and stands in contrast to the Catholic ideal of the monastic life, whose object is to transcend the demands of mundane existence."[7] To put it another way, the man who is "so heavenly minded that he is no earthly good" would not be a Calvinist. Weber was well aware that no single factor could explain the flourishing of market economies in some nations and the stagnation of other nations. However, the other factors that can help explain the emergence of capitalism are powerful indeed. Weber's critics have argued that he underappreciated the Catholic contributions to the emergence of capitalism. Financial innovation, a "capitalist spirit," and corresponding business success were to be found in Roman Catholic areas such as northern Italy, while one of the most stringently Calvinist areas in the world, Scotland, remained relatively undeveloped.[8] There were also those financially successful Calvinists who were good stewards but not ascetics—they did not mind copious consumption.

Murray Rothbard believed, *contra* Weber, that Calvin's idea of the calling did not bring about capitalism, but that it may have affected economic thought by glorifying labor. Calvinistic Great Britain produced Adam Smith, a liberal Presbyterian who, following David Hume, came close to a labor theory of value:

> The value of any commodity ... to the person who possesses it, and who means not to use or consume it himself, but to exchange it for other commodities, is equal to the quantity of labor which it enables him to purchase or command. Labor, therefore, is the real measure of the exchangeable value of all commodities.[9]

Later, Karl Marx would incorporate the error of the labor theory of value into his own work, with disastrous consequences. Marx reasoned that if labor was the source of all wealth, then if the capital owner extracted any of the value of production for himself, it must have been unjustly

---

7. Anthony Giddens, in introduction to Weber, *Protestant Ethic*, xii.
8. See Murray N. Rothbard, *Economic Thought before Adam Smith*, vol. 1 (London: Edward Elgar, 1995), 142.
9. Adam Smith, *An Inquiry into the Nature and Causes of the Wealth of Nations* (1776; repr. Indianapolis: Liberty Press, 1981), 47.

extracted from the worker. The work of economists such as Jean-Baptiste Say, Jules Dupuit, William Stanley Jevons, and Leon Walras eventually pushed economic thought toward utility theory as a replacement for the labor theory of value. With utility theory, the value of any good or service may differ from person to person, depending on how useful it is to the individual. Value is therefore not something to be discovered, but is rather imputed to the good or service by the valuer. Furthermore, because buyers and sellers may place different values on the same good, mutually beneficial exchange is possible. This was clear at least as far back as Aristotle,[10] though it took more than two thousand years for economic thought to fully embrace the idea.

In contending that Calvinism encourages a labor theory of value, Rothbard essentially follows Emil Kauder:

> Calvin and his disciples placed work at the center of their social theology. . . .
> All work in this society is invested with divine approval. Any social philosopher or economist exposed to Calvinism will be tempted to give labor an exalted position in his social or economic treatise, and no better way of extolling labor can be found than by combining work with value theory, traditionally the very basis of an economic system. Thus value becomes labor value, which is not merely a scientific device for measuring exchange rates but also the spiritual tie combining Divine Will with economic everyday life.[11]

While praising diligent, purposeful labor, Calvinism may have encouraged the accumulation of capital. Weber noted the Calvinistic emphasis on success in one's vocation as well as the de-emphasis on consumption. Encouraging production in a vocation and asceticism in consumption leads to several problems, which adversely affected Adam Smith's thought and intrigued Weber. Clearly, whatever is produced that is not consumed immediately is saved. Saving per se became important to a flaw in Smith. As Edwin West wrote, "Smith, like a prudent steward of a Scottish aristocrat's estate, could hardly disguise a strong personal preference for much

---

10. Aristotle, *Nichomachean Ethics*, 1133a5–30.
11. Emil Kauder, *A History of Marginal Utility Theory* (Princeton, NJ: Princeton University Press, 1965), 5.

private frugality, and therefore for 'productive labor,' in the interests of the nation's future accumulation."[12]

This saving inevitably leads to capital accumulation. A society possessing relatively large amounts of capital will become more specialized in production. Laborers will require larger markets to practice their specialized trades, and producers of specialized capital and consumer goods will require larger populations into which to sell their products. As Adam Smith pointed out, the division of labor is limited by the extent of the market. As capital increased, so that pressure for a larger market increased.

To the extent that Calvinism encouraged capital accumulation, it would also generate a group of capital owners who had an interest in the preservation of property rights over their capital. This developing interest group would not only encourage modifications in the civil law to protect that property from depredations by thieves and by the state, but would put pressure on Protestantism itself to emphasize individual property rights as opposed to coercive collectivism. It is this last point that H. M. Robertson is arguing when he writes that the "doctrine of the 'calling' did not breed a spirit of capitalism. The spirit of capitalism was responsible for a gradual modification and attrition of the Puritan doctrine."[13] It may be that capitalism reinforced Calvinism as much as Calvinism reinforced capitalism.

Ekelund and Hebert point out that even the Protestant form of worship and the rejection of the Catholic calendar may have had an impact on economic growth:

> Generally . . . Protestant rituals were simpler, with less pomp and pageantry, and churches were less elaborate. Far fewer resources were devoted to Protestant churches compared to the great Roman Catholic cathedrals of Europe. It is quite possible, moreover, that Protestantism's rejection of the numerous feast days sanctioned by the Catholic Church led to an increase in the number of work days, thereby increasing labor inputs under Protestant regimes. Additionally, the system of "indulgences for pilgrimages" to churches and holy places declined dramati-

12. Edwin G. West, *Adam Smith* (New Rochelle, NY: Arlington House, 1969), 173.
13. H. M. Robertson, *Aspects of the Rise of Economic Individualism* ([1933]; Cambridge: Cambridge University Press, 1959), 27.

cally in Protestant countries, a factor that also might have contributed to economic growth.[14]

Calvin may have inadvertently fostered economic freedom in another, much broader way. By furthering the Reformation, Calvin promoted a competitor to the Roman Catholic Church. Ernst Troeltsch, who argued that the Protestant Reformation had perpetuated a "medieval spirit" by trying to resist modernization, contended that the Reformation had unintentionally modernized Europe. The modernizing influences were "mainly indirect and unconsciously produced effects . . . even in accidental side-influences, and again in influences produced against its will."[15] Robert Nelson, drawing parallels between ascetic Calvinist Puritanism and the modern environmentalist movement, notes that of all the effects of Calvinism,

> one of the most important impacts was simply the removal of the authority of the Roman Catholic church over wide areas of Europe, thereby opening a new latitude for experimentation in all kinds of social and intellectual matters. Calvin would very likely have been disturbed—horrified might be the better word—at many of the features of modernity that today are attributed partly to the legacy of Calvinism. In this distaste for modern developments, Calvin would now be able to find some surprising new compatriots—an apparently growing number of people who believe that the Americas before Columbus, other primitive societies around the world, the "natural" relations among the creatures of the animal world, and it seems virtually any premodern and/or animal existence is possessed of a higher moral standing than our current civilization.[16]

It is unimaginable that Calvin would have attributed a moral superiority to heathen primitive societies, and Calvin was certainly no primitivist. Thus, the parallels Nelson draws between Calvinist asceticism and

14. Robert B. Ekelund Jr. and Robert F. Hebert, *A History of Economic Theory and Method*, 5th ed. (Long Grove, IL: Waveland Press, 2007), 91.

15. Ernst Troeltsch, *Protestantism and Progress: A Historical Study of the Relation of Protestantism to the Modern World* (Boston: Beacon Press, 1958), 87.

16. Robert H. Nelson, "Environmental Calvinism: The Judeo-Christian Roots of Eco-Theology," in Roger E. Meiners and Bruce Yandle, eds., *Taking the Environment Seriously* (Lanham, MD: Rowman and Littlefield, 1993), 251.

undeveloped societies are weak indeed. Yet it is ironic that Calvinistic asceticism may have inadvertently promoted the luxurious consumption characteristic of so many capitalistic nations.

Calvin on Mercantile Activity

Calvin had reservations about merchant activity. His writings evince not a little vituperation toward businessmen. Gary North avers that Calvin "had little respect for businessmen in general," whom he called "'those robbers' who hope for a catastrophe in order to raise the prices of their goods."[17] However, though Calvin may have had little regard for the businessman's self-interest, he was far from condemning that activity as a vocation. In fact, compared with many of his time, Calvin bore little enmity toward merchants. As Stone notes,

> Calvin's real world involved shopkeepers, traders, and craftsmen as well as clerics and academics. He was relatively free of the medieval distaste for commerce as he was of Luther's preference for the pastoral life. His world was that of urban commerce and he affirmed it. The exchange of money and goods was affirmed. The institution of money itself was not suspect. God had provided the institution for the good of humanity.[18]

It would be difficult, also, to explain the remarkable increase in the numbers of merchants working in Calvin's Geneva if Calvinistic policies toward merchants were unfriendly. E. William Monter finds an increase in merchants from 50 in 1536 to 180 by the late 1550s.[19]

Freedom of conscience led Calvin to defend the freedom of those agreeing to a contract to determine the terms of their agreement. As North writes, "Calvin . . . favored the general principle of the *cov-*

17. Gary North, "The Economic Thought of Luther and Calvin," *JCR* 2, 1 (Summer, 1975): 98.

18. Ronald H. Stone, "The Reformed Economic Ethics of John Calvin," in Robert L. Stivers, ed., *Reformed Faith and Economics* (Lanham, MD: University Press of America, 1989), 41–42.

19. E. William Monter, *Calvin's Geneva* (New York: John Wiley & Sons, 1967).

enant; covenanting men should be limited by consciences unrestricted by multitudinous legal pronouncements."[20] North also notes, "The *conscience* of man, while not completely autonomous and sovereign, was given a new role to play in the administration of property. . . . [C]onscience had more responsibility and fewer guidelines to direct human action."[21]

Calvin grasped some of the essentials of economics that allowed business to prosper. McGrath explains,

> Although he did not develop an "economic theory" in any comprehensive sense of the term, he appears to have been fully cognizant of basic economic principles, recognizing the productive nature of both capital and human work. He praised the division of labor for its economic benefits and the way it emphasizes human interdependence and social existence. The right of individuals to possess property, denied by the radical wing of the Reformation, Calvin upheld.[22]

Calvin's defense of private property (in opposition to the Anabaptists of his time who favored abolishing private property) is seen in the following selection from *Four Last Books of the Pentateuch*, Exodus 16:17:

> For it is necessary for the preservation of human society that each should possess what is his own; that some should acquire property by purchase, that to others it should come by hereditary right, to others by the title of presentation, that each should increase his portion in proportion to his diligence, or bodily strength, or other qualifications. In fine, political government requires, that each should enjoy what belongs to him.[23]

Later in the same chapter, Calvin indicates that turning wealth toward the benefit of the poor is to remain a voluntary act, not coerced by anyone.

20. North, "The Economic Thought of Luther and Calvin," 98.
21. Ibid.
22. McGrath, "Calvin and the Christian Calling," 31–35.
23. John Calvin, *Four Last Books of the Pentateuch*, in Stivers, *Reformed Faith and Economics*, 76.

> And Paul also, wisely makes the distinction, in enjoining that there should be an equality, not arising from a promiscuous and confused use of property, but by the rich spontaneously and liberally relieving the wants of their brethren, and not grudgingly or of necessity.[24]

Calvin apparently had a hazy understanding of something Adam Smith would point out two and a half centuries later—that unintended good could arise from a badly motivated activity. He noted, "Something that is neither blessed nor desirable in itself can become something good for the devout."[25] In this way, even the merchant driven by self-interest could produce something good.

McGrath observes, "A culture of free enterprise flourished in Geneva, in large part thanks to Calvin's benign attitude towards economics and finance."[26] However, it would be a mistake to classify Calvin as an advocate of *laissez-faire* economic policy. Calvin may have avowed the legitimacy of business in general, but he saw such a substantial role for economic regulation that he cannot be considered an unqualified advocate of free markets.[27] The development of Calvinist thought in later centuries may have provided support to greater economic freedom, but Calvin himself saw ample reason for governments to intervene in the economy. The Geneva municipal government supported a hospital (which also served as an orphanage, welfare office, and public health service), provided public education, regulated prices, and limited printers' prices (evidently for the benefit of the church's own publications).[28] Jeannine Olson notes that public welfare in Geneva was largely coincident with similar changes elsewhere in Europe:

> Social welfare in Geneva resembled welfare organization in many other early modern Europe cities of the times in its conversion of urban welfare systems from decentralized institutions run by religious orders to centralized systems controlled by city councils. In cities that became

24. Ibid.
25. John Calvin, quoted in McGrath, "Calvin and the Christian Calling," 31–35.
26. Ibid.
27. See, e.g., Fred Graham, *The Constructive Revolutionary: John Calvin and his Socio-Economic Impact* (Atlanta: John Knox Press, 1971), 127–44.
28. Stone, "The Reformed Economic Ethics of John Calvin," 43.

Protestant like Geneva this conversion often coincided with the local Reformation; it was necessary to replace the welfare functions of the Roman Catholic religious orders. Thus, when Geneva became Protestant, the city's welfare institutions were taken under the control of the city council and centered in the city hospital. The creation of the *Bourse française* represented somewhat of a departure from this tendency toward centralization, because the Bourse was supervised by deacons and pastors and financed independently of the city council.[29]

Stone observes that Calvinistic interventionism was broad in its reach. "Beyond the welfare system and education the work of Calvin and the pastors reached out to suggestions for railings to protect children on stairs and balconies. Fires and chimneys were regulated and efforts were made to clean the town and for street repair." There was also "strict regulation prohibiting the recruitment of mercenaries from Geneva."[30]

We see that the modern Christian Left has not had to look far for support in Calvin's work. Indeed, there is much in the economic thought in Calvin's time to warm the heart of an interventionist. Calvin was not unlike many scholastics and some other Reformers such as Martin Luther. On Luther's 1524 essay "Trade and Usury," Gary North comments:

> Its perspective is medieval. Like the scholastic commentators before him especially those of the twelfth and thirteenth centuries, he opposed free pricing. Merchants may not follow the rule of buying low and selling high. "On such a basis trade can be nothing more than robbing and stealing the property of others. . . . The rule ought to be, not, 'I may sell my wares as dear as I can or will,' but, 'I may sell my wares as I ought, or is right and fair.'" The problem for Luther's analysis, as it had been with the earlier scholastics and canonists, concerned the ethical limits of fairness. How dear may the merchant sell?[31]

Five years later, in the Greater Catechism, Luther would write of the market as a "den of thieves," where "everyone makes use of the market

---

29. Jeannine E. Olson, *Calvin and Social Welfare: Deacons and the Bourse Francaise* (Selinsgrove, PA: Susquehanna University Press, 1989), 12.
30. Stone, "The Reformed Economic Ethics of John Calvin," 43.
31. North, "The Economic Thought of Luther and Calvin," 79.

in his own willful way, proud and defiant, as though he had a good right to sell at as high a price as he chose, and none could interfere."[32] Luther's economic thought was a mess, and many of the other economic thinkers of the time were not much better. Calvin did not advance economic thought by a revolutionary casting off of all that was unbiblical or logically untenable about medieval economics. He absorbed and reflected the milieu of sixteenth-century Christian social thought. It is the substantial burden of remaining error in Calvin that gives the modern Calvinistic Left a justifiable link to Calvin's social policy.[33]

Some of this may be seen in Calvin's comments on what today would be called a "living wage." In the *Old Testament Harmony*, Calvin wrote,

> Humanity is recommended to us in general lest, while the poor labour at our service, we should arrogantly abuse them as if they were our slaves, or should be illiberal and stingy towards them, since nothing can be more unjust than that, when they have served us, they should not at least have enough to live upon frugally.[34]

However, Calvin stops short of turning this moral requirement into a legal obligation. Calvin, according to François Dermange, "explic-

---

32. Martin Luther, "Greater Catechism" (1529), in Henry Wace and K. A. Buchheim, eds., *Luther's Primary Works* (London: Hodder and Stoughton, 1896), 72.

33. Some of these links, however, are specious. For instance, David Little argues from some of Calvin's statements on community, justice, and charity that Calvin would have advocated progressive taxation. As many on the Christian Left are prone to do, Little infers from exhortations to generosity that the state should be involved in broad-based redistribution of wealth. Recognizing to some extent his own non sequitur, Little can only plead that Calvin, to be consistent, might be inclined to redistribute via progressive taxation since he advocated state intervention in some other cases. Given temporal and logical inconsistencies in Calvin, this is a stretch. Even Little admits that Calvin's "emphasis upon free consent in economic and other social relationships does, as we say, run into conflict with the countervailing emphasis upon a mandatory economic order," and that Calvin's thought on these matters was ambivalent and incomplete. See David Little, "Economic Justice and the Grounds for a Theory of Progressive Taxation in Calvin's Thought," in Stivers, *Reformed Faith and Economics*, 61–84.

34. John Calvin, *Old Testament Harmony*, 3.114, on Deut. 24:14–15, quoted in François Dermange, "Calvin's View of Property: A Duty Rather Than a Right," in Edward Dommen and James D. Bratt, eds., *John Calvin Rediscovered: The Impact of His Social and Economic Thought* (Louisville: Westminster John Knox Press, 2007), 39.

itly distinguishes this religious interpretation of justice from legal and political justice. God summons consciences to appear before his judgment seat, not before an earthly judge, and hence one must say that this law is 'spiritual.'"[35] This distinction is lost on many morally concerned statists today, who often act as though any moral requirement must, if at all practical, be a legal requirement as well. It is a non sequitur with terrible consequences.

Left-leaning Christians today often commit a double error in their reading of biblical passages on justice. First, the justice of the distribution of property is determined by observing outcomes rather than processes. Wealth may be obtained without coercion by voluntary labor and contract, but the distribution is considered unjust if it is unequal. Second, the injustices committed by the state in the process of redistributing this wealth are assumed to be less problematic than the initial market injustices. As Ronald Stone writes,

> The welfare of the people . . . is a clear responsibility of the government as Calvin understood it. The tendency toward governmental control of business is clear in Calvin's writings and actions. Tendencies of many later-day Calvinists toward affirmations of laissez-faire economics and social Darwinism do not seem to have a grounding in Calvin. The cruelty of unregulated social Darwinism certainly is not consistently compatible with Calvin's teachings.[36]

Neither, of course, would socialism be "consistently compatible with Calvin's teachings." Calvin was inconsistent on the applications of his theology, particularly if his thought is examined over several decades. In practice, while the Genevan public hospital was funded by the municipal government, there were important church-based alternatives revealing Calvin's high regard for nongovernmental charity. For example, the Bourse Francaise, which cared for refugees, the poor, disabled, or orphaned in Geneva, was a privately funded organization.[37] Furthermore, other than through taxes levied on everyone,

35. Dermange, "Calvin's View of Property", 40.
36. Stone, "The Reformed Economic Ethics of John Calvin," 45.
37. See Hall, *The Legacy of John Calvin*, 16–17.

Calvin objected to compulsory extraction of wealth from the rich to give to the poor.

> Calvin . . . reminds us that charity does not dispense with justice. His purpose is to condemn judges who want to "depart from equity in favour of the poor," in the name of the gospel, and "follow out a foolish idea of mercy" by favoring the poor. In the name of justice, there should not be any question of providing for the needs of the destitute by causing harm to the wealthy. The Reformer agrees with Paul: while the wealthy have a duty to give alms, one must not compel them to share their possessions. Whatever may be the merit of charity, and the concern to free the poor from tyranny, one should not become less upright by even a hair's breadth.[38]

Stone's linking of Darwinism with laissez-faire policies is similarly unfair. Policies that allow resources to be allocated according to voluntary arrangements in the marketplace tend to result in resources going to their highest-valued uses, at least according to the information about value made available through market prices. Policies that replace market allocation with coercion, as all state-run redistribution does, tend to result in resources going to the uses most valuable *to the civil magistrates* in charge of distribution, without benefit of price information. If there is a Darwinian-style competition in resource allocation, competition to please customers for the sake of profit (so that the most efficient producers survive) is merely replaced by competition to obtain political power (so that the most efficient wealth brokers survive). The Darwinian competition does not disappear when coercive power is granted to the state, no matter what the constitutional arrangements for the assignment of that power may be.

Democratic processes to assign coercive power to political representatives do not ensure that the resources will be allocated with any more justice than the market process. The problem with social Darwinism is *not* that the more productive individuals tend to accumulate a greater scope of authority over resources. This can be no more objectionable than, say, idea Darwinism, in which the best ideas are listened to and acted upon. Rather, the problem with social Darwinism is that authority over resources

---

38. Dermange, "Calvin's View of Property," 43.

is not an end in itself. Good stewardship includes the meeting of needs that are not communicated well through a system of market prices. The individual has a requirement to be generous to the poor, for example. This does *not* imply the employment of coercive power to extract wealth from those unwilling to be as generous as the wielders of that power believe they should be.

In this, modern scholars who find consistency between Calvin and free market policies *do* have grounding in Calvin. Calvin was aware (especially after witnessing state-sponsored persecution of Protestants) of the necessity of limits on the civil magistrate. These limits are further examined later in this chapter.

Calvin and the Calvinists on Usury

Calvin made a lasting advance in economic thought when he criticized medieval usury prohibitions. Calvin was certainly not the first to attack the usury doctrine, and he was not consistent in doing so, but he did contribute to the ending of an unbiblical and socially destructive ban. At a time when restrictions on interest requirements were being eroded by exceptions and qualifications, Calvin appealed to conscience, asserting that civil authority could not restrict the terms of a lending agreement.

Calvin knew enough from his contact with the business world to recognize the absurdity of the medieval argument that money was "sterile." The sterility of money meant that money itself could not generate a return, so that a payment on the use of money necessarily made the borrower worse off. Unlike Luther before him, however, Calvin saw that having the use of money for a time would give the borrower the ability to buy and sell at a profit before returning the money. As long as that profit was possible, money could not be sterile. "The profit is not in the money itself," Calvin wrote, "but in the return that comes from its use."[39]

Rejecting the idea that restrictions on interest in the Mosaic law were applicable in detail today,[40] Calvin argued only that interest should not be

---

39. Quoted in Stone, "The Reformed Economic Ethics of John Calvin," 41.
40. Calvin's view on law was essentially in the natural law tradition. Calvin did not regard any of the Old Testament civil law as binding on Christians today, except for the civil

charged on loans to the poor.[41] Of course, with Calvin's strong view of the authority of the state, any civil law restricting interest payment must be followed. Like Luther, Calvin's Geneva capped interest rates at 5 percent. Some time later, the maximum was raised to 6.67 percent.[42]

Calvin was inconsistent. If interest payments were legitimate except in the case of loans to the poor, Calvin should not have objected to someone being a professional moneylender. Yet he did object. It would fall to later Calvinists to remedy this inconsistency. The Dutch Calvinist Claude Saumaise, a.k.a. Claudius Salmasius (1588–1653), justified not only professional moneylending, but also interest-bearing loans to the poor. Saumaise

---

implications of the Ten Commandments. That summary of the law was, he believed, written on the consciences of human beings, so that insofar as even a secular authority followed that natural law, it could meet with Christian approval. See *Institutes*, 4.20.16. See also Dermange, "Calvin's View of Property," 44–48.

41. Calvin developed seven restrictions on interest, discussed briefly by Christoph Stückelberger: "The first restriction is that 'the poor should not be charged interest nor should anyone be under constraint who is afflicted by disaster or is in a situation of utter need through their poverty. . . . The second restriction is that those who lend should not be so set on gain that they are in default in necessary charitable works, nor so concerned to put their money in safe keeping that they fail to recognize the value of their poor brothers and sisters. . . . The third restriction is that [in the case of an interest-bearing loan] nothing should happen that does not accord with natural justice, and should not be found to be appropriate everywhere when we look at the matter in accordance with Christ's injunction (i.e. what you want others to do for you etc.). . . . [The fourth restriction is that] the borrower should make as much or more profit from the borrowed money [as the creditor]. . . . Fifthly, let us not consider what is allowable in terms of received common custom, nor assess what is right and fair by the iniquitous standards of the world, but let us use the Word of God as a precept. . . . Sixthly, let us not consider only what is of advantage to the individual with whom we have to deal, but consider also what is expedient for the public, for quite clearly the interest paid by a trader is a public allowance. Thus, one must properly determine that the contract is of service generally, rather than harmful. . . . Seventhly, let us not break the standard that the civil laws of the region or locality allow—though that is not always enough, because these laws permit things that they would not be able to correct or suppress by forbidding them. So we have to prefer fairness, which cuts back on excesses." Christoph Stückelberger, "Calvin, Calvinism, and Capitalism," in Dommen and Bratt, *John Calvin Rediscovered*, 128–29.

42. Economic theory would predict that the outcome of a cap on interest rates would be a shortage of lending, that is, that would-be borrowers would find it difficult to find a loan. Calvin and others who supported such caps replaced high-interest loans with the impossibility of finding a loan at all. Of course, "gifts" to lenders and other methods of evading the restrictions were not uncommon under these circumstances, and probably reduced some of the problems created by the caps.

saw that having more moneylenders meant more competition, and thereby lower rates. It was logical, then, that more professional moneylenders would be more advantageous to the poor.[43] In his trenchant manner, Saumaise wrote, "I would rather be called a usurer, than be a tailor."[44]

The Old Testament forbade only interest charged to fellow Jews, and that apparently for charitable loans (see, e.g., Lev. 25:35–37), so many of the medieval strictures Calvin would have dropped had no basis in divine law anyway. But in imposing interest rate caps, Calvin (like Luther) was going beyond the Mosaic law. Calvin had insisted that lenders use the Bible as a guide in determining what is "right and fair" with regard to interest rates, neglecting what should have been obvious to a biblical scholar like himself—that the Bible says nothing of what rate is right or fair. Interest is either permitted or forbidden, and usury, properly defined, is the charging of interest *of any amount* where it is forbidden. Never does the Old Testament impose a limit on interest rates.

Earlier scholars, largely in the Roman Catholic scholastic tradition, had in essence arrived at the same views as Calvin. Conrad Summenhart (1465–1511) argued in 1499 for dramatically increasing the number of exceptions to the basic prohibition on usury. It was useful, however, for Calvin to discard the formal ban. Murray Rothbard, no friend of Calvinism, praised Calvin for at least dispensing with the ecclesiastical prohibition on interest.

> The odd result was that hedging his explicit pro-usury doctrine with qualification, Calvin in practice converged on the views of such scholastics as Biel, Summenhart, Cajetan and Eck. Calvin began with a sweeping theoretical defence of interest-taking and then hedged it about with qualifications; the liberal scholastics began with a prohibition of usury and then qualified it away. But while in practice the two groups converged and the scholastics, in discovering and elaborating upon exceptions to the usury ban, were theoretically more sophisticated and fruitful, Calvin's bold break with the formal ban was a liberating breakthrough in Western thought and practice. It also threw the responsibility for applying teachings on usury from the Church or state to the individual's conscience. As

43. Rothbard, *Economic Thought before Adam Smith*, vol. 1, 144.
44. Ibid., 145.

Tawney puts it, "The significant feature in his [Calvin's] discussion of the subject is that he assumes credit to be a normal and inevitable incident in the life of a society."[45]

Calvinism and the Limits on the Civil Magistrate

The Calvinistic doctrine of total depravity applied equally to private citizens and to the civil magistrate, and led to the conclusion—if not with much consistency in Calvin himself, then eventually in his followers—that the civil magistrate's power should be carefully circumscribed. Early on, Calvin held to the view that the king was above the law, the doctrine of *princeps legibus solutus est*. However, Calvin gradually reversed himself. Although he was attracted to the idea of an enlightened civil magistrate with substantial power, Calvin was suspicious enough of the character of governing officials to recommend a separation of powers. This was evident as early as 1536 in his *Institutes* (the final edition cited is that of 1559), and in 1543, in his civic reform requiring the agreement of two local councils before a law could be enacted.[46] In the *Institutes*, Calvin wrote,

> I will not deny that aristocracy, or a system compounded of aristocracy and democracy, far excels all others, not indeed of itself, but because it is very rare for kings so to control themselves that their will never disagrees with what is just and right; or for them to have been endowed with such great keenness and prudence, that each knows how much is enough. Therefore, men's fault or failing causes it to be safer and more bearable for a number to exercise government, so that they may help one another, teach and admonish one another; and, if one asserts himself unfairly, there may be a number of censors and masters to restrain his willfulness.[47]

As Calvin preached in 1562, "Pride blinds [princes] so totally that they think they ought to be put in the rank of God."[48]

---

45. Ibid., 141.
46. Hall, *The Legacy of John Calvin*, 24.
47. *Institutes*, 4.20.8.
48. John Calvin, Sermon 29, *Sermons on 2 Samuel: Chapters 1–13*, trans. Douglas Kelly (Edinburgh: Banner of Truth, 1992).

This proverb has been used by tyrants for a very long time: "what matters is will, not reason." In other words, they consider themselves bound by no laws. . . .

[R]ulers judge everything to be legitimate for themselves and do not consider themselves bound by the law of God, nor do they consider his worship to pertain to themselves. Herein they are terribly mistaken. . . . Even though the power of earthly princes be great in this world, still they must realize that they are ministers and servants of God and the people.[49]

Calvin, by this date, was attracted to the idea of an enlightened civil magistrate following the rule of law. In 1561, Calvin advocated a republican style of government, citing Deuteronomy 1 as support.[50] Yet, although Calvin gravitated toward popular election of public officials (not so far as to reject monarchy), he took a dim view of the capacity of ordinary, nonpolitical individuals even to think about constitutional matters, writing, "Obviously, it would be an idle pastime for men in private life, who are disqualified from deliberating on the organization of any commonwealth, to dispute over what would be the best kind of government in that place where they live."[51] Furthermore, Calvin believed that even to think of changing the form of government under which one lived was "foolish" and "harmful."[52]

Calvin was not a revolutionary, in that he taught nonresistance to government, at least by individual citizens. In the *Institutes*, he wrote that "it is our duty to show ourselves compliant and obedient to whomever he sets over the places where we live,"[53] and in his *Commentaries on Romans*

---

49. Ibid.

50. On Deut. 1:14–16, Calvin wrote: "Hence it more plainly appears that those who were to preside in judgment were not appointed only by the will of Moses, but elected by the votes of the people. And this is the most desirable kind of liberty, that we should not be compelled to obey every person who may be tyrannically put over our heads; but which allows of election, so that no one should rule except he be approved by us. And this is further confirmed in the next verse, wherein Moses recounts that he awaited the consent of the people, and that nothing was attempted which did not please them all." Charles Raynal and John Leith, eds., *Calvin Studies Colloquium*, trans. Douglas Kelly (Davidson, NC: Davidson College Presbyterian Church, 1982). Unfortunately, Calvin failed to see that the democratic process is no guarantee of liberty. Even democratically elected officials can be tyrants.

51. *Institutes*, 4.20.8.

52. Ibid.

53. Ibid.

he blamed the people under a tyrant for the tyranny: "For since a wicked prince is the Lord's scourge to punish the sins of the people, let us remember that it happens through our fault that this excellent blessing of God is turned into a curse."[54] However, Calvin did not rule out resistance by lesser magistrates.

> I am speaking all the while of private individuals. For if there are now any magistrates of the people, appointed to restrain the willfulness of kings . . . I am so far from forbidding them to withstand, in accordance with their duty, the fierce licentiousness of kings, that, if they wink at kings who violently fall upon and assault the lowly common folk, I declare that their dissimulation involves nefarious perfidy, because they dishonestly betray the freedom of the people, of which they know that they have been appointed protectors by God's ordinance.[55]

Calvin's followers, furthermore, became extremely revolutionary, some even defending the assassination of tyrants.[56] Kelly writes,

> Calvin . . . was determined to show that true Protestants were loyal to the civil magistrate and were in no sense political revolutionaries. This desire to vindicate fellow evangelicals from the charge of political radicalism is undoubtedly part of the reason why Calvin was exceptionally conservative all of his life in strongly opposing revolutionary movements against bad rulers. . . . Calvin eagerly dissociated himself from John Knox's more radical stand for civil resistance in Scotland in the late 1550s. Calvin's

54. John Calvin, *Commentaries on the Epistle of Paul the Apostle to the Romans*, quoted in in John T. McNeill, ed., *Calvin on God and Political Duty* (Indianapolis: ITT Bobbs-Merrill, 1956), 85–86.

55. *Institutes*, 4.20.31.

56. David Hall provides a listing of eight important works that "legitimized the idea of citizen resistance against governmental expansion that exceeded proper limits," largely from those who had direct contact with Calvin: Martin Bucer's *De Regno Christi* (1551), John Ponet's *A Short Treatise of Political Power* (1556), Christopher Goodman's *How Superior Powers ought to be obeyed of their subjects; and wherein they may lawfully by God's word be disobeyed and resisted* (1558), Peter Viret's *The World and the Empire* (1561), Francois Hotman's *Francogallia* (1573), Theodore Beza's *De Jure Magisterium* (1574), George Buchanan's *De Jure Regni Apud Scotos* (1579), and Hubert Languet's *Vindiciae Contra Tyrannos* (1579). Hall, *The Legacy of John Calvin*, 24.

thought underwent some evolution on this point in the 1560s, however, during the religious wars in France.[57]

In 1561, commenting on Daniel 6:22, Calvin writes, "For earthly princes lay aside their power when they rise up against God, and are unworthy to be reckoned among the number of mankind. We ought, rather, utterly to defy them than to obey them."[58]

One of the more revolutionary followers of Calvin, Philippe du Plessis Mornay (1549–1623), believed that the purpose of civil governments was to protect the natural rights of the people. This included that cornerstone of a free market economic system, the right to private property. Furthermore, that right and others could not be fully alienated from the people, as the people merely delegate their sovereignty and may reclaim it (via lower magistrates) if the ruler becomes tyrannical.

Calvin's view of the limited role of the civil magistrate, even with its inconsistencies when it came to specific policy issues, may have been one of his most important and lasting contributions. Calvin apparently recognized some of the dangers inherent in civil government, even while defending that government against revolutionary Protestant sects. To the extent that Calvin prescribed safeguards against that inherent danger, such as separation of powers, republicanism, and the inalienable authority of lesser magistrates vis-à-vis the greater magistrates, he provided the groundwork for Western society's institutional bulwarks against central planning.

E. Calvin Beisner has contended, in the context of environmentally oriented central planning, that such planning contradicts another Christian moral standard: to avoid pride. To claim that a bureaucrat or a committee of bureaucrats can have sufficient knowledge to plan an economy is to lay claim to one of the attributes of God: omniscience. Beisner wrote,

> Humility applied to environmental stewardship should lead us, in the light of the vast complexity of human society and the earth's ecosystems, to hesitate considerably at the notion that we know enough about

57. Kelly, *The Emergence of Liberty in the Modern World*, 11.
58. John Calvin, *Commentaries on the Prophet Daniel*, vol. 1 (Grand Rapids: Baker, 1979), 382.

them to manage them (as opposed to enforcing the rules of justice)—particularly that we are confident enough of our knowledge to assert our management preferences in place of the free choices of those who disagree with us.[59]

Calvin, with his skepticism about the capacity of human reason to arrive at a "right" solution to human problems, urged adherence to law. Law serves as a far more reliable guide to human behavior than our own independent reason, and when it is biblical law, it adds the confidence of divine revelation. Our own natures, totally depraved as they are, must submit to a wisdom outside ourselves. In the *Institutes*, Calvin reminds us that Paul, "with reference to both Tables of the Law . . . commands us to put off our own nature and to deny whatever our reason and will dictate."[60]

Earlier in the *Institutes*, Calvin acknowledges man's power of reason, but contends that it is severely limited:

> Since reason, therefore, by which man distinguishes between good and evil, and by which he understands and judges, is a natural gift, it could not be completely wiped out; but it was partly weakened and partly corrupted, so that its misshapen ruins appear. John speaks in this sense: "The light still shines in the darkness, but the darkness comprehends it not" [John 1:5]. In these words both facts are clearly expressed. First, in man's perverted and degenerate nature some sparks still gleam. These show him to be a rational being, differing from brute beasts, because he is endowed with understanding. Yet, secondly, they show this light choked with dense ignorance, so that it cannot come forth effectively.
>
> Similarly, the will, because it is inseparable from man's nature, did not perish, but was so bound to wicked desires that it cannot strive after the right.[61]

By extension, then, from Calvin's comments on self-renunciation and reason, our humility ought to extend so far as to respect the collective wisdom of others as embodied in law and convention, and to hold in

59. E. Calvin Beisner, *Where Garden Meets Wilderness: Evangelical Entry into the Environmental Debate* (Grand Rapids: Eerdmans, 1997).
60. *Institutes*, 3.7.3.
61. Ibid., 2.2.12.

highest regard the law of God. To assert our own capacity to reason independently through social problems (a large proportion of which would be *economic* problems, of course) would be to esteem too highly our own abilities to comprehend the complexities of human society and prescribe what is best.

Calvin referred to what he called natural instincts and "manifest reason" in his effort to explain the commonality of social conventions. He found evidence of this collective wisdom in the very existence of enduring laws and conventions, rather than in the individual's capacity to reassess and overthrow stale convention through his own genius. Concerning the study of "government, household management,[62] all mechanical skills, and the liberal arts," Calvin wrote,

> since man is by nature a social animal, he tends through natural instinct to foster and preserve society. Consequently, we observe that there exist in all men's minds universal impressions of a certain civic fair dealing and order. Hence no man is to be found who does not understand that every sort of human organization must be regulated by laws, and who does not comprehend the principles of those laws. Hence arises that unvarying consent of all nations and of individual mortals with regard to laws. For their seeds have, without teacher or lawgiver, been implanted in all men.[63]

Here Calvin deliberately passed by some important differences among men as to the form of laws, and the willingness of others to ignore those laws. However, most important here was his skepticism regarding the ability of men to improve upon these laws and conventions with raw reason. In the *Institutes*, he wrote,

> As philosophers have fixed limits of the right and the honorable, whence they derive individual duties and the whole company of virtues, so Scripture is not without its own order in this matter, but holds to a most beautiful dispensation, and one much more certain than all the philosophical

62. "Economics" comes from the Greek word meaning "household management," originally found in Xenophon.

63. *Institutes*, 2.2.13.

ones. The only difference is that they, as they were ambitious men, diligently strove to attain an exquisite clarity of order to show the nimbleness of their wit. But the Spirit of God, because he taught without affectation, did not adhere so exactly or continuously to a methodical plan; yet when he lays one down anywhere he hints enough that it is not to be neglected by us.[64]

Man's unassisted reason was not to be trusted. As he wrote, "Because our slowness needs many goads and helps, it will be profitable to assemble from various passages of Scripture a pattern for the conduct of life in order that those who heartily repent may not err in their zeal."[65]

For Calvin, then, reason undirected by biblical higher principles was prone to failure. Zeal, or good intentions, did not remove the tendency toward error. Order was not to be achieved by the reasoning of philosophers, but by following God's law. Biblical instruction, he wrote, has as a main aspect a "rule . . . that does not let us wander about in our zeal for righteousness."[66] Calvinism thus bred a conservatism with respect to social matters—tradition rather than novelty, duty rather than self-indulgence, adherence to rules rather than ad hoc judgments. The Calvinist's life is to be governed by deference to the wisdom of others, and most especially to the law of God. Thus we see in societies influenced by Calvinism a number of institutions that acknowledge the superiority of convention over reason, for example, a judicial tradition of *stare decisis*, requiring a strong regard for precedent in adjudication.

Calvin's theological writings on the ethical and intellectual limitations of man thus have profound implications for economics, although he did not explicitly recognize many of them or even demonstrate consistency in his own policy conclusions. The innate decentralization of economic knowledge defies any attempt to centralize knowledgeable control.

Market-based economies use prices to condense and communicate the information dispersed across billions of individuals, most of whom are complete strangers to one another. Prices represent a summary of assessments of the value of different resources, goods, and services. In an important essay published in 1945, the economist Friedrich A. Hayek

64. Ibid., 3.6.1.
65. Ibid.
66. Ibid.

observed that the problem of communicating relevant information to any central economic planner is perhaps insurmountable, because the most pertinent information is frequently of the sort that cannot be recorded and transmitted to a central economic bureau. Economists, Hayek said, had been seeking the best economic arrangement, "if we possess all the relevant information, if we can start out from a given system of preferences, and if we command complete knowledge of available means."[67] Hayek pointed out that this approach is misguided, because no one ever possesses all the relevant information or has certainty of individual preferences. Even today, those who would plan economic activity are incited to overconfidence by volumes of aggregate statistics and streams of other data. The planners do not realize how profoundly they limit their own abilities by stifling the prices that convey the most important information. Although Calvin did not recognize all the implications of his doctrine of total depravity, policymakers today who appreciate Calvin's ideas would be skeptical of their own capacity to organize an economy.

Conclusion

Calvin's best contributions to economics and political philosophy may have come where he remained closest to his area of relative expertise—theology. His inconsistency and confusion seemed to grow as he stepped farther from his theological foundations, although he did make an important stride forward in his thoughts on usury. Ultimately, however, his doctrine of total depravity, his theology of work, and the attack on the secular/sacred dichotomy may have been of greater importance than his views of particular economic policy issues. Also, though Calvin (especially early in his life) held to an untenable position on the authority of the civil magistrate, the development of Calvin's theology led to better results among many of his followers.

Calvinism's contribution to the moral and legal security of property rights is of great value. By emphasizing vocational success and saving, Calvinism encouraged capital accumulation—and capital accumulation

---

67. Friedrich A. Hayek, "The Use of Knowledge in Society," *American Economic Review* 35, 4 (Sept. 1945): 519.

may have led to pressure for more secure property rights. Calvin was inconsistent enough on property rights that modern leftists can find in Calvin's work plenty of ammunition against the free market.

However, Calvinism's association with property rights is not all an accident of interest group pressures. By favoring Christian liberty and the freedom of conscience, Calvin removed some of the barriers to the freedom of contract. The moral objections Calvin had with some contractual terms (e.g., a failure to provide a "living wage") did not always lead him to advocate state intervention into those terms. And, in opposition to the communist experiments of his day, Calvin found support for private property in the Bible.

Calvin will frustrate any reader who attempts to find a thoroughgoing defense of laissez-faire policy, much less a consistent support for statism. Yet despite his inconsistencies, Calvin aided the development of the morally informed economic policy that characterizes historical classical liberalism today.

5

CALVINISM AND LITERATURE

LELAND RYKEN

The idea of a Calvinistic approach to literature might seem a difficult case to make. Norman R. Cary's survey *Christian Criticism in the Twentieth Century: Theological Approaches to Literature* yields no Calvinistic "school" of literary theory.[1] Yet I can recall two events from my past that point in the direction of a discernible Calvinistic approach to the composition and study of literature.

When a person who was then my colleague in the English Department at Wheaton College reviewed a book by Calvin Seerveld, he was highly critical of it. As a person of Anglo-Catholic convictions, he expressed disbelief that anyone could write a Christian apology for the arts without mentioning the incarnation of Christ as a cornerstone of that apology. I remember thinking that this did not constitute a marvel at all. On further

1. Norman R. Cary, *Christian Criticism in the Twentieth Century: Theological Approaches to Literature*, Literary Criticism Series (Port Washington, NY: Kennikat, Associated Faculty Press, 1976).

reflection it occurred to me that the reason Seerveld's approach seemed natural was that I shared his Calvinistic orientation.

A second anecdote centers on my own book, *The Liberated Imagination: Thinking Christianly about the Arts*.[2] The book was used as a textbook by a cluster of music professors at a Reformed college. Because I teach at Wheaton rather than a Reformed college, the professors made no identification of me with their own tradition, although they resonated with my approach to the arts. When it became known that I was of Christian Reformed background, one professor is reported to have blurted out, "I *knew* it."

Because there is no discernible school of literary theory stemming from Calvin as its source, it is easy to overlook the relevance of Calvinism in formulating a Christian approach to literature and its study. This is where my two anecdotes prove useful, for they alert us that scholars of Calvinistic conviction do view literature and its study in a way that sets them apart from other Christian approaches. Furthermore, writing this essay led me to see for the first time the degree to which my own approach to literature and its study has represented a Calvinistic approach.

In the discussion that follows, I have outlined the ways in which Calvinistic thought yields a Christian poetic ("philosophy of literature"). This poetic is essentially what I have advocated for four decades. In some instances Calvinism has been an influence on my thinking, while in other cases I will note compatibility rather than conscious indebtedness.

Calvin yields relatively few statements that relate directly to literature and the arts, but there are just enough seminal statements to serve my purpose. To show that there has been a tradition of Calvinistic thought through the centuries, I will quote selectively from leading thinkers in the Calvinistic tradition spanning three centuries, including Jonathan Edwards, Abraham Kuyper, and Francis Schaeffer.

The Cultural Mandate

We know that we were created for the express purpose of being employed in labour of various kinds, and that no sacrifice is more pleasing to God

2. Leland K. Ryken, *The Liberated Imagination: Thinking Christianly about the Arts* (Wheaton, IL: H. Shaw Publishers, 1989).

than when every man applies diligently to his own calling. (John Calvin, commentary on Luke 10:38)

As I sat in Christian school classrooms in rural Iowa, I was told that Calvinism was distinctive in having "a world and life view." The details of this were never spelled out for me, although I sensed from the way in which the phrase was voiced by the authority figures in my life that something important was at stake. At the outset of my teaching and writing career I encountered the idea from a different angle, and this time it assumed a seminal importance in my thinking about literature and the arts.

What I learned is that Christianity encompasses both a missionary mandate (summarized in the Great Commission) and a cultural mandate. The urtext for a cultural mandate is Genesis 1:26–28, which narrates how God commanded Adam and Eve to have dominion over the earth. In Calvinistic thought, this is not only an agricultural command, having to do with the literal ground, but also a cultural command. Thus extended, the statement means that humankind has been placed by God over the entire creation, including that part of it produced by people (usually called *culture*). A search of sources quickly reveals that the idea of a cultural mandate belongs almost exclusively to the Calvinistic or Reformed tradition, where it is a commonplace.[3] The importance of the idea of a cultural mandate to the pursuit of literature is incalculable. To begin, it gives literature a place to stand. If culture is God-intended and God-sanctioned, so is literature. Furthermore, if the pursuit of literature is not simply permitted but commanded, its legitimacy is even more strongly asserted. This is how I understood my interest in literature once the idea of a cultural mandate had been established in my thinking.

The view that God has given his followers not only a missionary mandate but also a cultural mandate undercuts at once the sacred-secular dichotomy that has characterized much non-Reformed

3. I have found no reference to the cultural mandate in Calvin's writings. It would appear, therefore, that the phrase is a product of Calvinism after Calvin. That it belongs largely to Calvinistic thought is corroborated by Nancy Pearcey's observation that when she lectures on the culture mandate, "many people say that they have never encountered the concept before." Nancy Pearcey, *Total Truth: Liberating Christianity from Its Cultural Captivity* (Wheaton, IL: Crossway Books, 2005), 399.

evangelical thinking. I have often seen the following statement by C. S. Lewis quoted, and in fact in my early writings I quoted it myself with approval: "The Christian knows from the outset that the salvation of a single soul is more important than the production and preservation of all the epics and tragedies of the world."[4]

I no longer quote the statement with approval. For one thing, Lewis presupposes that the epics and tragedies of the world cannot be *the means by which* God brings a person to belief. When I was commissioned to write an essay on literature and the spiritual life, I polled Christians in my circle of acquaintances regarding the role of literature in their spiritual lives. I quickly discovered a substantial group for whom imaginative literature had played a crucial role in their coming to salvation in Christ—some thought just as much so as someone's coming to faith at an evangelistic crusade. More generally, the statement by Lewis shows an inadequate view of the cultural mandate that God gave to the human race. If the human race is to have dominion over the earthly order, every sphere and act of dominion is worthy. There is no warrant for arranging activities into a hierarchy. If God commands something, it is worthy. It is not inherently in competition with the missionary mandate.

A complementary Calvinistic doctrine reinforces the idea of the cultural mandate, namely, the doctrine of vocation or calling. The teaching of the Reformers on vocation is well thought out and nuanced, but its basic outline is simple. The leading ideas, as articulated by Calvin, are as follows: (1) God is sovereign in the events of a person's life. Part of this sovereignty is that the tasks that come to people in their lives are "appointed duties" (named "callings") that have been "assigned . . . by the Lord."[5] (2) Because God is a person's "guide in all these things," our daily undertakings are not simply self-contained tasks but are part of a religious service to God, with the result that if "you obey your calling" it will "be reckoned very precious in God's sight."[6] (3) No vocation is more sacred than another; in Calvin's words, "it is all one in the sight of God what a person's manner [i.e., vocation] is in this world, inasmuch as this

4. C. S. Lewis, *Christian Reflections* (Grand Rapids: Eerdmans, 1967), 10.
5. *Institutes*, 3.11.6.
6. Ibid.

diversity does not hinder agreement in piety."[7] According to Georgia Harkness, whereas Luther had asserted the possibility that one can "serve God *within* one's calling," Calvin took the bolder step of claiming that one can "serve God *by* one's calling."[8]

The application of the Calvinistic doctrine of vocation to literature is far-reaching. It elevates the life of the writer and teacher of literature to a status of importance in God's sight, and therefore in the sight of writers and teachers themselves. The Calvinistic tradition gave poet Chad Walsh the conceptual framework and vocabulary for saying that the writer "can honestly see himself as a kind of earthly assistant to God (so can the carpenter), carrying on the delegated work of creation, making the fullness of creation fuller."[9] My repertoire of public addresses includes one called "The Christian Writer's Calling." In it, I begin by delineating Reformation ideas about vocation, which I then apply to the activities that a literary author performs. Without the framework of Reformation ideas on vocation, I would be left with only a humanly concocted collection of ideas about writers and their work, with no theological authority behind my assertions.

Calvin's endorsement of culture and championing of the idea of vocation may seem remote from the production and study of literature, but they are not. Throughout my career, Calvinistic ideas on the cultural mandate and vocation have provided my basic platform on which to be a spokesman for literature, free from anxiety about whether my literary vocation is a legitimate Christian pursuit. Not to have had that confidence would have subverted my enterprise at every turn. A Calvinistic worldview freed Francis Schaeffer to assert that "a work of art has a value in itself," independent of its "propagation of a particular message," not existing "solely [as] a vehicle for some sort of self-conscious evangelism."[10] Scholars in

7. John Calvin, *Calvin's Commentaries*, trans. William Pringle (Grand Rapids: Baker, 1999), 20, 25. All quotations from Calvin's commentaries are from this multivolume set.

8. Georgia Harkness, *John Calvin: The Man and His Ethics* (Nashville: Abingdon, 1958), 179.

9. Chad Walsh, "The Advantages of the Christian Faith for a Writer," in Leland Ryken, editor, *The Christian Imagination: The Practice of Faith in Literature and Writing* (Colorado Springs: WaterBrook, 2002), 169.

10. Francis Schaeffer, *Art and the Bible* (Downers Grove, IL: InterVarsity, 1973), 33, 37, 61.

non-Reformed evangelical circles who believe in a missionary mandate but not a cultural mandate have generally carried a burden of anxiety about the value of literature in itself.

The Doctrine of Creation

> Because sculpture and painting are gifts of God, I seek a pure and legitimate use of each, [as] things which the Lord has conferred upon us for his glory and our good.[11]

Earlier I recalled the occasion when my colleague marveled at a book on aesthetics that did not highlight the incarnation of Jesus, as the Anglo-Catholic tradition has always done. My own view is that, while certain essential points about art and literature can be deduced and illustrated from the incarnation of Jesus in human flesh, other Christian doctrines establish those points more directly and convincingly.

Literature begins in an author's creativity. Authors create worlds of the imagination that do not exist before the author calls a literary work into existence. That is why literary theory (especially in the last two centuries) has focused so heavily on creativity as a subject of inquiry. One cannot conceive of literature and the arts without thinking about creativity.

The mystery of how works of great art come into being is so intriguing that an interest in literature and the arts inevitably raises the question of the creative process. Interviews with authors have become an important critical genre in the modern era, and such interviews almost universally wind their way to an inquiry into how authors compose and how specific literary works came into being. The titles of books and essays confirm how important the world at large regards it to understand the creative process: *Creativity: Flow and the Psychology of Discovery and Invention*; "The Making of a Poem"; *Dostoyevsky and the Creative Process*; *The Creative Process*; *Fifty Contemporary Poets: The Creative Process*.

When we ask how the high value that the arts place on creativity fits into a Christian worldview, I believe that the two are in total agreement.

11. *Institutes*, 1.11.12

We reach that conclusion partly by looking at the first chapter of the Bible, where we learn that God is a Creator who pronounced his handiwork "very good" (Gen. 1:31). If we then trace references to God's work throughout the Bible, we find that he is a being whose essence is to declare, "Behold, I am doing a new thing" (Isa. 43:19), culminating in his creation of a new heaven and new earth in imagery that echoes the creation story of early Genesis (Rev. 22:1–5).

An important aspect of the creation story is God's creation of man in his image. The key text is Genesis 1:26–27, where God is recorded as saying, "Let us make man in our image," and where the author narrates poetically, "So God created man in his own image, in the image of God he created him." The chief attribute of God that we know about when we read this passage is that he is a creator. Within its narrative context, therefore, the most obvious thing that God and people have in common is their ability to create. By implication, creativity is a gift that God conferred on people.

If we ask what theological tradition has made most of the twin ideas of God as creator and people as *imago dei* as cornerstones of literary theory, the answer is that it is the Reformed tradition. No single sentence of literary theory has encapsulated more of my own thinking than the following statement by Abraham Kuyper: "As image-bearer of God, man possesses the possibility both to create something beautiful, and to delight in it."[12] Kuyper elaborated the concept as follows: "That artistic ability, that art-capacity . . . can have room in human nature, we owe to our creation after the image of God. . . . So we may imitate God's handiwork. . . . It is our privilege as bearers of His image, to have a perception of this beautiful world, artistically to reproduce, and humanly to enjoy it."[13]

A later representative of this Calvinistic viewpoint is Francis Schaeffer. In his monograph *Art and the Bible*, Schaeffer echoes the themes of Kuyper. One of these themes is that "both God and man create," that "the word *create* is appropriate" for what the artist does, and that works of art are "expressions of the nature and character of humanity . . . the outworking of the creativity that is inherent in the nature of man."[14] Secondly,

---

12. Abraham Kuyper, *Lectures on Calvinism* (Grand Rapids: Eerdmans, 1931), 142.
13. Ibid., 156–57.
14. Schaeffer, *Art and the Bible*, 35–36.

Schaeffer is able to root in the doctrine of creation his view that "Christian art is by no means always . . . art which deals with religious themes." He writes, "Is God's creation totally involved with religious subjects? What about the universe? the birds? the trees? the mountains? . . . When God created out of nothing by his spoken word, he did not just create 'religious' objects."[15]

When we turn to the writings of Calvin, we find the same orientation. The key ideas are as follows: (1) Because God is the creator and ruler of creation, "all the arts emanate from Him, and therefore ought to be accounted divine inventions."[16] (2) The arts are not autonomous human abilities but are gifts that God confers on people; in commenting on the artists who produced the handiwork for the tabernacle, Calvin writes that "whatever ability is possessed by any emanates from only one source, and is conferred by God."[17] (3) Artistic ability is part of God's image in people: "the many pre-eminent gifts with which the human mind is endowed proclaim that something divine has been engraved upon it."[18] (4) By virtue of bearing the image of a creative God, humans are capable of genuine creation: they possess the "energy and ability . . . to devise something new in each art or to perfect and polish what one has learned from a predecessor."[19]

Calvinistic thinking about divine and human creativity allows us to steer a middle course between two extremes on the current scene. The Romantic movement of the early nineteenth century elevated autonomous human creativity all out of proportion, even to the point of deifying it. The Calvinistic tradition puts human creativity in its place under God and treats it as a gift of which people are stewards. In this regard it is important to note that Calvin regularly refers to the arts as a gift from God, as when he speaks of "God's gift freely offered in these arts" and of the arts as "gifts the Lord left to human nature."[20]

15. Ibid, 59.
16. *Comm.*, 3.3.291.
17. Ibid., 3.3.291–92.
18. *Institutes*, 1.15.2.
19. Ibid., 2.2.14.
20. Ibid., 2.2.16.

But there is also currently a perverse debunking tradition among certain segments of evangelicalism that disparages the concept of human creativity, even to the point of denying that it exists. The views of the Calvinistic tradition outlined above serve as a corrective to this misconception also. In the words of Francis Schaeffer, "it is important to understand that both God and man create. Both make something."[21]

A final importance of the doctrine of creation is that it provides a theological explanation of why people create. We need empirical inquiry to explain *how* people create, but purely secular attempts to explain *why* they create turn out to be frivolous. Calvin's discussion of the matter provides three impeccable explanations. One is that a creative God created people in his image: God equips artists "according to the character that he bestowed upon each kind by the law of creation."[22] Secondly, God endows artists with the gift of artistry: regarding the artists who worked on the tabernacle Calvin asserts that "God had already conferred acuteness and intelligence on the artificers in question."[23] Thirdly, God's Spirit equips even unbelieving artists: "no one excels even in the most despised and humble handicraft, except in so far as God's Spirit works in him."[24]

Common Grace

We ought not to forget those excellent benefits of the divine Spirit, which he distributes to whomever he wills, for the common good of mankind. (*Institutes*, 2.2.16)

As with the doctrine of creation, the doctrine of common grace represents a distinctive contribution of Calvinism to literary theory. Whereas the doctrine of creation speaks particularly to the *production* of works of literature, common grace relates more to the *reading and study* of works already composed. Nearly all of the writing on common grace has been produced by theologians in the Calvinistic (and even Dutch) tradition—

21. Schaeffer, *Art and the Bible*, 35.
22. *Institutes*, 1.1.16.
23. *Comm.*, 3.3.292.
24. Ibid., 3.3.291.

Calvin himself and names such as Hodge, Berkhof, Kuyper, Van Til, and Osterhaven.[25] The doctrine of common grace holds that God endows all people, Christian and non-Christian alike, with a capacity for the true, the good, and the beautiful.

Calvin himself is the best starting point, and we can discern three leading threads in his thinking on the subject. First, non-Christian writers are capable of expressing what I call the true, the good, and the beautiful, with the result that "whenever we come upon these matters in secular writers, let that admirable light of truth shining in them teach us that the mind of man, though fallen and perverted from its wholeness, is nevertheless clothed and ornamented with God's excellent gifts."[26] Secondly, and as an extension of the first idea, we can affirm truth wherever we find it: "All truth is from God; and consequently, if wicked men have said anything that is true and just, we ought not to reject it; for it has come from God."[27]

Thirdly, the Spirit of God is the ultimate source of all that is good in literature, and we can honor God as that source. Calvin writes, for example, "If we regard the Spirit of God as the sole fountain of truth, we shall neither reject the truth itself, nor despise it wherever it shall appear, unless we wish to dishonor the Spirit of God."[28] And again, "We cannot read the writings of the ancients . . . without great admiration. . . . But shall we count anything praiseworthy or noble without recognizing at the same time that it comes from God?"[29]

The importance of common grace for the literary enterprise is immense. It means first that we do not need to inquire into the religious orthodoxy of an author before we can affirm what is worthy in what such an author has produced. Wherever we find the true, the good, or

25. A primer on the Calvinistic doctrine of common grace includes the following sources (arranged chronologically): Charles Hodge, *Systematic Theology* (1887; repr. London: James Clarke, 1960), 2.654–75; Herman Kuiper, *Calvin on Common Grace* (Grand Rapids: Smitter, 1928); Louis Berkhof, *Reformed Dogmatics* (Grand Rapids: Eerdmans, 1932), 2.22–32; Cornelius Van Til, *Common Grace* (Philadelphia: Presbyterian and Reformed, 1954); M. Eugene Osterhaven, "Common Grace," in Carl F. H. Henry, ed., *Basic Christian Doctrines* (New York: Holt, Rinehart and Winston, 1952), 171–77. Abraham Kuyper's book *Common Grace* is unavailable in English.

26. *Institutes*, 2.2.15.

27. *Comm.*, 21.300–1.

28. *Institutes*, 2.2.15.

29. Ibid.

the beautiful, we can applaud it. This is far from universally accepted by Christians. Among earnest believers I often sense an uneasiness, if not outright hostility, toward works of literature authored by non-Christians. The lineage of this uneasiness goes back to some of the church fathers, who struggled with the question of how to reconcile their Christian faith with their upbringing in classical culture. Some of them rejected classical culture. The doctrine of common grace also leads us to conclude that we can and should spend time reading secular literature as well as avowedly Christian literature for our edification and delight.

Finally, it is not uncommon to run across the sentiment that Christians (or Calvinists!) are somehow to blame for the fact that they are not the best writers in the world. We could as well try to assign blame for Christians' not being the best athletes or pianists or cooks. The truth is as Calvin asserted: "whatever ability is possessed by any [artist] . . . is conferred by God,"[30] who "distributes" his gifts "to whomever he wills."[31]

Beauty

> In grasses, trees, and fruits, apart from their various uses, there is beauty of appearance and pleasantness of odor. (*Institutes*, 3.10.2)

From the beginning of my teaching and writing about literature, I have championed the importance of beauty in literature and art. I had no more than planted my flag for the cause of beauty when it fell out of fashion as an aesthetic value. I never wavered in my devotion to beauty as a leading ingredient of the literary experience, and one of the few things that have gone well in my discipline during the past four decades is that beauty has made a deserved comeback as an aesthetic value among scholars who theorize about literature and art.

In my first book of literary theory, I followed my introductory chapter with a daring move that reflected my convictions. I gave priority to "Literature and the Quest for Beauty" and gave this explanation: "I have placed this chapter on beauty early in the book for an important reason:

30. *Comm.*, 3.3.291–92.
31. *Institutes*, 2.2.16.

beauty is the dimension of literature that is always getting shortchanged in literary criticism."[32]

The Bible, of course, is the primary text on beauty. Genesis 2:9 speaks volumes: "Out of the ground the LORD God made to spring up every tree that is pleasant to the sight and good for food." Here is God's design for human well-being, and it includes two complementary things—the useful and the purely aesthetic. The conditions for the good life have never changed since that moment in Paradise. That God values both the utilitarian and the aesthetic is evident in the kind of world that he created.

Numerous other tributaries flow into the Bible's endorsement of beauty. One is in the descriptions of the art that adorned the Old Testament tabernacle and temple, including passages that attribute beauty to those places (Ex. 28:2; Ezra 7:27; Ps. 96:6; Isa. 60:13). Other passages ascribe beauty to God as one of his attributes (e.g., Ps. 27:4; Ezek. 16:14–15, 17). The words *beauty*, *beautiful*, and *beautify* appear approximately 120 times in English translations of the Bible, in a predominantly positive way.

While the Bible is the primary text for establishing the purely aesthetic side of literature as a value, I was strongly influenced to champion the cause by writers in the Calvinistic tradition. Calvin himself gave us a classic formula when he called the earthly creation the theater of God's glory.[33] In affirming the legitimacy of beauty and our enjoyment of it, Calvin famously wrote,

> If we ponder to what end God created food, we shall find that he meant not only to provide for necessity but also for delight and good cheer. . . . Has the Lord clothed the flowers with great beauty that greets our eyes, the sweetness of smell that is wafted upon our nostrils, and yet will it be unlawful for our eyes to be affected by that beauty, or our sense of smell by the sweetness of that odor? . . . Did he not, in short, render many things attractive to us, apart from their necessary use?[34]

32. Leland Ryken, *Triumphs of the Imagination: Literature in Christian Perspective* (Downers Grove, IL: InterVarsity, 1974), 33.
33. *Institutes*, 3.10.2.
34. Ibid..

Even more impressive than these brief comments by Calvin are the ideas of Jonathan Edwards, for whom beauty is such a central theological concept that a scholar named Roland André Delattre wrote a whole book on it titled *Beauty and Sensibility in the Thought of Jonathan Edwards.*[35] The book is filled to overflowing with evocative quotations from Edwards on beauty, along with extensive analysis of his thought on the subject. All of that is beyond the scope of my discussion here, but the following statement was a cornerstone for my thinking on the theological importance of beauty for the literary enterprise: "For as God is infinitely the greatest being, so he is allowed to be infinitely the most beautiful and excellent: and all the beauty to be found throughout the whole creation, is but the reflection of the diffused beams of that Being who hath an infinite fullness of brightness and glory."[36]

Calvin and Edwards were not the end of Calvinistic influence on me in regard to beauty. Abraham Kuyper likewise produced classic statements on the importance of beauty in his lectures on Calvinism. Here is one of them: "the beautiful . . . has an objective existence, being itself the expression of a Divine perfection. . . . We know this from the creation around us. . . . For how could all this beauty exist, except created by One Who preconceived the beautiful in His own being, and produced it from His own Divine perfection?"[37] Kuyper also wrote, "After the Creation, God saw that all things were good. Imagine that every human eye were closed and every human ear stopped up, even then the beautiful remains, and God sees it and hears it."[38]

The Calvinistic endorsement of beauty as an aesthetic criterion has a double significance for literature. One application focuses on writers of literature. If beauty of form is as important as the Calvinistic tradition affirms, the writer's labors to perfect the formal properties of a work are validated. Ernest Hemingway rewrote the conclusion to his novel *A Farewell to Arms* seventeen times in an effort to get it right. Welsh poet

35. Roland André Delattre, *Beauty and Sensibility in the Thought of Jonathan Edwards: An Essay in Aesthetics and Theological Ethics* (New Haven: Yale University Press, 1968).

36. Jonathan Edwards, *The Nature of True Virtue*, in *The Works of Jonathan Edwards* (New Haven: Yale University Press, 1989), 8.550–51.

37. Abraham Kuyper, *Lectures on Calvinism*, 156.

38. Ibid.

Dylan Thomas made more than 200 handwritten manuscript versions of his poem "Fern Hill." Can a literary author justify the time spent in polishing the technique of a piece? If we affirm the importance of beauty, the answer is yes.

A parallel exists for readers and literary critics. That works of literature possess beauty of form and technique is indisputable. What is open to decision is whether this aspect of literature is deserving of attention. If we affirm beauty as an aesthetic property, the way is open for readers and critics to give their attention to the formal aspects of literary works. Since beauty is essentially nonutilitarian, the moment we elevate beauty of form we open the door to a hedonistic defense of literature (a defense of literature that rests on pleasure and enjoyment). The hedonistic defense of literature has been a hallmark of my own literary theory, and it has been buttressed by a Calvinistic viewpoint.

Truth in Literature

It pleased the Lord to hallow his truth to everlasting remembrance in the Scriptures alone.[39]

A former chairperson of my English Department once theorized that there were two major approaches within our department to the integration of the Christian faith and literary study. He labeled them the incarnational and perspectival approaches. The first of these believes that if literature professors are Christians, whatever they do with literary works represents an integration of their discipline with the Christian faith. The second label implies that integration does not happen automatically but requires conscious analysis and application of intellectual criteria to works of literature.

This dichotomy is useful in seeing what distinguishes a Calvinistic approach to literature. One of the types of truth that literature embodies is truthfulness to human experience. Literature can be said to *incarnate* the truth about reality. Loosely speaking, literary theorists in the Catholic and Anglican traditions are likely to focus on this aspect of literature. This approach is sometimes called *sacramentalist* as well as *incarnational*.

39. *Institutes*, 1.7.1

For theorists in this tradition, the fact that literature embodies human experience in distinctly artistic forms is sufficient to make it religious and/or Christian. The concepts of myth, symbol, and sacrament are considered the important aspects of the integration of literature and the Christian faith. What matters is the inherent nature of literature and its affinities to the Christian faith. Here are two specimen statements: (1) "Literature and religion are indeed close together in their areas of interest. Both use symbols [and are] mythic."[40] (2) "No clear line can be drawn between poetry and religion, if only because religion properly involves the whole of life and the total man. . . . In the last analysis religious expression and poetry have it in common that they testify to reality, and by symbolic means."[41]

A perspectival approach does not question that truthfulness to reality and human experience constitutes one of the main values of literature, but it disagrees that this fact constitutes an adequate integration of literature and the Christian faith. A Calvinistic approach to literature refuses to waive the criterion of intellectual truth as an important aspect of literary analysis. In other words, the intellectual content of literature needs to be identified and assessed.

I think it is self-evident that doctrine and the intellectual content of the Christian faith have mattered supremely to adherents of Calvinism. The intellectual rigor and complexity of Calvin's *Institutes* suggest the flavor of the tradition that has stemmed from Calvin. An important part of this orientation is the conviction that ideas need to be weighed, and truth needs to be differentiated from error. Applied to literature and the arts, this mind-set produces a comment like this one from Francis Schaeffer:

> The fact that something is a work of art does not make it sacred. . . .
> As Christians, we must see that just because an artist—even a great
> artist—portrays a world view in writing or on canvas, it does not mean
> that we should automatically accept that world view. . . . The truth of a

40. Cleanth Brooks, "Christianity, Myth, and the Symbolism of Poetry," in Finley Eversole, ed., *Christian Faith and the Contemporary Arts* (Nashville: Abingdon, 1957), 105.

41. Amos Wilder, "Poetry and Religion," in Eversole, *Christian Faith and the Contemporary Arts*, 113–14.

world view presented by an artist must be judged on separate grounds than artistic greatness.[42]

Once we accept that the ideas embodied in literature need to be tested by intellectual criteria of truth and error, the question naturally arises as to what constitutes the standard by which ideas should be judged. I think that anyone familiar with the literary theory and criticism that I have produced will at once agree that a distinguishing feature has been the degree to which I appeal to the Bible as my primary source for ideas about literature and my assessment of specific works of literature. While assigning primacy to the Bible might be broadly evangelical rather than specifically Reformed, it is nonetheless the case that we owe the principle of the primacy of the Bible to the Reformation.

Calvin is one of the fountains from whom the primacy of Scripture became established in Christian thought. In an essay titled "Calvin and the Holy Scriptures," Kenneth Kantzer notes more than a dozen instances in which Calvin refers to the Bible in such terms as "unerring standard," "the infallible rule of [God's] holy truth," "the certain and unerring rule," and the Bible's "unerring certainty."[43] In the *Institutes*, Calvin quotes from the Old Testament 2,474 times and from the New Testament 4,330 times.[44] Calvin himself wrote that "the church recognizes Scripture to be the truth of its own God," with the result that "it unhesitatingly venerates Scripture."[45]

Literary theorists and critics who accept such a view of biblical authority are likely to advertise their distinctiveness as they analyze works of literature. When a literary critic appeals to the Bible as the official repository of Christian truth, the effect is very different from when critics appeal to the creeds of Christendom, or to specific theologians such as Augustine and Tillich, or to no religious authority at all but simply to the inherent qualities of literature (such as symbolism and myth). Additionally, to sub-

---

42. Schaeffer, *Art and the Bible*, 41.

43. Kenneth Kantzer, "Calvin and the Holy Scriptures," in John F. Walvoord, ed., *Inspiration and Interpretation* (Grand Rapids: Eerdmans, 1957), 142.

44. John T. McNeill, *The History and Character of Calvinism* (London: Oxford University Press, 1967), 213.

45. *Institutes*, 1.7.2.

scribe to the Bible as the final court of appeal in questions of intellectual truth results in a certain tough-mindedness when literary scholars assess the truth claims found in works of literature.

The literary imagination did not escape the effects of the fall. I can imagine that some of my readers would have expected me to say more about that than I have. My response is multiple. (1) When I actually ply my trade as a literary critic in the Calvinistic tradition, discerning truth from error in specific works of literature constitutes a much larger share of my effort than the foregoing apology for literature has hinted. (2) The effects of the fall on the literary enterprise represent an abuse of literature and are not a comment on the inherent nature of literature. (3) As an extension of that, one cannot construct a defense of literature based on the abuses of it. (4) The emphasis within Calvinism on human depravity carries a built-in curb on viewing literature with naïve optimism; the wonder is that Calvin consistently expresses such a positive attitude toward culture and the arts.

Summary: A Calvinistic Approach to Literature

Let this be our principle: that the use of God's gifts is not wrongly directed when it is referred to that end to which the Author himself created and destined them for us, since he created them for our good. (*Institutes*, 3.10.2)

It is by now evident that even though published sources acknowledge no Calvinistic school of literary theory and criticism, such an approach nonetheless exists. I have also come to see that I approach literature from within that tradition. The summary that follows is therefore partly validated by the fact that it comes from a practitioner of the approach that I describe. I need to observe also that, while up to this point in my essay I have divided the material into distinct topics, those topics are actually intertwined and make up a coherent whole.

A Calvinistic approach to literature begins at a broad level of belief that culture is good in principle, having been instituted by God. Additionally, God calls his creatures to pursue their vocations in the various spheres that make up culture, with literature being one of these spheres. The gift that this outlook primarily confers is a tremendous confidence in the legitimacy and value of composing and studying literature. Speaking personally, I have never had doubts about the worthiness of my calling as a Christian teacher and critic of literature.

This embracing of a cultural mandate is part of the broader doctrine of creation. The doctrine of creation affirms the earthly order as having value in God's sight. This has a large significance for the literary enterprise because the subject of literature (including the literary anthology that we know as the Bible) is human experience, embodied as concretely as possible. I move in Christian circles where the human element in life and the Bible is often disparaged, as though only God matters. As a counter, I have with increasing regularity found myself quoting the opening sentence of Calvin's *Institutes*, with its declaration that true knowledge "consists of two parts: the knowledge of God and of ourselves."

Additionally, the idea of humankind's creation in the image of God provides a theological explanation for why authors create, and an assurance that human creativity is a gift implanted in people by God. This need not move in the direction of idolatry but can be subsumed under the notion of stewardship of God's gifts. In the words of Renaissance poet Sir Philip Sidney, "Let us give right honour to the heavenly Maker of that maker [the writer], who, having made man to His own likeness, set him beyond and over all the works of that second nature," that is, the world of the literary imagination.[46]

By just a slight extension, the idea of the cultural mandate and the doctrine of creation reach out to embrace the Calvinistic emphasis on common grace. This, too, gives literary enthusiasts a place to stand. If God reveals himself in the entire created order, through the work of unbelievers as well as believers, the realms of gold (John Keats' metaphor for the world of imaginative literature) become open for Christians to traverse. This gives the lie to a common misconception that Calvinism's preoccupation with human depravity inevitably produces a negative view of literature and human culture. The "world and life view" that was touted

46. Sir Philip Sidney, "An Apology for Poetry," in Charles Kaplan, ed., *Criticism: The Major Statements* (New York: St. Martin's, 1964), 114.

in my grade school and high school education results in a balanced view that is capable of seeing both good and bad in what it encounters in the world and in literature.

With the legitimacy of literature firmly established, the further question becomes what aspects of literature are deserving of attention. The world at large will doubtless be surprised to know that the Calvinistic tradition has given prominence to beauty as an aesthetic value. For me personally it has even provided a platform for the hedonistic defense of literature on the grounds of enjoyment and human enrichment.

But of course the question of intellectual truth cannot be waived simply because works of literature are beautiful and enjoyable. Literary authors are not only truthful to human experience; they also offer an interpretation of the experiences that they portray. These viewpoints—ultimately adding up to a worldview—need to be tested by a standard of biblical truth. When we make that exploration, it turns out that whereas the morality of most of the literature that I teach is broadly Christian, the values and worldview are not. The genius of a Calvinistic approach to literature is that it does not obligate us to reject everything in an author or work of literature simply because we cannot approve of everything.

I will end by quoting a statement that I made in my first book of literary theory. When I wrote it, I was unaware of the degree to which I was writing under the influence of my Calvinistic heritage: The pursuit of the arts, including literature, is a great calling. The abundant life begins now and permeates the whole person, including his or her artistic impulses.

6

CALVIN'S LEGACY IN PHILOSOPHY

WILLIAM C. DAVIS

Calvin would probably be sorry to learn that this chapter exists, at least at first. Nearly every mention of "philosophy" in his *Institutes* and *Commentaries* is negative, so he might prefer that his legacy in philosophy be the demise of the discipline. To the dismay of many besides Calvin, philosophy has not withered away. Non-Christian, pagan philosophical systems have multiplied with abandon since the sixteenth century. Even more surprising to Calvin, however, might be the growth and proliferation of Christian—even Reformed Christian— philosophical schools and systems. In this chapter I will summarize some of the most important ways that Calvin's influence continues to be felt in the work of philosophers. I will focus on Calvin's abiding impact in epistemology and metaphysics, and even in these areas my treatment will be selective. Much more might be said about Calvin's legacy in the philosophical subdisciplines of ethics (as in the Christian hedonism of John Piper's *Desiring God*), aesthetics (as in Nicholas Wolterstorff's *Art in Action* or Hans Rookmaaker's *Modern Art and the Death of a Culture*),

114

and political philosophy (as in Roy Clouser's *The Myth of Religious Neutrality* or James Skillen's *In Pursuit of Justice*).[1] Even a partial survey of Calvin's continuing influence in epistemology and metaphysics will show that philosophers are deeply in Calvin's debt, not only for his insights but also for the tradition of academic inquiry founded on his methods that his followers continue to pursue.

Calvinism as a Tradition of Inquiry, not a Philosophical School

Calvin's principal goal in his *Institutes* and *Commentaries* was to provide a systematic biblical foundation for pastoral practice.[2] Because of this, it is likely that he would be dismayed to find that his writing was taken by some of his followers as a foundation for philosophical speculation as well. Speculative philosophy can too easily become detached from pastoral concerns, and we should deplore the use of Calvin's work as an excuse for devising arid and lifeless solutions to sophistical puzzles. But speculative philosophy does not have to be dry or pastorally dead. For philosophers concerned to engage genuine problems with the pastoral matters of apologetics, human freedom, and personal eschatology, Calvin's work lays a foundation that would be widely appreciated, and surely he would not despise the practical direction that the philosophical reflection of his followers often took after his day.

---

1. John Piper, *Desiring God* (Colorado Springs: Multnomah Books, 2003); Nicholas Wolterstorff, *Art in Action: Toward a Christian Aesthetic* (Grand Rapids: Eerdmans, 1980); Hans Rookmaaker, *Modern Art and the Death of a Culture* (Wheaton, IL: Crossway Books, 1994); Roy Clouser, *The Myth of Religious Neutrality: An Essay on the Hidden Role of Religious Belief in Theories* (Notre Dame, IN: University of Notre Dame Press, 2005), esp. 269–302; James Skillen, *In Pursuit of Justice: Christian-Democratic Explorations* (New York: Rowman & Littlefield, 2004). Calvin's legacy in architecture is also surprisingly extensive. My awareness of this legacy is a result of the work of my student Luke Irwin. His essay on this legacy is at http://www.covenant.edu/docs/academics/philosophy/studentwork/Irwin_on_Calvin_and_Architecture.pdf. I was alerted to the significance of John Piper's place in Calvin's legacy by my student Nathan Newman. His essay on Calvin and Piper is at http://www.covenant.edu/docs/academics/philosophy/studentwork/Newman_on_Calvin_and_Piper.pdf.

2. *Institutes*, 1.11.1; "John Calvin to the Reader," 4; and "Prefatory Address to King Francis," 12–13.

For Calvin and the late middle ages, "philosophy" most often referred to the exercise of autonomous reason, that is, human reason detached from the correcting work of divine revelation.[3] As later Calvinists, including Dooyeweerd, would echo, Calvin, however, distinguished *philosophy* from *Christian philosophy* precisely over the question of dependence on God's revelation.[4] For Calvin, "Christian philosophy" is possible only where inquiry into philosophical questions submits to the Holy Spirit and to God's revelation in nature and special revelation in the Word.[5] Enlightenment enthusiasm for autonomy rather than dependence made the eighteenth and nineteenth centuries especially inhospitable for self-consciously Calvinist work in philosophy.

Through three centuries of Enlightenment thinking about "good" philosophy, Calvin's legacy in the discipline of philosophy has been carried forward more as a tradition of inquiry than as a body of conclusions about philosophical theories. Calvin's influence in purely philosophical matters is easiest to trace in the subdiscipline of epistemology, where his fruitful suggestions about our dependence on God's revelation for all our knowledge and the crippling effects of the fall are still matters of close scrutiny.[6] But on closer inspection, even in epistemology his legacy is more a matter of method than a received view or philosophical system.

Epistemology

Calvin's *Institutes* opens with sweeping epistemological claims. Not only does everyone know of God,[7] but knowledge of God is tightly con-

3. For a helpful explanation of Calvin on philosophy, see Charles Partee, *Calvin and Classical Philosophy*, Interpretation Bible Studies (Louisville: Westminster John Knox Press, 2005).

4. Herman Dooyeweerd, *In the Twilight of Western Thought* (Nutley, NJ: Craig Press, 1980), 1–60, opens with a section titled "The Pretended Autonomy of Philosophical Thought." R. J. Rushdoony's "Introduction" to his edition of Dooyeweerd's work highlights the problem of autonomous reasoning.

5. Calvin held that submission to the Holy Spirit and God's Word is necessary for Christian philosophy, but it is not sufficient. *Institutes*, 3.7.1–3 calls for self-renunciation as well.

6. Herman Bavinck, *The Philosophy of Revelation* (Whitefish, MT: Kessinger Publishing, 2008), gives his 1908–9 Stone Lectures in which he develops Calvin's emphasis on revelation in epistemology. For a recent extension of this theme to the natural sciences, see Tim Morris and Don Petcher, *Science and Grace* (Wheaton, IL: Crossway Books, 2006), 207–42.

7. *Institutes*, 1.1.3.

nected to knowledge of self.[8] Calvin wastes no time imagining or answering skeptical objections. Instead, he focuses on the pastoral implications of this "duplex" knowledge: we are all worshipers; we all know God and we know ourselves; and left to ourselves we will worship idols of our own devising.[9] Since the fall of Adam and Eve, our ability to know is compromised, and the only remedy for our epistemic defects is the work of the Holy Spirit correcting our thoughts and affections by applying the Word of God to our minds and hearts. In this ambitious program Calvin opens a new chapter in Western epistemology. For biblical and pastoral reasons, he takes for granted that knowledge of self and knowledge of God are common features of human life. He also assumes without argument that knowledge does not depend on the mediation of priests or intellectuals.

Because Calvin's aims are pastoral, he is willing to give theoretical questions relatively little attention. As a result, it is much easier to be confident about the outline of a Calvinist epistemology than it is to insist on details about definitions and mechanisms. For example, Calvin clearly held that all people find themselves wrestling with some kind of awareness of God's existence. He is much less specific about how he thinks this awareness arises. Similarly, the corruption of human faculties resulting from the fall is a crucial part of Calvin's claims about human social and religious existence. But the exact ways that this corruption arises and spreads receive less attention. From a pastoral point of view, it makes sense to focus more on the fact of the need than on the precise mechanisms that nurture and sustain it. Yet even with a pastoral focus, it is evident that three themes in Calvin's work have had and will have a significant impact on the development of Western philosophy. These three are the centrality of God's Word for our knowledge, the universality of the knowledge of God and faith as a kind of knowledge, and the noetic effects of the fall. I will consider each of these in turn.

The Authority of Scripture

For Calvin, all knowledge depends on revelation. What we come to know about the world around us by experience or reflection depends on

8. Ibid., 1.1.1.
9. Ibid., 1.1.10.

general revelation. Although non-Christians tend to think we wrest this knowledge from the world by our own powers without any need for divine help, Calvinist philosophers recognize our dependence on God graciously giving us the ability to make sense of the world, sustaining those abilities, and maintaining the orderliness of the world itself. God's work in general revelation is so uniform, however, that it is easy to take it for granted. Even Christian philosophers in the Enlightenment era were liable to write as if human powers were sufficient in themselves to master scientific matters.[10] Confidence in these powers grew as scientific inquiry began to make human existence more comfortable and efficient in the eighteenth century. Increased confidence in science and the scientific method of inquiry grew to the point that many philosophers were willing to believe that unaided human reason and experience can serve as the ultimate standard against which all knowledge claims are judged.[11]

When Calvin was writing, before the rise of science as the ultimate standard, his embrace of the authority of Scripture did not seem remarkable. Even in his day, though, it was bold; and it remains a bold position today even after the waning of abject confidence in science. Calvin asserted the unique authority of Scripture despite the opposition of the Roman Catholic Church. The Roman church hierarchy had taught for years that the authority of the Bible depends on the approval of the church. Calvin turned that dependence around, asserting that the authority of the church extends only as far as it is consistent with God's Word.[12] The ultimate standard against which all knowledge claims are to be judged is the self-authenticating Word of God.[13]

Calvin did not separate God from his Word. In this, he followed the reasoning of Hebrews 6: God's promises (God's Word) can rest on nothing

10. One example is Thomas Reid, *An Inquiry into the Human Mind on the Principles of Common Sense*, ed. D. Brookes (University Park, PA: Pennsylvania State University Press, 2003); also George Turnbull, *The Principles of Moral Philosophy*, 1740 ed. (Hildesheim, Germany: Georg Olms Verlag, 1976).

11. David Hume, *A Treatise of Human Nature*, ed. L. A. Selby-Bigge, 2nd ed. (Oxford: Clarendon Press, 1978), first published 1739–40; also Antoine-Nicholas de Condorcet, *The Progress of the Human Mind* (Chicago: G. Lander, 2009), first published 1795.

12. *Institutes*, 1.7.2.

13. I will use "Scripture," "Bible," and "Word of God" interchangeably for simplicity. Although the terms are not coextensive, the differences do not affect my claims in this chapter.

more certain than God himself. Calvin acknowledges the Bible as self-authenticating because it is God's Word.[14] He recognizes that this leads naturally to another question. How do we know that the Bible is God's Word? For Calvin, the answer is the internal testimony of the Holy Spirit. We know the Bible is the Word of God because God the Spirit assures us.[15] Although this answer is unlikely to be satisfying to those who have not been assured by the Spirit, Calvin's position is philosophically tight. The only authority that *could* authorize the Word of God is God himself. No other authorities are called upon or smuggled in.

Calvin's philosophical followers have accordingly shared a very high view of the authority of God's Word. As Descartes was heralding the dawn of the modern era in his *Meditations*, the Westminster divines offered a Calvinist alternative. Searching for a self-authenticating starting point independent of the Roman Catholic Church, Descartes chose to start with his clear and distinct ideas. He accepted all that is immediately evident to his self-consciousness as the self-authenticating touchstone of truth.[16] The Westminster Confession of Faith acknowledges all that is "expressly set down in Scripture" as the starting point.[17] Most philosophers since that split in the 1640s have followed Descartes. Rather than having their systems rest ultimately on the truth of God's Word, they have tried to find a way to make "what is immediately evident" to our minds the final authority. The result has been well-documented frustration.[18] For the purposes of this essay, however, the philosophically less traveled path blazed by Calvin is much more interesting.

Modern epistemologists have sought among natural human powers for a trustworthy, self-authenticating source of knowledge. Calvinist

14. *Institutes*, 1.7.5, in which Calvin refers to Isa. 43:10 and 54:13 for support. On the authority of Scripture in Calvin see B. B. Warfield, *Calvin and Augustine* (Philadelphia: Presbyterian and Reformed, 1956), 70–79.

15. *Institutes*, 1.7.4.

16. Rene Descartes, *Discourse on Method and Meditations on First Philosophy* (Miami: BN Publishing, 2008), Second Meditation especially. For concise explanations of Descartes' epistemology, see Frederick Copleston, *History of Philosophy* (New York: Doubleday, 1994), 4.90–115, as well as Gordon Clark, *Thales to Dewey* (Unicoi, TN: Trinity Foundation, 1989).

17. *The Westminster Confession of Faith* (Glasgow: Free Presbyterian Publications, 1973), 1.6.22.

18. Lesslie Newbigin, *Proper Confidence* (Grand Rapids: Eerdmans, 1995), 29–44, gives a concise summary.

philosophers have been alone in starting from the self-authenticating Word of God. This didn't happen right after Calvin, however. Until the twentieth century, the appeal of modernist optimism was so great that Christian epistemologies were comfortable trusting some human ability alongside God's Word. Jonathan Edwards was impressed with the power of natural reason.[19] Thomas Reid and many followers in the nineteenth century leaned on the reliability of mature "common sense" to defeat skepticism and provide a starting point for knowledge.[20] It is not until the work of Cornelius Van Til, John Frame, Gordon Clark, and Alvin Plantinga in the twentieth century that Christian philosophers offer theories of knowledge that give the Word of God the place set aside for it in Calvin's system.

Van Til's "Christian Epistemology" is ably developed in the work of John Frame. Their theory of knowledge is dominated by God's absolute right to exercise his lordship over all things, including knowledge claims.[21] Not only is God himself the standard of truth, his Word is the only infallible, self-authenticating source of truth. Because of this, God's criteria for "truth" and "knowledge" must be presupposed in an act of worshipful submission before any knowledge claims can be made. Those who claim to know anything without submitting to God's lordship demands are rebels who succeed only on "borrowed capital."[22] Apart from insisting on the futility of epistemology apart from submission/presupposition, however, Van Til did not work out a detailed theory of knowledge.

Gordon Clark's "Dogmatism" gave more details, but in his zeal to silence skeptics, Clark in his epistemology makes many important knowledge claims impossible. Clark's approach is straightforward: we only know what is stated explicitly in Scripture and what can be deduced from Scrip-

19. Jonathan Edwards, *A Treatise Concerning Religious Affections*, in John E. Smith, Harry S. Stout, and Kenneth P. Minkema, *A Jonathan Edwards Reader* (New Haven: Yale University Press, 1995), 137–71.

20. Thomas Reid, *Essays on the Intellectual Powers of Man*, ed. D. Brookes (University Park, PA: Pennsylvania State University Press, 2002); see also William C. Davis, *Thomas Reid's Moral Epistemology on Legal Foundations* (London: Thoemmes Continuum, 2006).

21. Cornelius Van Til, *A Christian Theory of Knowledge* (Nutley, NJ: Presbyterian and Reformed, 1969); John Frame, *The Doctrine of the Knowledge of God* (Phillipsburg, NJ: Presbyterian and Reformed, 1987).

22. Cornelius Van Til, *Christian Theistic Evidences* (Phillipsburg, NJ: Presbyterian and Reformed, 1969), 69.

ture by "good and necessary consequences."[23] Radical skepticism is defeated from the outset because the Word of God authorizes itself as a source of knowledge. The rules of "good and necessary consequences" are authorized (Clark insists) because they are used by the biblical authors. As a result, Clark's dogmatism allows him to claim that he *knows* that God exists, that Jesus is the Christ, and that Jesus was raised from the dead. But while these are crucial items of knowledge for Christians, Clark's epistemology struggles with other important truths. For example, Clark admitted that he did not *know* that Christ died for Gordon Clark. Because "Gordon Clark" is not mentioned in Scripture, he had no way to deduce *from Scripture* any conclusion that mentioned him. He didn't even know that he existed. Clark saw the rules of logic used in Scripture and so felt authorized to use those rules himself. He was not willing to follow the gospel writer Luke's example and use what he learned from sense experience and eyewitness testimony to extend what he counted as knowledge (see Luke 1:1–4). Clark's zeal for a Calvinist epistemology cannot be questioned; but the value of his dogmatism is limited by its unavoidable slide into skepticism about the application of spiritual truths to our lives today.

The most recent attempt to develop an epistemology that takes the self-authenticating authority of Scripture seriously comes in the "extended" version of Alvin Plantinga's "A/C Model" in *Warranted Christian Belief*.[24] The details of Plantinga's approach are explained in the next section. Here it is sufficient to note two features of Plantinga's use of Scripture. First, Plantinga acknowledges the necessity of Scripture for our knowledge of spiritual truths. Although he insists on the adequacy of sense perception, rational intuition, memory, and our other powers to give us knowledge of the world, Plantinga recognizes that some truths can only be known by the work of the Holy Spirit through the Scriptures. We know that Jesus rose from the dead, for example, because when we read Luke 24 the Holy Spirit reveals to our minds and seals to our hearts the truth that Jesus was raised. Our other powers are insufficient to apprehend this truth, as Calvin asserts in the *Institutes:* "the things pertaining to our salvation are

23. Gordon Clark, *A Christian View of Men and Things* (Grand Rapids: Baker, 1981), 318–22.

24. Alvin Plantinga, *Warranted Christian Belief* (Oxford: Oxford University Press, 2000), 241–89.

too high to be perceived by our senses, or seen by our eyes, or handled by our hands."[25] Second, Plantinga explicitly adopts Calvin's insistence that God's Word is self-authenticating.[26] The authority of God's Word does not depend on its being found acceptable to autonomous reason, or the senses, or community consensus. Some of Plantinga's theological conclusions are distressing (about Free Will, or God's limitations in creation, for example), but the role that he gives Scripture in his epistemology is a promising development of a key Calvinist theme.[27]

Knowledge of God[28]

Calvin's Genevan Catechism opened with the question, "What is the chief end of man?" The answer to this question was, "To know God by whom he was created."[29] Calvin clearly sees the knowledge of God as a vital pastoral concern. It has long been a central concern of philosophers, and the knowledge of God is the only area of philosophy today where Calvin is known by name in a positive way. The philosophical world today knows Calvin for only three ideas, and two of them are unwelcome. The two unwelcome ideas are freedom-destroying predestination and the depressing idea that humans suffer from depravity. The one positive idea philosophers attribute to Calvin is the *sensus divinitatus*, the epistemological doctrine that humans find belief in God somehow inevitable. This counts as a positive idea even for non-Christian philosophers because most philosophers find skepticism annoying. The idea that knowledge of God depends on a distinct perception-like power is intriguing. Calvin gets the credit for claiming that we have this ability, and philosophers are still debating his claims.

25. *Institutes*, 3.2.41.
26. Plantinga, *Warranted Christian Belief*, 259–66, gives an extended discussion of Calvin on the self-authentication of Scripture.
27. For more about Plantinga on free will and creation, see his *The Nature of Necessity* (Oxford: Oxford University Press, 1974), esp. 169–83.
28. I am indebted to my student Lauren Fritz for research support for this section. Lauren's essay, "John Calvin's *Sensus Divinitatus* and the Apologetic Task," is at http://www.covenant.edu/docs/academics/philosophy/studentwork/Fritz_on_Calvin's_Senus_Divinitatus.pdf.
29. John Calvin, The Genevan Catechism (1536), available at http://www.ondoctrine.com/2cal0504.htm.

What Calvin says about our immediate knowledge of God echoes Paul's words in Romans 1. Calvin writes

> That there exists in the human mind, and indeed by natural instinct, some sense of Deity, we hold to be beyond dispute, since God himself, to prevent any man from pretending ignorance, has endued all men with some idea of his Godhead, the memory of which he constantly renews and occasionally enlarges, that all to a man, being aware that there is a God, and that he is their Maker, may be condemned by their own conscience when they neither worship him nor consecrate their lives to his service.[30]

Following Paul's example, Calvin highlights the universality of the knowledge of God in order to assert universal culpability for failing to worship God. Calvin's focus is *that* all know that there is a God who deserves worship. He is not giving a detailed account of *how* the knowledge arises. One part of Calvin's legacy in the discipline of philosophy consists in efforts to work out the epistemological details surrounding Calvin's provocative, Pauline claim.

During the early modern period of philosophy (1640–1800), Descartes claimed in his *Meditations* that we all have an idea of an infinite, perfect creator of all things. He held that this idea is placed there directly by God, as if God were leaving behind a signature on his handiwork.[31] Descartes does not say how the belief arises, whether by instinct or by some other faculty; and fuzziness about *how* the belief arises eventually led philosophers away from Calvin's approach. Following Descartes, it was still expected that knowledge of God was widespread, but philosophers became dissatisfied with Calvin's suggestion that instinct, perception, or even memory produces the belief. Descartes' position that the idea of God is innate also fell out of favor. In his *Essay Concerning Human Understanding*, Locke rejects all innate ideas, and he argues that knowledge of God is universally available by demonstration from self-evident principles.[32]

30. *Institutes*, 1.1.3.
31. Rene Descartes, *Meditations on First Philosophy*, Third Meditation.
32. John Locke, *An Essay Concerning Human Understanding* (New York: Oxford University Press, USA, 1977), 4.3.18.

With the exception of Scottish "Common Sense" philosophers such as Thomas Reid, generations of Christian philosophers followed Locke's example.[33] Although *belief* in God may arise from a kind of instinct, *knowledge* of God's existence was thought to depend on a demonstration, a proof. Some of the most significant Calvinist philosophers of the last three hundred years held essentially this position. Among them are Jonathan Edwards, Charles Hodge, B. B. Warfield, John Gerstner, and R. C. Sproul.[34] Enlightenment thinking about knowledge made it hard for Christian philosophers and theologians to resist the conclusion that knowledge required (epistemic) *justification*; and demonstrative proof was thought to be the most powerful kind of justification. As it turned out, however, giving a demonstrative proof of God's existence *from uncontroversial premises* has been hard to do. If it is possible at all, very few Christians have done it. So if we only *know* God exists by giving a proof, then few people—including Calvin—know that God exists.

Calvinist philosophers and others sympathetic to Calvin's account of our knowledge of God have most often moved away from looking for a demonstrative proof to justify belief in God. Instead, they have questioned the assumption that knowledge always requires a justification aimed at satisfying skeptics. Herman Bavinck's *Our Reasonable Faith* (1909) took this approach. Bavinck insisted that our knowledge of God

> obviously has its own peculiar character. It is different from all other knowledge that can be obtained, and the difference is not one of degree but of principle and essence ... [It] differs from the knowledge of created things in its origin and object and in its essence and effects.[35]

Knowledge of God differs in essence from other knowledge because it involves love for God, not merely the possession of information. This knowledge also differs from other knowledge because it depends on faith.

33. For an account of the role of Scottish Common Sense Philosophy in the nineteenth century, see James McCosh, *The Scottish Philosophy* (Hildesheim, Germany: Georg Olms Verlagsbuchhandlung, 1966).

34. A clear summary and defense of this position is given in R. C. Sproul, John Gerstner, and Arthur Lindsley, *Classical Apologetics* (Grand Rapids: Zondervan, 1984).

35. Herman Bavinck, *Our Reasonable Faith* (Grand Rapids: Baker, 1956), 26.

"It is the product not of scientific study and reflection but of childlike and simple faith."[36]

Similar accounts of our knowledge of God can be found in the works of other philosophers in the twentieth century. One of the earliest followers of Bavinck was the Reformed theologian Cornelius Van Til, whose ideas were later developed by Greg Bahnsen, John Frame, and Scott Oliphint.[37] For these "Presuppositionalists," knowledge of the God of the Bible and submission to his lordship are the beginning of all knowledge and meaning. Although all people know God from what has been revealed in creation, true knowledge of God (rather than suppression in unrighteousness) depends on faith worked in us by the Holy Spirit. More recently, self-consciously Calvinist philosophers such as Paul Helm (*Faith and Reason*) and Esther Lightcap Meek (*Longing to Know*) have worked to develop the epistemological details of our awareness of God's existence.[38]

The work of Van Til, Frame, Helm, and Meek is well known among Calvinist and some evangelical philosophers. But Calvin's legacy in philosophy today is most widely known through the work of Plantinga, Wolterstorff, and the (so-called) Reformed Epistemologists.[39] Blending Thomas Reid's common sense foundationalism with a Bavinck-like Dutch confidence, Plantinga's *Warrant and Proper Function* develops a broad epistemological strategy in which Calvin's *sensus divinitatus* is analogous to other faculties such as sight and hearing. As a result, our belief in God's

36. Ibid., 31.

37. Van Til, *A Christian Theory of Knowledge*; Greg Bahnsen, *Pushing the Antithesis* (Powder Springs, GA: American Vision, 2007); John Frame, *The Doctrine of the Knowledge of God*; and K. Scott Oliphint, *Reasons (for Faith): Philosophy in the Service of Theology* (Phillipsburg, NJ: P&R Publishing, 2006).

38. Paul Helm, *Faith and Reason* (New York: Oxford University Press, USA, 1999); Esther Lightcap Meek, *Longing to Know* (Ada, MI: Brazos Press, 2003).

39. Alvin Plantinga, *Warrant: The Current Debate* (Oxford: Oxford University Press, 1993); Alvin Plantinga, *Warrant and Proper Function* (Oxford: Oxford University Press, 1993); Plantinga, *Warranted Christian Belief*; Alvin Plantinga and Nicholas Wolterstorff, eds., *Faith & Rationality: Reason & Belief in God* (Notre Dame, IN: University of Notre Dame Press, 1983). "Reformed Epistemology" is "Reformed" in the sense that it originally (in Plantinga's 1980 paper, "The Reformed Objection to Natural Theology," read to the American Catholic Philosophical Association) aimed to build on Calvinist insights in epistemology. In his "Introduction" to *Faith & Rationality*, Wolterstorff admits that the system is called "Calvinist epistemology" or "Reformed epistemology," "not very felicitously," 7.

existence is "properly basic" when it arises from our natural, instinctive sense of God's presence.

For Plantinga, knowledge of God's existence is like our knowledge that other minds exist, or that the tree I see outside my window exists. Not only do we find ourselves believing in the existence of other minds and trees without constructing rational proofs, we know they are there *without constructing rational proofs*. These beliefs are warranted not because they follow logically from other (more basic) beliefs. Rather, they are warranted because they are produced by faculties (1) functioning properly (that is, as designed), (2) in the environment for which they were designed, and (3) successfully aimed at the truth by their Designer. Looking out my window, I find myself believing there is a tree outside. If this belief is the result of my senses functioning as God designed them to work, and if God made my eyes to apprehend the truth about the external world, then my belief is warranted. Plantinga argues that a belief can be warranted even without a justification. So because knowledge is warranted true belief, I can know that there is a tree outside even if I can't produce a proof for it.[40]

Our knowledge of God, according to Plantinga, meets all of these conditions. The natural instinct Calvin calls the *sensus divinitatus* is the part of our cognitive equipment that God designed and gave us to produce in us beliefs about his existence. The environment for which it is designed includes God's magnificent creation. Merely from the things that were made, all people know of—or are culpable for repressing the knowledge of—God's existence. So when I see the multitude of stars on a clear night and think, "There must be a God," it is appropriate to say that I *know* that God exists. It is appropriate to say this even if I cannot begin to give an argument that would reason from the splendor of the heavens as a premise to the existence of God as a conclusion. I know because the belief arose in the same natural way that my belief in the tree outside my window arose.

40. This "proper functionalist" theory of knowledge is developed in detail in Plantinga's *Warrant and Proper Function*. Plantinga's critics include both Christians and non-Christians. See Paul Helm, *John Calvin's Ideas* (New York: Oxford University Press, 2006), 209–45; Richard Swinburne, "Plantinga and Warrant," *Religious Studies* 37, 2 (June 2001): 203–14. Steve Wykstra, "'Not Done in a Corner': How to Be a Sensible Evidentialist about Jesus," *Philosophical Books* 43, 2 (Oxford: Blackwell, 2002), 92–116.

It should not be surprising that philosophers have criticized Plantinga's approach to the knowledge of God. Non-Christians have attempted to argue that the *sensus divinitatis* is too different from less-controversial faculties (such as sight and memory) to count belief in God as properly basic *even if* God exists. Christian philosophers have objected that Plantinga leaves too little room for the rational arguments for God's existence found in natural theology.[41] The strength of these objections is still a matter of debate among both Christian and non-Christian philosophers. What is not debatable, though, is the importance of Plantinga's proper functionalism in the current epistemological discussions. The attention that Plantinga's work is getting is significant to Christian philosophy for at least two reasons. First, Plantinga's work places Calvin's claims about the *sensus divinitatis* in the thick of current debates about the nature of knowledge. Revival of interest in Calvin on this subject has led philosophers to examine Calvin's treatment of other issues as well.

The second significant feature of Plantinga's use of Calvin concerns the way Plantinga extends his analysis beyond knowledge of God's existence to other Christian beliefs. In *Warrant and Proper Function*, Plantinga develops a theory of knowledge that shows how the *sensus divinitatis* is rightly counted among the faculties of our "design plan." When it functions properly, this faculty generates warranted belief about God's existence. In *Warranted Christian Belief*, Plantinga identifies *faith* as another God-given module of our belief-forming equipment.[42] Plantinga's discussion of faith as a source of knowledge also follows Calvin's *Institutes*. Plantinga argues that when it is functioning properly, faith is the faculty by which the Holy Spirit reveals to our minds and seals to our hearts the truth of God's Word.[43] So, for example, Plantinga insists that he *knows* that Jesus rose from the dead because when he reads in the Bible, "He is not here, he is risen," he finds himself believing that Jesus rose from the dead. More than just having the belief, he finds his heart moved by the splendor of

---

41. Michael L. Czapkay Sudduth, "The Prospects for 'Mediate' Natural Theology in John Calvin," *Religious Studies* 31, 1 (March 1995): 53–68; and Michael L. Czapkay Sudduth, "Plantinga's Revision of the Reformed Tradition: Rethinking our Natural Knowledge of God," *Philosophical Books* vol. 43, 2 (Oxford: Blackwell, 2002), 81–91.

42. Plantinga, *Warranted Christian Belief*, 246–52, 290–94.

43. *Institutes*, 3.2.7; Plantinga, *Warranted Christian Belief*, 251–52.

the reality. Neither the belief nor the affection is the result of rational argumentation. The belief and the affection are the work of the Holy Spirit through the repaired cognitive faculty designed to apprehend this spiritual truth.

The details of Plantinga's account of faith as a source of knowledge go well beyond Calvin's discussion of faith. In part, this is because Plantinga draws on the work of Jonathan Edwards on the role of affections in our knowledge of spiritual truths.[44] But even where Plantinga's epistemology extends beyond Calvin and Edwards, his conclusions are usually well within the spirit and intent of Calvin's claims in the *Institutes*. Concerning our knowledge of God via the *sensus divinitatus* and our knowledge of the great truths of the gospel through the reading of God's Word, Plantinga's work has extended Calvin's philosophical legacy as much as any other current author.

The Noetic Effects of the Fall

The Enlightenment was optimistic about human powers almost to the point of giddiness. Calvin is less enthusiastic about the ability of fallen humans to do the good and think about reality adequately. While most philosophers admit that humans are fallible, Calvin is known for a much more pessimistic view that emphasized the depth and extent of the brokenness of our faculties. The general terms epistemologists use for the whole basket of abilities that we use to form beliefs is "noetic endowment" or "noetic equipment." The term "noetic" refers to wisdom or understanding. It ranges beyond mere ideas or beliefs to affections, disposition, practical awareness. Going beyond the mere formation of ideas is important for understanding Calvin's contribution to epistemology, since he never treats belief apart from action or choice. This is evident in *Institutes* (1.15.8), where the first activity of intellect is distinguishing between good and evil. Conscience is a chief function of our noetic endowment. Physical eyesight is another part of our noetic endowment. Although it was compromised in the fall, spiritual sight by faith can also be a part of our noetic equipment. The noetic effects of the fall include all the ways that the fall impaired the equipment we use to form beliefs and affections.

---

44. Plantinga, *Warranted Christian Belief*, 294–323

Although the biblical data are limited, we can piece together some of the noetic powers that Adam and Eve possessed before the fall. Calvin mentions Adam and Eve's pre-fall abilities in order to highlight our post-fall epistemological *disabilities*. He notes, for example, that prior to the fall Adam and Eve enjoyed clear perception of heavenly (or spiritual) things.[45] In order for them to commune with God (walking in the garden), God's presence must have been evident with a clarity we do not experience now. In his work of naming the animals, Adam demonstrates an untainted capacity for faithful stewardship of the garden. In addition to using language to exercise dominion, Adam also displayed the ability to love faithful service to God. In his first address to Eve, Adam shows a facility with language that is both poetically subtle and spiritually perceptive. Prior to the fall, Adam and Eve saw spiritual realities (beings, values, meanings), loved what is truly lovely, and were able to express these powers without selfishness, division, or idolatry.[46]

The fall of Adam and Eve from this lofty state is beyond explanation. With all their noetic advantages—both cognitive and affective—it is impossible to give a sufficient reason or to suggest a mechanism that would move them from joyful trust to desperate rebellion.[47] In addition to the self-inflicted injuries they experienced in the fall, God also imposed a covenantal curse on them and their children. None of our faculties—including reason!—is free from corruption. This means we cannot use any faculty (reason, the senses, self-consciousness, etc.) as the standard against which the other faculties are calibrated or corrected. The limitations and distortions that now plague human thought and affection do not give us an excuse for our sinful behavior toward God and others; but they are deep enough to leave us epistemologically dependent on God's grace. For Calvin, these consequences are obvious features of the biblical narrative. More than being just finite, humans are fallen. Because of this, we must look outside ourselves for a standard and for correction.

45. *Institutes*, 1.15.3–4.
46. Calvin, *Commentary on Genesis*, vol. 1 (Forgotten Books, 2007), concerning Genesis 1:26.
47. John Milton, *Paradise Lost* (New York: Penguin Classic, 2003), offers Satan's pride as an explanation for the fall that goes well beyond the biblical data.

For most philosophers, this is an unacceptably negative conclusion about our abilities.

For spiritual matters, fallen human powers are not just inept; they lead us to embrace unlovely falsehoods. With earthly matters, however, things are different. Concerning physical perception and the common affairs of life, Calvin notes that our noetic equipment is practically reliable. We can find our way about without crashing into things; we can find and grow food; we successfully reproduce; and we construct civil societies capable of enduring. Calvin's discussion of our post-fall powers highlights this difference between spiritual and earthly matters.[48] More recent Calvinist philosophers have proposed that the depth of the fall's impact on our powers runs along a continuum. Kuyper, Dooyeweerd, and Clouser argue that sin's impact on our noetic affairs is most disruptive in religious matters, and that it diminishes as the subject matter gets farther and farther from religious matters. The disciplines of math and physics, they propose, are less compromised by the fall than the disciplines of economics and ethics.[49]

The corruption of our noetic powers is both an individual and a communal problem. Self-love and idolatry are encouraged by the example of others, and we all too easily believe that our tribe's opinions and practices are superior to the opinions and practices of other tribes.[50] Twentieth-century critics of modern optimism about human reason have picked up this Calvinist theme, emphasizing the communal dimension of our noetic dysfunction. Christian philosophers such as Merold Westphal have credited Calvin for alerting the Western philosophical world to our brokenness.[51] But Calvinist warnings about the noetic effects of the fall went unheeded by nearly every Enlightenment philosopher. Throughout the modern period, Calvin's legacy in philosophy included being a minority voice urging caution. With the demise of Enlightenment optimism and

48. *Institutes*, 2.1.4–11.

49. Abraham Kuyper, *Lectures on Calvinism* (Grand Rapids: Eerdmans, 1931); Dooyeweerd, *In the Twilight of Western Thought*; and Clouser, *The Myth of Religious Neutrality*.

50. Stephen Moroney, *The Noetic Effects of Sin: An Historical and Contemporary Exploration of How Sin Affects Our Thinking* (Lanham, MD: Lexington Books, 1999).

51. Merold Westphal, "Taking St. Paul Seriously: Sin as an Epistemological Category," in T. P. Flint, ed., *Christian Philosophy* (Notre Dame: University of Notre Dame Press, 1990), 216.

the rise of postmodern and pluralist pessimism, it is likely that Calvinist philosophers will need to balance their account of our epistemic brokenness with observations about the epistemic abilities that humanity retained after the fall.

Metaphysics: Free Will and Divine Providence[52]

Both Christian and non-Christian philosophers have found parts of Calvin's epistemology useful and worthy of further development. Calvin's metaphysical positions have not been nearly as well received.[53] Calvin's biblical emphasis on God's glory complicates any attempt to give a philosophically careful explanation of human freedom. The problem of the relationship between human freedom and God's providential control of all things goes back at least to Augustine's *De Libero Arbitrio*.[54] Calvin's doctrine of divine providence makes the challenge especially great. By insisting on God's complete independence of all things outside his own nature and the completeness of God's decree, Calvin leaves room only for theories of human freedom that affirm the compatibility of God's meticulous providence and morally significant human freedom.[55] In the generations immediately following Calvin, such "compatibilist"

52. I am indebted to my student Colby Wilkins for significant research support and helpful observations. Colby's essay on Calvin's legacy in debates about free will is at http://www.covenant.edu/docs/academics/philosophy/studentwork/Wilkins_on_Calvin_and_Compatibilism.pdf.

53. An entire section could be devoted to Calvin's impact on philosophical inquiry into the relationship between body and soul, and the problems of personal identity and human immortality. Calvin is wrongly accused of passing along an uncritically platonic hatred of the physical body. A good place to start in understanding this issue and vindicating Calvin's view would be John Cooper's *Body, Soul, and Life Everlasting: Biblical Anthropology and the Monism-Dualism Debate* (Grand Rapids: Eerdmans, 2000); Paul Helm, *John Calvin's Ideas*, 129–56; and Margaret R. Miles, "Theology, Anthropology, and the Human Body in Calvin's *Institutes of the Christian Religion*," *Harvard Theological Review* 74, 3 (1981): 311.

54. Augustine, *On Free Choice of the Will* (Indianapolis: Hackett Publishing, 1993), 3.4.11. For a contemporary statement of this "simple foreknowledge" position, see David P. Hunt, "Divine Providence and Simple Foreknowledge," *Faith and Philosophy* 10, 3 (1993): 394–414.

55. Calvin's compatibilism is clear both in his *Institutes* (1.17.3–5, 2.3.13–14, 2.4.8, 2.5.1–19) and in his work *The Bondage and Liberation of the Will: A Defense of the Orthodox Doctrine of Human Choice against Pighius* (Grand Rapids: Baker, 1996).

approaches to free will were embraced even by those outside Reformed circles.[56] Jonathan Edwards' *Freedom of the Will* defended the Calvinist position, albeit without embracing the label "Calvinist."[57] After the eighteenth century, however, Christian philosophers largely joined the rest of the philosophical world in rejecting Calvin's compatibilism. Because of this, accounting for human freedom remains one of the principal challenges facing Calvinist philosophers.

The problem of "free will" has changed since Calvin's time. In the sixteenth century, concerns about "freedom" centered on whether or not fallen humans retain the ability to *do the good*. God's providence was not the most obvious threat to human freedom; it was God's curse on Adam and Eve that posed the bigger hurdle. Against the Roman Catholic claim that our wills could do the good in our own strength, Calvin joined Luther in insisting that free will is a slave *to sin*. One of the blessings of inclusion in Christ is deliverance from this bondage. Instead of being slaves to sin, God's people are slaves to righteousness. Philosophers today would not recognize this as a solution to the problem of "free will," but for Calvin it was the heart of the solution.[58]

The current philosophical problem of "free will" has its origin in a seventeenth-century shift in focus on what it means to be free. Instead of

56. A "compatibilist" holds simply that real human freedom and some kind of determinism are compatible. Leibniz, for example, was a compatibilist, as were the Roman Catholic Scholastics. Philosophers who reject compatibilism usually hold a "libertarian" position, according to which real freedom is possible only if determinism is false. Concerning Leibniz's analysis of Thomas, Molina, and Banez, see Jack D. Davidson, "Untying the Knot: Leibniz on God's Knowledge of Future Free Contingents," *History of Philosophy Quarterly* 13, 1 (January 1996): 89–116.

57. Jonathan Edwards, *A Careful and Strict Inquiry into the Modern Prevailing Notions of Freedom of the Will, Which Is Supposed to Be Essential to Moral Agency, Virtue and Vice, Reward and Punishment, Praise and Blame* (originally published 1754), in John E. Smith, Harry S. Stout, and Kenneth P. Minkema, *A Jonathan Edwards Reader* (New Haven: Yale University Press, 1995). On being a Calvinist, Edwards writes, "The term 'Calvinist' is in these days, among most, a term of greater reproach than the term 'Arminian'; yet I should not take it at all amiss, to be called a Calvinist, for distinction's sake: though I utterly disclaim a dependence on Calvin, or believing the doctrines which I hold, because he believed and taught them; and cannot justly be charged with believing in everything just as he taught," 193.

58. *Institutes*, 2.4 and 2.5, as well as *The Bondage and Liberation of the Will*. See also Paul Helm, "Calvin and Bernard on Freedom and Necessity: A Reply to Brummer," *Religious Studies* 30, 4 (Cambridge: Cambridge University Press, 1994), 457–65.

treating freedom as the ability to do the good, philosophers and theologians came to see freedom as the ability *to do otherwise* (than one in fact did). On this definition, people are truly free only if they could really have done otherwise than they did. For example, William Farel *freely* demanded that Calvin remain in Geneva only if Farel had the power *not* to make that demand. It would not be enough to say that God might have ordained that Farel not make the demand. In that case, it was God, not Farel, who had the power. In order for Farel to have the power to do otherwise (and be free in this new sense), then the choice had to be entirely, finally, up to Farel. Determining whether Farel (or anyone) has this kind of power turns out to be tricky; but for the last two hundred years this definition of freedom has dominated the philosophical discussion. Outside of Reformed circles, it is now widely thought that this kind of freedom—called "libertarian freedom"—is a necessary condition for being held morally responsible.[59] So unless a person has this kind of power, then nothing he or she does is morally significant, and he or she cannot be morally praised or blamed for his or her actions.

The last extended defense of the older view of freedom was given by Jonathan Edwards in his *Freedom of the Will* in 1754. Edwards argued for theological determinism, the view that God determines all that occurs including what humans will. He defined free actions as those done according to one's will. His position was a Calvinist compatibilism, and his reasoning rested on a biblical understanding of God's perfect freedom. God, he insisted, is perfectly free even though God is unable to do other than what is perfect. Edwards rejected the need to define human freedom in terms of the ability to will otherwise on the grounds that such a definition would set up a vicious regress. A person would be free only if she could have willed to will to will to do otherwise, etc.[60]

Edwards' Calvinist analysis of human freedom passed out of philosophical favor quickly. His account of God's sovereign decree was out of step with the humanistic drift of Enlightenment thought, and Kant soon

---

59. One of the clearest statements of the connection between libertarian freedom and moral responsibility is given by Peter van Inwagen in *An Essay on Free Will* (Oxford: The Clarendon Press, 1983).

60. Edwards, *Freedom of the Will*, 206–8.

(1781) offered a compatibilist bridge to the pure libertarian approach to freedom that now dominates philosophical discussion. Christian philosophers and theologians prior to Kant consistently argued that only God has libertarian freedom. This is because only God is perfectly independent. God alone has the power entirely within himself to choose otherwise. Only a being entirely independent of God could have this kind of power. Non-Christian philosophers such as Roderick Chisholm have openly accepted the conclusion that humans must have God-like autonomy if they are to be held responsible.[61] Until very recently, Christian philosophers were unwilling to go this far. But the pull of the Kantian assumption has proven to be powerful. Driven by the conviction that moral responsibility requires libertarian freedom, most Christian philosophers now endorse libertarian accounts of human freedom that exclude—sometimes pointedly exclude—God's decree as the determiner of human events.[62]

To their credit, most Christian philosophers recognize that a freedom that makes humans radically independent of God raises serious questions about God's omniscience and providence. Until just the last few years, most Christian philosophers followed the early Augustinian approach to God's knowledge of the future and his providential governance of all things. In his De Libero Arbitrio, Augustine explained God's perfect knowledge of future events in terms of God (passively) looking ahead. God knew the future by foresight. This is now called the "Simple Foreknowledge" solution.[63] In order to preserve human freedom, God's providence was limited to all the events not determined by human free choices. Although this elevates human decisions to the level of God's decisions (in autonomy and power), many have followed Kierkegaard in seeing this as a proof of

61. Roderick Chisholm, "Human Freedom and the Self," reprinted in R. C. Hoy and L. N. Oaklander, Metaphysics (Belmont: Wadsworth Publishing, 1991), 364: "If we are responsible, and if what I have been trying to say is true [that freedom means the power to will otherwise], then we have a prerogative which some would attribute only to God: each of us, when we act, is a prime mover unmoved."

62. Thomas Flint, "Two Accounts of Providence," in Divine and Human Action: Essays in the Metaphysics of Theism, ed. by Thomas V. Morris (Ithaca, NY: Cornell University Press, 1988), 175–76.

63. John Sanders, "Why Simple Foreknowledge Offers No More Providential Control Than the Openness of God," Faith and Philosophy 14, 1 (1997): 26.

God's power: God is so great that he can create beings that are radically independent of him.[64]

Calvinist philosophers are not usually persuaded by the claim that God's glory is increased by having the ability to make beings upon whom he then must depend. On this view, although God knows all, God must passively *learn* from his creatures what their independent wills have determined. And Calvinists have not been alone in seeing that the Simple Foreknowledge solution is philosophically unstable. In order for God timelessly to know that Farel would demand in 1536 that Calvin stay in Geneva, it had to be timelessly true that Farel would demand in 1536 that Calvin stay in Geneva. Timeless truths cannot be otherwise. So even if God's knowledge is merely passive foresight, Farel could *not* have done otherwise. Because of this, most evangelical philosophers now concede that the Simple Foreknowledge picture is not sufficient to preserve libertarian freedom. Many also concede that they must choose from among three options: Calvinist Determinism, Molinism, and Open Theism.[65]

For both Molinists and Open Theists, defense of our libertarian freedom leads to a willingness to adjust our understanding of God's

64. Søren Kierkegaard, *Concluding Unscientific Postscript* (Princeton, NJ: Princeton University Press, 1974), 232. His most explicit statement can be found in his *Journals and Papers*, ed. and trans. by Howard V. Hong and Edna H. Hong (Bloomington, IN: Indiana University Press, 1970), citation number 1251: "Only omnipotence can withdraw itself at the same time it gives itself away. . . . He to whom I owe everything has in fact made me independent." Kierkegaard did not deal with the objection that "God has the power to make an absolutely independent being" is incoherent in just the way "God has the power to make a stone He cannot lift" is incoherent.

65. Molinism is the position advanced by Luis de Molina in the sixteenth century. See his *Liberi Arbitri cum Gratiae Donis, Divina Praescientia, Providentia, Praedestinatione et Reprobatione Concordia* (The Harmony of Free Will with Divine Grace, Divine Foreknowledge, Providence, Predestination, and Reprobation), 1588. An English translation of the crucial Part IV has been made by Alfred J. Freddoso in Luis de Molina, *On Divine Foreknowledge* (Ithaca, NY, and London: Cornell University Press, 1988). An unusually clear explanation of Molina's doctrine of middle knowledge and its implications for providence and predestination can be found in Thomas Flint's "Two Accounts of Providence," in Morris, *Divine and Human Action*, 147–81. Clear statements of the Open Theist position can be found in Clark Pinnock, Richard Rice, John Sanders, William Hasker, and David Basinger, *The Openness of God* (Downers Grove, IL: InterVarsity Press, 1994), and John Sanders, *The God Who Risks: A Theology of Divine Providence* (Downers Grove, IL: InterVarsity Press, 1998).

independence. In both cases, human freedom is equated with God's free-dom.[66] A man who made wind-up worshipers would be pathetic, but God is not a man. The Bible repeatedly warns against judging God by human standards. More than that, Isaiah calls us to take comfort in the profound difference between God and us. God's ways are not our ways precisely in that God will forgive where we will not (Isa. 55). Beyond the inappropriateness of casting God in our image (for example in depicting God as yearning for a close relationship with us as if he were a needy parent and we are stubborn teenagers), the libertarian position requires the conclusion that some good things (such as true worship) do *not* come ultimately from God. The Bible teaches that every good thing comes from God (James 1:17). If God had to wait for human wills to choose true worship, then at least that good thing would not come from God.

Calvinist philosophers have been among the minority of philosophers arguing that morally significant human freedom and some kind of determinism are compatible. But Calvinists are not the only compatibilists, and while compatibilists often share lines of argument, some versions of compatibilism are biblically unacceptable. The most influential compatibilist argument in the last forty years was given by Harry Frankfurt. In a deft series of stories, Frankfurt shows that moral responsibility is possible even when someone does *not* have the power to do otherwise.[67] The story has perplexed so many libertarians that it is worth sketching the details here:

Suppose that a man named Black takes whatever steps necessary to ensure that a man named Jones will choose to act in one way rather than another. (For example, Black may implant a microchip in Jones' brain that delivers a crippling shock to Jones whenever he considers not acting in the specific way Black wants.) Suppose further that Black's device never has to do anything because Jones chooses to do as Black

66. For more on the biblical inadequacy of the Molinist and Open Theist views of God's foreknowledge, see Paul Helm, *The Providence of God* (Downers Grove, IL: InterVarsity Press, 1994), 55–61; John Frame, *The Doctrine of God* (Phillipsburg, NJ: P&R Publishing, 2002), 160–89; and my brief article, "Does God Know the Future?" *Modern Reformation* (Sept.–Oct., 1999).

67. Harry G. Frankfurt, "Alternate Possibilities and Moral Responsibility," *The Journal of Philosophy* 66, 23 (Dec. 4, 1969): 829–39. The crucial counterexample begins on page 836.

wanted. In that case, Jones is clearly responsible for the choice, but could not have done otherwise. Frankfurt's conclusion is that the plausibility of this story shows that the ability to do otherwise is not a necessary condition for moral responsibility.

This story aids the Calvinist cause by showing that our intuitions about moral responsibility do not *require* that we have the ability to do otherwise. It thus opens up the possibility that we could be morally free even if we are unable to do otherwise (because God's decree takes it ultimately out of our power). But Frankfurt's story only shows that the libertarian intuition is too hasty. It does not solve all the problems that a Calvinist approach to freedom raises. Two of these problems deserve to be highlighted here because they are likely to dominate the next generation of Calvinist philosophical work on human freedom: (a) how can God hold us morally responsible for choices that find their ultimate origin in God's eternal decree, and (b) how can Calvinists avoid the charge that the doctrine of God's eternal decree produces a fatalistic form of determinism?

Concerning the first problem, human responsibility for acts decreed by God, Calvinist philosophers will have to start with the Bible's claims about human freedom. General revelation alone will not be sufficient to clarify the relationship between God's decree and our free choices because nothing in creation gives an adequate insight into God's prerogatives and purposes. Frankfurt's story raises questions about the necessity of the ability to do otherwise for morally significant freedom, but the story still suggests that Jones is the ultimate author of the free choice. Calvinists cannot pretend that God's decree only plays a role in the cases where Jones independently chooses not to do otherwise. Jones always does as God decrees, and Jones is not the ultimate cause of the choice. Calvinists hold that Jones is morally responsible even though God's decree determines the choice. This picture is offensive to most people, since it means Jones is morally guilty for all of the sins Jones commits even though they were decreed by God. But the biblical reality is even worse. Not only is Jones guilty, but God is not. God retains the credit for all of Jones' morally upright choices, but the guilt for sins falls only on Jones.

The justice of this arrangement is perplexing until we remember that God is not another creature. As the Lord and creator, God has the authority to order all things as he sees fit. The question is not whether God's ways make sense to our rational intuitions; it is rather whether our intuitions will conform to God's claims about his ways. Because of this, God's Word must have the last say. Three passages speak to the issue of human freedom and God's decree especially clearly. In Acts 2:22–24, Peter argues that Jesus was delivered up to death by sinful men according to the determinate counsel and foreknowledge of God. In Ephesians 2:1–10, Paul argues both that salvation is entirely the work of God's grace and that God prepared our good works in advance for us to walk in them. In Romans 9:6–24, Paul answers the charge that God is unjust for determining to punish Pharaoh's disobedience even after God hardened Pharaoh's heart. Paul makes it clear that the hardening served the purpose of advancing God's glory, and yet Pharaoh is justly punished. In all of these cases God's decree is compatible with the moral responsibility of the humans involved.[68]

It is because of this biblical evidence that Calvinists such as Edwards reject libertarian accounts of freedom and assert instead that freedom for humans consists in the ability to act according to our will. External coercion or constraint *imposed by other creatures* undermines freedom and responsibility. God's eternal decree does not limit or remove our responsibility. In the end, freedom is not the sort of thing that can be shared. In order for humans to be radically free in the libertarian sense, God would have to be dependent on human wills. God would have to learn from us what we will do. Our wills would be absolute sources of goodness, and thus God would not be the only source of goodness. God could be sure that his purposes would be achieved only if his plans did not depend on any free human choices. The Bible does not suggest that God is limited in any of these ways. Indeed, it asserts that God does not learn or wait, and that His plans are sure to be fulfilled even though they include our free, responsible choices.

The second challenge facing Calvinist accounts of human free will is the threat of fatalism. God's eternal decree and meticulous providence

68. For an extended discussion of the implications of these passages for a Calvinist compatibilism, see John Calvin Wingard, "Morally Significant Freedom, Moral Responsibility, and Causal Determinism: A Compatibilist View," *Testamentum Imperium* 2 (2009): selection no. 12 (URL: http://www.preciousheart.net/ti/2009/index.htm).

determine every event of human history. It might seem to follow that human effort and deliberation are pointless. God's will is unavoidable. Whether I work hard or not, all will go as God has decreed. Christians are rightly dissatisfied with the Stoic or Muslim who makes no effort and simply says "what will be will be" or "as Allah wills." Many Christian philosophers have concluded that the Calvinist approach to human freedom leads to the same kind of quietist fatalism.

A Calvinist answer to this challenge must start with the admission that Calvinists have not always resisted the temptation to fall into *hyper-Calvinism*. Hyper-Calvinists use God's comprehensive eternal decree as an excuse to ignore the Bible's call for diligent action. Lazy or despairing responses to God's sovereign decree are at least a kind of practical fatalism, and Calvinists must fight this temptation by careful attention to Scripture. Calvinist compatibilism differs from Stoic fatalism in at least two important ways, and both ways depend on the personal character of God's decree. Stoic quietism flows from the belief that the Logos determining all events is impersonal, detached, and uninterested. The God of the Bible is personal, engaged, and loving. More than that, the God of the Bible is wise, and he wills both the ends and the means. God does not bring things about *in spite of* or *apart from* human free will. Instead, God brings things about by means of human free will. He ordained that Farel freely demand that Calvin stay in Geneva, thus bringing about Farel's demand through Farel's decision to make the demand. A Calvinist understanding of free will leads to zealous activity (as willed by God), not to inactivity.

At this point, the most common response from evangelical philosophers is that the Calvinist position makes humans into mere puppets and God into a cruel puppet master.[69] To see the pull of this response, suppose that I built a machine and strapped a cat into it. Suppose also that I used the machine to force the cat to shred a friend's expensive rug. In this case, the cat would not be morally responsible for the damage. If I were then to inflict a painful punishment on the cat for its "crime," my actions would be terribly cruel. For philosophers with libertarian expectations

69. Charles K. Cannon, "'As in a Theater': Hamlet in the Light of Calvin's Doctrine of Predestination," *Studies in English Literature, 1500–1900* 11, 2, Elizabethan and Jacobean Drama (Spring, 1971): 211, mentions this common objection. Internet references to the problem are less subtle: http://www.bcbsr.com/topics/calvinism_heresy.html.

about freedom, it would be at least as unjust and cruel if God's decree determined events and he were then to punish people for carrying out the crimes that God decreed.

The Calvinist answer must focus on the faulty libertarian assumption that we have no evidence about how God thinks about the relationship between his will and our actions. If God's Word was silent on this matter, we would have to depend on our intuitions about puppets and puppet masters. But God's Word is not silent. In Romans 9 (and Jer. 18:1–4, which Paul echoes), humans are likened to clay in the hands of a potter. In this analogy, humans have no more independence than a puppet. Despite this, God commits some pots to destruction *for his glory*. This is a hard word, but a similar picture is given elsewhere in Scripture (cf. Isa. 29:16; 46:10; 1 Kings 22:13–40; Job 42:2; Acts 2:23; 4:28). Rather than using our feelings about our freedom to correct our reading of Scripture, we ought to use Scripture to correct the conclusions we reach on the basis of our feelings.

What, after all, would be so bad about being a puppet in the service of God's glory? It would be hideously demeaning to be a puppet completely controlled by another creature, but God is not just another creature. God is God. Calvin's legacy in the ongoing philosophical discussions about free will exerts its influence most of all on these points. God's glory, knowledge, and independence are more important than human autonomy and dignity. And our intuitions need to submit to God's Word and not the other way around. Calvinist philosophers must work to explore the implications of these biblical demands even when the conclusions are unpopular. Although it is unlikely that theological compatibilism will attract a wide following among non-Christian philosophers, the future of Calvinist metaphysics must hold fast to the supremacy of God's lordship and the ultimate authority of God's Word.

Conclusion: The Future of Calvinist Philosophy

Five hundred years after his birth, Calvin's work continues to play an important role in the development of Western philosophy. Even though his views are sometimes mischaracterized or misunderstood, his insistence on God's glory and the dependence of fallen humans on God's grace is still widely influential. Neither of these themes (God's glory and human depravity) will ever be welcome among secular philosophers. But precisely because Calvin's Pauline doctrine of the *sensus divinitatus* is correct about the universal knowledge of God's existence and power, Calvinist philosophy will always be compelling even when it is unpopular. The challenge for future Calvinist philosophers is to engage the philosophical world more and more confidently. The waning of modernism has diminished the stigma so long associated with open dependence on God's Word and the recognition of spiritual sight as a source of knowledge. The philosophical world is questioning old, narrow secular assumptions. Calvinists and other Christian philosophers who take the bad news about sin and the good news of the gospel seriously cannot expect to be popular. But we can and should hope to follow Calvin's example and bring God's Word to bear on philosophical problems and assumptions. Calvin might not have wanted to have a philosophical movement bearing his name; but he would be pleased to see his commitment to God's glory and God's Word continuing to make a difference in the discipline of philosophy.[70]

70. I am indebted to my colleague in the Philosophy Department at Covenant College, John Calvin Wingard, for help in developing this chapter. The students in my spring 2009 Calvin seminar at Covenant provided hours of discussion and helpful research as well. In addition to those mentioned in the notes above, this seminar included Sam Belz, Anna Cameron, Nathan Davis, Peter Garriott, Ross Meyer, Anna Phillips, Justin Richards, Graham Svendsen, and Bryce Wilkins.

7

CALVIN, POLITICS, AND POLITICAL SCIENCE

PAUL MARSHALL

Is There a Calvinist Approach to Politics?

There are, of course, continuing disagreements about almost every important theorist. But, as in his own lifetime, Calvin still seems to provoke not only different views about his work and life, but often radically opposite views. Political theorist Michael Walzer correctly observed that "virtually all the modern world has been read into Calvinism: liberal politics and voluntary association; capitalism and the social discipline on which it rests; bureaucracy with its systematic procedures and its putatively diligent and devoted officials; and finally all the routine forms of repression, joylessness and unrelaxed aspiration."[1] There are still ongoing, contesting interpretations of the nature, status, place, and influence of Calvin's view

---

1. Michael Walzer, *Revolution of the Saints: A Study in the Origins of Radical Politics* (Cambridge: Harvard University Press, 1982), 300.

of politics.[2] In particular, even though the very term "political science" was probably coined by the Calvinist Althusius, several contemporary political theorists argue that Calvin had nothing original to say about politics. Because this view is widespread, it must be addressed—especially since this attempted marginalization of Calvin is based on a parochial and dogmatic a priori secular rejection of his, or, indeed, any robust Christian theory of politics.

Perhaps the most notable exponent of the view of Calvin's unoriginality is Quentin Skinner, whose *The Foundations of Modern Political Thought* is probably the most influential recent English language survey of sixteenth- and seventeenth-century political theory. Skinner asserts that no "Calvinist theory of revolution," which has often been regarded as the most interesting of Calvin's teaching on politics, really existed.[3] We need to be careful about what Skinner means here. To be sure, he has "no doubt that the revolutionaries of early modern Europe were in general professed Calvinists" or that there was a "theory of popular revolution developed by the radical Calvinists in the 1550s" that shaped "the mainstream of modern constitutionalist thought." He even refers to Locke's *Two Treatises of Government* as "the classic text of radical Calvinist politics." His point is not that Calvinists were ignorant or had no interesting and complex theories; it is rather that "there are virtually no elements in the theory which are specifically Calvinist." The theories held by Calvinists may indeed have been—and in fact were— very important, but Calvinist beliefs did not add anything important to their views. Calvinists may have held interesting and influential views, but they were not *specifically Calvinist* views. Instead their theories "were almost entirely couched in the legal and moral language of their

2. See John Witte, *The Reformation of Rights: Law, Religion, and Human Rights in Early Modern Calvinism* (Cambridge: Cambridge University Press, 2007), 39–42.

3. Quentin Skinner, *The Foundations of Modern Political Thought* (Cambridge: Cambridge University Press, 1978), 1.15. See also his "The Origins of the Calvinist Theory of Revolution," in B. C. Malament, ed., *After the Reformation: Essays in Honor of J. H. Hexter* (Philadelphia: University of Pennsylvania Press, 1980), 309–30. For an overview of Skinner on Calvin, see my "Quentin Skinner and the Secularisation of Political Thought," in *Studies in Political Thought* 2, 1 (Fall 1993): 85–104.

Catholic adversaries" or else could even be "largely a repetition of the Lutheran constitutional theory."[4]

While, for Skinner, Calvinists were certainly influential, their influence was merely one of passing on ideas that they had borrowed. Thus, although Calvinists influenced Locke, they did so only in a derivative way. The important line of influence was that "the concepts in terms of which Locke and his successors developed their views of popular sovereignty and the rights of revolution had already been largely articulated and refined over a century earlier in the legal writings of such radical jurists as Salamonio, in the theological treatises of such Ockhamists as Almain and Mair." In fact, Skinner is not even saying that the Calvinists were mere conduits of others' theories, for he gives them credit for "distinctive contributions" in tackling the question of the relation between the office and the person of a magistrate and in their permissiveness concerning who may lawfully resist a tyrant. Notwithstanding, he insists that such contributions and innovations were not themselves particularly Calvinist but were adaptations *within* a conceptual structure borrowed from Catholics. For Skinner, Calvinists were certainly innovative, but not in a Calvinist way.[5] He argues that, to an "almost paradoxical extent . . . radical Calvinists relied on a scheme of concepts derived from the study of Roman law and scholastic moral philosophy."[6] In short, Skinner says there is nothing original or unique in Calvinist political theory; hence, in a precise sense, there is no Calvinistic political theory.

The reason that Skinner holds to this influential view is not because of a superior grasp of Calvin's thought but because he simply defines political thought in such a way as to read out any Calvinist contribution *by definition*. Skinner wants to give a survey of political thought, but he also wants "to indicate something of the process by which the modern concept of the State came to be formed," to show how "the main elements

---

4. Skinner, *The Foundations of Modern Political Thought*, 1.15.239, 2.210.323. Similarly, Plamenatz maintained that "Calvin's political theory . . . is lucid, consistent, systematic, and entirely second-hand." John Plamenatz, *Man and Society* (London: Longman, 1963), 1.57. See the comments of Oliver O'Donovan in his *Desire of the Nations* (Cambridge: Cambridge University Press, 1996), 210–11.

5. Skinner, *The Foundations of Modern Political Thought*, 1.225.230, 2.51.347–48.

6. Ibid., 15; see also 2.74.

of a recognisably modern concept of the State were gradually acquired."[7] This other aim gives rise to the title of his main work, *The Foundations of Modern Political Thought*, which means that it is, *inter alia*, an attempt to explore what founds the modern state.

Given these aims, it is important to know what Skinner means by "modern." For Skinner, a "State . . . conceptualised in distinctively modern terms" would be "the sole appropriate object of its citizens' allegiances" and have "no rivals within its own territories as a law-making power and an object of allegiance." Hence Skinner's "modern concept of the state" implies, *inter alia*, the exclusion of any religious beliefs from the core of political theory. Hence, for Skinner modern political theory requires not only the separation of church and state but a state that has "no rivals as an object of allegiance." It requires a way of theorizing about government that is secular in the sense that it excludes any religious reasoning.[8]

But, clearly, many of the principal texts of sixteenth-century political theory have not significantly shaped modern categories and conceptions (unless, in a Whig fashion, we simply define "principal texts" as those that have influenced the modern age). Such works, important in their own time but uncongenial to self-described "modern" people, would in principle be included under Skinner's first aim of "an outline account of the principal texts of the period" but not under his second aim of showing "the process by which the modern state" came about. Thus two of the aims of his major work are in tension. Illuminating the "process" requires ignoring or downplaying texts, no matter how original, that are distant from modern conceptions, while "outlining principal texts" requires highlighting and expounding the same. In the case of Calvinism, Skinner has confused these two aims by downplaying that which

---

7. Ibid., 9.

8. Ibid., 1.9n1, 1.10, 2.211, 240, 351–52. He also suggests that "purely civil or political" authority is "repudiated" by a closer relation between allegiance in church and state." Quentin Skinner, "The State," in T. Ball, J. Farr, and R. L. Hanson, eds., *Political Innovation and Conceptual Change* (Cambridge, Cambridge University Press, 1987), 90–131, esp. 122. On Skinner's understanding of political thought, see J. Tully, ed., *Meaning and Context: Quentin Skinner and His Critics* (Princeton, NJ: Princeton University Press, 1988). Hancock maintains that "Skinner interprets modern politics—politics freed from religion—simply as 'pure' politics." Ralph Hancock, *Calvin and the Foundations of Modern Politics* (Ithaca: Cornell University Press, 1989), 10.

is not congenial to "modern," meaning "secular," minds while implying that it does not really exist.

Given such a definition of political theory, Calvin must be excluded simply by definition since he does not approach the study of politics in the approved modern manner. He certainly does not have a "theocratic" conception of the imposition of biblical law, something that he firmly and explicitly condemns: "The law of God given through Moses is (not) dishonored when it is abrogated and new laws are preferred to it . . . for the Lord . . . did not give that law to be proclaimed among all nations and to be in force everywhere. Rather we must make our laws with regard to the condition of times, place and nation. . . . How malicious and hateful toward public welfare would a man be who is offended by such diversity."[9] Instead of positing a state that has "no rivals within its own territories as a law-making power and an object of allegiance," he declares that the church, while not normatively a rival, is certainly another "object of allegiance." He roots a creative understanding of politics squarely within a Christian view of the world. In this he reflects much about the Reformation and Protestantism itself.

In fact, Calvin's key contributions to the study of politics come not from the detailed particulars of legal theory but from the way he embedded politics in a Christian, particularly Protestant, worldview or cosmology. Calvin's major contributions came in what we might now call a political sociology that reframes the nature of political action.

Protestantism and Society

Calvin's thought, while having distinctive elements, is rooted in the general themes of Protestantism. While the Reformers concentrated on theology, doctrine, personal life, and the church, when they sought to reassert the primacy of faith and the primacy of Scripture, they also thereby produced changes, often inadvertently, and sometimes not the ones they wanted, in the understanding of the "self," the structure of the family, education, science, literature, ethics, economics, and politics.

9. *Institutes*, 4.20.16. See also 4.20.3.

For example, the emphasis that each person could be related directly to God through the mediator Jesus Christ had a variety of effects, of which I will mention just two, both of which relate first of all to the church itself. One was that, while the church was elevated, it was also in a sense dethroned, at least as an organization. It was no longer, in principle, regarded as the head, the highest body, the leader of society. Hence the question of the relation of different institutions in society has opened up. Another effect, especially pronounced in the Free Church tradition, was to stress the dimension of the church as a body of believers. This encouraged what we might call, loosely, more democratic structures. Many commentators have found the roots of modern democracy and constitutionalism in this ecclesiastical move, especially as transmitted through Calvinism and Puritanism.

Perhaps this dethroning may better be described as the dethroning of the priesthood and the monastic orders. In later medieval Catholicism, the priest, monk, and nun tended to be seen as the ones who were, potentially at least, truly holy. They were an elite who could devote their lives to spiritual things. Other people and other forms of life were good, vital, and necessary, but were held to be of a lower spiritual order. Almost without exception Protestants, including Calvin, criticized this division of a lower and a higher life and asserted the potential equality of all ways of life. Whereas medieval Christians usually used the term "vocation" to refer only to the priesthood and to religious orders, Protestants stressed that all tasks and ways of life were "vocations," "callings," "professions."[10]

This reassertion of all work and ways of life as equal avenues of Christian service orientated Christians toward a divine vocation in the world. One of the accusations of heresy against William Tyndale, for example, was that he had claimed, "There is no work better than another to please God: to pour water, to wash dishes, to be a souter (cobbler) or an apostle, all is one; to wash dishes and to preach is all one, as touching the deed to please God." This charge appeared to be aimed at Tyndale's own assertion,

10. See Paul Marshall, *A Kind of Life Imposed on Man: Vocation and Social Order from Tyndale to Locke* (Toronto: University of Toronto Press, 1996); Paul Marshall, "Calling, Work and Rest," in M. Noll and D. Wells, eds., *Christian Faith and Practice in the Modern World: Theology from an Evangelical Point of View* (Grand Rapids: Eerdmans, 1988), 199–217, 324–28.

later quoted by William Perkins, that "if thou compare deed to deed, there is a difference betwixt washing of dishes, and preaching of the word of God; but as touching to please God, none at all: for neither this nor that pleaseth, but as far forth as God hath chosen a man, hath put his spirit in him, and purified his heart by faith and trust in Christ."[11]

Similar themes were consistently propounded by Luther, who wrote: "If you are a manual laborer, you find that the Bible has been put into your workshop, into your hand, into your heart. It teaches and preaches how you should treat your neighbor . . . just look at your tools . . . at your needle and thimble, your beer barrel, your goods, your scales or yardstick or measure. . . . and you will read this statement inscribed in them . . . You have as many preachers as you have transactions, goods, tools, and other equipment in your house and home."[12]

Calvin's Worldview and Society

If we approach Calvin to understand how his views fit together in a Christian worldview, then a distinct approach to society emerges. Calvin's vision of the sovereignty of God sets the tenor of his thought, including his social and political thought. Reflecting the Protestant conceptions just described, it produces three basic interrelated motifs. One is that God is sovereign over *everything* in the world. The second is that, because sovereignty resides only in God, no earthly institution can claim final sovereignty for itself. The third is that God's sovereignty requires an active, voluntary human response in each area of life.

Concerning the sovereignty of God, one of Calvin's central themes is that the world, and all that is in it, is created by, is ordered by, points toward, and can be used to give honor to God and succor to man: "The infinite wisdom of God is displayed in the admirable structure of heaven and earth." The "end for which all things were created" was that "none of the conveniences and necessaries of life should be wanting to men.

11. William Tyndale, "Parable of the Wicked Mammon" (1527), in *Doctrinal Treatises and Introductions to Different Portions of the Holy Scriptures* (Cambridge: Parker Society, 1848), 98, 102.

12. Martin Luther, *Luther's Works*, vol. 45 (Philadelpia: Fortress Press, 1962), 39–40.

In the very order of the creation the paternal solicitude of God for man is conspicuous."[13]

This focus on the order of the entire creation tends to undercut any ascetic rejection of the world. It also tends to undercut any scheme of nature and grace wherein certain parts of the world, or certain types of activity such as piety or contemplation, are treated as necessarily more holy than others. At times, Calvin still retains a nature/grace scheme and treats churchly activities as a higher realm than others. Nevertheless a major thrust of his work is devoted to stressing God's integral sovereignty over every dimension of life. Hence he says that "civil authority is a calling not only holy and lawful before God, but also the most sacred and by far the most honourable of all callings in the whole life of mortal men."[14]

For Calvin the world is designed as an ordered whole in which man is placed as lord in voluntary subjection to the will of God. Bohatec even refers to his "*Pathos der Ordnung,*" his passion for order.[15] As Wolin says, "the general concept of order was a premise common to both religious and political society." The overall method Calvin employed for bringing the two societies into some kind of congruence was to treat them both as subject to the general principle of order, or, as André Biéler says, "The believer's religious life and material life are both subjected to the same order of God."[16]

Within this ordered world, Calvin stresses that all human activities are to be "callings" and are, as such, equal in the eyes of God. As with Luther, Tyndale, and other Protestants, this equality pertains to human activities themselves, but it also extends to the organizations and institutions to which human callings give rise and in which they are lived out and manifest. Every part of life is to be lived in responsibility to God and, therefore, no activity or institution can claim to be the full mediator between God and humanity. This differentiation applies to society generally, for "the

---

13. John Calvin, "Argument" of *Commentary on Genesis*, vol. 1 (Grand Rapids, Eerdmans, 1948), 57, 96.

14. *Institutes*, 4.20.4, 59. See D. Little, *Religion, Order and Law: A Study in Pre-Revolutionary England* (New York: Harper and Row, 1969), 42.

15. Josef Bohatec, *Calvin's Lehre von Staat und Kirche* (Breslau, Marcus, 1937).

16. S. Wolin, *Politics and Vision: Continuity and Innovation in Western Political Thought* (Boston: Little, Brown, 1960), 179–80; André Biéler, *La Pensée Economique et Sociale de Calvin* (Geneva, Librarie de l'Universite, 1961), 154.

Maker of the world has given . . . [the human race], as it were, a building regularly formed, and divided into several compartments."[17] "The community at large is divided, as it were, into so many yokes, out of which arises mutual obligation."[18]

In relating these callings to one another, Calvin pictures society as composed of functionally diverse but mutually supportive groups defined by vocation. He sums up the duty of one person to another as the duty of "mutual subjection"—there should be among all a "universal bond of subjection." "God has bound us so strongly to each other that no man ought to endeavour to avoid subjection; and wherever love reigns mutual services will be rendered." "I do not except even kings and governors, whose very authority is held for the service of the community . . . all should be exhorted to be subject to each other in their turn."[19]

This subjection to one another, and equality of ways of life and activities, lead to a stress that no institution should have a primacy of authority over others. As Carney notes:

> There would seem to be a common character to all associations in Calvinist political literature. This common character is neither individualist nor absolutist. It begins neither with the self-evident rights of individuals nor with the *a priori* authority of rulers. Rather it asks what is the vocation (or purpose) of any association, and how can this association be so organized as to accomplish its essential business. Authority (or rule) becomes a function of vocation; and great care must be taken to provide constitutional structures, both ideological and institutional, that authority not become unduly weak or corrupt.[20]

17. John Calvin, Commentary on 1 Peter 2:13–16, in *Commentary on Hebrews, I and II Peter* (Grand Rapids, Eerdmans, 1963), 269.

18. John Calvin, Commentary on Ephesians 5:21–27, in *Commentary on Galatians and Ephesians* (Grand Rapids: Eerdmans, 1957), 317.

19. Ibid., 316–17. See also G. Spykman, "Pluralism: Our Last Best Hope?" in *CSR* 10 (1981): 99–115; G. Spykman, "Sphere Sovereignty in Calvin and the Calvinist Tradition," 189–206, in D. Holwerda, ed., *Exploring the Heritage of John Calvin* (Grand Rapids: Baker, 1976); Bohatec, *Calvin's Lehre von Staat und Kirch.*

20. F. S. Carney, "Associational Thought in Early Calvinism," 39–53 of D. B. Robertson, ed., *Voluntary Associations* (Richmond: John Knox Press, 1966), 46.

Combined with this stress on the sovereignty of God and mutual subjection is Calvin's emphasis on *usefulness*. He is not, of course, a utilitarian, but rather he emphasizes that we must use the diverse gifts that God has given us. "It is not the will of the Lord that we should be like blocks of wood . . . but that we should apply to use all the talents and advantages which he has conferred upon us." This stress means that Calvin has a functional view of economic life rather than a hierarchical one. What is true of the economy is true of institutions in society generally. They are not to be arranged in a hierarchical order reaching up to God, but are arranged side by side supporting one another in mutual service to God in their specific vocations. All work, all vocation, all institutions, are all equally *Coram Deo*. This produces what Beyerhaus refers to as the "thoroughly levelling" effect of Calvin's emphasis on the sovereignty of God.[21] One result of this Calvinist conception of sovereign order was "that a society could be at once well organized, disciplined, and cohesive and yet be without a head."[22] Calvin's society did not need a supreme head; that was reserved to God.

The actual lines that Calvin seeks to draw between activities and institutions, especially those between church and state, can seem quite jumbled, especially to the "modern" mind. But, he consistently emphasized that there is a "great difference between the ecclesiastical and civil power" so that it would be "unwise to mingle these two which have a completely different nature."[23] Hence, as Little points out, "even in the ideal conditions of Geneva, Calvin never allowed the Church to become organizationally coterminous or identical with the magistracy. To a degree unknown in Zwingli's Zurich, Luther's Germany, or Hooker's England, Calvin maintained the independence of the Church over against civil society."[24]

---

21. Little, *Religion, Order and Law*, 60. Beyerhaus is quoted on 45.

22. S. Wolin, "Calvin, The Political Education of Protestantism," 191.

23. *Institutes*, 3.19.15, 4.2.1–2, 4.11.3. See the discussion by John Witte, *Religion and the American Constitutional Experiment* (Boulder, CO: Westview Press, 2000), 48–49; and John Witte, *God's Joust, God's Justice: Law and Religion in the Western Tradition* (Grand Rapids: Eerdmans, 2006), 380.

24. Little, *Religion, Order and Law*, 78. See also Biéler, *La Pensée Economique*, 129–30; Francois Wendel, *Calvin: Origins and Development of His Religious Thought* (London: Collins, 1963), 74; O'Donovan, *Desire of the Nations*, 210–11.

Human Response

Calvin's stress on equality necessarily comports with his emphasis on voluntariness and human responsibility. He stressed that a Christian's obedience should not in the first place be given fearfully because of the penalties of the law, nor be given grudgingly to earn salvation, nor be given nervously to prove salvation. Instead, obedience should be given thankfully in response to God's gift of grace in Jesus Christ:

> part of Christian liberty is that the consciences do not observe the law, as being under any legal obligation; but that, being liberated from the yoke of the law, they yield a voluntary obedience to the will of God. . . . They will never engage with alacrity and promptitude in the service of God unless they have previously received this liberty.[25]

This free obedience is all the greater because we are not, in the first place, subjects of God nor servants of God: we are, rather, children of God:

> See how all our works are under the curse of the law if they are measured by the standard of the law! But how, then, would unhappy souls gird themselves eagerly for a work for which they might expect to receive only a curse? But if, freed from this severe requirement of the law, or rather from the entire rigor of the law, they hear themselves called with fatherly gentleness by God, they will cheerfully and with great eagerness answer, and follow his leader. To sum up: Those bound by the yoke of the law are like servants assigned certain tasks for each day by their masters. These servants think they have accomplished nothing, and dare not appear before their masters unless they have fulfilled the exact measure of their tasks. But sons, who are more generously and candidly treated by their father, do not hesitate to offer them incomplete and half done and even defective works, trusting that their obedience and readiness of mind will be accepted by their fathers, even though they have not quite achieved what their fathers intended. Such children ought we to be, firmly trusting that our services will be approved by our most merciful Father, however small, rude, and imperfect these may be.[26]

25. *Institutes*, 3.19.4.
26. Ibid., 19.5.

While it might seem paradoxical to the modern mind, precisely because of Calvin's assertion of the bondage of the human will to sin, he also repeatedly calls for a free and voluntary response to God.[27] For Calvin, as long as mankind lives in a state of sin, there must of course still be an order of coercion. However, concomitant with and beyond this, as Little says, "the realm of the free conscience—as a key to the whole question of order—is ultimate, and provides the guidelines for understanding God's plan and his work in the world. . . . Nothing is surer than that the Kingdom of God, toward which all things move, includes overcoming the engines of coercion in favour of voluntary obedience."[28] This stress on a free and voluntary response affects Calvin's entire view of society. He sums up the duty of one person to another as the duty of "mutual subjection"—there should be among all a "universal bond of subjection." "God has bound us so closely to each other that no man ought to endeavour to avoid subjection; and wherever love reigns mutual services will be rendered."[29]

Calvin's view of economic activity illustrates this pattern of mutual servitude. While, because of the fall, work is often hard and painful, yet it was given by God at the beginning explicitly as a gift and responsibility to humankind. Work should be taken up willingly and mutually as service to God and our fellows. Commerce itself is a natural way for people to commune with one another: "it is not enough when one can say, 'Oh I work, I have my trade, I set the pace.' This is not enough; for one must be concerned whether it is good and profitable to the community and if it is able to serve our neighbours. . . . And this is why we are compared to members of a body."[30] "The life of the Godly is justly compared to trading,

27. See also David Little, "Calvin and the Prospects for a Christian Theory of Natural Law," in G. Outka and P. Ramsay, eds., *Norm and Context in Christian Ethics* (New York: Scribners, 1968), 175–97.

28. Little, *Religion, Order and Law*, 53. See also M. E. Chenevière, *La Pensée Politique de Calvin* (Geneva: Slatkine, 1970), 93–94.

29. John Calvin, Commentary on Ephesians 5:21 in John Calvin, *Commentary on Galatians and Ephesians* (Grand Rapids: Eerdmans, 1957), 316–17. See R. Wallace, *Calvin's Doctrine of the Christian Life* (Grand Rapids: Eerdmans, 1959), 157.

30. John Calvin, Sermon on Ephesians 4:26–28, quoted in F. Graham, *The Constructive Revolutionary: John Calvin and His Socio-Economic Impact* (Richmond: John Knox Press, 1971), 80–81.

for they ought naturally to exchange and barter with one another in order to maintain intercourse."[31]

André Biéler, in his classic work on Calvin's social and economic views, summarizes him thus:

> "God has created man," Calvin says, "so that he may be a creature of fellowship." . . . Companionship is completed in work and in the interplay of economic exchanges. Human fellowship is realized in relationships which flow from the division of labour wherein each person has been called of God to a particular and partial work which complements the work of others. The mutual exchange of goods and services is the concrete sign of the profound solidarity which unites humanity.[32]

This free and voluntary principle is illustrated strikingly in marriage. Calvin has what John Witte calls the "first comprehensive covenantal model of marriage."[33] His *Ordonnances sur les Mariages* declares "that no father may force his children into whatever marriage may seem good to him without their good pleasure and consent, but that the son or daughter who may not wish to accept the party which the father may wish to give him, may excuse himself . . . and the refusal will not entail any punishment by the father."[34] If the children marry without parental consent then, provided they are of legal age and that the lack of consent was due to "the negligence or over-rigour of their parents," a dowry and financial settlement must still be made "as if they had consented."

The same motif occurs even with reference to divorce: "Although from antiquity the right of the woman has not been equal to that of her husband in case of divorce, since according to the witness of the apostle the obligation is mutual and reciprocal pertaining to the marital bed [*la cohaibation du lict*], and because in that regard the wife is not more subject to her husband than the husband to the wife; if a man is

31. John Calvin, *Commentary on the Harmony of Matthew, Mark, Luke*, 3 vols. (Grand Rapids: Eerdmans, 1972), 2.441–45.

32. Biéler, *La Pensée Economique et Sociale de Calvin*, 321.

33. Witte, *God's Joust, God's Justice* (Grand Rapids: Eerdmans, 2006), 380.

34. Quoted in Graham, *The Constructive Revolutionary*, 153.

convicted of adultery and the wife demands to be separated from him, it should be granted her as well."[35]

Political Action

So far, we have not addressed Calvin's view of politics per se but rather his view of society as one wherein each part is called to reflect the order and glory of God, each part is differentiated according to vocation and none is the center of God's rule on earth, and each part is to be taken up by the free, committed, and voluntary response of God's people. While this is not politics per se, it has major implications for how we understand politics and, indeed, transforms how we understand politics.

One political effect was produced by Calvin's stress on the committed activity of *all* God's people. As Walzer notes, what Calvinism produced "tended to be practical and social, programmatic and organizational. Manifestos, exhortations, polemics—these were the forms of its literary expression; covenants, assemblies, congregations, and holy commonwealths—these were the results of its organizational initiative." What was new in Calvinism was the idea that "organized bands of men might play a creative part in the political world . . . reconstructing society according to the word of God or the plans of their fellows." This was a distinct view; it did not enter at all into the "thought of Machiavelli, Luther or Bodin. In establishing the state, these three writers relied exclusively upon the prince, whether they imagined him as an adventurer, a Christian magistrate, or a hereditary bureaucrat. All other men remained subjects, condemned to political passivity."[36]

Wolin makes a similar point, although couched in rather revolutionary language—that the Reformers were leaders of mass movements and "among the first to attempt to catalyse the masses for the purpose of social action. . . . consider, too, the political implications of the Reformation as a broad movement of revolt directed against an established order, a revolt

---

35. Quoted in Graham, *The Constructive Revolutionary*. See also Ernst Troeltsch, *The Social Teaching of the Christian Churches* (London: George Allen & Unwin, 1931), 922

36. Walzer, *Revolution of the Saints*, 1–2, 25–26. See also O'Donovan, *Desire of the Nations* (Cambridge: Cambridge University Press, 1996), 210–11.

whose success depended upon radicalizing the masses into disaffection with existing authorities and institutions ... hardly a trace of these notions can be found in Machiavelli or Hobbes."[37]

Liberty and Democracy

Calvin's view went beyond transforming popular, engaged political action, innovative and important as that is. While strictly avoiding seditious language, he continually voiced scepticism about kingship. Because of the dangers of a monarch becoming proud or overbearing, Calvin writes that the "vice or inadequacy of men thus renders it safer and more tolerable that many hold the sway so that they may mutually be helpers to each other, teach and admonish one another, and if one asserts himself unfairly, the many may be censors and masters, repressing his wilfulness."[38] Elections are very useful in order to maintain such mutual admonishment, hence:

> the condition of the people most to be desired is that in which they create their shepherds by general vote. For when anyone by force usurps the supreme power, that is tyranny. And where men are born to kingship, this does not seem to be in accordance with liberty. Hence the prophet says: we shall set up princes for ourselves; that is, the Lord will not only give the Church freedom to breathe, but also institute a definite and well ordered government, and establish this upon the common suffrages of all.[39]

In turn, the liberty out of which springs such suffrage is itself a great and central good. Calvin describes it as "more than half of life."[40] Hence "if we

---

37. Wolin, "Calvin, The Political Education of Protestantism," 19. See also C. M. N. Eire's discussion of the implications of Calvinist iconoclasm in his *War Against the Idols: The Reformation of Worship from Erasmus to Calvin* (Cambridge, Cambridge University Press, 1986), chaps. 6 and 7; D. Little, "A Christian Perspective on Human Rights," in A. A. An-Na'im and F. M. Deng, eds., *Human Rights in Africa: Cross Cultural Perspectives* (Washington, DC: The Brookings Institution, 1990), 59–103, especially 77, 89–97.

38. *Institutes*, 4.20.8; J. T. McNeill, *John Calvin: On God and Political Duty* (Indianapolis: Bobbs-Merrill, 1956), xxii.

39. John Calvin, Commentary on Micah 5:5, quoted in McNeill, *God and Political Duty*, xxii-xxiii.

40. John Calvin, Commentary on Deuteronomy 24:7, *Commentaries on the Four Last Books Of Moses: Arranged in the Form of a Harmony* (Grand Rapids: Eerdmans, 1948).

have the liberty to choose judges and magistrates, since this is an excellent gift, let it be preserved and let us use it in good conscience. . . . Let those to whom God has given liberty and freedom use it . . . as a singular benefit and a treasure that cannot be prized enough."[41] "This is the most desirable kind of liberty, that we should not be compelled to obey every person who may be tyrannically put over our heads; but which allows of election, so that no one should rule except he be approved of by us."[42] This liberty even extends to the making of law. As noted earlier, Calvin maintains that God did not intend that the Mosaic law should be "proclaimed among all nations and to be in force everywhere." It is up to us, guided by our faith, to "make our laws with regard to the condition of times, place and nation."[43]

The system of government that Calvin advocated was not a democracy. It has been described as a "conservative democracy" or, in his own terms, "aristocracy, or aristocracy tempered by democracy." In modern terms, we should simply describe it as a republic. The American system is, for example, a mixture of monarchic (the presidency), aristocratic (the Senate), and democratic (the House) elements. Calvin, perhaps strangely, given his stress on human responsibility and action, does not exhort his readers to erect such a system; he merely tells them that it is a good system and that if they live in one then they should count themselves blessed and give thanks to God.

He also stresses subjection to the ruler. Whatever political system we live in, it is our duty to honor and obey the ruler as a minister of God. Mankind is sinful and so God has providentially provided a political order to punish evildoers and check the spread of sin. We are subject to this order and to the coercion that it necessarily involves. It is possible to resist, and perhaps even overthrow, an unjust ruler, but this should not be done by the population at large but only those in subordinate authority—the "lesser magistrates."[44]

This praise of liberty and stress on obedience are constant themes in Calvin's, and Calvinist, thought: "While Calvin's thought invariably 'slips'

41. Calvin, quoted in McNeill, *God and Political Duty*, xxiv.
42. John Calvin, Commentary on Deuteronomy 1:16, *Commentaries on the Four Last Books Of Moses: Arranged in the Form of a Harmony* (Grand Rapids: Eerdmans, 1948).
43. *Institutes*, 4.20.16. See also 40.20.3.
44. Ibid., 4.20.31.

one way or the other, both directions are always present, and each acts as a qualification and condition upon the other." This means that there must always be political coercion and control, but that this coercion is in constant tension with the new order brought into being as a free response to the Word of God, which is "a voluntary, harmonious community in which election rests with the elect." Ideally, Calvin wanted a consensual polity in church and state, but this ideal is always held back by the reality of sin. The resulting demand is for "a polity which checks sedition, on the one hand, but guarantees 'maximum feasible participation' on the other. Such an arrangement, application to both Church and State, is a combination of democracy and aristocracy. This form of government presupposed, primitively, to be sure, a system of checks and balances whose importance was not lost on later Calvinist, and non-Calvinist political thinkers."[45] As Marci Hamilton puts it: "Calvinist theology taught the Framers . . . that the paradoxical elements of distrust and hope could be brought together to good effect."[46] The support by most colonial Calvinist preachers for the new constitution was hence more than opportunism or cultural assimilation: it reflected features of a Calvinist view of the political order.

Althusius

The shifts that Calvin introduced in understanding politics is well illustrated by Althusius, who developed a distinct notion of political science, and may even have coined the term.[47] Althusius' Calvinism is not merely an incidental aspect of his biography or theology. The Calvinist themes of the sovereignty of God over all associations and all sciences, of the differentiation of associations and sciences according to vocation, and of the mutual supportiveness of all associations and sciences underlie and shape

45. Little, *Religion, Order and Law*, 72, 76, 167.
46. Marci A. Hamilton, "The Calvinist Paradox of Distrust and Hope at the Constitutional Convention," in Michael McConnell, Robert F. Cochran, and Angela C. Carmella, eds., *Christian Perspectives on Legal Thought* (New Haven: Yale University Press, 2001), 293–306; the quote comes from 306.
47. F. Carney, "Associational Thought in Early Calvinism," 40–41, maintains that similar themes can be found in the writings of Hofman, Mornay, Beza, Buchanan, Ponet, Vermigli, Zanachuis, and Rutherford.

his work. Althusius followed Calvin in stressing a functional view of social institutions as distinct from a hierarchical view, and he argued that this differentiation requires a corresponding differentiation of the sciences that study these institutions. For Althusius, "We should make sure that we render each science its due."[48] While churches require theology, politics requires its own political science, a discipline rooted in a Christian understanding of the world and specifically devoted to its own unique subject matter. This differentiation of theology, political science, and other disciplines is not intended to separate other disciplines from the Bible and from Christian faith since Althusius stresses that religious commitments shape not only theology but also political science, jurisprudence, ethics, and so forth. Althusius weaves the sciences together carefully:

> Therefore in so far as the substance of sovereignty or of the Decalogue is theological, ethical or juridical, and accords with the purpose and form of those arts, so far do those arts claim as proper to themselves what they take for their use from the Decalogue and the rights of sovereignty. . . . I claim the Decalogue as proper to political science in so far as it breathes a vital spirit into symbiotic life, and gives form to it and conserves it, in which sense it is essential and homogeneous to political science and heterogeneous to other arts. So I have concluded that where the political scientist ceases, there the jurist begins, just as where the moralist stops the theologian begins, and where the physicist ends the physician begins. No one denies, however, that all arts are united in practice.[49]

As Hueglin notes, in this conception, "political science has a distinct right to interpret the word of God because the two tables of the Decalogue pertain to piety and justice." Indeed, as Skillen notes, "The . . . contribution of Althusius comes not from his calling politics away from divine authority and revelation but from his insistence that the church is not that divine authority and does not have a monopoly on the Scriptures."[50]

48. Althusius, "Preface to the First Edition (1603)", in F. Carney, ed., *The Politics of Johannes Althusius* (Boston: Beacon Press, 1964), 1–2.

49. Ibid.; also "Preface to the Third Edition (1614)," in Carney, 9. See also 69, 74.

50. Thomas O. Hueglin. "Have We Studied the Wrong Authors? On the Relevance of Johannes Althusius," in *Studies in Political Thought* 1 (Winter 1992): 75–93, esp. 81; James W. Skillen, "The

The result is something that even Skinner describes as "a recognisably 'modern' conception of 'politics' as a sphere of enquiry with its own distinctive subject matter."[51]

Althusius also shaped federalism.[52] Daniel Elazar argues that his *Politics* "was the first book to present a comprehensive theory of federal republicanism rooted in a covenantal view of human society derived from, but not dependent on, a theological system. It presented a theory of polity-building based on the polity as a compound political association established by its citizens through their primary associations on the basis of consent rather than a reified state, imposed by a ruler or an elite." Furthermore, "Althusius serves as a bridge between the biblical foundations of Western civilization and modern political ideas and institutions. . . . Althusius confronts the same problems of modern politics without jettisoning or denying the biblical foundations."[53]

The currently much discussed notion of "subsidiarity," loosely understood as the principle that matters ought to be handled by the least-centralized competent authority, has usually been attributed to Catholic social thought. However, no less than a European Union research team, led by the EU's then-President Jacques Delors, concluded that its origins lay in Calvinism, especially Althusius.[54]

Althusius was able to develop an original social theory which incorporated original political theory, as well as perhaps being the first user of the

---

Political Theory of Johannes Althusius," in *Philosophia Reformata* 39 (1974): 170–90. See also the comments of P. S. Pieter Sjverds Gerbrandy, *National and International Stability: Althusius: Grotius: van Vollenhoven* (Oxford: Oxford University Press, 1944), 7.

51. Skinner, *The Foundations of Modern Political Thought*, 2.341. He also emphasizes that another Calvinist, George Buchanan, said similar things a generation before.

52. Thomas Hueglin, "Johannes Althusius: Medieval Constitutionalist or Modern Federalist?" *Publius* 9, 4 (1979): 9–41. Otto von Gierke regarded Althusius as a pivotal figure in the development of modern constitutionalism. See his *The Development of Political Theory* (New York: Norton, 1939), 71.

53. Daniel Elazar, "Althusius's Grand Design for a Federal Commonwealth," in *Politica: An Abridged Translation of Politics Methodically Set Forth and Illustrated with Sacred and Profane Examples*, ed. and trans. Frederick S. Carney (Indianapolis: Liberty Fund, 1995), xxxv. See also Thomas Hueglin, "Covenant and Federalism in the Politics of Althusius," in Daniel J. Elazar and John Kincaid, eds., *The Covenant Connection: From Federal Theology to Modern Federalism* (Lanham, MD: Lexington Books, 2000), 31–54.

54. Ken Endo, "The Principle of Subsidiarity: From Johannes Althusius to Jacques Delors," *Hokkaido Law Review* 44, 6 (1994): 629–32, 553–652.

term "political science." He did so not only as a committed Calvinist but also as one whose thought was shaped deeply by Calvinist principles.

Conclusions

For Calvin, the whole creation is equally under God's sovereign will, the institutions of society are not arranged hierarchically but are differentiated according to vocation and so are to be arranged side by side in mutual support, and God's work is carried out by the free, voluntary obedience of God's people.[55] Political and religious thought formed a continuous realm of discourse in which the major unifying element was a general concept of order. Within this overall scheme "political society was to be rescued from limbo by being restored to a wider, ordered frame. It was to become a part of the Christian cosmology."[56] God's sovereign rule is over *all* institutions and associations. Since each of these institutions is differentiated according to its vocation, and God is not mediated exclusively through one of them, then none can claim sovereignty over the others.[57]

This led to a stress on moving politics from being simply an elite occupation to one that is participatory. It also led to a covenantal view of politics that has created modern federalism. It also led to the creation of political science as a discipline. Calvin reshaped politics and the study of politics, not in the details of sovereignty and rebellion, but by situating politics and political action as a response of human beings who freely submit themselves to God and thus seek to transform the social, economic, and political order so that it might reflect God's order.

55. F. Carney, *The Politics of Johannes Althusius*, 39–53.
56. Wolin, "Calvin, The Political Education of Protestantism," 168, 179, 180
57. Spykman, "Pluralism: Our Last Best Hope?" *CSR* 10 (1981): 99–115.

8

CALVINISM AND SCIENCE

DON PETCHER

John Calvin lived and taught in Geneva well before the rise of modern science. Indeed, he died in 1564, the very year Galileo Galilei was born! Although Nicolas Copernicus's *De Revolutionibus Orbium Coelestium*[1] was published posthumously in 1543, there is some uncertainty as to whether Calvin was even aware of it.[2] As Davis Young puts it, "It is undeniable that Calvin was fully immersed in the medieval geocentric worldview. There is no hint of Copernicanism here."[3] Calvin's silence on Copernicus, however, did not stop Andrew Dickson White from writing in 1896 in his *History of the Warfare of Science and Theology in Christendom* that

1. *On the Revolutions of the Heavenly Spheres.*
2. The consensus of historians seems to be that either Calvin was not aware of Copernicus's treatise, or he did not consider it within his expertise to comment. Davis A. Young, *John Calvin and the Natural World* (Lanham: University Press, 2007), 44–49.
3. Ibid., 34.

Calvin took the lead in his commentary on Genesis, by condemning all who asserted that the earth is not at the center of the universe. He clinched the matter by the usual reference to the verse of Psalm 93, and asked, "Who will venture to place the authority of Copernicus above that of the Holy Spirit?"[4]

In trying to make a case for his warfare thesis, White was merely passing down hearsay from other authors, for such a statement is not found in any of Calvin's writings.[5] Reijer Hooykaas, who was among the first to discover White's error, tells us that when he first read the quote, he was suspicious because it did not seem to fit with Calvin's own view of interpretation.[6] The lesson here is one of presumption, as some historians assumed that in throwing off the allegorical interpretive methods of the medieval scholastics, the Reformers would have to resort to literal interpretations. White clearly had a nineteenth-century axe to grind in portraying science and theology at war. Although this "warfare thesis" has proven to be a false estrangement by the most recent historical studies, any Christian working in science nowadays must face the lingering effects of its legacy, for many still think science and religion are at war to this day.

In contrast with White's caricature, Calvin's approach leaves much more room for common sense, allowing science substantial freedom while maintaining a high view of Scripture. Thus from the point of view of a scientist such as I am who celebrates being in the Calvinist tradition, Calvin set the stage for a rich understanding of science.[7]

4. Andrew Dickson White, *A History of the Warfare of Science with Theology in Christendom*, vol. 1 (New York: Appleton, 1896), 127. Taken from Davis A. Young, *John Calvin and the Natural World*, 45.

5. For a recent summary of the story, see Davis A. Young, *John Calvin and the Natural World*, 43–49.

6. R. Hooykaas, *Religion and the Rise of Modern Science* (Vancouver: Regent College Publishing, 1972), 121.

7. We omit here a discussion that Calvin, as a "man of his times," often argued for what we would call a "God of the gaps," that is, invoking God when there seems to be no other explanation. For example, as described by Young, in *John Calvin and the Natural World*, 160, in his argument about how the earth could maintain a stability at the center of the universe, he invoked God's ongoing miraculous providential power. Here I would also like to mention Charles Coulson and his John Calvin McNair Lectures of 1954, in Charles Coulson, *Science and Christian Belief* (London: Oxford University Press, 1955). The "God of the gaps" problem was a major theme of the first lecture. Such arguments

Calvin and Science

Perhaps the most central doctrine summarizing Calvin's thought is the doctrine of the sovereignty of God over all of creation. One way this has come down to us is through the Calvin-motivated statement, "All truth is God's truth, wherever it may be found,"[8] or as Abraham Kuyper put it in the nineteenth century, "There is not a square inch in the whole domain of our human existence over which Christ, who is Sovereign over *all*, does not cry: 'Mine!'"[9]

Within God's sovereignty is the central theme of God's providence, which in turn undergirds Calvin's notion of God's "radical sustenance" of creation, a concept important in understanding how to view those regularities we call laws of nature. As Hooykaas put it,

> In Calvin's *Institutes* (Book I, chap. 16, 4) he states in the chapter on Providence that God's fatherly hand is in all things that happen; the stars could do no harm, all fear is groundless, for God reigns. The order comes from God, but the deviations from this order, the *extra*-ordinary events, are likewise from him. From this point of view there is no essential difference between ordinary events, such as the sequence of day and night; extraordinary events, such as earthquakes; and miraculous, or even unique, events—"Sun, stand thou still." In Calvin's writings there is no talk about super-natural acts or interventions; God's Providence is "obscured" by those who connect it with special acts only.[10]

are nowadays discouraged, for many times things that were ascribed to actions by God have subsequently been explained through "natural" processes. It is important in Calvinist thought to realize that God is involved at every level in His creation, including those "natural" processes.

8. This phrase is usually attributed to Augustine. Two similar expressions are, "All truth is of him who says 'I am the truth,'" in the preface of his *Christian Doctrine*, section 8, and, "A person who is a good and true Christian should realize that truth belongs to his Lord, wherever it is found, gathering and acknowledging it even in pagan literature, but rejecting superstitious vanities and deploring and avoiding those who 'though they knew God did not glorify him as God,'" which appears in *Christian Teaching* II.75.

9. Abraham Kuyper, "Sphere Sovereignty," the inaugural address for the Free University of Amsterdam, repr. in Abraham Kuyper, *A Centennial Reader* (Grand Rapids: Eerdmans, 1998), 488.

10. R. Hooykaas, *Religion and the Rise of Modern Science*, 108.

This puts Calvin at odds with those who advocate a strict separation between the "natural" and the "supernatural" that continues to play a role in the thinking of most of us. We will argue in what follows that there is good reason to return to Calvin![11]

Science is essentially about knowledge,[12] a subject that Calvin spends a lot of time expounding.[13] In Calvin's day, the Renaissance already had an effect on how knowledge was viewed. As William Bouwsma puts it, "Their general result was a humanization of theology based on a recognition of the limits of human understanding and an awareness that theology, however sublime its subject, is nevertheless a *human* enterprise, that it sees only darkly, not face to face."[14] Calvin was well aware of these developments, and it became basic to his thought.[15] He therefore held that the fall affected reason and knowledge: "But Paul (Rom. iii. 10) teaches that corruption does not reside in one part only, but pervades the whole soul, and each of its faculties,"[16] and, "We have need of the assistance of the law, since all that is sound in our understandings is corrupted; so that we cannot perceive what is right, unless we are taught from some other source."[17]

How do we obtain knowledge? As Bouwsma tells us, Calvin rejected a lot of what passed for knowledge in previous ages, and in its place, he formulated another conception.

> If the personality is conceived as a mysterious unity, knowing must be
> reconceived as a function of the whole, above all involving its "center," the

11. For a fuller account of this issue, see Tim Morris and Don Petcher, *Science and Grace* (Wheaton: Crossway, 2006), chap. 5.

12. The word "science" (in French as well as in English), which was derived from the Latin root *scientia*, meant knowledge in general, thus referring to all areas of academic enquiry, and Calvin typically used it this way.

13. In Calvin's *Institutes*, knowledge was an important part of the subject matter, for he spent a good part of Book I discussing knowledge of God, and a large portion of Book II dealing with knowledge in relation to Christ.

14. William J. Bouwsma, *John Calvin: A Sixteenth-Century Portrait* (New York: Oxford University Press, 1988), 153.

15. Ibid.

16. John Calvin, Commentary on Genesis 3:6, *Commentary on Genesis* (Grand Rapids: Baker, 1979), 1.155.

17. Ibid., 4.455.

heart. Unlike philosophical knowledge, a knowledge of the heart is not coldly objective but suffused with feeling. Faith, as knowledge, is thus, for Calvin, not simply "a common assent to the evangelical history"; it involves "the heart rather than the head and the affections rather than the understanding."[18]

Bouwsma also brings out that Calvin allowed something he called "experimental knowledge," that which is derived from experience, to work together with the "knowledge of faith." Finally, Bouwsma tells us:

Because empirical knowledge is *affective*, it is also *effective*: with this insight Calvin clarified and strengthened the instrumentalism of Renaissance culture. The belief that knowledge is "for use" dissolved the boundary between the contemplative and active life; it brought biblical scholarship and theological reflection out of the study and into the world.[19] Calvin praised "the liberal arts and sciences" as "a most useful instrument not only for piety but for daily life."[20]

Thus in contrast with the Enlightenment philosophy to come, with its pretended autonomy of reason and experience, Calvin provides an approach to knowledge through the heart, which means that it must have a personal component; it rests on faith.

Calvin was definitely "pro science."[21] Although he acknowledged that "natural reason never will direct men to Christ,"[22] in one of his own versions of "all truth is God's truth," he held that

If we regard the Spirit of God as the sole fountain of truth, we shall neither reject the truth itself, nor despise it wherever it shall appear, unless we wish

18. Bouwsma, *Sixteenth-Century Portrait*, 157–58.

19. Bouwsma here cites E. David Willis, "Rhetoric and Responsibility," in Calvin's Theology," in *The Context of Contemporary Theology: Essays in Honor of Paul Lehmann*, ed. A. J. McKelway David Willis-Watkins (Atlanta: John Knox Press, 1974), 52–53. See Bouwsma, *Sixteenth-Century Portrait*.

20. Commentary on 1 Corinthians 8:1, cited in Bouwsma, *Sixteenth-Century Portrait John Calvin*, 159.

21. For a general discussion, see Davis A. Young, *John Calvin and the Natural World*, 192–205.

22. John Calvin, Commentary on John 1:5, as quoted in Young, *John Calvin and the Natural World*, 2.

to dishonor the Spirit of God. . . . Those men who Scripture calls "natural men" were, indeed, sharp and penetrating in their investigation of inferior things. Let us, accordingly learn by their example how many gifts the Lord left to human nature even after it was despoiled of its true good.[23]

Here at once we see Calvin's commitment to the notion of common grace, i.e., that knowledge from creation is open to all who study, while at the same time he acknowledges that the fall has affected creation. While Calvin gives ample motivation for the study of creation, that it lifts us to loftier thoughts of the Creator and teaches us about him—and of course that it can aid us in this life—in view of the fall, he also puts forward a posture of humility: "God has made such a masterpiece that we should admire it, confessing that we cannot comprehend a thing so high and so profound and secret."[24] So Calvin advocated an appropriate humility in both knowledge and in science.

However, there is an advantage to the believer, for Calvin maintained that while a certain type of knowledge is obtainable by the "natural man," true wisdom can only come through knowledge of Christ, for "where Christ is not known, men are destitute of true wisdom, even though they have received the highest education in every branch of learning: for their knowledge is useless until they truly 'know God.'"[25] The Scriptures then act as spectacles to aid us in coming to an understanding of God: "so Scripture [like spectacles], gathering together the impressions of Deity, which, till then, lay confused in their minds, dissipates the darkness, and shows us the true God clearly."[26] Similarly, "For as an eye, either dimmed by age or weakened by any other cause, sees nothing distinctly without the aid of spectacles, so (such is our imbecility) if Scripture does not direct us in our inquiries after God, we immediately turn vain in our imaginations."[27] Thus if the Scriptures are to serve as our spectacles for knowing God, and knowing God is necessary for true wisdom in studying creation, this establishes a relation between Scripture and investigations of science. In a certain sense then, as Colin Gunton has emphasized more recently, all of knowledge is revelation.

23. *Institutes*, 2.2.15, as quoted in Young, *John Calvin and the Natural World*, 4–5.
24. *Serm.* 96 on Job, 433, as quoted in Bouwsma, *Sixteenth-Century Portrait*, 155.
25. *Comm.* on Isa. 33:6.
26. *Institutes*, 1.6.1.
27. Ibid., 1.14.1.

[W]e, being who and what we are cannot know unless we are taught by that which is other than we, and that means by the Spirit of God. . . . Though nature is relatively passive under our enquiry . . . it remains true that knowledge of her comes as gift, and is therefore a species of revelation. . . . If there is revelation of the truth of the world, it is because the Spirit of truth enables it to take place. To put it another way, the creator Spirit brings it about that human rationality is able, within the limits set to it, to encompass the truth of creation. We therefore neither control nor create our knowledge, even though the concepts by which we express it are in part the free creations of our minds. Does it not then follow that all knowledge depends on disclosure or revelation.[28]

And because all knowledge ultimately comes from the same source, then properly interpreted, there can be no conflict. Thus Calvin's formulation is somewhat different from the more usual "two books"[29] view of the likes of Galileo and Francis Bacon, in that Calvin gives a special role to Scripture.

Finally, very important for understanding Calvin's approach to the relation between Scripture and science is his doctrine of accommodation. The basic question is this: In what way should we expect Scripture to speak to us about the workings of creation? On the one hand, Calvin is very clear that in his view, Scripture makes no mistakes, and everything that is said is completely trustworthy as coming with God's authority. On the other hand, he held that in Scripture, God accommodates to us in our understanding, and therefore Scripture speaks in ways that make sense to us. For according to Calvin, God communicated with us in "a rough popular style" using "popular language," or even "childishly"[30] so as not to obscure his message, a message that is to teach us the way of salvation. Thus, for Calvin, at the heart of God's accommodation is his message of love; the main purpose is pedagogy, not an effort to reconcile difficult passages for the purpose of apologetics or science.[31]

---

28. Colin E. Gunton, *A Brief Theology of Revelation* (Edinburgh: T&T Clark, 1995), 34–35.

29. This is the view that we have two "books" of data, the book of Scripture and the book of nature.

30. Young, *John Calvin and the Natural World*, 162.

31. Ibid., 164.

A couple of examples should suffice to illustrate the point. First, take Calvin's commentary on Genesis 1:16:

> If the astronomer inquires respecting the actual dimensions of the stars, he will find the moon to be less than Saturn; but this is something abstruse, for to the sight it appears differently. Moses, rather adapts his discourse to common usage. For since the Lord stretches forth, as it were, his hand to us in causing us to enjoy the brightness of the sun and moon, how great would be our ingratitude were we to close our eyes against our own experience.[32]

This shows that Calvin was aware of the science of the day, and he clearly advocates that the purpose of Moses' description of the heavens was not to lay out the science for us, but rather to make contact with the everyday experience of the hearers. Equally illustrative on this point is Calvin's silence on whether or not the astronomical science of the day, that is, Aristotelian or Ptolemaic astronomy, should be criticized. He clearly saw differences in these accounts from the Mosaic system, and hence they could be said to be at odds with the Bible's representation of astronomy. However, since he held that the language used by Moses was an everyday language, he did not take this to mean that the language should be taken as to teach a literal astronomy, so as to contradict the "scientific" systems of the day. This may also be in part the reason he never engages Copernican astronomy; to him there was apparently no biblical issue.[33]

So, although Calvin did not think the Scriptures were intended in general to speak to what we now know as "scientific" issues, his followers in later years rightly continued to hold a high view of Scripture, for, "In general, the 'biblicism' of the Reformed Christians was not concerned with scientific topics, and in seeking the data of science solely in the book of *creation*, they followed the example of one of their main teachers, John Calvin."[34]

Thus Calvin provided an impetus to look outside the Scriptures for answers to scientific questions. We conclude that Calvinism provides

---

32. As quoted in ibid., 180.
33. Motivated by Hooykaas, *Religion and the Rise of Modern Science*, 120–21.
34. Hooykaas, *Religion and the Rise of Modern Science*, 117. Hooykaas refers here to Calvin's commentaries on Gen. 1:15; Ps. 19:4–6; 24:2.

a robust worldview upon which to base a thorough grounding for our understanding of creation and the practice of science.

Calvinists in Science and the Rise of Mechanism

Do Calvinists have an advantage in the enterprise of science?[35] Although the Reformed countries had more freedom[36] than their Catholic counterparts, and their ties to the authority of tradition were somewhat weakened, the rise of modern science saw men of all persuasion contributing in various respects. Certainly in every age prominent Calvinist scientists have participated, but it is difficult to claim a discernible benefit in contributions. This is no doubt because in the end it is creation that speaks, and we all study the same creation. More important is what happened in this collective development of modern science and how it may have affected our own view of creation. In regard to the rise of modern science in the early modern period, I will focus on three things: the rise of the mechanistic philosophy, the discovery that the earth has a history,[37] and the separation of the "natural" from the "supernatural."

The scientists at the time of Calvin were largely the inheritors of attitudes toward science dominated by those of Christianized Greek origin; Calvin gave us no new radically Christian science. However, in the two centuries following Calvin's death, Johannes Kepler (1571–1630) and Galileo Galilei (1564–1642) contributed to a new understanding of the heavens, and, bolstered by the mathematically formulated laws of motion

35. R. K. Merton famously raised a similar issue in 1938, when he noticed a seeming overbalance of Puritans in the body that was to become the Royal Society in seventeenth-century England, and he conjectured that the Puritan faith held something special in fostering the rise of modern science. Hooykaas, *Religion and the Rise of Modern Science*, 98. The thesis, now known as "Merton's thesis," has been discussed often in the literature, and the general attitude nowadays among historians is that it is difficult to make the thesis stick. John Hedley Brooke, *Science and Religion: Some Historical Perspectives* (Cambridge: Cambridge University Press, 1991), 110–15.

36. In the Reformed countries, there was no mechanism such as the Index (list of banned books) for control of publishing, because there was no central authority to exercise such censorship.

37. For an excellent summary of the history of this period, see Davis A. Young and Ralph F. Stearley, *The Bible, Rocks, and Time: Geological Evidence for the Age of the Earth* (Downers Grove, IL: IVP Academic, 2008), chap. 3.

and the law of gravity of Isaac Newton (1642–1727), a new philosophy, the so-called mechanistic philosophy,[38] was on the rise. In contrast with the Platonic worldview in which the world of perfect forms and hence "perfect mathematics" played a large role, and to the Aristotelian world-view in which the "final cause" or purpose of an object was important, the mechanistic philosophy imagined the world running according to in-built laws, much like a machine. In this context, scientists, including prominent Christians in the Calvinist tradition,[39] began to ask new questions concerning the formation of the earth. Various issues arose concerning what was dominant in forming the earth as we find it: waters from above or upheaval from below? uniform processes over long periods or catastrophes? how to interpret the embedding of fossils in the various strata? Concerning the latter, for the first time, scientists began to come to terms with the fact that fossils were remainders from living creatures, and that the earth had a history. It may come as some surprise that there was no strong reaction by the Calvinists against the emergent understanding that the earth's history was evidently a long one, but this fact probably resides in the Calvinist attitude of taking science seriously and Calvin's doctrine of accommodation.

While early proponents of the mechanistic philosophy such as Robert Boyle (1627–91), who was a contemporary of Newton and in the Calvinist tradition, upheld a strong view of God's "radical sustenance" of the laws of nature, some apparently went too far. According to Hooykaas, some began to argue from Calvin's doctrine of predestination to the notion of determinism:

> They state that the Calvinist system contains a belief in immutable law, which it has in common with the system of natural science; thus the doctrine of God's foreknowledge is held to have strengthened the belief in

38. Pierre Gassendi (1592–1655) and René Descartes (1596–1650) were early advocates of such a philosophy. See, e.g., Margaret J. Osler, *Divine Will and the Mechanical Philosophy* (Cambridge: Cambridge University Press, 1994).

39. The list includes Robert Boyle (1627–91) in physical science and geology; Jean-André Deluc (1727–1817) of Geneva; John Playfair (1748–1819) of Edinburgh; Joseph Townsend (1739–1816), an evangelical clergyman; William Buckland (1784–1856), an Anglican clergyman; and Louis Agissiz (1807–73) of Switzerland. See Young and Stearley, *The Bible, Rocks, and Time*, chap. 3.

natural law. This argument seems to rest on a serious misunderstanding, as it more or less identifies predestination with determinism. Certainly the two theories have in common the implication that nothing happens by chance; but whereas the one is concerned with God's free will and implies that God, who is beyond time, has foreknowledge of what He wills, the other is a form of necessitarianism; the former stresses the reign of Jahveh, the latter that of fate and necessity.[40]

Hooykaas points out the error often made in the past, e.g., by Thomas Aquinas and William of Conches, that order is attributed to rationality, and therefore considered as necessary. In Calvin, rather, the subject of order is dealt with under "providence," as a sign of God's loving care for his creatures, rather than under the topic of predestination.[41] The point I wish to make here is that as the mechanistic philosophy became more dominant in the nineteenth century, it became increasingly difficult to distinguish mechanism from deism, and for those willing to live with ambiguous beginnings, it opened the door to atheism. But what is theologically wrong with determinism? In a mechanistic deterministic universe, the beginning conditions of creation plus the deterministic laws hold all the information needed to absolutely predict the future. In other words, everything that comes to pass is already built in from the beginning! This flies in the face not only of Calvin's rich doctrine of providence, in which God is thoroughly involved at every step of the working of the universe, but also of God's freedom to carry out his purposes. In a world that is not deterministic, the future is not already built into the past, so there is a freedom in the created universe that is hitherto undetermined. Thus the universe can admit to all sorts of creaturely freedoms which are genuinely free in and of themselves. It is only God in his providence who brings about his certain purposes for his creation, not through the laws of nature per se, but through his eternal decrees. As I have argued elsewhere,[42] the regularities in the universe are therefore not to be considered as built-in natural laws at all, but patterns of regularity that God lovingly covenants

---

40. Hooykaas, *Religion and the Rise of Modern Science*, 107. Hooykaas cites Merton on this point in 151n28.

41. Ibid., 108.

42. Morris and Petcher, *Science and Grace*, chaps. 5–6.

with his creation to uphold in his radical sustenance.[43] This understanding in no wise removes God from the day-to-day upholding of the universe, but establishes his freedom in doing so.

There is another hidden danger in the move to mechanism relating back to an old medieval problem that arose from the question of what God is capable of doing; for example, can he lie or change the past?[44] Such questions arise out of dilemmas inherited from the neo-Greek notion of God as a "necessary God."[45] The resolution at that time lay in the formulation of God's "two powers," his "absolute power" (all that he can do) and his "ordained power" (what he ordains to do). With the move to voluntarism,[46] and the loss of focus on a necessary world, this distinction became somewhat passé in the thirteenth and fourteenth centuries. In the subsequent rise of the mechanistic philosophy, the usage of the terms gradually began to be co-opted for another purpose. While originally the "ordained power" was a subset of God's "absolute power"—meaning that he could do (practically) anything, but he only wills to do certain things—with the new focus on "laws of nature," the "ordained power" gradually came to be viewed as the "ordinary power"[47] in contrast with his absolute power. So originally his ordained power included everything he ordained, including miracles, whereas after the shift his ordinary power came to be used to describe the "normal" workings of things, expressed in the laws

43. See *Science and Grace*, 143. In our original work, we developed the Calvinist doctrine of creation in terms of the Trinity, so our full definition was, "A law of nature is God's sustaining of, or man's description of, that pattern of regularity that we observe in nature as God works out His purposes towards His own ends in His covenant faithfulness, through His Son, the eternal Word, by means of His Spirit." Space does not allow me to elaborate on the wider points of creation in the present article.

44. For a full account of this story, see Morris and Petcher, *Science and Grace*, chap. 5.

45. A necessary God, sometimes referred to as "the God of the philosophers," is one who must of necessity be the way he is. Then the suspicion might be that he would of necessity also have to create, and his creation would also be necessary and not contingent.

46. Voluntarism in this context refers to the realization that God's creation is not necessary in the sense that it had to be a certain way. Therefore logic alone is not sufficient to uncover its secrets, but rather we must "look"; voluntarism encourages an experimental attitude toward creation.

47. Even Martin Luther used this terminology, using "absolute" and "extraordinary" on the one hand as opposed to "ordained" and "ordinary" on the other. Francis Oakley, *Omnipotence, Covenant, and Order: An Excursion in the History of Ideas from Abelard to Leibniz* (Ithica, NY: Cornell University Press, 1984), 56.

of nature. By this move, the miracles, once a part of the "ordained" power, were relegated to his "absolute" power, setting up a dualistic notion of God's actions. Thus the rise of mechanism was accompanied by a natural/supernatural split. Calvin would not have seen things this way, and neither would most Calvinists today!

This situation resulted in an unfortunately common "habit of the mind" cemented into our collective cultural memory. There is now a tendency to think in terms of creation working according to mechanistic laws, very much as a deist might think, but then to relegate "supernatural" activity to a "violation" of these laws in some sense. With this dualistic thinking, it is very easy to think of the "normal" world as independent of God for the most part, and this has a depersonalizing effect on our attitude toward God's working in the world. Calvin might advise us to train ourselves to see God's Spirit working at all times in upholding every aspect and detail of creation, thereby restoring us to the true wonder that is everywhere around us. Scientists are thus reminded that we are investigating the very work and will of God!

Calvinism in the Age of Modernist Science[48]

By the mid-nineteenth century, the view that the earth had a lengthy history had become rather well accepted, among Christians and non-Christians, and the mechanistic philosophy had become the dominant mode of thinking within scientific circles. Within this mechanistic mindset, the new geology offered a view toward the historical development of the earth, a kind of "evolution" so to speak. With so many fossils that were considered ancient and apparently appearing in a definite succession, it should be no surprise that a number of scientists began to speculate that life might also have an evolutionary history. Charles Darwin wasn't the first;[49] he was merely the first to provide a framework for evolution

48. *Modernist science*, that which occurred in the *modern* period of the nineteenth and early twentieth centuries, is as opposed to *modern science*, which usually refers to the twentieth-century physics of relativity, quantum mechanics, and beyond.

49. Indeed, Darwin's own grandfather, Erasmus Darwin (1731–1802), expressed such ideas, as did Jean-Baptiste Lamarck and others. See, e.g., Brooke, *Science and Religion*, 212–25.

to which others were receptive.[50] His notion was that the environment of a species plays a role as to whether that species survives, a process he termed "natural selection." He did not give an account of how changes occur, but merely that they do occur, and as they do, natural selection would come into play. Darwin's views are in the mechanist tradition for, as John Hedley Brooke reminds us,

> Charles Darwin concluded his *Origin of Species* (1859) with the proclamation that there was grandeur in his view of life. From a simple beginning, in which living powers had been "breathed into" a few forms or even one, the most beautiful and wonderful organisms evolved.

Brooke goes on to tell us that Darwin confessed in a private letter that when he said "breathed into" he had no intention of using a biblical metaphor; he meant that the few forms had "appeared by some wholly unknown process." Thus his view was that, after some unspecified beginning, life evolved according to laws of nature without the aid of outside intervention.

When Darwin's proposal hit the presses in 1859, it became generally accepted in the scientific community within a relatively short period of time. There were of course both scientific and theological objections.[51] Among theologians reacting to Darwin, perhaps none in the evangelical community was more prominent than Charles Hodge, who held the chair of exegetical and didactic theology at Princeton Seminary. Hodge was one of the most visible evangelicals of his time in the United States and a great

---

50. While Darwin had been working on the idea longer, Alfred Russel Wallace developed the same idea independently. Since Darwin had not published yet when Wallace sent him a manuscript, friends encouraged Darwin to publish simultaneously with Wallace. Thus, scientifically speaking, credit should be given to both men, although Wallace was always very gracious, attributing the credit to Darwin. However, in contrast with Darwin, Wallace apparently never accepted that man was descended from animals.

51. One of the more potent scientific arguments was from William Thomson (later Lord Kelvin), a devout churchman. Thomson used his understanding of thermodynamics to estimate that the earth could be at most 100 million years old. Although much older than the young earth estimates derived from the Bible, his number is far less than needed for Darwin's theory and was worrying to Darwinists. It was not until the discovery of radioactivity and the nuclear force that the argument was proved to be fallacious. Brooke, *Science and Religion*, 285.

defender of Calvin. He was also a product of the American nineteenth-century Enlightenment optimism, which held a high view of science. At the same time, though, a liberal development was trying to employ "scientific methods" to critique the biblical texts (i.e., "higher criticism"). Hodge was understandably quite critical of this movement, because he contended that rather than sitting in judgment of Scripture, biblical scholars should use Scripture as data, or "facts," much as the material world "out there" acts as the data to provide the facts of science. As he put it,

> The true method of theology is, therefore, the inductive, which assumes that the Bible contains all the facts or truths which form the contents of theology, just as the facts of nature are the contents of the natural sciences. It is also assumed that the relation of these Biblical facts to each other, the principles involved in them, the laws which determine them, are in the facts themselves, and are to be deduced from them, just as the laws of nature are deduced from the facts of nature. In neither case are the principles derived from the mind and imposed upon the facts, but equally in both departments, the principles or laws are deduced from the facts and recognized by the mind.[52]

Thus it was not a question of the validity of applying the scientific method to theology, but rather a question of using the appropriate scientific method on the "data" of theology. His attitude was that the facts speak for themselves, whether they are the facts of astronomy or theology. So Hodge had a high view of science and a high view of the Bible, both inherited from his Calvinist tradition, and it was from this perspective that he approached the discussions about the antiquity of the earth and Darwin's theory. Hodge was also rather explicit that science could in some cases be an aid to interpret Scripture,[53] but would not contradict it if properly interpreted: "As the Bible is of God, it is certain that there can be no conflict between the teachings of the Scriptures and the facts of science. It is not with facts but with theories, believers have to contend. . . .

52. Charles Hodge, *Systematic Theology*, vol. 1 (Peabody, MA: Hendrickson, 1999), 17, as quoted in Morris and Petcher, *Science and Grace*, 61.

53. Charles Hodge, *What Is Darwinism?* ed. Mark A. Noll and David N. Livingstone (Grand Rapids: Baker, 1994), 53–54.

These theories [of the past] have either proved to be false or to harmonize with the Word of God, properly interpreted."[54]

Although Darwin's *Origin of Species* was published in 1859, Hodge did not react in print for some fifteen years, with the exception of some discussion of Darwin in his *Systematic Theology* (1871–73). In 1874, Hodge published a book-length monograph titled *What Is Darwinism?*[55] Hodge did not attack Darwin by direct reference to Scripture; rather, he began with a kind of worldview analysis, arguing that Darwin's theory is actually a broad theory of the universe, its origins, and existence, to be contrasted with what a biblical view would entail. After some philosophical and scientific arguments he brought out "the grand and final objection" that Darwin's theory is based on random mutation, and therefore there is no pretense of design or progress or purpose. His concluding remarks include the oft-quoted passage,

> We have thus arrived at the answer to our question, What is Darwinism? It is Atheism. This does not mean, as before said, that Mr. Darwin himself and all who adopt his views are atheists; but it means that the theory is atheistic, that the exclusion of design from nature is, as Dr. Gray says, tantamount to atheism.[56]

In this closing argument, Hodge refers to Asa Gray, a well-known Harvard botanist and evangelical who had wholeheartedly embraced Darwin's theory, provided that God is its author and design is not omitted. Thus in attacking the lack of purpose in Darwin's theory rather than evolution in general, in a sense Hodge leaves the door open for some form of theistic evolution. As we shall see from some of his followers, this attitude persisted among the Calvinists, to some extent continuing to this day.

54. Charles Hodge, *Geology and the Bible*, 1872, as quoted in Mark A. Noll, ed., *The Princeton Theology, 1812–1921* (Grand Rapids: Baker, 2001), 144. Hodge follows this up by describing the Copernican revolution and how it changed our views, and then speculates about how the more recent geological data may bring about a change in interpretation of Scripture on the age of the earth.

55. One can only speculate as to why he waited that long, but perhaps he just did not see it as a pressing issue, or perhaps it was because it took fifteen years for Darwin's theories to become reasonably established, thus raising questions among evangelicals.

56. Hodge, *What Is Darwinism?* 156–57.

Another Calvinist of note who also taught at Princeton and took some interest in science was Benjamin B. Warfield (1851–1921), a student of and eventual successor to Charles Hodge. Warfield took an active role in the fight against liberalism and contributed to *The Fundamentals*, a series of essays that came out between 1910 and 1915, funded by a rich philanthropist and written by some of the leading evangelicals of the day in order to defend evangelicalism (or "fundamentalism" as it was then known) against modernism. An interesting aspect of these essays, as surprising as it may seem, is that evolution was not an issue. While Warfield did not address scientific issues in his contributions to these essays, his view is quite similar to another Calvinist contributor, James Orr.

Orr (1844–1913), a well-known Scottish Presbyterian and Calvinist, was tasked to write the article titled "Science and the Christian Faith." As the evangelical spokesperson for science, Orr, like Hodge, did not speak primarily against evolution. Rather, he laid out a broader view of science from an evangelical perspective, first disputing the thesis that Andrew Dickson White and others had put forward, that science and religion are at war. To this he pointed out the tremendous number of scientists in the recent and distant past who were devout Christians. Of supposed conflicts between science and the Bible, he affirms, "the supposed disharmony with the truths of the Bible was an unreal one, early giving way to better understanding on both sides, and finally opening up new vistas in the contemplation of the Creator's power, wisdom, and majesty."[57] Orr then argues that miracles cannot be ruled out by any a priori pronouncement such as the "uniformity of nature." Next, in a section on Scripture and science, he says quite appropriately,

> What is the *general relation* of the Bible to science? . . . Here, it is to be feared, mistakes are often made on both sides—on the side of science in affirming contrariety of the Bible with scientific results where none really exists; on the side of believers in demanding that the Bible be taken as a text-book of the newest scientific discoveries, and trying by forced methods to read these into them.[58]

57. James Orr, "Science and the Christian Faith," in *The Fundamentals* (Grand Rapids: Baker, 2000), 1:336.
58. Ibid., 1:340.

In a reflection of Calvin's doctrines of accommodation and providence, he goes on to clarify,

> The Bible clearly does not profess to anticipate the scientific discoveries of the nineteenth and twentieth centuries. Its design is very different; namely, to reveal God and His will and His purposes of grace to men, and, as involved in this, His general relation to the creative world, its dependence in all its parts on Him, and His orderly government of it in Providence for His wise and good ends. Natural things are taken as they are given, and spoken of in simple, popular language, as we ourselves every day speak of them. The world it describes is the world men know and live in, and it is described as it appears, not as, in its recondite researches, science reveals its inner constitution to us. Wise expositors of the Scriptures, older and younger, have always recognized this, and have not attempted to force its language further.[59]

In order to demonstrate that last point, Orr cites a well-known passage from Calvin's commentary on Genesis 1, noting that Calvin "wrote before the Copernican system of astronomy":

> He who would learn astronomy and other recondite arts, let him go elsewhere. Moses wrote in a popular style things which, without instruction, all ordinary persons indued with common sense are able to understand.... He does not call us up to heaven, he only proposes things that lie open before our eyes.[60]

In order to demonstrate his thesis, Orr refers to the two "revolutions" of science, the Copernican and the geological, which had already been largely accepted by the evangelical community. In the following quote, we see how Orr assessed the latter development in his time:

> But things, as in the case of astronomy, are now better understood, and few are disquieted in reading their Bibles because it is made certain that the world is immensely older than the 6,000 years which the older chronology gave it. Geology is felt only to have expanded our idea of the vastness

59. Ibid.
60. As quoted in Ibid., 1.340–41.

and marvel of the Creator's operations through the aeons of time during which the world, with its teeming populations of fishes, birds, reptiles, mammals, was preparing for man's abode—when the mountains were being upheaved, the valleys being scooped out, and veins of precious metals being inlaid into the crust of the earth.[61]

Here, writing in defense of the evangelical tradition, Orr reveals his confidence that the old age of the earth is largely accepted among evangelical Christians.

Finally, Orr addresses the issue of evolution. Here, and in his other essay in *The Fundamentals* titled "The Early Narratives of Genesis," Orr brings out several interesting points. For example, in the former, he raises issues that he expects could not be explained by science in principle, i.e., the origin of life, the transition to consciousness, and the transition to rationality, personality, and moral life in man. In the latter, he speaks of biblical teachings that science does not deny, viz., that man is the crown and summit of God's creation, that there is a unity to the human race, and that man is made in God's image. He concludes that in general "the narratives of Creation, Fall, and Flood, are not myths, but narratives enshrining the knowledge or memory of real transactions,"[62] and supports this by saying that "if the story of [the fall] were not in the Bible, we would require to put it there for ourselves in order to explain the condition of the world as it is."[63] While he thus allows for much freedom in interpreting the details, and, like Hodge, he denies that Darwin's mechanistic account could be the whole story, he concludes by saying there is no conflict between science and the Bible.

Perhaps no other nineteenth-century figure has championed Calvinism more than Orr's contemporary, the Dutch theologian, author, professor, and politician, Abraham Kuyper (1837–1920). Kuyper was immensely interested in science and scholarship, and recognized that there was a battle, but not between science and the Bible. Rather the battle was between Christianity and modernism. This led him to formulate his own warfare thesis, not between Christianity and science, but between these

61. Ibid., 343–44.
62. Ibid., 240.
63. Ibid., 239.

two worldviews. He elaborated on this in his 1898 Stone lectures,[64] titled simply, *Lectures on Calvinism*:

> Two *life systems* are wrestling with one another, in mortal combat. Modernism is bound to build a world of its own from the data of the natural man, and to construct man himself from the data of nature; while, on the other hand, all those who reverently bend the knee to Christ and worship Him as the Son of the living God, and God himself, are bent upon saving the "Christian Heritage." This is *the* struggle in Europe, this is *the* struggle in America, and this also, is the struggle for principles in which my own country is engaged, and in which I myself have been spending all my energy for nearly forty years.[65]

Underlying this struggle, Kuyper maintained, was the Calvinist principle of *antithesis*, which entails the struggle between the kingdom of God and the kingdom of this world which is in all of us and all institutions. Rather than suggesting that science was devoid of faith, Kuyper suggests that all science must depend on faith:

> Every science in a certain sense starts from faith . . . . Every science presupposes faith in self, in our self-consciousness; presupposes faith in the accurate working of our senses; presupposes faith in the correctness of the laws of thought; presupposes faith in something universal hidden behind the special phenomena; presupposes faith in life; and especially presupposes faith in the principles, from which we proceed; which signifies that all these indispensable axioms, needed in a productive scientific investigation, do not come to us by proof, but are established in our judgment by our inner conception and *given with our self-consciousness*.[66]

Thus for Kuyper, science is always based on faith in a number of things. By faith, Kuyper says, he "does not mean the 'faith in Christ Jesus' in its saving efficacy for the sinner, nor yet the 'faith in God' which is fundamental to all religion, but that formal function of the life of our

64. The Stone Lectures are given at Princeton every year.
65. Abraham Kuyper, *Lectures on Calvinism* (Grand Rapids: Eerdmans, 1931), 11.
66. Ibid., 131–32.

soul which is fundamental to every fact in our human consciousness."[67] In addition, the two life systems result in two different sciences; he identified the stark difference between these two as having to do with whether or not a "disturbance" (i.e., the fall) had taken place:

> Hence it follows that the conflict is not between faith and science, but between the assertion that the cosmos, as it exists today, is either in a *normal* or an *abnormal* condition. If it is normal, then it moves by means of an eternal evolution from its potencies to its ideal. But if the cosmos in its present condition is *abnormal*, then a *disturbance* has taken place in the past, and only a *regenerating* power can warrant it the final attainment of its goal. This, and no other is the principal antithesis, which separates the thinking minds in the domain of Science into two opposite battle-arrays.[68]

Despite the difference in the two sciences, Kuyper points to common grace as the way that science can still be done together , as S. U. Zuidema notes:

> Common grace checks the operation of sin and the curse on sin, and in principle makes possible again the unfolding of creation's potentialities and the development of the creature. It fosters this unfolding, nourishes it, strengthens it. It makes for a "grace-endowed nature";[69] nature remains nature . . . but common grace curbs the destructive operation of sin and postpones the curse on nature; in fact, in the realm of the temporal and the visible it even enables people to do the good, the moral good, the civic good, opening up the possibility of progress in the life of creation. Thus, next to the stemming of sin and curse, common grace in Kuyper's view also operates for "progress": it serves and promotes cultural development and progress, and makes these possible.[70]

However, common grace only goes so far. Although we share certain things such as sense data and reason, eventually differences will arise.

---

67. Abraham Kuyper, *Principles of Sacred Theology*, trans. J. Hendrik de Vries (Grand Rapids: Eerdmans, 1954), 125.

68. Kuyper, *Lectures on Calvinism*, 132.

69. S. U. Zuidema, "Common Grace and Christian Action in Abraham Kuyper," *Communication and Confrontation* (Toronto: Wedge Publishing, 1972), 65.

70. Ibid.

What has been well done by one need not be done again by you. It is at the same time important that, though not hesitating to part company as soon as principle demands it, the two kinds of science shall be as long as possible conscious of the fact that, formally at least, both are at work at a common task. . . . The formal process of thought has not been attacked by sin, and for this reason *palingenesis*[71] [rebirth] works no change in this mental task.

There is but one logic, and not two . . . . [This one logic] contributes in two ways important service in maintaining a certain mutual contact between the two kinds of science.

In the first place, from this fact it follows that the accuracy of one another's demonstrations can be critically examined and verified, in so far at least as the result strictly depends upon the deduction made. By keeping a sharp watch upon each other, mutual service is rendered in the discovery of logical faults in each other's demonstrations, and thus in a formal way each will continually watch over the other. And on the other hand, they may compel each other to justify their points of view over against one another.[72]

Out of this emerges a kind of recipe for doing science with unbelievers. We are to understand the methods of investigation and their reliability, and at the same time maintain a critical attention to the places where faith commitments creep in. Thus separating the two, however imperfectly, we can promote a dialog concerning both what can be concluded, and what the fundamental assumptions are behind the conclusions. Such a dialog in and of itself may not convert people to our point of view, but at least it will remove the unjustifiable certainty upon which they rest, leaving them without excuse. What a wonderful rich view of the scientific enterprise has Calvinism wrought through Kuyper's eyes![73]

71. *Palingenesis* is the Greek word for "rebirth" or "born again."
72. Kuyper, *Principles of Sacred Theology*, 159–60.
73. We should not leave this section without mentioning Herman Dooyeweerd, a student of Kuyper who took his seminal ideas much further in an attempt to establish a clearly Calvinist approach to academics and science. He spearheaded an interesting Calvinist movement in the twentieth century that raises issues concerning science. See Herman Dooyeweerd, *A New Critique of Theoretical Thought*, trans. David H. Freeman and William S. Young (Nutley, NJ: Presbyterian and Reformed, 1969), and Herman Dooyeweerd, *Roots*

Modern Science, Contemporary Issues, and Insights

Since the nineteenth century, there have been several substantial developments in science. In the early twentieth century, physics underwent "revolutions" in the development of quantum theory and in "big bang" cosmology. In biology, we are right now seeing rapid developments and new understandings in the field of genetics and the human genome.

When Edwin Hubble's 1929 data supported the idea of an expanding universe, the then-popular "steady state" theory was in trouble.[74] By extrapolating back in time, the expanding universe implies that it must have had a beginning, now known as the "big bang."[75] At the time, many Christians rejoiced, pointing to the theory as evidence for creation, and as disproving the idea that the universe had always existed as it was. Ironically, some Christians today view the big bang with suspicion, lumping it in with biological evolution as a godless theory. This is certainly a good indication of how attitudes among evangelicals could and did change in the course of the twentieth century.

The discovery of quantum theory has opened up a very interesting view of God's creation as we learn that at the subatomic level objects do not follow the intuitions we gain from our experience of the everyday world around us. All quantum objects exhibit both wave and particle natures in a way that seems paradoxical, and everyday properties such as position, momentum, and angular momentum (or spin) can no longer be said to have definite values without a measurement.[76] In addition, in the quantum theory, mysterious instantaneous correlations exist between par-

---

of Western Culture: Pagan, Secular, and Christian Options, trans. John Kraay (Toronto: Wedge Publishing Foundation, 1979).

74. Einstein had even put an ad hoc constant (the "cosmological constant") into his general relativity theory to try to find a steady state solution to the equations. Once he heard about the expanding universe, and that if this ad hoc constant were omitted his equations would allow for solutions in agreement with the data, he called the addition of the cosmological constant his greatest mistake. Ironically, we now know that the universe is actually speeding up in its expansion, which suggests a non-zero although small value for the cosmological constant.

75. "Big Bang" was originally a pejorative term coined by Fred Hoyle (in a 1949 radio broadcast) to criticize the theory to which he did not subscribe. However, the term stuck.

76. There is one formulation of quantum mechanics, from David Bohm, that does not suffer from this problem, although it is at the expense of severe nonlocality, in the sense that every particle must be viewed as being affected by every other particle in the universe instan-

ticles, and these have been well verified by experiment.[77] Quantum theory therefore undermines the mechanistic philosophy, bringing an element of randomness into our understanding of what we can know about the world. Even though the mathematics of the quantum theory is well defined, its interpretation is anything but agreed upon. However, the apparent randomness need not be a source of concern for Calvinists. On the contrary, to me the quantum theory has opened up a new, rich approach to God's created world, illustrating wonderfully that the story of the universe is not one of a deterministic mechanism completely controlled by initial conditions. Thus the future is "open" to God's personal actions; it is not entirely prescribed by impersonal laws and past conditions. This seems to fit well with the Calvinist doctrine of providence combined with radical sustenance. For in quantum theory, a closer look at the inner structure of matter seems to reveal a freedom for God to determine outcomes of physical events which would not follow necessarily from the laws. I would also expect to see such "openness" at other levels of our descriptive laws of nature, for God's creation cannot be reduced to just the physical.[78]

The analysis of the human genome is proceeding at a rapid pace, with new interpretations coming out all the time. It is an exciting area not only to seek new data, but also to work through new questions being raised about how God designed and coded information in his sovereign and divine plan for humanity. What we see at present is multiple interpretations of the data, and the near future promises to be very interesting in terms of both scientific understanding and dialog.

These developments in science flesh out more fully what was hinted at by Calvin, and made more explicit by Kuyper—that science is affected by worldview.[79] As Del Ratzsch has pointed out,

---

taneously and at all times. For an overview of this and other issues, see, e.g., Nick Herbert, *Quantum Reality* (Harpswell, ME: Anchor, 1987).

77. The phenomenon, known as entanglement, is related to Bell's inequality. This is also discussed in Nick Herbert, *Quantum Reality*, 1987.

78. For example, animal behavior is not predetermined entirely by so-called "laws" of nature, but it is presumably not through quantum processes alone that animal freedom arises. That would be a reductionism.

79. So if science can no longer automatically be claimed to be grounded as inherently objective and neutral by virtue of its method or some other reason, then the burden to explain exactly why it works is incumbent on each worldview. As we argue in our book *Science and*

Science is done by humans and it cannot escape what is inescapably human. Our science is limited to humanly available concepts, humanly available reasoning, humanly shaped notions of understanding and explanation and humanly structured pictures of what the world must be like. How could it be otherwise? Science seems to have a serious and incurable case of the humans.[80]

This should be no surprise to the Calvinist, for if knowledge depends on the orientation of the human heart as Calvin maintained, then the antithesis between the kingdom of God and the kingdom of this world will always be present in the scientific enterprise. We should go on to ask, what other aspects of thinking about science have we inherited that are not in keeping with our Calvinist tradition?

Let us return then to one of the most subtle issues we have inherited in the philosophy of science, the tendency to think of our world as a big machine running according to built-in laws. This unfortunate controlling metaphor predisposes us to demean the ever-ongoing work of God, and prevents us from seeing the wonder that is everywhere around us. Further, the mechanistic mind-set tends to make us ignore the "natural," to restrict God's present-day work only to a category called "supernatural." Not only does this create a false dualism of God's activity, it also has ramifications in some respects in our cultural discussion concerning science. For if there is really no such strict division between "natural" and "supernatural," then all arguments based on the division become suspect.

Perhaps the most glaring issue that continually faces us is the notion that science and religion are somehow at war, and that current scientific endeavors in general should be looked at with suspicion or even skepticism. The primary impetus for the "warfare" notion came from nineteenth-century scholars such as Andrew Dickson White and John William Draper,[81] who wished to discredit religion in the face of the then-rising star of

---

Grace, Calvinist theology provides a strong foundation for a robust theology of science. Abraham Kuyper in the nineteenth century already had understood the main effects of the antithesis with regard to science.

80. Del Ratzsch, *The Battle of Beginnings* (Downers Grove, IL: Intervarsity Press, 1996), 129.

81. See David C. Lindberg and Ronald L. Numbers, eds., *God and Nature* (Berkeley and Los Angeles: University of California Press, 1986), 1–3.

modern science. Since that time, we have understood more clearly that science cannot be divorced from worldview,[82] and that in some sense there is no way of separating "the humans" out of the scientific enterprise.[83] The Calvinist position has always been that God speaks through his creation as well as his Word, so that, rightly understood, studying creation will only be an aid to our Christian faith. Since there is only one source of knowledge, there can be "no final conflict."[84]

Let me now return to an issue brought up by Calvin that is relevant for our present-day discussions. In 1550, in a tract titled *Concerning Scandals*, Calvin picked up on the theme of "stumbling blocks" in Romans 16:17:

> Since the way to live has been laid down for us by God, and we are obliged to him to follow it, it may be compared to a road or a race track. This gives rise to another metaphor: obstacles of all kinds, whether they divert us from the right direction, or keep us back by being in the way, or provide the means for making us fall, are called "scandals [i.e., stumbling blocks or obstacles]."[85]

Because of such obstacles, Calvin saw the necessity of humbling ourselves to become fools in this world:

> By "being fools" we do not mean stupid; nor do we direct those who are learned in the liberal sciences to jettison their knowledge, and those who are gifted with quickness of mind to become dull, as if a man cannot be a Christian unless he is more like a beast than a man. The profession

82. This issue is related to the move to postmodernism and the contribution of science concerning that move. For an overview, see Morris and Petcher, *Science and Grace*, chap. 2.

83. This is related to the demarcation problem of science, that there is no definition that would be accepted by philosophers in general that would draw a line between science and non-science. This is largely related to the issue of worldviews and judgment calls.

84. "No Final Conflict" is the title of a lecture given by Francis Schaeffer, in which he outlined what he considered to be limits and freedoms for the Christian concerning science. His limits sound rather like those of James Orr, that there was a real Adam, a real fall, and so on. However, he sees the possibility of an old earth, physical death before the fall, and other freedoms that seem to be born out by science. A version of this lecture is reprinted in *The Complete Works of Francis Schaeffer* (Westchester: Crossway Books, 1982), 117–48.

85. The word *scandal* here is a direct transliteration of the Greek word that is often translated "stumbling block" or, as in the NIV version of the Romans passage above, "obstacle." John Calvin, *Concerning Scandals*, trans. John W. Fraser (Grand Rapids: Eerdmans, 1978), 8.

of Christianity requires us to be immature, not in our thinking, but in malice (1 Cor. 4:20). But do not let anyone bring trust in his own mental resources or his learning into the school of Christ; do not let anyone be swollen with pride or full of distaste, and so be quick to reject what he is told, indeed even before he has sampled it.[86]

This admonition is relevant to our scientific knowledge claims of course, but equally so to our general tendency to think that we know more about the world than we do.[87]

That being said, an underlying science/Christianity warfare attitude continues to play itself out in the young earth creation debates (which have even been a source of intra-church squabbles) and the issues of intelligent design. As we have demonstrated above, after the rise of modern science, by employing the principle of accommodation and taking science seriously, Calvinists as a whole have never made the age of the earth an issue. The situation is still borne out in Calvinist denominations, for to my knowledge, not one has taken a dogmatic young earth position. As an example, in the Presbyterian Church in America, a study committee on the length of days in Genesis 1 presented a report to the PCA General Assembly in 1999 that commended several potential interpretations of Genesis, most of which do not constrain the length of days or the age of the earth.[88] Several other Calvinist denominations, notably the Orthodox Presbyterian Church, have issued similar publications.[89] (In fact, the young earth movement as a scientific movement is a relative newcomer, which has its origins largely from outside Calvinist circles.[90])

86. Ibid., 18.

87. A discussion of this can be found in Calvin's Commentary on 1 Cor. 1, for example, in the context of divisions in the church.

88. The report can be found at http://www.pcahistory.org/creation/report.html (last viewed July 25, 2009)

89. The OPC Report of the Committee to Study the Views of Creation can be found at http://opc.org/GA/CreationReport.pdf (last viewed July 25, 2009). I would also like to note that from the time Darwin's theory was introduced, evangelical Calvinists have had reservations about Darwinism and believe that this issue should be properly understood as separate from the age of the earth.

90. This may be surprising to some readers. The present-day young earth movement as a scientific movement grew initially from a "prophecy" from the Seventh-day Adventist founder Ellen G. White in the nineteenth century, and only slowly gained impetus in the twentieth century. It was not even an issue in the Scopes evolution trial of 1925, for William Jennings Bryan admitted to an old earth view. The movement gained impetus in the publishing of *The Genesis Flood* by

In light of the important Calvinist teaching of accommodation and its underlying attitude that the Bible speaks to us in an everyday language rather than with specialized scientific intentions, we are advised to avoid speculative approaches that read current science into its pages. Such approaches would include claims that the Bible intends to teach scientifically that the Genesis "days" must be literal twenty-four-hour days,[91] as well as teachings that claim to find the modern big bang theory in some detail within its pages.[92] If we insist on those positions, they can even become stumbling blocks to the gospel. I think Calvin would admonish us to handle these issues lovingly and with proper respect, rather than to appear before the watching world as combatant people who lack humility in our knowledge claims about science.

The intelligent design movement (ID) has perhaps in recent years shifted the emphasis away from young earth/old earth arguments to the question as to whether design can be observed in the creation that we study. In *The Design Revolution*, Bill Dembski succinctly describes what the movement attempts to show:

> The fundamental claim of intelligent design is straightforward and easily intelligible: namely, *there are natural systems that cannot be adequately explained in terms of undirected natural forces and that exhibit features which in any other circumstance we would attribute to intelligence.*[93]

Henry Morris and John Whitcomb in 1961. For a summary of the history of the movement, see Ronald Numbers, *The Creationists: From Scientific Creation to Intelligent Design* (Cambridge: Harvard University Press, 2006). However, it is important to note that the young earth movement as a scientific movement should not be confused with the issue of the interpretation of the days in Genesis. Indeed, each denominational study report referred to above affirms the literal twenty-four-hour-day interpretation as one of the acceptable choices.

91. Whatever the merits to the present-day movement as a scientific enterprise, there are many popular myths associated with it that have been debunked but continue to be passed on among the churches, and serve to discredit the movement in wider circles. We should be more attentive to getting our stories right before the watching world, lest we discredit our Lord and Savior! For a recent attempt at a thorough portrayal of the scientific case for an old earth, and a discussion of many of the popular myths, see Young and Stearley, *The Bible, Rocks, and Time* (Downers Grove, IL: IVP Academic, 2008).

92. This view has been popularized by Hugh Ross and his "Reasons to Believe" ministry, http://www.reasons.org/ (last viewed July 30, 2009).

93. William Dembski, *The Design Revolution* (Downers Grove, IL: InterVarsity Press, 2004), 27 (emphasis Dembski's).

The issue of intelligent design[94] is not only about affirming the existence of design, for all Christians would maintain that the universe is designed, even if it were through an evolutionary process. Rather the issue is whether the detection of design can be quantified in some sort of objective manner. This involves, in part, attempts to quantify the study of information in the universe. In my opinion, this is certainly a worthy question to raise within the general attitude of scientific investigation, and can lead to some extremely interesting and potentially fruitful questions about nature itself. However, there are also inherent drawbacks to the program as it stands. For one thing, every design argument that has been put forward thus far involves judgment calls of the sort for which worldview matters substantially. Thus a Christian may be more inclined in a given situation to judge that something is designed, but a materialist may look at the same argument and judge that there is a plausible explanation through law and chance. Unfortunately, design theorists have often given the impression that if materialists would only be more objective, they would see the need for intelligent design behind nature. This would imply that perhaps the materialists are being less than honest in their thinking.[95]

The notion of objective proof is itself a throwback to the modernist hope for a neutral objective science, which we have learned from Kuyper is not possible, since underlying faith is always at work. Thus there will always be a judgment call, and the more speculative the claim, the more divided the judgment. We may talk about probabilities for particular judgment calls, but there is no neutrality to draw on.

So we ought not to expect more of the design arguments than they can deliver. Just as in the days of natural theology when a reasonable inference was made to the existence of a designer God, it was found to be impossible to get to the God of the Bible from the "bottom up." The design theorists, when they talk about theism, sometimes have a tendency to lump all theisms together. But in view of our earlier discussion, this only leaves us with the question: knowing what we know about God and the gospel, is

---

94. The intelligent design movement is not a Calvinist movement, although there are some Calvinists who participate. Among others are Catholics and even agnostics.

95. In the preface of *The Design Revolution*, Dembski seems to embrace the notion that a Kuhnian revolution is at hand in science, and it revolves around intelligent design. Dembski, *The Design Revolution*, 19–21.

it faithful science to ignore the Triune Creator?[96] So as interesting as the intelligent design movement is for the Christian, the bottom line is that we should take it for what it is and not more. There will always be a naturalistic story even if it sounds unreasonable to us, and the reason is quite simple: For the Calvinist, whether we see design in the universe or not is not simply a matter to be determined through reason and experimentation alone, but ultimately it is a matter of the heart. So we end this section with a cheer and a warning. Bravo to the intelligent design theorists for opening up an intriguing and increasingly rich discussion about the nature of creation, much of which can serve as pre-evangelism for those skeptical of the Christian faith, as long as we as a church continue to be humble about our claims.

Finally, I would like to summarize by saying that for the Calvinist, science is a wonderful vocation. Scientists have the freedom and privilege of studying the very creation of God, informed by Scripture, yet knowing that what we find will not be a threat to our faith. If, as Hodge declares, science can also reciprocally aid us in our understanding of God's Word, then we are doubly blessed. The benefits apply to increasing our wonder at God's creation, to alleviating ills and improving our human condition in our fallen world, and to enriching our theological interpretation of God's Word. Even if we cannot say that Calvin definitively framed science in a unique way, he did provide a rich theological heritage for the doing of science; there is no greater heritage for the scientist than that of Calvinism. Thank God for the wonderful grace of the scientific enterprise.

---

96. This theme is pursued in Morris and Petcher, *Science and Grace*, chap. 4.

9

John Calvin's Impact on Business

Richard C. Chewning

Were John Calvin alive today he would undoubtedly be embarrassed by the attention given him for the 500th anniversary of his birth. He would surely say, "Whatever God-honoring understandings I may have had and shared with others, I believe they were but a free gift from him. I am but his humble servant." John Calvin was indeed blessed, and through him we have been blessed. God put in Calvin's heart the desire that the Word of God would become the sole shaper of his *worldview*—the focus of this volume.

The worldview of sixteenth-century Europeans was profoundly impacted by the preaching and writing of Calvin. Ideas regarding the earning of one's livelihood through *business* were in an unsettled state. Calvin's ideas about the conduct of business had a great impact on the prevailing worldview. And his thoughts generated significant behavioral responses that remain embedded in the minds of many in the twenty-first century, albeit generally in grossly perverted forms. To substantiate these points we will examine:

A. The antecedents to the worldview that was in place when Calvin (1509–64) became influential.

B. Three thoughts Calvin interjected into the worldview that had a significant impact on the economic thinking of his day:

1. Work was intended to *glorify* God—not a means of meriting salvation, but a means of manifesting the ability to work, with which God had endowed each human. ("Successful" work subsequently became tied to God's special blessing of election in the minds of many inside and outside the church, a widely adopted *perversion* of Calvin's teaching.)

2. Interest paid on money borrowed to enhance one's business was not to be thought of as usurious in nature but as "rent" for the use of another's capital, just as one might rent a building.

3. Profits are *good*. This was a revolutionary thought. They are a mark of good works and are to be used for beneficent purposes, the latter teaching being quickly forgotten.

C. The continuing impact of Calvin's thinking, perversions of his thinking, and threats of the annihilation of his thinking in the twenty-first century.

Using an analogy from human reproduction, John Calvin was born in the eighth month of the market economy's gestational period in the womb of culture. Many of the components necessary for a market system were in their late term, waiting to be born. Calvin was in the delivery room and assisted in the birth of the free market system.

It is important, however, that we not *baptize* an economic system with a particular biblical interpretation or anoint a particular economic arrangement with a false blessing. Notwithstanding, it is important to ask, Is the economic process being described compatible with biblical *values*? To answer this question we will identify six biblical values that appear to be highly compatible with free-market economics.

Biblical Values that Are Compatible
with Free-Market Economics

Freedom. Is there any condition of the human spirit more important to God than that of his image bearers' ability to enjoy the freedom to choose? The privilege of choice was granted to God's first image bearers from the day of their creation.[1] Indeed, granting choice to them seemed so important in the mind of God that he chose to endow humanity with the freedom to choose even knowing that its exercise would cause their death;[2] necessitate the incarnation of God the Son;[3] and require his Son's subsequent life, sorrow, death, and resurrection.[4] Indeed, it is hard to conceive of any ability that God provided his image bearers as being more important than having a free will—the freedom to choose within the limits of their *nature.*[5] Biblically, however, *freedom* is to be distinguished from *license,* where righteousness is disregarded. Biblically, true freedom is limited by the revealed character of God; apart from God's character and will, freedom has no constructive meaning.

Work. Work, family, and worship were all within the scope of our first parents' comprehension before their fall.[6] The fall polluted work in two ways. First, the created order fell along with our first parents and thereafter resisted yielding its benefits without humanity struggling to gain its latent blessings.[7] The created order now resisted yielding its potential. It fought back, if you like. But second, work itself became associated with toil and sorrow.[8] The Book of Proverbs is full of admonitions regarding work for the sluggard, the drunkard, and those without motivation.[9]

---

1. Gen. 2:15–17; 3:1–13.
2. Gen. 2:17; 3:19; Rom. 5:12.
3. John 1:1, 14, 29; 6:51; 8:58; 10:36; 20:30–31.
4. Matt. 28:5–6; Acts 2:24; 1 Cor. 15:3–4; 1 Peter 2:24.
5. The original "free will" died with our first parents' fall. The human will thereafter could be exercised only within the constraints of one's *nature*: fallen/alienated from God nature, or fallen/restored to God nature for the subsequent realignment of the perverted will to one that is God-centered, a degree-by-degree realignment.
6. Gen. 1:26–2:3.
7. Gen. 3:17–19; Rom. 8:20–22; Heb. 6:7–8.
8. Gen. 3:17; Job 5:7; 14:1; Eccl. 2:23.
9. Examples: Prov. 6:6, 9; 9:4–6; 13:4; 19:24; 20:1; 21:17; 23:20–21, 29–30; 26:15; 30:25–27; 31:4–5.

Some people, however, see work as providing the opportunity to disclose their belief in themselves; their thirst for wealth, security, and/or power; and their unintended repudiation of God as the Sovereign Provider.[10] Christians on the other hand often find work to be an integral aspect of their *redemption*. They serve God through their work, which glorifies him.[11] This last point was powerfully promoted by John Calvin.

Personal Initiative/Responsibility. Taking responsibility for one's conduct is a value of considerable importance in the Bible. A statement such as "aspire to live quietly, and to mind your own affairs, and to work with your hands" is not an unusual biblical exhortation.[12] God's conversation with Cain regarding his need to "do well" and for his need to "rule over" his own behavior set a standard for all God's image bearers.[13] We are to "do good to everyone" whenever the opportunity presents itself.[14] And taking the initiative to better one's position in life, if such an opportunity presents itself, is also commendable in the sight of God.[15] But whatever we do, we are to do it to the glory of God.[16]

Stewardship/Accountability. Biblically, our "dominion and rule" over God's created order is followed by a time of personal *accountability*. The world and all that is in it belongs to the Lord,[17] but our superintending activities over what is rightly God's are accompanied by the certainty that he will openly examine the record of our stewardship.[18] The intentions, thoughts, and motives that accompany every act of stewardship will be disclosed by the Lord at the time of our accounting.[19]

Charity. God has been our example: he has freely given us all things.[20] And he wants us to be generous and loving as he is: he gives temporal

10. Deut. 8:17–18; 1 Tim. 6:9–10.
11. 1 Cor. 10:31; Col. 3:17; 1 Peter 4:11.
12. Acts 18:3; Eph. 4:28; 1 Thess. 4:11; 2 Thess. 3:10–12; etc.
13. Gen. 4:7.
14. Gal. 6:10; Prov. 3:27.
15. 1 Cor. 7:21.
16. 1 Cor. 10:31; Col. 3:17; 1 Peter 4:11.
17. Ex. 19:5; Deut. 10:14; Ps. 24:1; 50:10–12; 1 Cor. 10:26.
18. Matt. 12:36; 16:27; Rom. 14:12; 1 Peter 4:5.
19. 1 Cor. 4:5.
20. Rom. 8:32.

blessings "on the evil and on the good," and "on the just and on the unjust."[21] Indeed, we are taught that "It is more blessed to give than to receive."[22] The Macedonians were commended by the apostle Paul for their generosity when he noted that "their deep poverty overflowed in the wealth of their liberality."[23] Being "liberal" in one's giving is called a gift from God[24] as it reflects God's own character and that which he desires us to emulate.[25] We will see later that Calvin strongly promoted the teaching of *charity*, but was largely ignored.

Freedom, work, creativity, personal initiative/responsibility, steward-ship, and charity are all values set forth in Scripture and have played a significant role in free market economies.

The Dominant Worldview Regarding Business Between the Fifth and Sixteenth Centuries

How did people in Europe provide for their material needs between the fall of Rome and A.D. 1600? The answer is a metamorphosing one. The Roman Catholic Church emerged after the collapse of Rome as the *only* surviving institution with any continuity of influence and power.

> The breakup of the Roman Empire was followed by political turmoil. Much of Europe was ushered into a period of genuine instability. What emerged were city states, feudal holdings and the divided lands of kings. These small regions were self sufficient and did not rely on economic or social interchange with one another. . . . The Roman Catholic Church . . . was . . . institutionally located within the boundaries of the majority of the independent "kingdoms" . . . [and] it alone remained as a unifying and stabilizing minister in the shifting tides of Europe.[26]

21. Matt. 5:45.
22. Acts 20:35.
23. 2 Cor. 8:2, NASB. Chaps. 8 and 9 commend the generosity of the churches in helping others in need.
24. Rom. 12:8.
25. Eph. 4:13, 24; Heb. 12:10; 2 Peter 1:4.
26. Richard C. Chewning, *Business Ethics in a Changing Culture* (Reston, VA: Reston Publishing, [1982] 1984), 31.

Along with the political dissolution of the Roman Empire came huge economic implosions. Safety and security broke down. Trade between cities became extremely hazardous. Common currencies and the rule of law disappeared. Disease and invading conquerors depopulated the countryside. As a result, survival through self-sufficiency became the norm.[27]

The "new" insular life gave rise to the *manorial estate*: thousands of acres of land ruled over by an abbot, baron, feudal lord, or self-proclaimed lord of the manor. The manor lord was not only the owner but also the "protector, judge, police chief, and administrator." His estate typically included a large manor house, a walled area that extended beyond the house and protected workshops where "cloth might be spun or woven, grapes pressed, food stored, simple . . . blacksmithing work performed, [and] course grain ground."[28] "Security" was the attraction and reward of the manor life. The peasants were helpless apart from the protection they received from the manor lord.[29]

There were also some scattered towns, even if in ruinous condition. Customs differed from town to town. Traveling merchants would come to the periodic fairs where trade was conducted in the towns. City burghers established *guilds*—the "trade, professional and craft organizations."[30] Guildmasters ran the guilds, which were made up of independent producers who worked in their own houses and banded together to elect a guild government that laid down the rules of business.[31] The *making of money was not* the driving force behind the guilds, however. Competition was to be avoided."The terms of service, the wages, the route of advancement of apprentices and journeymen were all fixed by custom."[32]

Economics in the medieval period was concerned with subsistence and did not play a dominant role in the social order. So what did? "It was the Church, the great pillar of stability in an age of disorder, *which constituted the ultimate authority on economics.* . . . [T]he economics of

27. Robert L. Heilbroner, *The Making of Economic Society*, 2nd ed. (Englewood Cliffs, NJ: Prentice-Hall, 1975), 30.

28. Ibid., 30–31.

29. Ibid., 32.

30. Ibid., 34.

31. Ibid., explanation added.

32. Ibid., 35.

medieval Catholicism was concerned not with credits and debits of suc-cessful business ... [but] with ... the souls of business operators."[33] R. H. Tawney believed that the assumption of that day was "economic interests are subordinate to the real business of life, which is salvation ... [and that] economic motives are suspect ... [and] need ... repression."[34] What could change such a perception?

Change in one's thinking requires a change in one's beliefs. In the tempo-ral things of life this is normally accompanied by a change in what is observed and experienced. In the context of making a living, the bartering process needed a substitute for the exchange of two products. It needed a monetary foundation. Money must be present if a market system is to exist.

Numerous "stimulators of change" were at work in this period. For example, traveling merchants brought with them, besides their products, tales of faraway places that fostered inquisitiveness and excitement.[35] The merchants also encouraged urbanization by attracting people to wherever they located. But those attracted to their activities were not officially part of the city or manor, so it was uncertain how they were to be taxed or assimilated into the social order. New ways of thinking had to be devised.[36]

During this period, thousands of peasants who went on the Crusades left home penniless but came home with money to spend. This introduced a modicum of economic freedom.[37]

Merchants traveling a hundred miles in Europe might cross a dozen "sovereignties each with different rules, regulations, laws, weights, mea-sures, [and] money." It required centuries to bring the scattered indepen-dent territories together to form larger political/economic entities.[38]

The emerging political powers began sponsoring overseas explo-rations beyond the known boundaries. Such adventures stirred the imagination of thousands.[39]

33. Ibid., 36, emphasis added.
34. R. H. Tawney, *Religion and the Rise of Capitalism* (New York: Harcourt, Brace & World, 1947), 31.
35. Heilbroner, *Making of Economic Society*, 46–47
36. Ibid., 47–48.
37. Ibid., 49–50.
38. Ibid., 50–51.
39. Ibid., 51–52.

The Roman Catholic Church, the *dominant* power in Europe,[40] taught that business was a dangerous place to spend one's time.[41] Profits were considered sinful. Lending money at interest was illegal. These restrictive practices existed because famines and plagues had created an environment where those with food gouged those without food.[42] The guilds established "just prices" and "just wages" under the oversight of the church.[43] It was the *protesting churches* that provided new ways of thinking.[44]

The feudal lords lived in an economic environment built on a system of *payments in kind* in which days of work paid one's taxes and rent. Money was not a part of economic exchange on the manors. The growing urban areas with their marketplaces, however, saw a rise in the use of money to create exchanges. So over time the "payments in kind" gave way to "payments in money." The economic system was slowly monetized, which changed the power structure.[45]

Labor, *land*, and *capital* became "commodities" with the monetization of economics. *Labor* slowly became a commodity for sale. *Land* holdings that had been taken through conquest or granted by a king gradually assumed a value that could be quantified in terms of money and sold. And the guildmasters gradually metamorphosed into merchant capitalists with their accumulated money.[46] Slowly, cooperative production began to supplant the craftsman,[47] and the profit motive emerged under the cover of *competition*.[48]

It was three hundred years later, however, before the Scottish moral philosopher Adam Smith (1723–90) provided a *moral* framework within which competition could be conceived of as a *natural* and *beneficial* economic agent. Smith believed that

40. Chewning, *Business Ethics in a Changing Culture*, 31.
41. E. A. J. Johnson and Herman E. Krooss, *The American Economy: Its Origins, Development, and Transformation* (Englewood Cliffs, NJ: Prentice-Hall, 1960), 21.
42. Heilbroner, *Making of Economic Society*, 41.
43. Johnson and Krooss, *The American Economy*, 30–34.
44. Chewning, *Business Ethics in a Changing Culture*, 32.
45. Heilbroner, *Making of Economic Society*, 55–57.
46. Ibid., 57–58.
47. Ibid., 61.
48. Ibid., 62–63.

the capitalist proprietor . . . was not [to be] regarded as a paragon of virtue. Indeed it was Smith's distrust of businessmen which led him to place so much emphasis on the desirability of competition. . . . [T]he best way to restrain the social evils arising from business unscrupulousness, Smith felt, lay in vigorous business competition whereby over-reaching by one ambitious entrepreneur would be nullified by lower prices or better commodities offered to the public by his competitors.[49]

Even though Adam Smith wrote his seminal work *An Inquiry into the Nature and Cause of the Wealth of Nations*, in 1776, it was seventy years later before it drew the attention of practitioners and policymakers who adopted its "philosophical rationalization" to justify their "unphilosophical desires."[50]

The many forces mentioned above interacted with each other over hundreds of years and became the feedstock for capitalism.[51]

John Calvin's Economic Interjections into the Sixteenth-Century Worldview

Many of the important concepts and forces necessary for a free-market system were gestating or already emerging in relatively immature forms at the time of Calvin's birth. There were also, however, enormous restraining counterforces at work, suppressing the full emergence and acceptance of several extremely important components necessary for a free market to flourish. These restraints were being maintained by the Roman Catholic Church.

It is also important to understand the surroundings in which John Calvin was born and lived. Edward Dommen has probably outlined that environment as well as anyone in his "Introduction" to *John Calvin Rediscovered*.

49. Johnson and Krooss, *The American Economy*, 102.
50. Ibid., 103.
51. There are hundreds upon hundreds of quality writings and books that describe the multitude of people, events, social and political institutions, habits, customs, laws, wars, trading activities, economic forces, plagues, and many hundreds of other parts that resisted and advanced the ferment and movements that gave rise to the notion of "free markets" and the benefits derivable from them.

John Calvin lived entirely in an urban environment and was bathed in the atmosphere of nascent capitalism. His parents were bourgeois of Noyon in northern France, where his father was an ecclesiastical administrator. John's early studies were not in theology but law and letters. When he found it prudent to leave France in early 1535, he went to Basel, a *great trading center*. When passing through Geneva in mid-1536, at the age of 27, he was induced to stay and organize the Reformed church there. Geneva was also a long-established *center of trade and finance as well as manufacturing*. When he was forced to leave in 1538, he settled in yet *another trading city*, Strasbourg, before returning in 1541 to Geneva, where he remained until his death in 1564. *In this setting, his everyday contacts called upon him to deal with the moral problems of an urban economy. As a result, he thought more deeply about the subject than the other leading reformers of his time.*[52]

The most important (but not the only) contributions Calvin made to the flowering of capitalism were his pronouncements regarding (1) *work,* (2) the appropriate payment of *interest,* and (3) a positive understanding of *profits.*

Calvin's Worldview on Work

The teachings propagated by the Roman Catholic Church at the time of Calvin's birth were so dominating that it is impossible for us today to existentially grasp just how absorbed the Europeans were with matters related to one's personal salvation.[53] The church had tied pious works (defined by the church) to one's salvation. Before the Reformation, the typical citizen believed that he or she was beholden to the church for salvation, and that was tied to religious works.

The tensions between the Reformers and the Catholic Church were numerous, but two issues dominated the Reformation. They were,

---

52. Edward Dommen and James D. Bratt, eds., *John Calvin Rediscovered: The Impact of His Social and Economic Thought,* Princeton Theological Seminary Studies in Reformed Theology and History (Louisville and London: Westminster John Knox Press, 2007), vii (emphasis added). Also see Tawney, *Religion and the Rise of Capitalism,* 104: "Calvinism was largely an urban movement."

53. Tawney, *Religion and the Rise of Capitalism,* 31.

according to the Reformers: (1) Scripture alone was to be the guiding light directing people's faith and practice of life, and (2) Salvation was a free gift of God—*grace* alone—and not related to works of merit. Both Luther and Calvin hammered away to maintain these truths. Calvin's pronouncements on works are laid out in his *Institutes* (3.14). There the relationship between works and salvation is made clear.

Martin Luther (1483–1546) and subsequently John Calvin (1509–64) broadened the focus on works by placing them in the context of being a "response activity" related to God's grace and mercy rather than a "required activity" for salvation. The two men, however, focused on very different applications of the place of works in a person's life. They stood together on the truth that one cannot please God by any works apart from Christ. But Luther popularized the understanding that work is a calling—the cobbler, mother, silversmith, milkmaid, farmer, chimney sweep, and sailor each have a calling as important as that of the monk, cardinal, pope, or king. But Luther did not include merchants and bankers and other business types in his articulations regarding God's calling in life[54] because he "hated commerce and capitalism."[55]

Luther conceived of work as part of the "natural order," which he thought of as being represented in the rural and agricultural settings of Europe. He never respected commerce.[56] Calvin on the other hand saw life in urban centers and the accompanying commerce and applied Scripture to the economic challenges encountered in this context.[57] But both agreed that salvation was a free gift of grace and not a matter of works. This newly articulated truth raised two very important questions in the minds of those focused on personal salvation. First, "What does God expect of me if works are not a prerequisite for salvation?" And second, "If I cannot earn my salvation, then how can I know I am saved?"

The first question was answered similarly by Luther and Calvin: God has given us the ability to work and he has providentially placed us in a position in life where we are to use our talents *to glorify him*. His glory was

54. Max Weber, *The Protestant Ethic and the Spirit of Capitalism* (London: George Allen and Unwin, 1948), 79–92.
55. Tawney, *Religion and the Rise of Capitalism*, 92.
56. Ibid., 92–102.
57. Ibid., 102–9.

"to be sought not by prayer only, but by action—the sanctification of the world by . . . labor."[58] This translated into the understanding that everything we do should be done to honor and glorify God. God's glorification was declared to be the chief and highest end of humanity.[59]

Luther and Calvin answered the second question, "How can I know I am saved?" in strikingly different ways. Luther taught that people were to believe God's Word and live by *faith*, which would bring them an inward assurance of salvation.[60] Calvin's teaching took a different turn. Calvin emphasized the doctrines of election and predestination,[61] which set in motion a response that transformed the economic culture. Calvin in essence said that salvation is God's business. So, "How can I be assured that I am saved?" was morphed into, "How can I be sure that I am one of God's elect?"

The differences between the teachings of Calvin and the interpretations and applications of his teachings made by his followers and opponents alike are often enormous. Many of the teachers and hearers of the doctrines of election and predestination got it wrong. Nevertheless, Calvin's teaching regarding these doctrines became a core element in the Reformers' struggle to change the Roman Catholic Church. But Calvin's teachings morphed into "Calvin*ism*," which for most observers became virtually indistinguishable from John Calvin's precise teaching.[62] R. H. Tawney goes so far as to say, "Like the author of another revolution in economic theory, he [Calvin] might have turned on his popularizers with the protest: 'I am not a Calvinist.'"[63]

The question, "How do I know if I have been saved?" demanded an answer, even though Calvin taught that if you believed in Christ's atoning death you should not be preoccupied with your salvation. You should simply

---

58. Chewning, *Business Ethics in a Changing Culture*, 35.

59. "The Larger Catechism, agreed upon by The Assembly of Divines at Westminster, with the Assistance of Commissioners from the Church of Scotland, as a part of the covenanted uniformity in religion betwixt the churches of Christ in the kingdoms of Scotland, England, and Ireland. 1648: this formalized the position of the reformers." *The Confession of Faith: The Larger Catechism; The Shorter Catechism; The Directory for Public Worship; The Form of Presbyterial Church Government* (Edinburgh and London: William Blackwood & Sons, 1969), 49.

60. Weber, *Protestant Ethic*, 110–13.

61. Tawney, *Religion and the Rise of Capitalism*, 108–9.

62. Weber, *Protestant Ethic*, 108–28.

63. Tawney, *Religion and the Rise of Capitalism*, 107.

"work hard" in order to glorify God.[64] The logic of the day quickly became this: *"Works are not a way of obtaining salvation, but they are indispensable as a proof that salvation has been attained."*[65] This understanding of the relationship between salvation and works released a motivational tidal wave of energy theretofore unknown. Those who misunderstood Calvin's teaching were for all practical purposes caught up in an early form of "prosperity theology."

Calvin's teaching regarding election and predestination was the distinguishing characteristic of Calvinism that dominated the cultural struggles in the developing countries of England, the Netherlands, and France in the sixteenth and seventeenth centuries.[66] Hence, "wherever the doctrine of predestination was held, the question could not be suppressed whether there were any infallible criteria by which membership in the *electi* could be known."[67] The answer seemed to come in two parts. First, to doubt if you were saved was evidence of an "imperfect faith." Second, the best means of growing in one's self-confidence was to engage in "intense worldly activity" that would create abundance,[68] a sign that God had favored the individual, which was often twisted into, "I am one of the elect."

Had not Calvin made it clear that works were not to be tied to salvation? Yes he had, but Calvinism taught various interpretations of Calvin and did not always teach with the care and accuracy of Calvin himself. Although Calvin was cautious in nuancing his thoughts, some of his followers were not. Their misreading of Calvin often became associated with Calvinism.

Hard work became a major transitional force shifting the balance of power away from the economic teachings of the Roman Catholic Church. A new economic worldview slowly emerged.

Calvin's Worldview on Interest

The word *interest* was synonymous with *usury* in the fifteenth century. Both the Roman Catholic Church and the early Reformers considered

---

64. Ibid., 96.
65. Ibid., 109, emphasis added. By implication, only the unsaved are slothful.
66. Weber, *Protestant Ethic*, 98.
67. Ibid., 110.
68. Ibid., 111–12.

lending at interest to be sinful. Excommunication from the church was the typical penalty for doing so—church law forbade it.[69] Tawney quotes Luther as saying, "The greatest misfortune of the German nation is easily the traffic in interest.... The devil invented it, and the Pope, by giving his sanction to it [in limited circumstances] has done untold evil throughout the world."[70] Tawney pointed out that Luther "would refuse *usurers* the sacraments, absolution, and Christian burial."[71] Likewise, the Huguenots and the Dutch church in the sixteenth century frequently excluded the Lombards (bankers) from communion because of their involvement in lending money for interest.[72]

"Interest/usury" as it was understood in the Middle Ages has probably been written about and discussed as much as any economic factor of that era. Moreover, the regulations regarding just wages and just prices and the prohibition of charging interest were all closely tied to the power and dictates of the Roman Catholic Church. The church was, from its perspective, attempting to prevent economic gouging by those who controlled the supply of food and other goods during the Middle Ages. The regulations on prices, wages, and interest were intended as decrees of compassion.[73]

The stumbling block that emerged over this great span of time, however, was the failure of the "rule makers" (guildmasters, feudal lords, and church) either to perceive that a new way of doing business was being birthed or that a new economic system was emerging that had the possibility of elevating the material well-being of everyone willing to join in the effort. Lord Acton gave a lecture at Cambridge in 1895 in which he said, "After many ages persuaded of the headlong decline and impending dissolution of society, and governed by usage and the will of masters who were in their graves, the sixteenth century went forth armed for untried experience, and ready to watch with hopefulness a prospect of incalculable change."[74] There was a mood afoot in Europe in the sixteenth century

69. Chewning, *Business Ethics in a Changing Culture*, 32.
70. Tawney, *Religion and the Rise of Capitalism*, 95, qualification added.
71. Ibid., 95, emphasis added.
72. Weber, *Protestant Ethic*, 201n29.
73. Heilbroner, *Making of Economic Society*, 41.
74. Lord Acton, *A Lecture on the Study of History*, delivered on June 11, 1895, at Cambridge, England (Bibliolife, 2009), 9.

that demanded change, and John Calvin "birthed" the idea that charging interest could carry with it a sense of *moral legitimacy*.

The following quote from R. H. Tawney is an accurate summary of what Calvin interjected into the thinking of those concerned about the marketplace in the sixteenth century.

> Legends are apt . . . to be as right in substance as they are wrong in detail, and both its critics and its defenders were correct in regarding Calvin's treatment of capital as a watershed. What he did was to change the plane on which the discussion was conducted, by treating the ethics of money-lending, not as a matter to be decided by an appeal to a special body of doctrine on the subject of usury, but as a particular case of the general problem of the social relations of a Christian community, which must be solved in the light of existing circumstances. The significant feature in his discussion of the subject is that he assumes credit to be a normal and inevitable incident in the life of [a commercial] society. . . . [He] argues that the payment of interest for *capital* is as reasonable as the payment of *rent for land*, and throws on the conscience of the individual the obligation of seeing that it does not exceed the amount dictated by natural justice and the golden rule. He makes, in short, a fresh start.[75]

Whenever Calvin preached on "interest/usury" from a biblical text such as Exodus 22:25 he remained faithful to the full intent of its pronouncements: "If you lend money to any of my people with you who is poor, you shall not be like a moneylender to him, and you shall not exact interest from him." But he expounded in private letters to those in commerce and from the pulpit his views on an appropriate form of interest in the capital markets. As economic transactions became monetized and bartering goods disappeared to a large degree, and capital (money) was being sought for investment purposes with the intent of creating new capital, this presented an entirely different setting in which to think about interest—people were *renting capital*. The broader community agreed, and a new concept of renting money emerged and flourished.

But others before Calvin had attempted to define money in a similar manner. Why did their efforts fail while Calvin's message succeeded?

75. Tawney, *Religion and the Rise of Capitalism*, 107–8, emphasis added.

There are three possible reasons why Calvin's thinking was accepted and advanced. First, the time was ripe for such thinking; second, his thinking was logical and seemed to reflect common sense; and third, Calvin's teachings and thoughts attracted a wide following and created a movement that became known as "Calvinism." Calvinism carried Calvin's teachings across Europe and into the New World—North America.[76] This last point is why even today there is often confusion between Calvin and Calvinism.

Calvin's Worldview on Profits

The relationship between profits and the presumed motives of those making profits is perhaps one of the biggest quagmires of impugned moral iniquity in existence. Those not engaged in an entrepreneurial enterprise generally attribute a selfish motive to those making a profit without considering the fact that a service cannot be maintained when there is no profit. A profit is to business what a healthy blood count is to the body. But profit making from antiquity until the time of Calvin was most often thought to be sinful. It was taken for granted prior to the sixteenth century that profits needed to be "limited, restricted, [and] warned against." It was deemed all right to make enough to maintain one's "place or station in society," but doing more than that was seen as revealing a spirit of avarice, which was considered a deadly sin.[77]

> The whole idea of profit, and indeed the possibility of profit, was incompatible with the position occupied by the great medieval land-owner [or those in the Church]. Unable to produce for sale owing to the want of a market, he had no need to tax his ingenuity in order to wring from his men and his land a surplus which would merely be an encumbrance, and as he was forced to consume his own produce, he was content to limit it to his needs. His means of existence was assured by the traditional functioning of an organization which he did not try to improve.[78]

76. Ibid., 102.
77. Ibid., 32.
78. Henri Pirenne, *Economic and Social History of Medieval Europe* (New York: Harcourt, Brace & World, Harvest Books, 1956), 63.

The worldview exposed in the quote above was pervasive for centuries before the life of John Calvin. Furthermore, prior to the Reformation the Roman church supported such thinking. Stated simply, making a profit was neither necessary nor the Christian thing to do. Business, while necessary, was seen by the church and the Christian community as a very dangerous place to spend one's life.[79] *What Calvin did was provide the entire "economic enterprise" with a new sanctification.*[80]

Calvin taught that profits were the fruit of one's labor. They represented a person's good work. And good work reflected God's grace in that person's life which in turn resounded to God's glory. So profits were not frowned upon by Calvin.[81] His thinking and teaching were transforming. He set people free to work hard and reap the benefits that naturally accrued from their endeavors. The real world's transformation from an exclusively agrarian economy into an agrarian/commercial economy had lacked an accompanying adjustment in the worldview of those engaged in the political theological/economic spheres of the time.

Those influenced by Calvin—bankers, manufacturers, traders, and eventually the church—took on a very different attitude toward profits and the resulting wealth. If their religion approved "diligence," it did not approve "indulgence." Wealth had an entirely different purpose. It was not to be squandered on one's pleasure or used to demonstrate one's superiority. The new worldview that respected profits promoted a new morality: *thrift*. It made savings, the conscious abstinence of spending for one's enjoyment, a virtue. This in turn made the investing of one's savings for productive purposes an instrument of piety as well as profit. A new concept of economic life was born. The old "ideal" of economic and social stability was replaced by the acceptance of economic growth and material improvement for everyone.[82]

A quote that demonstrates just how profound and transforming Calvin's thinking and teachings were on work, interest, and profits is the following statement made by John Wesley (1703–91) during a later time of religious revival.

---

79. Johnson and Krooss, *The American Economy*, 21.
80. Tawney, *Religion and the Rise of Capitalism*, 34.
81. Chewning, *Business Ethics in a Changing Culture*, 34.
82. Heilbroner, *Making of Economic Society*, 54.

I fear, wherever riches have increased, the essence of religion has decreased in the same proportion. Therefore I do not see how it is possible, in the nature of things, for any revival of true religion to continue long. For religion must necessarily produce both industry and frugality, and these cannot but produce riches. But as riches increase, so will pride, anger, and love of the world in all its branches. How then is it possible that . . . a religion of the heart, though it flourishes now as a green bay tree, should continue in this state? For the Methodists in every place grow diligent and frugal; consequently they increase in goods. Hence they proportionately increase in pride, in anger, in the desire of the flesh, the desire of the eyes, and the pride of life. So, although the form of religion remains, the spirit is swiftly vanishing away. Is there no way to prevent this—this continual decay of pure religion? We ought not to prevent people from being diligent and frugal; *we must exhort all Christians to gain all they can, and to save all they can; that is, in effect, to grow rich.* [83]

Calvin thus nurtured basic values such as work, wealth accumulation, thrift, investment, risk assumption, competition, and productivity. Calvin indeed had a profound impact on the formulation and acceptance of a new worldview regarding commerce.

The Remains of Calvin's Thinking in the Twenty-First Century: The Perversions and Threats to its Continuation

The Book of Amos reveals God's displeasure with the perversions that arise in *all* economic systems. The ubiquitous nature of sin, like a cancer, eventually destroys the equity (not equality) and justice of all systems created for the production and distribution of scarce resources. Amos delivered numerous pronouncements against the rich for the unjust ways they treated the poor. For the sake of space, the charges laid at the feet of the wealthy by God through the prophet Amos can only be mentioned here in a footnote.[84] But greed had replaced kindness and charity 750 years before the birth of Christ. The people in Amos' day experienced God's displeasure for their economic sins and other forms of idolatry.

83. Weber, *Protestant Ethic*, 175 (Weber's emphasis).
84. Amos 2:4–8; 3:11–15; 4:1–2; 5:10–13; 6:1–7, 11–14.

So how much of John Calvin's influence on commerce remains in the twenty-first century? Few people are aware of just how much of his influence is still with us, for the history of capitalism is mostly forgotten. Calvin's teachings regarding *work*, *interest*, and *profits* were extremely influential in the creation of an economic system whose efficiency, productivity, and profitability provided the greatest door to material prosperity ever experienced after the fall. However, the free market's very success, rooted in the freedom to pursue economic security, became dominated by the desires for material success. The following biblical warning has been forgotten: "Beware lest you say in your heart, 'My power and the might of my hand have gotten me this wealth.'... And if you forget the LORD your God and go after other gods and serve them and worship them, I solemnly warn you today that you shall surely perish."[85] Calvin's godly teachings have been abandoned for the most part.

However, Calvin's economic thoughts are still with us to a discernable degree, though they often have morphed into something that looks similar but have a totally different motivational base, or have been so perverted that they have no responsible connection to Calvin's teachings. The remnants of Calvin's thinking regarding work, interest, and profits can be described as follows:

Work. Martin Luther's pronouncements regarding work are with us to a greater degree than those of John Calvin. Luther's simple but biblical teachings that God made us to work, that work is honorable, and that work is a calling are still expounded from many evangelical pulpits.

Calvin, however, accentuated an entirely different spiritual truth. He not only added that people should work hard in their efforts to glorify God,[86] but also taught about election and predestination. These stirred the mind. The question became, "If I cannot earn my salvation by works then how can I know if I am one of the elect and am predestined for eternal life with Christ?" The popular answer became: "Works are not a way of obtaining salvation, but they are indispensable as a *proof that salvation has been attained.*"[87] So hard work and its fruits (wealth and status) became

---

85. Deut. 8:17, 19.
86. Tawney, *Religion and the Rise of Capitalism*, 96.
87. Ibid., 109, emphasis added.

the self-assuring measure of one's right standing with God. Calvin did not teach this connection but many of his interpreters did. The results were revolutionizing, and prosperity slowly became one of the "new idols" to be worshiped instead of the Provider God.

No one, to this author's knowledge, has ever sought to track the rate of decline in the impact of the doctrine of predestination on the behavior of Christians from the seventeenth century onward. It seems safe to say, however, that while the topic of predestination is still alive and occasionally discussed in a small corner of the larger Christian family, it is in all probability rarely tied to one's work ethic today.

But the work ethic is alive and well to the point of being an obsession in the life of many people. The person who is perceived to be continually hard at work, even beyond the bounds of necessity, is sometimes referred to as a workaholic. Hourly workers are now protected by law from working more than a limited number of hours per week unless overtime is paid. But the productivity per hour of work continues to rise because much of it is tied to increased efficiency accomplished through ever-advancing technology.[88]

Entrepreneurs on the other hand are almost expected to work 60, 70, or even 80 hours a week. Their personal assets are at risk. They are not on anyone's payroll. They are rewarded only for their successful hard work. They perceive of themselves as being on their own and at the mercy of the forces at work in the free competitive marketplace. They don't believe in handouts or luck. They tend to have faith in themselves. This represents the worldview of the secular humanists and all others who are not "looking to Jesus."[89] Indeed, entrepreneurs and small businesses are the driving and innovative forces in the marketplace. This has been widely studied and commented on.[90]

---

88. The Bureau of Labor Statistics, an arm of the U.S. Labor Department, publishes a plethora of statistics on the Internet that show long-term advancements in the output of labor. Americans are still hard workers, for the most part. There are exceptions where there is "organized protection."

89. Heb. 12:1–2.

90. William J. Dennis Jr., Bruce D. Phillips, and Edward Starr, "BNET Business Network: Small Business Job Creation: the Findings and Their Critics," in *Business Economics* (July 1994).

The residual fallout of John Calvin's teaching regarding work, and the twists given to it by his early followers, is still much evident at the beginning of the twenty-first century. But the heart and soul of his teaching regarding works *for the glory of God* and its quickly perverted *proof* (evidence) *of God's favor* has been dismissed by the secular humanists as "nonsense" and widely abandoned by the Christian community. Hard work is very much alive but is utilized for idolatrous purposes with an ever-declining reference to a desire to glorify God. This form of godliness without the spiritual substance remains!

Interest. The concept of usury that was such a part of people's consciousness in the sixteenth century has diminished over the past five centuries. This has been particularly true over the past fifty years. For example, the Truth in Lending Act was passed by Congress in 1968 to require banks and other lenders to clearly disclose the rate of interest they were charging small borrowers. Prior to this legislation, banks and other lenders were telling those getting consumer loans that they were, for example, paying 6 percent for the money borrowed when they were in fact paying 12 percent for a one-year loan. This went unnoticed by the vast majority of borrowers because they did not understand interest calculations. To illustrate, the lending institution would calculate the 6 percent charge on the original balance of a $600 loan (.06 x $600 = $36) and spread the year's interest payment over the 12 monthly payments (Interest per month: $36/12 = $3 per month; Principal payment per month: $600/12 = $50 per month or a total payment of $53 per month). This resulted in a total interest payment of $36 on an average outstanding principal balance of $300 ($600/2 = average outstanding balance of $300 over the course of the year). This meant that the borrower paid $36 of interest over the year for an average of $300, or $36/$300 = 12 percent per year.[91]

---

91. The author confronted his banker with this reality prior to passage of the Truth in Lending Act, and the banker told me the rate was only 6 percent. When told it was really 12 percent, he asked, "How do you know that?" I told him I taught corporate finance, and he smiled and said, "Oh!" About six months after passage of that act, I was invited to speak at a credit conference in Richmond, Virginia, and was asked after my address—during which I had made no reference to the act—what I thought of it. I responded by saying I was sorry that such legislation was found to be needed, but it was, and I thought it was a good piece of legislation. I was loudly booed.

To further illustrate the public's shifting thought regarding interest, the Commonwealth of Virginia had a constitutional limit on the interest a financial institution could charge a customer (6 percent) as late as the 1970s. During the Carter presidency (1977–81), U.S. Treasury Bonds reached the height of having to pay 13 percent per annum on 30-year bonds. Virginia and other states were forced to amend their constitutions regarding interest payments or they would have experienced massive outflows of money from their financial institutions.[92] Market forces govern interest rates today, not statutory laws.

The infusion of consumer credit cards into the market in the 1960s virtually killed any remaining public or private concerns regarding usury. Consumers today know that they are paying a 12 percent to 22 percent annualized rate of interest on unpaid balances on credit cards. Churches are for the most part saying nothing about this, and the general public accepts this as being perfectly normal.

Again, Calvin's understanding and teaching that interest paid on borrowed money used for productive purposes is nothing more than a justifiable *rent* payment is universally accepted. What is new is the acceptance of paying interest (rent) on money borrowed by consumers (rather than producers) for the purpose of consuming tomorrow's expected income today. There are ethicists who find nothing wrong with this "new rent" (usury?), but paying such interest is clearly poor stewardship of one's resources.

Profits. Calvin established the legitimacy of profits in the sixteenth century.[93] The legitimacy of profits stands perhaps even stronger at the beginning of the twenty-first century. But what has changed dramatically over the past 500 years is what is considered the acceptable use of commercial profits.

Calvin believed profits provided an opportunity for meeting one's *needs*; extending *charity* to those with *needs*; and *expanding one's productive capability* to create goods, services, and jobs. These were understood as bringing glory to God. It is the goal of bringing glory to God that has almost disappeared from the thoughts of those seeking profits today.

92. This author was employed by the Virginia State Legislature as a consultant to work on this issue.
93. Tawney, *Religion and the Rise of Capitalism*, 104.

Profit is the engine that creates goods, services, and jobs. However, in many sectors that is virtually the only area that remains connected to the thoughts of John Calvin. The idea of profits meeting the *needs* of the poor is not heard in the conversations in the marketplace today. Wages may be thought of as taking care of needs, but the average American has garnered such a high standard of living that *wants*, not needs, typically motivate expenditures. The expression "keeping up with the Joneses" has been a gospel for three generations. Thorstein Veblen, an economist at the University of Chicago, wrote *The Theory of the Leisure Class*[94] at the turn of the twentieth century. In it he coined the phrase "conspicuous consumption"—people with wealth displaying their "status" through their expenditures.

The amassing of wealth today is thought of as providing for a high standard of living and security for one's family. It is rarely discussed as providing care for those less fortunate. As a nation we are the most generous people on earth, but it must be added that we give away only 2.2 percent of our private income annually. We gave $306 billion in 2007, of which $102.3 billion was given to religious organizations and $40.3 billion to educational institutions. Of the $306 billion, $229 billion was given by individuals and the balance by corporations and foundations.[95] While the gross dollars given appear to be a lot, the percentage "sacrificed" is a small percentage of the wealth created that was available for voluntary redistribution to worthy causes.

Many Christians give both a tithe *and* an offering to God's works, but Calvin would be sorely disappointed by the published statistics regarding the giving to churches within the broad Christian community. On income that went up 215 percent between 1968 and 2005, the average family reduced the percentage of their giving to the church from 3.11 percent to 2.58 percent, a 17 percent reduction. The amount of church giving that went for benevolent purposes declined from 0.66 percent to 0.39 percent over the same period of time, a 41 percent decline in the amount given to

94. Thorstein Veblen, *The Theory of the Leisure Class: An Economic Study in the Evolution of Institutions* (Macmillan: New York and London, 1899).

95. All of the above data are from Giving USA 2007, the Annual Report on Philanthropy, published by the AAFRC Trust for Philanthropy.

help those in need.[96] Calvin's concern that profits be used for charitable purposes is clearly not reflected in these statistics.

Conclusion

John Calvin was the leader of those who understood that the "whole purpose of God"[97] is rooted in the absolute sovereignty of God. Calvin also believed that the law revealed in special revelation was to find its application in the midst of an ongoing culture that encountered in its daily affairs the laws of natural revelation. The two laws when correctly understood should work in harmony. The principles found in the revealed law did not change but the environment in which the natural law was encountered was ever changing. However, the ubiquitous nature of sin that was released with the fall of our first parents is always present to cloud the unification of the two laws.[98] Calvin was not a "situationalist," but he believed in applying God's revealed principles in ever-changing cultural situations.

Calvin, upon engaging the culture of his day in the context of the commercial centers, reshaped the application of the biblical revelation to work, interest, and profits. His teachings ushered in freedom to the economic impulses that were struggling to be released from constraints imposed by those who retained the medieval worldview. Calvin, however, saw another reality: his application of God's Word to the world he observed provided an economic freedom heretofore not experienced.

Calvin's teachings had a transforming impact in the sixteenth century, and their radiating force is still with us in the twenty-first century. To be sure, his teachings may have become so infected with the sin that accompanies the separation between God and the vast majority of those who prosper in the marketplace that the "root/fruit" connection has been largely severed. Work is rarely spoken of today as a means to honor and glorify God. Consumer credit, with its accompanying interest, has become

96. Data are from The Empty Tomb Inc.'s Web site, which has a table of the State of Church Giving through 2005. This table has information from the U.S. Bureau of Labor Statistics Consumer Expenditures Survey, with data from 1968 to 2005.
97. Acts 5:20; 20:20; 20:27.
98. Tawney, *Religion and the Rise of Capitalism*, 102–32.

a means of encouraging consumers to spend next year's income today, and it is perverted to a much larger degree than its commercial counterpart. Commercial lending still follows very closely the reasoning of Calvin. Profits, as used by the professional managers who govern many of our larger corporations, have drifted far away from Calvin's defined purposes—to meet people's needs, to be used for charity, and to provide more and better goods and services. Only the last reason for profits remains in the mind of most owners and managers, and this has put the cart before the horse. Goods and services have become the means to profits, and profits have become the end objective of most businesses.[99]

A snippet of a quote from the letter of John Wesley reproduced earlier expresses a profound reality: "I fear, wherever riches have increased, the essence of religion has decreased in the same proportion."[100] Apart from the persevering grace and mercy of God there would be none walking faithfully with Christ. But with the help of the indwelling Holy Spirit, Christ's redeemed brothers and sisters still seek the "mind of Christ" in the Scripture regarding work, interest, and profits. To God be the glory!

99. The question of John Calvin's continuing influence on the free-market system has interested this author for years. In 1963 I submitted to my dissertation committee a proposal titled, "An Investigation and Comparison of the Historic and Contemporary Church Ethic with the Contemporary Creeds and Practices of Modern Business." The third paragraph of that proposal stated: "Max Weber is one of the most widely known authors on the subject of business ethics. His essay *The Protestant Ethic and the Spirit of Capitalism* synthesizes the ethic which emerged from the teachings of the major Protestant churches during the Reformation. The dominant ethic he labeled the Protestant Ethic. The central core of the Protestant Ethic, as described by Weber, was found in the teachings of John Calvin. The question is often asked today, does the Protestant ethic still exist as a force in the economic community? This proposed study should go a long way toward answering this question." The focus of the study was intended to be confined to the Presbyterian church. Its seminaries, churches, and congregants were to be sampled and questioned. The Presbyterian church was selected because it above all other Protestant denominations drew its heritage from Calvin's teachings. In conjunction with the proposal, the following "hypothesis" was constructed: "The ethic that is being taught businessmen by the clergy of the Presbyterian church in the 1960s is different from that which was taught by John Calvin and the Presbyterian clergy during the Protestant Reformation. Furthermore, contemporary business ethics, as revealed in business behavior and practices, does not conform to the religious teachings of the Presbyterian church, i.e., past or present." The dissertation proposal was rejected by the committee on the grounds that the conclusions would in all probability prove to be *subjective* and *un-provable*, i.e., unquantifiable.

100. Weber, *Protestant Ethic*, 175.

10

Calvin and Music

Paul S. Jones

J ohn Calvin was not silent about music. His writings on the subject
have had a lasting influence on Protestantism in general, and on
the Reformed church in particular. The strength of this Reformer's
convictions shaped the development of music in several countries. Our
task is to discuss Calvin from within the discipline of music. Since five
centuries have passed, it behooves us to explore Calvin's own statements
and practices as recorded. In taking up this challenge we shall consider the
Calvinist worldview, Calvin's contributions to music and his teaching on
music in worship, the development of the Huguenot Psalter, the historical contributions to Western music of certain Calvinistic musicians, and
guiding principles for Christian musicians.

The Calvinist Worldview

At the core of Calvin's theology is the juxtaposition of man's total
depravity with God's irresistible grace. Our need for redemption is answered

with the salvation found in Christ, worked out through faith by grace alone via justification and sanctification—the work of the Holy Spirit. Calvin taught that holiness and piety should characterize the believer. The follower of Christ must shun worldliness and look to the Word of God as the authority for life and godliness. As B. B. Warfield put it:

> He who believes in God without reserve and is determined that God shall be God to him in all his thinking, feeling and willing—in the entire compass of his life activities, intellectual, moral and spiritual—throughout all his individual social and religious relations, is, by force of that strictest of logic which presides over the outworking of principles into thought and life, by the very necessity of the case, a Calvinist.[1]

James Montgomery Boice, pastor, theologian, and Calvinist, taught that the proper Christian worldview appears in Paul's doxology from Romans 11:33–36—that all things are from, through, and to God, and therefore every matter should be characterized by and result in glory to God alone (*soli Deo gloria*).[2] Immediately following that passage, Romans 12:1–2 describes our need for mind renewal and the call to present ourselves as living sacrifices. This requires the conforming of our daily activities and decisions to the will of Christ.

As Calvinists we describe the work for which God has fit us and given us a desire as our "calling"—full-time Christian ministry, irrespective of vocation. Calvin regarded all service offered to God as worship and the whole of life as an enactment of the grace of God.[3] This carries the idea of sacrificing ourselves daily in thought, word, and deed. The union of Christ with the believer is such that all that is Christ's is also ours in him. This mystical union is the work of the Holy Spirit, grafting us into Jesus more and more (through sanctification) until we are completely one with him.

1. B. B. Warfield, *Calvin as a Theologian and Calvinism Today*, quoted in A. N. Martin, *The Practical Implications of Calvinism* (Edinburgh: Banner of Truth, 1979), 4.
2. James Montgomery Boice, *Romans: An Expositional Commentary*, vol. 3 (Grand Rapids: Baker, 203), 1465–72.
3. Philip W. Buin, "Reformed Ecclesiology: Trinitarian Grace According to Calvin," in David Willis-Watkins, ed., *Studies in Reformed Theology and History* 2, 1 (Winter 1994): 27.

Calvin taught that obedience to Christ results in joy and that rejoicing should characterize the people of God. He was also a serious, earnest man who always tempered comments about enjoying God's gifts with warnings against their abuse. Yet he was no prude or killjoy. He celebrated marital union and sexuality in a day when scholars typically remained single. He supported biblical plays and even comedies in Geneva. He had, colleagues reported, a great sense of humor as well as a rather fiery temper. He enjoyed fine wine (sometimes provided by the city council in recognition of his labors). He liked to play darts, and he permitted games and other recreation on the Sabbath outside of service times, including shooting for prizes.[4] Calvin did not condone dancing, believing that it was lewd and lascivious. But Roman Catholic and other Protestant leaders frowned on dancing too.

Calvin was not the narrow, austere, utilitarian, legalistic theologian some make him out to be. He had a considerable capacity for pleasure, as is clear from his *Institutes*:

> Has the Lord clothed the flowers with the great beauty that greets our eyes and the sweetness of smell that is wafted upon our nostrils, and yet it is not permissible for our eyes to be pleased by that beauty, or our sense of smell by the sweetness of that odor? Did the Lord not distinguish colors, making some more lovely than others? Did he not endow gold and silver, ivory and marble, with a loveliness that renders them more precious than other metals or stones? Did he not, in short, render many things attractive to us, apart from their utility?[5]

Philip Ryken has written, "The doctrines of grace help to preserve all that is right and good in the Christian life: humility, holiness, and

---

4. Percy A. Scholes, "Calvin and Music," in *The Puritans and Music* (London: Oxford, 1934), 334, 343. Scholes draws some of this information from R. N. Carew Hunt's book, *Calvin* (London: Centenary Press, 1933), 149, 176, 186. Scholes states that it is "pretty clear from a reading of the records that the English and Scottish idea of the sanctity of the 'Sabbath' did not derive from Geneva. Any restrictions appear to have applied merely to service hours, and even so they were not always strictly enforced." Tim Keller echoes this when he writes, "Calvin believed that Christ so fulfilled the Sabbath that the Old Testament regulations regarding Sabbath observance are not really binding on worshipers today at all (the Puritans and the Westminster Confession, of course, disagreed sharply with him)." See Timothy J. Keller, "Reformed Worship in the Global City," in D. A. Carson, ed., *Worship by the Book* (Grand Rapids: Zondervan, 2002), 206.

5. *Institutes*, 3.10.2.

thankfulness, with a passion for prayer and evangelism. The true Calvinist ought to be the most outstanding Christian—not narrow and unkind, but grounded in God's grace and therefore generous of spirit."[6] This should be the worldview and practice of a Calvinistic musician.

Calvin's Contributions to Music and his Teaching about Music in Worship

Congregational Singing

Upon his 1536 arrival in Geneva, a medium-sized, sixteenth-century city of 13,000 people, Calvin established daily gatherings for psalm singing and expository preaching.[7] He and his older colleague Guillaume Farel agreed that the congregation should be singing psalms together, and they made such a request of the city council. The council agreed but was slow to act. When the two Reformers were expelled from Geneva in early 1538, congregational singing in church was still not the common practice. At this point, Farel went to Basel and Calvin to Strasbourg, where he encountered Martin Bucer (1491–1551). Calvin accepted Bucer's invitation to become pastor of the French refugee church in Strasbourg.

Bucer's German church included congregational singing on a grand scale. Although Calvin encountered congregational singing in Basel in 1535, in Strasbourg he heard 2,000 German Christians of all ages unite in song. These were under the direction of a precentor who led his choir of schoolchildren to aid the congregation. Imagine how powerful and moving this experience must have been for Calvin! In the Roman churches of the time priests chanted in Latin, and choirs of professional singers predominantly sang polyphonic choral music in Latin; there was neither congregational song nor any church music in the common tongue.

6. Philip Graham Ryken, *What is a True Calvinist?* (Phillipsburg, NJ: P&R Publishing, 2003), 6.

7. Derek Thomas, "Who Was John Calvin?" in Burk Parsons, ed., *John Calvin: A Heart for Devotion, Doctrine, and Doxology* (Lake Mary, FL: Reformation Trust, 2008), 24.

The *Strasbourg German Service Book* of 1525 contained numerous metrical psalms and hymns, including two hymns by Luther.[8] The 1537 version integrated all 150 psalms (in German) with festal hymns, morning and evening hymns, and catechetical hymns.[9] Calvin decided that something similar to the German church's congregational singing needed to happen in French churches.

In 1537, before his exile from Geneva, Calvin and the other ministers had written to the council:

> This way to proceed to this seemed good to us: if some children, to whom we have previously taught a simple church song, sing in a high, distinct voice, to which the people listen attentively, following with their hearts what is sung by mouth, until little by little they become accustomed to sing a song together.[10]

When the council in Geneva invited Farel and Calvin back, the Reformers made the introduction of congregational singing a condition of their return. A precentor leading musical worship with a choir of schoolchildren was one of the practices transferred from Strasbourg for Geneva. The Genevan Church Order puts it this way: "One must begin by teaching the little children, the congregation will then follow."[11]

There may have been other significant reasons to have a musical director. The exiled Dutch Reformed Church's Convent of Wezel (1568) states: "In places where there is a school, the schoolmaster will teach the youth of the church how to sing psalms. Then the congregation can sing along with

---

8. Martin Luther, called the "father of congregational song," had earlier written 36 chorales (hymns), some based on psalms, for Germanic congregations. He held that congregational song was a great outworking of the doctrine of the priesthood of all believers. The service book in Strasbourg also included others by Matthias Greiter, Wolfgang Dachstein, Johannes Englisch, Heinrich Vogtherr, and Ludwig Oehler. Martin Bucer's commentary on the Hebrew psalms had considerable influence on the Strasbourg psalmodists.

9. Hughes Oliphant Old, *Worship: Reformed According to Scripture*, rev. ed. (Louisville: Westminster John Knox, 2002), 43–44.

10. Aimé Louis Herminjard, ed., *Correspondance des Réformateurs dans les pays de langue française*: 602, 4:162f., as quoted in T. Brienen, "The Sung Prayers (1)" *RMJ* 12, 1 (January 2000): 17.

11. Ford Lewis Battles, *The Piety of John Calvin* (Phillipsburg, NJ: P&R Publishing, 2009), 143n27. This is found in Article 79 of the Genevan Church Order.

the children."[12] "Lacking this [a school] it will be expedient to appoint a precentor to lead the people in the singing and to moderate and regulate the same, particularly in places where the preacher is totally inexperienced in the art of music."[13] Many churches today would benefit by obtaining a skilled musical leader for the same reason.

The Psalters

Strasbourg Psalter, 1539. While in Strasbourg, Calvin versified six psalms for his four hundred-member French congregation. He also wrote two hymns, based on the Ten Commandments and the *Nunc dimittis,* and he penned a French version of the Creed in prose (versified later for the 1542 Genevan Psalter).[14] Some Genevan loyalists call the Strasbourg psalter-hymnal the "first edition of the Genevan Psalter." Published in 1539, the Strasbourg contained 19 psalms and Calvin's hymns and Creed with the title, *Aulcuns pseaumes et cantiques mys en chant* (*Some Psalms and Hymns Arranged for Singing*). It included standard liturgies for the Lord's Day, matins, vespers, baptism, and the marriage service.[15] Clément Marot (ca. 1496–1544), the most famous French lyric poet of the sixteenth century, had versified the other 13 psalms. In later editions, Calvin withdrew his own psalms in favor of Marot's superior verse. Marot studied Martin Bucer's commentary on the Psalms in order to understand the Hebrew text well enough to write beautiful poetic versifications.[16] Matthias Greiter, Bucer's precentor, probably compiled this psalter for Calvin.[17]

12. S. Vander Ploeg, "Psalmen Datheni," in *RMJ* 2, 2 (April 1990): 54, quoting Evert Westra, *Uit Sions Zalen. Een kerkmuzikale handreiking* (Baarn: Bosch & Keuning, 1966), 38.

13. Ibid., 54, quoting Westra, 39.

14. The Ten Commandments were in twelve stanzas with *Kyrie eleisons* intervening. The *Nunc dimittis* is the New Testament canticle of Simeon from Luke 2.

15. Old, *Worship,* 45.

16. Hughes Oliphant Old, in e-mail correspondence July 28, 2009, referring to Samuel Lenselink's book, *Les Psaumes de Clément Marot* (Assen: Van Gorcum, 1969), wrote, "The important thing about this work is that it shows that Clément Marot used Martin Bucer's commentary on the psalms as his guide to understanding the Hebrew text. It shows a much more positive relationship between Marot and the Reformation than the nineteenth-century church historians wanted to admit." Marot's translations were titled "The Psalms of David newly put into French according to the true Hebrew."

17. T. H. L. Parker, *John Calvin: A Biography* (London: J. M. Dent & Sons, 1975), 88. See more about Greiter below in the section on early Calvinistic musicians.

Although Calvin made the psalms a priority in this and successive volumes, he cannot be called an "exclusive psalmodist," for the hymns included here were his own. At the end of the Strasbourg a verse that referred to both psalms and hymns was included: *"Pseaume et chant je chanteray à un seul Dieu, tant que je seray"* (*Psalms and hymns will I sing before the only God as long as I am*). A later edition included a hymn that has been credited to Calvin, *Je te salue, mon certain Rédempteur* (sung in English as "I Greet Thee, Who My Sure Redeemer Art").[18]

Important observations can be drawn from Calvin's efforts. First, his hymns and psalms were written to existing melodies from the German Strasbourg collection. Calvin was taking ownership of the worship of his congregation, and was trying to do something helpful, probably quickly. Second, the tunes were chosen because they "pleased him the most" (preference and opinion were involved). Third, the hymns he versified were from both Old and New Testaments. Fourth, the Creed was not divinely inspired but was included anyway, making it an anomaly.

This is not the place to take up a full discussion of exclusive psalmody or the regulative principle, but I refer the reader to Vern Poythress's outstanding essay in which he concludes that the *biblical* position (based on the example, ministry, and singing of Christ himself) is that congregational singing may include *any words that communicate the teaching of Scripture*.[19] Poythress argues from Ezra 3:

> The essence of the regulative principle is that our worship must be in Christ: it is conformity in thought, word, and deed, heart, soul, mind, and strength, corporately and individually, to the sovereign, glorious, exalted ministry of Christ, as prophet, priest, and king, at the right hand of God. We insist that we do not go beyond Scripture, but with the wisdom of Christ seek to understand Scripture, when we say that this Scripture (as we have argued) enjoins us to sing with both the 150 and other songs, as the needs of teaching may require.[20]

18. Whether or not this is accurately ascribed to Calvin is a matter of debate.

19. See Vern S. Poythress, "Ezra 3, Union with Christ, and Exclusive Psalmody," in *WTJ* 37 (Fall 1974–Spring 1975): 74–93, 218–35. He states, "The point is, Christ sings New Testament words as well as the 150 psalms. He sings not only to God but among the nations" (91).

20. Ibid., 232.

Genevan Psalter, 1542 (Huguenot Psalter). First published in 1542 as *La forme des prières et chants ecclésiastiques* (*The Form of Prayers and Ecclesiastical Songs*), the Genevan Psalter became known as the Huguenot Psalter. The 1542 version included 35 psalms (30 by Marot and 5 by Calvin), Calvin's hymns on the Song of Simeon and the Decalogue, and Marot's version of the Creed in metrical form. The book begins with an important Preface, which deals with the order of worship, the administration of sacraments, and in the last section, singing. We will explore this Preface more below. In 1542, Marot, who was persecuted in France, fled to Geneva as a refugee and stayed a year. We are unsure of the circumstances, but he and Calvin met and decided to work together.

Genevan Psalter, 1543 (Huguenot Psalter). In 1543, the Psalter was reprinted with 50 psalms, twenty of which were new, with improvements made to Marot's previous 30—a productive year indeed.[21] All 50 were now Marot's, and his version of the Decalogue was included as were two "table songs" or Graces for mealtime and a setting of the Lord's Prayer. Each psalm had its own melody, with many of the new tunes composed by Guillaume Franc. These psalms were placed on a rotating schedule for worship so that each was sung once every 17 weeks. The Preface or Foreword dated June 10, 1543, was now almost twice as long as the previous year, and much that had been added to it concerned music. There were 140 words on music in the 1542 version and 917 in 1543.

In the Preface, also called "The Epistle to the Reader," Calvin describes the function and value of singing in the context of worship and makes a case for the priority of singing the Psalms of David. He cites didactic and doxological reasons for choosing the psalms, which at their core are christological. "In contrast to both scholastics and Anabaptists, Calvin argued for the substantial identity of God's revelation to the ancient Hebrews and to the Christians. . . . The Old Testament and thus the Psalms were interpreted Christologically and as prophetic of the life of the church."[22] Let us consider the Preface in closer detail.

---

21. Some sources say only forty-nine psalms were included in the 1543 version. Pidoux mentions fifty. Calvin withdrew his own versifications during the year as Marot wrote new ones to replace them.

22. James H. Nichols, "The Intent of the Calvinistic Liturgy," in John Bratt, ed., *The Heritage of John Calvin* (Grand Rapids: Eerdmans, 1973), 96 and 97ff. Poythress says the christological character of the canonic Psalter is not the question. "The question is whether one can do justice

The Preface to the Psalter (1543). For Calvin, singing was prayer. He thus includes song as one of the three essential elements of Reformed worship (preaching, prayer, and the sacraments). He opens the Preface with general church topics but then says,

> As to the public prayers, these are of two kinds: some are offered by means of words alone, the others with song. And this is not a thing invented a little time ago, for it has existed since the first origin of the Church; this appears from the histories, and even Saint Paul speaks not only of praying by word of mouth: but also of singing.[23]

With this statement Calvin establishes historical precedent for his view. He links it with Paul and the traditions of the early church. In fact, the Greek philosopher Plato, the apostle Paul, and the early church fathers, particularly Augustine (354–430), and John Chrysostom (ca. 347–407), influenced Calvin's thoughts about music. He quotes all four in the 1543 Preface. Calvin writes of music:

> There is hardly anything in the world with more power to turn or bend, this way and that, the morals of men, as Plato has prudently considered. And in fact we find by experience that it has a secret and almost incredible power to move our hearts in one way or another. Wherefore we must be the more diligent in ruling it in such a manner that it may be useful to us and in no way pernicious.[24]

For Calvin it is music's *emotional* power that is so significant. He writes, "We know by experience that song has great force and vigor to

to the unveiled character of Christ's revelation of the name of God in the New Testament." He says that Hebrews 2:12 "pictures Christ as singing to the congregation the account of the eschatological deliverance of God's chosen One (cf. the context of Psalm 22), which the Psalter speaks of only in provisional form." Poythress, "Ezra 3," 85. He adds, "Romans 15:9 confirms our statement that Christ sings the name of God in fullness to the congregation." Ibid., 86n10. Isaac Watts carried this christological aspect of the psalms a step further when in his psalm paraphrases he endeavored to make Christ's work explicit. Some have criticized Watts for this.

23. John Calvin, "Genevan Psalter: Foreword," in Oliver Strunk, ed., *Source Readings in Music History: From Classical Antiquity through the Romantic Era* (New York: Norton, 1950), 346. See also 1 Cor. 14:15.

24. Ibid., 347.

move (*d'esmouvoir*) and inflame (*enflamber*) the hearts of men to invoke and praise God with a more vehement and ardent zeal."[25] He then narrows his focus:

> Now in speaking of music I understand two parts, namely, the letter, or subject and matter, and the song, or melody. It is true that, as Saint Paul says, every evil word corrupts good manners, but when it has the melody with it, it pierces the heart much more strongly and enters within; as wine is poured into the cask with a funnel, so venom and corruption are distilled to the very depths of the heart by melody. Now what is there to do? It is to have songs not merely honest but also holy, which will be like spurs to incite us to pray to God and praise Him, and to meditate upon His works in order to love, fear, honor, and glorify Him.[26]

Although less optimistic than Luther, this is much like Luther's well-known statements:

> Music and notes, which are wonderful gifts and creations of God, do help gain a better understanding of the text, especially when sung by a congregation and when sung earnestly.

> We have put this music to the living and holy Word of God in order to sing, praise and honor it. We want the beautiful art of music to be properly used to serve her dear Creator and his Christians. He is thereby praised and honored and we are made better and stronger in faith when his holy Word is impressed on our hearts by sweet music.[27]

Like Luther, Calvin believes that music can teach the Word and is a concentrator of the text it carries.[28] The funnel imagery he bor-

---

25. Ibid., 346.

26. Ibid., 347–48.

27. Martin Luther, "Preface to the Burial Hymns (1542)," in Ulrich S. Leupold, ed. and trans., *Luther's Works*, American Edition, vol. 53: *Liturgy and Hymns* (Philadelphia: Fortress Press, 1965), 328.

28. Charles Garside Jr., "Calvin's Preface to the Psalter: A Re-Appraisal," *RMJ* 2, 4 (October 1990): 130. Reprinted from *The Musical Quarterly* 37 (1951): 566–77.

rowed from Plato's *Republic*.[29] The Spirit uses music to illuminate the mind and to grant understanding to the heart. Music can also be misused, however; and this is the danger against which Calvin warns the reader—music's capacity to deliver and reinforce damaging textual content. This danger can extend to all musical aspects (melody, harmony, rhythm, and form). But as William Edgar points out, "Calvin does not seem to have thought about musical structure as a crucial aspect of the content."[30]

Calvin then closes in toward his primary subject even more:

> Now what Saint Augustine says is true—that no one can sing things worthy of God save what he has received from Him. Wherefore, although we look far and wide and search on every hand, we shall not find better songs nor songs better suited to that end than the Psalms of David which the Holy Spirit made and uttered through him. And for this reason, when we sing them we may be certain that God puts the words in our mouths as if Himself sang in us to exalt His glory.[31]

The principles from the earlier preface are strengthened and further applied to church worship in 1543; moreover, Calvin expands his discussion to music *in all of life*. This would explain why the table songs were included:

> For even in our homes and in the fields it [singing] should be an incentive, and as it were an organ for praising God and lifting up our hearts to Him, to console us by meditating upon His virtue, goodness, wisdom, and justice, a thing more necessary than one can say.[32]

29. "So when someone gives himself over to musical training and lets the flute pour into his soul through his ears, as through a funnel, those sweet, soft, and plaintive harmonies we mentioned; and when he spends his whole life humming, entranced by song, the first result is that whatever spirit he had he softens the way he would iron and makes useful rather than useless and brittle." Plato, *Republic*, 3.411a.

30. William Edgar, *Taking Note of Music* (London: SPCK, 1986), 82–83. Though beyond the scope of this chapter, one could explore this in considerable detail—the manner in which the elements of musical structure communicate truth or other information.

31. Calvin, "Genevan Psalter: Foreword," 348.

32. Ibid., 346–47.

John Chrysostom contrasted the effects of *strange chants* or *licentious songs* "where demons congregate" to *spiritual psalms* where the singers find themselves "in the company of angels." He was not referring to church practice but to music generally. Calvin wrote: "Wherefore Chrysostom exhorts men as well as women and little children to accustom themselves to sing them [the psalms], in order that this may be like a meditation to associate them[selves] with the company of the angels."[33]

Had Calvin's thinking expanded so much in a year? Perhaps people were asking him about music outside of worship, necessitating additional teaching. At a fundamental level, Calvin wanted his people to revel in the joy of the Christian life, to rejoice in the work of God's Son on their behalf in all places and times, which is why he says:

> In the first place, it is not without reason that the Holy Spirit exhorts us so carefully by means of the Holy Scriptures to rejoice in God and that all our joy is there reduced to its true end, for He knows how much we are inclined to delight in vanity. Just as our nature, then, draws us and induces us to seek all means of foolish and vicious rejoicing; so, to the contrary, our Lord, to distract us and withdraw us from the enticements of the flesh and of the world, presents to us all possible means in order to occupy us in that spiritual joy which He so much recommends to us.[34]

Near the end of the Preface, Calvin addresses the world, not just believers, offering a final purpose for the Psalter:

> But may the world be so well advised that instead of the songs that it has previously used, in part vain and frivolous, in part stupid and dull, in part foul and vile, and consequently evil and harmful, it may accustom itself hereafter to sing these divine and celestial hymns with the good king David.[35]

Calvin abhorred vanity, frivolity, and stupidity, and frequently protested against such things in his writings. Here he relates these to secular

33. Ibid., 348.
34. Ibid., 347.
35. Ibid., 348.

song. How much more would he have railed against them characterizing worship music!

Calvin's fears about music and his resulting strictures, sadly, have frequently discredited his good ideas concerning it. As Edgar points out:

> He shared this fear of music with the Church Fathers, who were hostile toward the use of instruments in worship. . . . The problem for us is that there is much truth in the fear expressed. Music does have a particular power to move, and it is therefore to be handled with great care by those who make use of it. Nevertheless that is not sufficient reason to put it at a distance. At any rate, rather than focus the same intensity of reforming zeal on music and the arts, many Protestants since Calvin's time have failed to deal biblically and wisely with music.[36]

Calvin was not an enemy of the arts as some have claimed. One opponent, the nineteenth-century Protestant preacher Orentin Douen, referred to Calvin as the "Pope of Geneva . . . an enemy of all pleasure and distraction, even of the arts and of music."[37] Even at the five hundredth anniversary of Calvin's birth on July 10, 2009, while people came from all over the world to pay tribute, Genevans themselves organized an outdoor play where, at the conclusion, a stone statue of Calvin was berated for his repressive rule. What stood out to one American pastor, to quote the *Wall Street Journal*, was "Geneva's antipathy to Calvin—not ambivalence, antipathy."[38] Unfortunately that sentiment is rather widespread, although it is more often the fault of Calvinists who have mishandled his teaching than of Calvin himself.

While Calvin may have frustrated his learned musical colleagues at times by insisting on unison singing in worship rather than permitting already implied four-part harmony to be heard (let alone settings requiring greater artistry), he was *not* against art or music. The Preface delivers his candid thoughts:

36. Edgar, *Taking Note of Music*, 83.

37. Orentin Douen, *Clément Marot et le psautier Huguenot. Études historiques littéraires, musicales et bibliographiques* (Paris, 1878–79), 1.377, as quoted in Charles Garside Jr., "Calvin's Preface, to the Psalter" 124.

38. David Skeel, *Wall Street Journal*, July 31, 2009.

Now among the other things proper to recreate man and give him plea-sure, *music is either the first or one of the principal*; and we must think that it is a *gift of God* deputed to that purpose. For which reason we must be the more careful not to abuse it, for fear of soiling and contaminating it, converting it to our condemnation when it has been dedicated to our profit and welfare.[39]

This statement resonates with Luther's view of music as one of God's greatest gifts, second only to theology and next to the Word of God itself in significance, although Calvin does not go that far. However, Calvin was not a musical theologian praising his art as Luther often did, but rather a lawyer-philosopher-theologian untrained in music.[40] This makes Calvin's statements in praise of music all the stronger. As Jeremy Begbie puts it, "Calvin's caution about music arises from his vigorous respect for music's particular and potent eloquencies."[41]

Genevan Psalter, 1551 (Huguenot Psalter). In 1551 another version of the Psalter was published (*Pseaumes octante trois de David*), with 83 psalms, 34 of these written by Theodore de Bèze (1519–1605), who succeeded Marot in 1548. Calvin wanted Marot to versify all 150 psalms, but Marot could not tolerate living conditions in Geneva and left. Bèze reports the personal role Calvin played in passing Marot's torch to him: "On the urgings of the great Dr. Johan Calvin, I have completed the rhyming of the psalms in French verses, begun by Clé-ment Marot, undisputed prince of the French poets of his time."[42] We must credit Calvin with engaging the finest poets and musicians he could find for this important work. If only evangelical and Reformed

39. Calvin, "Genevan Psalter: Foreword," italics added.
40. Garside, "Calvin's Preface to the Psalter," 128.
41. Jeremy Begbie, "Music, Word and Theology Today: Learning from John Calvin," in Lyn Holness and Ralf Wustenberg, eds., *Theology in Dialogue: The Impact of the Arts, Humanities, and Science on Contemporary Religious Thought*, Essays in Honor of John W. de Gruchy (Grand Rapids, Eerdmans, 2002), 19.
42. Pierre Pidoux, "History of the Genevan Psalter II," *RMJ* 1, 2 (April 1989): 33. A translation and reprint by permission of Librarie Droz S.A. Geneva. Psalm versification proceeded at a much slower pace after Marot. A reprint in 1554 added six psalms, and a seventh was added in 1557, but none of these were given new melodies. This became a trend, with 25 of the psalms of the 1562 version using repeated melodies rather than being assigned unique tunes. Bèze was responsible for 101 of the final psalm versifications.

churches followed those high standards today! The expanded *Psalter* spread the singing of the psalms over 25 weeks instead of 17, rendering earlier versions useless.[43]

Louis Bourgeois, musical editor for the 1551 Psalter, used the opportunity to correct printing errors in earlier versions of the music. He also simplified some melodic lines to make them more intuitive for the average singer, brought unity to the notation by retaining just two different note values and their corresponding rests, and made improvements to the layout. He replaced 12 previously used melodies with new ones that he composed, and altogether made changes in 23 existing melodies.[44] This caused a ruckus with the civil authorities, which we shall discuss more below. Bourgeois was also the composer for Bèze's new psalm versifications.

Genevan Psalter, 1562 (Huguenot Psalter). There are 125 different melodies for the 150 psalms in the complete 1562 Genevan Psalter. The variety of metric strophe-forms and verse structures necessitated differing melodies and meters.[45] Interestingly, the creedal hymn is no longer found in the 1562 Psalter.[46] Calvin, apparently, was changing his view regarding what should be sung in worship. By now 27,400 copies of the Huguenot Psalter had been printed in Geneva alone. It went through 19 Genevan editions, seven more from Paris, and three from Lyon.[47] Like a good general mobilizing his army for Reformation throughout Francophone lands, Calvin sent forth the Huguenot Psalter. "Realizing that a line sung from a psalm would touch the head and heart more deeply than a phrase read from the *Institutes*, Calvin used the Psalter to combine word and music."[48] This 1562 *Psalter* set

---

43. Pidoux, "History of the Genevan Psalter," 34.

44. Bernard Smilde, "The Psalms of Israel: Inspired and Inspiring," in *RMJ* 7, 4 (October 1995): 110. Translated from the Dutch and reprinted by permission of the author.

45. Pidoux says there are 116 different tunes. Some report 124 and others, 126. There are 109 or 110 different meters for these; only 3 meters are used more than twice!

46. Begbie, "Music, Word, and Theology," 12. Begbie mentions the table songs (which actually were Marot's and included by 1543), but says the Creed did not make it into the 1542 version. He is correct that Calvin's did not, but Marot's was included.

47. Herman J. Selderhuis, *John Calvin: A Pilgrim's Life* (Downers Grove, IL: InterVarsity, 2009), 241.

48. Ibid.

the standard for subsequent French Reformed psalters as well as those in English, Dutch, German, and Hungarian.[49]

The Psalm Tunes and the Influence of the French Renaissance

The psalm melodies were written in the ancient church or "psalm" modes. Calvin desired this connection with the early church, which had adapted these Greek-modified modes from the Jewish eight-tone, synagogue system. The desire to revive earlier practice is typical of Calvin's humanistic training. To Renaissance ears, these modes carried associated rhetorical meaning.[50] In 50 of the psalm tunes, fragments of Gregorian material can be found, while in 11, ancient hymns are recognizable.[51] A cultural-musical-ecclesiastical tradition of the Middle Ages and earlier was continued in these settings. Psalm singing is thereby intrinsically linked to Calvin's program of restoring the face of the ancient church.[52]

Something should be said about the way Calvin's musical reforms were influenced by Renaissance musical values, particularly the early Renaissance before sacred music became so polyphonically complex that even the Roman Catholic Church called for its reform.[53] These values include simplicity, a word-note relationship where music serves the text, clarity,

49. Joel R. Beeke, "Calvin on Piety," in Donald K. McKim, ed., *The Cambridge Companion to John Calvin* (Cambridge: Cambridge, 2009), 138–39. The Anglo-Genevan psalter is still used in Canadian Reformed Churches as the *Book of Praise*, and it employs all the Genevan tunes.

50. For example, the Phrygian mode was linked with texts where confession of sin or pleas for mercy were primary, whereas the Mixolydian mode fit texts associated with heaven, the immensity of God, and human response to such things (such as Ps. 19). In some early editions the names of the modes were printed as superscriptions with each psalm. This served as an indicator for the psalm's central theme. The Ten Commandments were set, fittingly, to a Hypomixolydian melody, a mode connoting expectation or a looking up in full confidence with a joyful certainty. See Jan Smelik, "Sing, All You Saints, With One Accord," in *RMJ* 2, 1 (January 1990): 12.

51. Smilde, "The Psalms of Israel," 110. As an aside, it is interesting that a new Roman Catholic book, *Les rossignols spirituels* (1616), called singers to reclaim the musical property "stolen" from them by the Huguenots! When one considers the limitations imposed by the psalm modes and the work necessary to match theological ideas with them, repetition and phrases that seem to quote Gregorian chant would understandably occur, even unintentionally, particularly when the composers already knew such chant melodies.

52. Begbie, "Music, Word, and Theology Today," 5.

53. I refer here to the brief passage from the documents of the Council of Trent (1545–63); cf. note 75 below.

intelligibility, and historical rootedness. We find those very attributes in the French psalters and Lutheran hymnbooks. Garside confirms this:

> Calvin's Preface, far from being at odds with the Italian and French Renaissance, is actually a formulation of musical thought quite consonant with certain of the musical ideas of the humanists. . . . It reveals itself as a document written certainly by a great religious Reformer. Nevertheless, it is in complete accord with one of the leading humanistic musical trends of the sixteenth century.[54]

In a sense, the Psalter's concepts were musically up-to-date, even visionary for an ecclesiastical volume, because the soon-to-come Baroque period appealed to historical Greco-Roman practice with even greater earnest.[55]

The music for the Psalter sounded unlike secular music of the day—also part of Calvin's goal. He wanted church music to have *pois et majesté* (weight and majesty) rather than being *léger et volage* (light and frivolous).[56] He said that music to entertain people at one's table should sound different from psalms sung in the church "in the presence of God." Calvin makes a

---

54. Garside, "Calvin's Preface to the Psalter," 131–32.

55. By this I mean the reforms of the Florentine Camerata and others, the invention of monody, *basso continuo*, figural notation, the *secunda prattica*, musical-rhetorical figures, and so forth. Hughes Oliphant Old, in e-mail correspondence July 28, 2009, suggested another reason for the big changes in church music: "Other Christian humanists like Erasmus and his disciples could not abide the 'music of the monks' as they called it. They did not like the ascetic nature of chant as it had been developed in monastic communities, so they avoided it." Calvin wrote, "What shall we then say of chanting, which fills the ears with nothing but an empty sound? Does any one object, that music is very useful for awakening the minds of men and moving their hearts? I own it; but we should always take care that no corruption creep in, which might both defile the pure worship of God and involve men in superstition." John Calvin, *The Book of Psalms*, translated from Latin and collated with the author's French version by James Anderson, vol. 1 (Grand Rapids: Christian Classics Ethereal Library, www.ccel.org), passage on Ps. 33:2. At least in chant the monks and priests were singing the biblical text as it appeared in the Vulgate, rather than versifications, and they chanted the psalms in their entirety every week. But because chant was so intrinsically tied to the Roman church, the Reformers abandoned it. It may not have served their expressive purposes or the natural accents of multiple languages either.

56. John Calvin's sermon on 2 Sam. 6, quoted in Alain Perrot, *Le visage humain de Jean Calvin* (Geneva: Labor et Fides, 1986), 204, reads: "nous connaissons par experience que le chant a grande force et vigueur d'émouvoir et d'enflamber le coeur des hommes pour invoquer et louer Dieu d'un zéle plus vehement et ardent. Il y a toujours à regarder que le chant ne soit pas léger et volage, mais ait poids et majesté."

distinction between music for corporate worship and the rest of life. As with Chrysostom, Calvin understood melody to function like a funnel for the Word—a text sung to a good melody could penetrate deeper than one only verbally experienced. He wrote in the *Institutes*:

> And surely, if the singing be tempered to that gravity which is fitting in the sight of God and the angels, it both lends dignity and grace to sacred actions and has the greatest value in kindling our hearts to a true zeal and eagerness to pray. Yet we should be very careful that our ears be not more attentive to the melody than our minds to the spiritual meaning of the words.[57]

The tunes of the Huguenot psalms are typically simple, stepwise, and stay within the span of an octave. The melody-text relationship is predominantly monosyllabic. But it is the rhythms of the psalm tunes that are most captivating. The 1562 Psalter employs much syncopation, to the point that some (including Elizabeth I) referred to its tunes snidely as "Genevan jigs." Variety was achieved through the alternation of duple and triple groupings of notes. Syncopation occurred with one long note between two short notes or two long notes between two short ones. Vitality and energy characterize the rhythm of these psalm settings.

The rhythms had a greater purpose, however, consistent with musical sensitivities of the day—they fit the French language. An important technique being used in French art music around this time was *musique mesurée*. This was the musical analogue to the poetic movement *vers mesuré*.[58] In

---

57. *Institutes*, 3.20.32. Calvin's point is well taken. Even today we can be drawn as much or more to the music of a hymn or psalm as to its text. We must engage our minds as we sing to avoid this pitfall, and instruments must play and phrase in such a way as to make the text clear.

58. In Oliver Strunk's *Source Readings in Music History*, rev. ed., ed. Leo Treitler (New York: W. W. Norton, 1998), 338, we read, "The humanist impulse to emulate ancient models led to a number of Renaissance experiments with quantitative verse in modern languages. None of these was more influential than the *vers mesurés à l'antique* and accompanying *musique mesurée* pioneered from 1567 to 1570 by the poet Jean-Antoine de Baïf (1532–89) and composer Joachim Thibault de Courville (d. 1581). Baïf believed that the fabled ethical effects of ancient music arose from the quantitative measuring of poetic lines and its reflection in musical rhythm. His measured verse in French assigned long or short values to each vowel according to certain orthographic rules; these values were to be conveyed in homophonic musical settings by rhythmic ratios of 2:1. The result in many settings was a

musique mesurée long vowels versus short vowels (and their syllables) in the text were set in a musical ratio of 2:1 (precisely what Bourgeois had done for the 1551 Psalter). Since the meter of the verse was usually flexible, the result was a musical style best transcribed without a prescribed meter, which sounds to our ears as though it has rapidly changing meters. This also explains why trying to fit other languages to the French tunes creates accentual and other poetic problems. The breadth and quality of melodies and metric forms in the 1562 Psalter is unmatched in any other metrical psalter.

Calvin placed singing at the heart of the church.[59] A printed table appearing in the 1562 Psalter reveals that the psalms were sung nonconsecutively but in their entirety, within a period of 25 weeks, or twice annually (Sunday mornings, Sunday afternoons, and Wednesday evenings).[60] This means that between 16 and 30 stanzas were sung in any given service—roughly the equivalent of five hymns of up to 6 stanzas each. Praise-oriented psalms were employed on Sundays and penitential psalms were reserved for Wednesdays.[61]

Surprisingly, there is no intentional relationship between this psalm-singing schedule and the sermon being preached.[62] Psalm singing was included as an *element of worship*, not according to the church year or the *lectio continua*.[63] In other words, the singing of psalms was an essential

---

freely additive rhythm, little constrained by metrical regularity, whose resonance can be heard in the early-seventeenth-century *air de cour* and even in the recitative of later French opera. Baïf translated the Psalter in measured verse and wrote at least three volumes of *chansonettes mesurées*." Frances Yates points out: "The same musicians of the [French] Academy who set the *chansonettes mesurées* to music provided also a measured music, based on exactly the same supposedly 'antique' principles, to match the measured psalms." See Frances A. Yates, *The French Academies of the Sixteenth Century* (London: The Warburg Institute, 1947), 66.

59. Parker, *John Calvin*, 87.

60. Pierre Pidoux, "Polyphonic Settings of the Genevan Psalter: Are They Church Music?" *RMJ* 7, 2 (April 1995): 46.

61. Jan R. Luth, "Aspects of Congregational Singing," *RMJ* 4, 4 (October 1994): 111.

62. Beeke contradicts this with his statement, "Psalters were assigned to each service according to the texts that were preached" ("Calvin on Piety," 138), but I have found no sources to corroborate that idea and many that dispute it. I am also unsure whether he is referring to various editions of the Psalter or specific psalms.

63. Some churches today read through the Book of Psalms sequentially as we do at Tenth Presbyterian in Philadelphia, a reading that is not tied directly to the sermon. But the schedule for singing psalms in Calvin's Psalters was not consecutive or sequential.

service element in its own right. Even this schedule for psalm singing, however, was not binding; in fact, Calvin recommends that latitude be given to other congregations:

> The established custom of the region, or humanity itself and the rule of modesty, dictate what is to be done or avoided in these matters. . . . Similarly, the days themselves, the hours, the structure of the places of worship, what psalms are to be sung on what day, are matters of no importance.[64]

This extended to church polity itself as Calvin wrote in his *Commentary on 1 Corinthians*:

> Let there be no ambition, no obstinacy, no arrogance or contempt for other churches, but on the contrary, let there be striving for edification, let there be moderation and common sense; and then nothing about variety in usages will call for blame.[65]

> Each church is free to establish whatever form of organization is suitable and useful for itself, for God has prescribed nothing specific about this.[66]

William Bouwsma writes that for common worship, Calvin's rule of convenience was such that he "was usually content, therefore, to recommend general principles of worship that individual churches might apply in accordance with their various and changing needs."[67] Calvin wanted people to become Christians, not Calvinists. He would be dismayed at much of what has been legislated and done through the years in his name.[68]

Calvin definitely concurred with Paul's exhortation to sing and pray with both heart and mind—with spirit and understanding (1 Cor. 14:15). He wrote,

64. *Institutes*, 4.10.31.

65. Calvin, *Commentary on 1 Corinthians* (1 Cor. 14:26), quoted in William J. Bouwsma, *John Calvin: A Sixteenth-Century Portrait* (New York: Oxford, 1988), 223.

66. Ibid., on 1 Cor. 11:2. Luther said similar things about Lutheran services and use of the *Deutsche Messe*.

67. Ibid., 224.

68. Consider the talented musicians in Wales during the Welsh Revival, for instance, persuaded to leave their livelihood because they were told it was "of the devil."

Now the heart requires the intelligence, and therein, says Saint Augustine, lies the difference between the singing of men and of birds ... the peculiar gift of man is to sing knowing what he is saying. After the intelligence must follow the heart and the affection, which cannot be unless we have the hymn imprinted on our memory in order never to cease singing.[69]

In summary, Calvin believed worship should involve the congregation joyfully singing metrical Psalms of David in unison. These psalms should be sung without instruments, monosyllabically, in ancient modes, and according to historical principles. They should be understood and memorized. He explained his near-exclusive focus on the canonical psalms by appealing to Augustine and Chrysostom. As Hughes Oliphant Old points out, Calvin does not appeal to the authority of Scripture on this matter.[70] Calvin believed that church music should serve the text, and he included a choir of children directed by a knowledgeable, professional musician to lead the people's musical worship.

Calvin's Genevan Liturgy

Calvin established a liturgy for Geneva's three parishes, influenced by Martin Bucer's liturgy for Strasbourg. Calvin wanted to celebrate the Lord's Supper weekly and pleaded to have it at least monthly, but the council in Geneva refused, limiting the sacrament to four times annually (which was already more frequent than the once-yearly communion typical in the medieval period).[71] Calvin's order of worship looked something like the following when the Lord's Supper was included (events in italics were not included for regular services):

69. Calvin, "Genevan Psalter Foreword," 348.
70. Old, *Worship*, 45.
71. Jan R. Luth, "Where Do Genevan Psalms Come From?" *RMJ* 5, 2 (April 1993): 36–37. See also Parker, *John Calvin*, 86; and W. Robert Godfrey, *John Calvin: Pilgrim and Pastor* (Wheaton, IL: Crossway, 2009), 71. These and other sources disagree slightly on this liturgical order and terminology, but the substance is similar. I have attempted to combine them where possible. Derek Thomas also says that Calvin instituted a monthly observance of the sacrament, in "Who Was John Calvin?" 24.

Invocation/Call to Worship (Ps. 124:8)
Confession of Sins/Absolution
Singing of Ten Commandments (the first four, then prayer, then the rest)
Prayer for Illumination (leading into the Lord's Prayer)
Singing of Metrical Psalms
Extemporary Prayer
Text and Sermon
Extemporary Bidding Prayer
Collection of Alms
Detailed Prayer with Paraphrase of the Lord's Prayer
Preparation of Elements During the Singing of the Apostles' Creed
    Words of Institution
    Instruction and Exhortation
    Consecration Prayer
    Fraction and Delivery
    Communion
    Post-Communion Prayer (of Thanksgiving)
Singing of Metrical Psalms
Benediction (Aaronic Blessing, Numbers 6:24–26)

Timothy Keller says that Calvin's goals for corporate worship may be reduced to three words that mark a middle road between Anabaptist and Lutheran models: simplicity, transcendence, and edification.[72] Robert Godfrey suggests four principles that Calvin desired for worship: the centrality of the Word of God, simplicity, spiritual ascent, and reverence.[73]

Calvin, the Organ, and Instruments

Calvin did not approve of organs or other instruments in worship. In a sermon on 1 Samuel 18, he put it this way:

It would be a too ridiculous and inept imitation of papistry to decorate the churches and to believe oneself to be offering God a more noble ser-

72. Keller, "Reformed Worship in the Global City," 212n53.
73. Godfrey, John Calvin, 80–86.

vice in using organs and the many other amusements of that kind.... All that is needed is a simple and pure singing of the divine praises, coming from heart and mouth, and in the vulgar [common] tongue.... Instrumental music was tolerated in the time of the Law because the people were then in infancy.[74]

His stated objection is the relationship between the organ and Roman services. Fascinatingly, the Roman Catholic Church came close to Calvin's thinking with the Council of Trent's (1545–63) declaration:

They shall also banish from churches all those kinds of music, in which, whether by the organ, or in the singing, there is mixed up any thing lascivious or impure ... so that the house of God may be seen to be, and may be called, truly a house of prayer.[75]

To be accurate in our assessment of Calvin's position, or that of the later Synod of Dort (1618–19), we must recall that the organ was not used for congregational singing in Roman churches either. Only a part of it (one manual) accompanied the choir of professional singers when such singers were not performing *a cappella*. This part of the organ was seldom large enough to accompany congregational singing, supposing there had even been such a thing. The organ was actually a concert instrument only fully used at non-service times.

Therefore, Calvin's rejection of the organ in ecclesiastical settings was really a rejection of:

1. professional, Latin-singing, Roman Catholic choirs performing polyphonic choral works, amounting to worship by proxy for the common people, in a verbal and musical language that was incomprehensible to them;
2. organ recitals of secular/church music being given in Roman churches at times other than during services.

74. As quoted in "Calvin and Music," in Percy A. Scholes, *The Puritans and Music* (London: Oxford, 1934), 336.
75. J. Waterworth, ed. and trans., *The Council of Trent: The Canons and Decrees of the Sacred and Ecumenical Council of Trent* (London: Dolman, 1848), 161.

He had never experienced a good organ being played skillfully as a support to congregational song; probably no one had. The organ was under suspicion in this age in general.[76]

Calvin's stance regarding other instruments, is more complex. His reasoning that Hebrew worshipers were permitted instruments because of their spiritual infancy seems difficult to support biblically. In sermons on Job 21, Calvin reveals his thinking about instruments. Job reads, "They take the timbrel and harp, and rejoice at the sound of the organ" (Job 21:12, KJV). To this Calvin comments, "Some people can enjoy themselves without losing their self-control but here Job tells us that the wicked turn to abuse the gifts and graces of God. . . . The flute and tabor and similar things are not blameworthy in themselves, but only their abuse by men, who most commonly turn them to bad ends." He then pleads for his hearers to "use the good things that God has made for us in such a way that we may not be led to cease to aspire to Heaven."[77] He also wrote in his commentary on Psalm 33:2,

> For even now, if believers choose to cheer themselves with musical instruments, they should, I think, make it a point not to dissever their cheerfulness from the praises of God. But when they frequent their sacred assemblies, musical instruments in celebrating the praises of God would be no more suitable than the burning of incense, the lighting up of lamps, and the restoration of the other shadows of the law.[78]

In these passages Calvin teaches that instruments are gifts of God, but because they can be misused, they must be banned from worship—

---

76. Scholes says "conclusively" that Calvin and the other leaders in Geneva had no objection to use of the organ outside church services. The Eastern church barred its use, the Roman Catholics reflected on its abuse, even Luther was lukewarm toward it. The Dutch churches were forbidden to remove their organs (because they were the property of the civil authorities), so these were retained for psalm-playing before and after services, but not during. In Scotland, Calvinists removed organs from churches, but rather than destroying them as works of the devil, they sold them to individuals for private use in the home. In Geneva, the organ of the monastery at Rive (decreed to be removed) took almost twenty years (1544–62) of attempts to negotiate its sale before it was eventually sold bit by bit for scrap metal. In the meantime it was stored at St. Pierre's (the cathedral where Calvin preached). In other words, there was no immediate panic to remove such a "papal" object. Scholes, *The Puritans and Music*, 337.

77. Ibid., 339–40.

78. Calvin, *The Book of Psalms*, in Anderson, vol. 1, passage on Ps. 33:2.

although they are fine outside of worship. His view on wine was different, although wine was used for communion. He knew the dangers of alcohol but said, "If wine is a poison to the drunkard, does that mean we are to have an aversion to it? Please, no. We do not let that spoil the taste for us, for on the contrary, we delight in the taste of wine!"[79] He believes that instruments were used under the law but should not continue in gospel times.

In his commentary on Psalm 71:22, however, Calvin states that he believes the Holy Spirit has *forbidden* instruments in worship:

> We are not, indeed, forbidden to use, in private, musical instruments, but they are banished out of the churches by the plain command of the Holy Spirit, when Paul, in 1 Corinthians 14:13, lays it down as an invariable rule, that we must praise God, and pray to him only in a known tongue.[80]

Would not the Holy Spirit have given instruction to put away such "immature" expressions of praise in the most direct and clear terms? Evidently Calvin understood this to be the case when Paul speaks of the uncertain sound in 1 Corinthians 14. Calvin believed instruments had their own "voice" but, because it was not a human voice carrying the intelligible words of Scripture, it was "uncertain."[81]

Calvinistic Musicians and the History of Western Music

As we have seen, Calvin was involved strategically with the development of the Huguenot Psalter. He also was blessed with gifted poets

79. Selderhuis, *John Calvin*, 162, from Erwin Mülhaupt, ed., *Supplementa Calviniana, Sermons inédits* (Neukirchen: Neukirchener Verlag, 1961), 6.39. Good for Calvin! To this, one would have to reply, however: "If instruments are a poison for Catholics with their Marian songs and religion of works, must the Reformed have an aversion to them? Please, no, for we delight in the sounds of instruments supporting psalms, hymns, and the gospel of grace!"

80. Calvin, *The Book of Psalms*, vol. 3, passage on Ps. 71:22.

81. However, in this passage Paul is teaching about the use of tongues in worship without an interpreter. If Calvin's analogy holds up, skilled players would serve as the "interpreters" of such instrumental sounds for those not fluent in the musical language. Most parishioners today are aided in their worship of God by organs and instruments that are *skillfully* played, as was David's aim for the Levites who played worship instruments, and as the Psalms themselves require (Ps. 33:1–4). Instruments played less than skillfully are a different matter.

and musicians to realize his ideas. His followers in other European countries and in North America expanded on these ideas to produce various psalters and elaborate church music that Calvin could not have imagined! It is noteworthy that the first book published in the New World was the Puritans' metrical Bay Psalm Book of 1640. What follows is a brief survey of some of the primary historical contributors to music in the Reformed tradition in several lands.

Switzerland

Guillaume Franc (1520–70). Franc was a Parisian musician who arrived in Geneva to open a music school shortly before Calvin's return. He was likely the composer of tunes for Marot's new texts in the 1543 Psalter, and he was editor of both the 1542 and 1543 versions, where he made some changes in the Strasbourg material. Probably at Calvin's urging, Franc was given an official contract with a wage increase and became Geneva's Precentor.[82] He was responsible for teaching psalm tunes to the schoolchildren. Calvin's *Ordonnances Ecclésiastiques* (Ecclesiastical Ordinances) of November 1541 contained an article about this: "It will be desirable to introduce ecclesiastical songs in order to better incite the people to prayer and to the praise of God. To begin with the little children shall be taught, and then in the course of time the whole church will be able to follow."[83] Franc also composed numerous melodies for the Lausanne collection of 1565, and since many of the 1542 tunes were retained in later editions, one must surmise that Franc was an admirable composer. The wage increase was not enough to live on, however, and Franc left Geneva in 1545.

Louis Bourgeois (ca. 1510–ca. 1559, aka Loys Bourgeoy). Bourgeois, who arrived in Geneva from Paris as a refugee, was a greater musician than Franc. He became Precentor in 1545, a post he initially shared with Guillaume Fabri. Fabri's work was not suitable, and so Bourgeois became

82. Which led Pierre Pidoux, on the basis of corroborating information, to determine that Franc is the likely composer of these tunes.

83. Pierre Pidoux, "The History of the Origin of the Genevan Psalter (I)," *RMJ* 1, 1 (January 1989): 6. Translation and reprint by permission of Librarie Droz S. A. Geneva.

responsible for all of it and remained in Geneva until 1552. He harmonized the Psalter homophonically in four parts, and published these in 1547 as *Pseaulmes Cinquante, de David Roy et Prophete*....[84] These psalms all used the 1542 texts of Marot. *Pseaulmes Cinquante* was published in Lyon, not because of friction with Calvin as some have reported, but because the Brothers Beringen were equipped to do such music printing.

Bourgeois's alterations to the 1551 Psalter got him into trouble. He signed and added a "Warning" (*Avertissement*) about the changes at the end of this version. However, he had not consulted the civil authorities before going to print and was promptly incarcerated upon the book's release once the council learned of his alterations. Calvin interceded on Bourgeois's behalf, prompting authorities to release him after just one day in jail. Apparently Bourgeois's changes met with Calvin's approval because they were retained in 1562. Bourgeois left Geneva in 1552 because of a lack of funds. Apparently even the greatest of Calvin's musicians was underpaid in Geneva.

"Maistre or Maître Pierre"—*an unknown who likely was Pierre Davantès (d. 1561)*. "Maistre Pierre" was one of the best-known of medieval farces, so perhaps this is a nickname for someone. Davantès worked on the 1562 Psalter. He obtained a three-year license in 1560 for a new type of music printing; reportedly, this featured an easier method of singing psalm stanzas without having to refer to the first. He also printed the biblical text alongside the rhymed version, and included the superscripts of the psalms.[85] "Maistre Pierre" was twice mentioned in the accounts of the Hôpital (a charitable institution in Geneva) as "the precentor" who was paid "for putting the psalms to music." For the 1562 version he included the work of some others, wrote his own melodies, and made use of Gregorian hymns as Bourgeois had done (notably, for Psalms 86 and 141). Some melodies were used twice, one was used three times (66, 98, 118), and another was used four times (24, 62, 95, 111).[86]

---

84. *Fifty Psalms of David, King and Prophet, set to music by Louis Bourgeois, in four voices in equal counterpoint, consonant with the word.*

85. Pierre Pidoux, "The History of the Origin of the Genevan Psalter (III)," *RMJ* 1, 3 (July 1989): 66. Translation and reprint by permission of Librarie Droz S. A. Geneva.

86. Smilde, "The Psalms of Israel," 110.

France

Matthias Greiter (ca. 1494–1550) and *Wolfgang Dachstein (ca. 1487–1553)*. These German musicians were friends who composed some of the tunes for the German Strasbourg Psalter, nine of which were utilized in the Genevan Psalter. Greiter was the Kantor/Precentor of Bucer's church at Strasbourg, and was likely the musical editor for Calvin's French Strasbourg Psalter. Dachstein was a renowned organist at the Strasbourg Cathedral and then at St. Thomas's who had studied theology in Erfurt at the same time as Luther. Dachstein encouraged Greiter to become Protestant. Both men "converted" back to Catholicism (to retain work to support their families) during the suspension of Protestantism in Strasbourg (1549–60).

Claude Goudimel (ca. 1514/20–72). Goudimel was not one of the tune makers for the Genevan Psalter, but he is often so credited because his compositional oeuvre is thoroughly engaged with that volume. He was one of the greatest composers of his day. He arranged most of the *Psalter* three times in addition to composing a large number of chansons, motets, and mass settings.

In 1551 eight of his polyphonic psalm settings were published by Nicholas du Chemin. They provided recreation and edification for those musicians who were able to tackle such difficult music "at home." From 1557–61, eight volumes of *Livres de Pseaulmes* were published by Le Roy & Ballard, each with about eight polyphonic psalms. For his 1562 publication (*Psaumes*), Goudimel wrote new homophonic settings as Bourgeois had done.[87] They were published in part books—one book for each of the four parts. In 1564 the *150 Pseaumes de David* were published. When he came upon a repeated tune, Goudimel wrote a variant polyphonic setting rather than repeating his homophonic version. A 1565 reprint in Geneva, known as the "Jaqui-Psalter," included all four voices in a single volume with the following preface:

> We have added three parts to the psalm tunes in this volume: not that
> they may be sung thus in the church, but that they may be used to rejoice

---

87. This 1562 version is often confused with the Genevan Psalter, but it is not the same. This Goudimel collection was published in Geneva the same year as the psalter but includes harmonizations for the 83 psalms of the 1551 psalter.

in God particularly in the homes. The one part, which should not be at fault, inasmuch as it is the tune used in the Church, remains in its entirety, as if it were the only part.[88]

These settings laid the foundation for the accompaniment practice to which we are accustomed today.[89] His "Jaqui" settings were not reprinted for almost 100 years, but according to Genevan Psalter scholar Pierre Pidoux, there was a great revival of his music with 10 reprints for Geneva and the surrounding areas alone.[90] This renewed interest was sparked by the new title, which added the words, "now arranged for the use of those who wish to sing in parts in church."[91] Goudimel, a Huguenot, died for his faith in late August 1572, in Lyon, as the St. Bartholomew's Day Massacre spread from Paris to the provinces.

Claude LeJeune (ca. 1528–1600). Orentin Douen's two-volume work, *Clément Marot and the Huguenot Psalter* (Paris, 1878–79) lists 13 editions of four- and five-part settings of psalms published between 1601 and 1664 by Claude LeJeune, the most important French composer of the late Renaissance, who set psalm versifications by Bèze, Marot, and Baïf. LeJeune composed settings for all 150 psalms. Some other renowned composers of polyphonic or homophonic settings of the psalms at this time include Clément Jannequin (ca. 1474–ca. 1560), Philibert Jambe-de-Fer (ca. 1515–ca. 1566), and Orlando di Lasso (1532–94). By the end of the century more than 2,000 settings of the Genevan texts and tunes had been produced.

88. A. G. Soeting, "Claude Goudimel," *RMJ* 2, 4 (October 1990): 118.

89. Lucas Osiander published a book of *Geistliche Lieder* (sacred songs) in 1586 that included 50 four-part settings of these psalms, but moved the melody (*cantus firmus*) from the tenor (where it had resided with Bourgeois and Goudimel and almost all Renaissance music) to the soprano voice. Osiander's chorale book was soon followed by the important collections of Hans Leo Hassler (1608) and Michael Praetorius (1609).

90. There were editions in 1664, 1667, 1668, 1690, 1701, 1739, 1746, 1748, 1755, and 1759.

91. Goudimel even made it to the New World in 1774 via an edition printed in the Colonies, "A Collection of the Psalm and Hymn Tunes." This was a reprint of the unison psalter, "*The Psalms of David . . . for the use of the Reformed Dutch Church in the City of New York*" (1765), but it contained Goudimel's four-part settings. See Soeting, "Claude Goudimel," 122.

The Netherlands

Jan Pieterszoon Sweelinck (1562–1621). Sweelinck was the most significant Dutch musician of his day. Although he wrote toccatas and fantasias and other music, he championed the Genevan psalms and was renowned for his organ variations on them. He published three books of vocal psalm settings in Renaissance style, with a fourth, *Cantiones sacrae* (1619), calling for *basso continuo* in the new Baroque style. A gifted organist, he earned the title "Phoenix of organ playing" because the so-called "dead" organs sprang to life out of the ashes when he played. He was also nicknamed the "maker of organists" because he was sought as a teacher by so many young German organists.[92]

Sweelinck's father, Peter Swybertszoon, was organist of the Oude Kirk (Old Church) in Amsterdam. Upon his death, Jan became organist in 1578 at the age of 15, and eventually was named the Precentor of Amsterdam. His variation technique on the Genevan tunes removed much opposition toward the organ. Ecclesiastical objections waned once the playing was ennobled, as organ players became thoughtful artists. "The former 'barbarian' with his 'wanton song' had become 'the master, who gracefully played a psalm on various stops,' and the 'superstitious Mary motets' were replaced by 'sober, edifying pieces.'"[93] Sweelinck's pupil, Paul Siefert (1586–1666), also composed two volumes of psalm motets.

Petrus Dathenus (ca. 1531–88). Dathenus, also known as Peter Datheen, was a Flemish-born, Genevan-trained preacher who felt called to the causes of the Reformation and purposed to give the Dutch a psalter. He served as chaplain to Frederick III in Heidelberg. Dathenus's psalter (1566) was not based on the Hebrew but on French versifications by Marot and Bèze. He attempted to retain an identical number of syllables as the French, but in so doing he disregarded Dutch prosody conventions entirely, resulting in over 7,000 misplaced accents and many *enjambments* that disrupted the text.[94] A Dutch translation from the Hebrew with

92. Manfred Bukofzer, *Music in the Baroque Era* (New York: Norton, 1947), 75.

93. Norma Vanderpol, "The Psalms, the Organ, and Sweelinck," *RMJ* 1, 1 (January 1989): 14.

94. S. Vander Ploeg, "Psalmen Datheni" 56, quoting Cornelius P. Van Andel, *Tussen de Regels* ('s-Gravenhage, 1968), 59.

new tunes to fit Dutch grammar would have been a better choice, Marot and Bèze had undertaken in French. Instead, the Synod of Dort upheld Dathenus's version.[95]

This decision resulted in many woes for Dutch congregational singing. The linguistic/musical incongruity led to multiple versions of the psalter being used simultaneously with parishioners singing from whichever version pleased them. Singing reportedly became quite atrocious. In 1641, Constantijn Huygens published a booklet calling for the use of the organ in worship (see below). He wrote that the congregation's singing "often sounds more like howling and screeching than singing . . . they make an ugly, roaring sound. The tones are all mixed up, like different birds singing at the same time. The tempos clash like well-buckets, the one goes up as the other goes down. There is much screaming as if it were a matter of drowning out all others."[96]

Constantijn Huygens (1596–1687). Huygens was a Dutch diplomat, poet, composer, and secretary to two princes. He was one of the most prolific writers of the Dutch Golden Age. In 1641 he called for the reintroduction of the organ in Dutch church services. Under edict of the various synods, the Dutch organs were played only after worship services. Huygens wanted these post-service recitals to cease and the organ to be played to aid the severely failing congregational singing *during* the service, under strict church control. He wanted organ preludes, postludes, and offertories, but only music based on Genevan psalm-tunes. This functional use of the organ in Dutch services influenced the use of organ in Lutheran lands, and it greatly aided the development of Baroque organs in the North German and Netherlands region. These organs were geared more to congregational song than the Catholic instruments further south. As a result, Dutch organ builders were sought throughout Lutheran lands as the masters of ecclesiastical organ building.

95. H. Hasper, *Een Reformatorisch Kerkboek* ('s-Gravenhage, 1941), 59. Dathenus' version included the Ten Commandments, the Lord's Prayer, the twelve Articles of Faith, the New Testament canticles, and one hymn, "*O Godt die onse Vader bist*," the use of which was left to the discretion of individual churches.

96. Constantijn Huygens, *Ghebruyck en onghebruyck van 't orgel in de Kercken der Vereenigde Nederlanden*, ed. F. L. Zwaan (Leiden, 1641). Verhandelingen der Kon. Ned. Akademie van Wetenschappen, afd. Letterkunde, new series, vol. 84 (Amsterdam/London, 1974).

Germany

Ambrosius Lobwasser (1515–85). Lobwasser was a professor at Köningsberg and translator of Marot's and Bèze's psalms into German. His translation, published in 1573 in Leipzig with the Goudimel-Jaqui harmonies, was a huge success. It spread these "German" psalms throughout German Switzerland. In 1675 Ulrich Sultzberger published a Lobwasser edition in Bern in which the psalms were transposed into the same key, the melody was moved to the soprano, and embellished harmonies were reduced to note-against-note.

The Swiss *Collegia Musica* (music societies) were formed out of a desire to sing the four-part Lobwasser psalms. Those who learned the four-part psalms in *Collegia* soon began to practice part-singing during worship. This led to four-part singing being introduced in Reformed churches throughout Switzerland. Singing in parts was already the practice in Great Britain and Germany, although most Dutch churches resisted it. Before long there was a French version of the Sultzberger as well. Groups of wind instruments often accompanied these psalms for congregational singing. Lobwasser's very popular edition was reprinted 66 times, the last in 1824.

Joachim Neander (1650–80). Neander (born Neumann) was a German Reformed Calvinist teacher and a writer of both hymns and hymn tunes. He authored more than 60 hymns, including his famous "Praise to the Lord, the Almighty" (a paraphrase of Psalms 103 and 150), one of the greatest hymns of praise of the church worldwide, which was translated into English by Catherine Winkworth in 1863. Neander died from tuberculosis at the age of 30.

Johann Sebastian Bach (1685–1750). While the great Lutheran church musician was not a Calvinist, for a time Bach worked in the Reformed court of Cöthen (1717–23). During this period he wrote the six Brandenburg concerti, two orchestral suites, the French Suites, Book I of the *Well-Tempered Clavier*, and many other chamber, instrumental, and keyboard works. While these are considered "secular" in that they have no immediate tie to church music, Bach wrote them for the glory of God, penning "s.D.g." (for *soli Deo gloria*) after their concluding measures. Certainly in his writing of the sacred cantatas, where Bach "preached" passages from the gospels and epistles through his compositional hermeneutic, his emphasis on the Word of God is congruent with both Calvin and Luther.

Felix Mendelssohn (1809–47). Mendelssohn was also a Lutheran, but he married Cécile, the daughter of French Huguenot pastor Auguste Jeanrenaud. They married in a Reformed church on the Goetheplatz in Frankfurt am Main. Felix wrote one hymn for the Reformed church, at the request of the minister who married them, which was published in the Huguenot hymnbook, *Recueil de cantiques chrétiens* (1849). Mendelssohn set numerous psalms; most of these are grand concert settings with soloists, choirs, and orchestra. His Jewish heritage may have drawn him toward the Psalms, particularly because his grandfather, Moses Mendelssohn (1729–86), translated the Book of Psalms into German.

Interacting with Calvin's Musical Ideas

Ultimately, as John Piper reminds us, nothing was more important to Calvin than God's supremacy over all things. "The essential meaning of John Calvin's life and preaching is that *he recovered and embodied a passion for the absolute reality and majesty of God.*" [97] Calvin's premises concerning music grew out of his theology. He was right about many things—the necessity of singing psalms, the importance of the worshiper's heart, the emotional power of music, the gravity of approaching a holy God in worship. Some may think Calvin's strictures for congregational singing were too narrow; on the other hand, had they been heeded they would have prevented the vain, frivolous, and sometimes nonsensical congregational music one finds in many churches today. Calvin would be appalled.

The primary flaw with Calvin's near-exclusive psalmody position is its inconsistency regarding hymnody. If the divinely inspired canonical psalms are the only legitimate sung prayer, does it not follow that *spoken* prayer in worship should be limited to the canonical psalms as well? However, if *extemporaneous* spoken prayer is permitted, and if congregational

---

97. John Piper, *John Calvin and His Passion for the Majesty of God* (Wheaton, IL: Crossway, 2009), 16, emphasis added.

singing is an act of prayer, then good Christian hymnody, which is carefully constructed *written* prayer, should be entirely permissible. Hymnody used in worship has less chance of being theologically incorrect than an extemporaneous prayer because it provides opportunity for careful review prior to use.[98] But even greater support for the inclusion of newly written hymns is found in its corollary—the *pre-written*, non-inspired prayers that were included in Genevan worship.

Perspectives of the Calvinistic Musician

Although Calvin does not address the *discipline* of music per se, a Calvinistic perspective has direct bearing on the life of a musician. For example, God is sovereign over all things, so the outcome of a performance, audition, competition, or interview is in his hands. We need not be fearful (Isa. 41:10), and human assessment is not our only consideration.

A great temptation in auditions, competitions, or even college recitals is to measure oneself inappropriately against others. A healthy understanding of someone else's gifts, including the recognition that "I may never be *that* good," does not mean we should be disheartened by the present level of our own development.[99] Nor should we be proud. These gifts are not ours—they are from, through, and to God—for his glory alone (Rom. 11:36). Having confidence is necessary, but pride leads to destruction (Prov. 16:18). If we have worked diligently to do our best, sought the Lord, and committed our efforts to him, we have done our part. Ultimately, we must accept the outcome as God's will in the matter and rest in him.

As Calvinists we know that we have a calling; so, irrespective of what we face, we can rest in his provision for that calling. In discour-

---

98. That said, pastors and musicians should be diligent in vetting worship music before utilizing it. A second inconsistency is the assumption that the canonical psalms are more fitting for worship than other biblical songs. The Bible is full of other divinely inspired songs of praise: Old and New Testament canticles (Songs of Moses, Miriam, Hannah, Zechariah, Mary, Simeon, etc.), prophecy, poetry, and hymns of Christ. The Bible includes them. Why should we exclude them?

99. I frequently remind Christian students that they do not know whether the Lord has entrusted them with one, five, or ten talents, as in Jesus' parable (Matt. 25:14–30). All they know for sure is that they are responsible for what they have been given. So that is the question—are we investing that with which we have been entrusted for God's glory?

aging situations we can find comfort in knowing that we are serving as we have been called. When there are multiple opportunities and the "right" choice is not obvious after prayer and wise counsel, one should follow the path that seems best until God redirects. If we seek a decision that will bring him glory and commit our way to him, he will direct our paths (Ps. 37:5).

We should strive for God's glory in every occasion to use our abilities and take great joy in the outworking of our calling. People should see Christ in the way we live and perform. We know that all things work together for the good of those who love him (Rom. 8:28). We know that with the Word of God as our standard we have a means by which to judge whether something is wholesome and God-honoring or not. We understand salvation to be God's work, not our own. We know that God's kingdom and plan are much larger than we are; and, there is nothing binding on the conscience except what is specified by Scripture. These truths play out in numerous practical ways for the Calvinistic musician.

We must trust God and his Word. He alone knows our future, and he has plans to prosper us, not to harm us (Jer. 29:11). He has ordained the paths we shall walk, and seeks to glorify himself through us. What he has for us is best. Why would we want anything less? Calvinism, then, should be the most freeing of all faiths!

Guiding Principles for Christian Musicians

A Calvinistic musician ought to realize that he or she is entrusted with one of God's greatest gifts—given for God's glory and man's pleasure, not for our glory and man's applause. For church musicians, the Word of God is central to our work; and our work is essential to corporate worship. Because singing is so often prayer, we must *mean* and *understand* what we are singing. A lapse in either element (intention or comprehension) has often rendered the singing of psalms or hymns irrelevant, even *irreverent*.[100] We must communicate the truths of the texts through music and avoid music that is trite, inane, or in conflict with the words. Worship extends to all of life, and in everything God must receive glory (1 Cor. 10:31).

100. Paul S. Jones, *Singing and Making Music: Issues in Church Music Today* (Phillipsburg, NJ: P&R Publishing, 2006), 13.

We have a mandate to teach children psalms and hymns. This will strengthen the church and be a lifelong asset for young worshipers. We should share our musical expertise with young people generally through teaching. Music can also teach spiritual truth (Eph. 5:19). As such it is an ally with the pulpit ministry, not a competitor. So as musicians we must engage our pastors and other church leaders, joining with them to uplift the name of Christ with excellent music for our congregations. Corporate worship music should be in line with Calvin's goals for worship: simplicity, transcendence, reverence, edification; and its expression should be rooted in gratefulness for Christ's redemptive work and in a love for others. As Joel Beeke puts it, "The worship of God is always primary, for one's relationship to God takes precedence over everything else. That worship, however, is expressed in how the believer lives his vocation and how he treats his neighbor."[101]

By God's grace, we must fight our internal enemies—pride, doubt, fear of failure, a critical spirit, despondency, and lust in its many forms. The *fear of man* and the *praise of man* are perhaps the two greatest pitfalls for musicians. We crave praise, and we hate to think that our performance or skill is being negatively critiqued. We permit our self-worth to be influenced by these factors. We are guilty, at times, of accepting God's glory for ourselves. We can just as easily not recognize when God has used us for his glory, and fail to give him thanks for the privilege. When accepting an audience's applause, even in the exhilaration of a good performance we should recall that we are but dust and give grateful praise to God. We must not compromise our faith or morality in the midst of pressure from secular management or directors of one sort or another. Fear for our own reputation or for the next "gig" is the fear of man. Our identity must be rooted in Christ, and in him we will be able to withstand both praise and criticism.

Calvin would prescribe balance and common sense in these matters. One must work hard and have self-discipline; of that there is no doubt. But if one never has fellowship with the church or reads theology or enjoys the beauties of a new day because he or she is practicing around the clock or studying without breaks, what does such a person have to share? Often

101. Beeke, "Calvin on Piety," 145.

the musicians who *move* us are not those with flawless technique, but those who communicate truth—because they have suffered and triumphed, because they have lived life. Our union with Christ and our engrafting into his church necessitate our engagement with fellow believers. The communion of the saints fosters spiritual growth.

Any composer, conductor, teacher, singer, or instrumentalist worth his salt realizes that all of life's experiences inform one's capacity to communicate musically. Engaging with various cultures' people, food, and customs; reading diverse books; having quiet time with the Lord; listening to other great artists perform; walking in the morning woods; watching an ocean sunset; sharing a friend's hurt; making a baby smile; and even grieving a great loss—all our experiences inform our minds and souls, and all are gifts of God ordained for our enrichment and for his glory. A Calvinist, musician or otherwise, embraces all of this with thankfulness for God's grace toward us.[102]

102. The author would like to express his gratitude to Samuel Hsu, Mary Beth McGreevy, and Hughes Oliphant Old for their helpful review of this material.

MEDICINE: IN THE BIBLICAL TRADITION OF JOHN CALVIN WITH MODERN APPLICATIONS

FRANKLIN E. (ED) PAYNE, MD

John Calvin's life was almost certainly cut short by many severe physical problems. Without doubt, greater comfort and function could have been provided by modern remedies. In this sense it is ironic that all the best of modern science and medicine is a direct legacy from Calvin. Since his time other Calvinists have made considerable contributions to the advancement of medicine, notably Cotton Mather and Abraham Kuyper, whose thoughts we will review briefly below. In addition, we will find that the Ten Commandments, upon the meaning of which Calvin expanded as perhaps no other before him, have considerable application to modern medicine, even to the extent of correcting certain "standards" of medical practice.

From the outset, the question must be asked of a Reformed worldview in general, and a Reformed medicine in particular, whether Calvin's heritage has stagnated. Within Reformed circles, one sometimes hears the phrase "Reformed and still reforming," but are we? The Enlightenment[1] started around the year 1700, and it has played havoc with what the Reformation started. While the Counter-Reformation of the Roman Catholic Church seemed only to strengthen the Reformation, the Enlightenment has had a major damaging effect. If one goes into almost any Reformed confessional church and asks her officers and her congregants to define and discuss the *ordo salutis* or the five *solas* of the Reformation, the answers may well be disappointing. Precise theological understanding rarely exists, even in Reformed circles, except among teaching elders. If congregants are thus deficient in their grasp of basic tenets of the faith, how much more so would one expect their understanding of ethics or worldview to be lacking, for these are at least one step removed from basic theological issues.

If this observation seems far removed from medicine, we need only consider the psychosomatic unity of a person. A person's health is greatly dependent on his belief system, what he "trusts and obeys." If this trust is fuzzy and nondescript, he is likely to sin by "any want of conformity unto, or transgression of, the law of God." Sin always has consequences for both body and soul, as we will see in our review of the Ten Commandments.

"Always reforming?" Most Reformed churches rest on documents that are three to four centuries old: for example, the Westminster Confession of Faith and the Heidelberg Catechism. While this book and other events celebrate 500 years since Calvin's birth, the United States and many other Western democracies may be "slouching towards Gomorrah."[2] The country that was birthed by the Reformation has become predominantly pagan! How could this happen? How could the truth that freed men's souls, and then by philosophical consequence freed them in civil law, have become derailed?

The relevance of medicine to the more primary issues in the United States is more direct than might appear at first glance. Two years ago, the cost of medical care in this country passed $2 trillion.[3] That is 16

---

1. From a biblical perspective, "Endarkenment" would be more accurate.

2. Borrowed from the title of Robert Bork's book, *Slouching Towards Gomorrah* (New York: ReganBooks/HarperCollins, 1996).

3. I am not always going to reference my statistics. Anyone can go to any search engine, type in the relevant key words, and find this information.

percent of the Gross Domestic Product. In religious terms, we have exceeded the tithe to the worship of our bodies, spending more than five times more for medical and health care than we give to charitable causes. The largest item in many state budgets is Medicaid. On a simply economic basis, the government's role in welfare and redistribution of possessions is the most central civil and social issue of the day. Payment for medical and "health" services is a large and growing portion of this welfare.

The central issue in medicine and any other worldview area (ethic)[4] *is what the Bible says.* This principle is the most basic and fundamental to the Christian faith. More than any other *sola*, it was the foundation of the Reformation and John Calvin's legacy for the future. *But even many of today's Reformed believers have compromised on this foundation.* One hears, "All truth is God's truth," and, "The Bible is true in every area to which it speaks." While these are true statements, they are most often compromises to a wider application of biblical truth. The first tries to equate biblical truth with scientific (frequently psychological) truth, when science, by definition and design, can never determine truth.[5] The second mostly limits the Bible to soteriological and narrowly defined theological truths, not history, science, economics, civil laws, and other areas in worldview. Relative to medicine, there is the problem of omission. Although controversial, certain theonomists have done more than any other group to spur Reformed theologians to think anew about the social and legal application of biblical law to society today. Most Reformed conferences and books do not address medical-ethical or medical worldview issues. We praise God that this book does. But both completeness of worldview and the depth of current problems in medicine demand that medical issues be addressed in light of the Calvinistic belief of *sola Scriptura*.

4. Biblical ethics and biblical worldview are one and the same. One could also posit that the Cultural Mandate, the Great Commission, the Kingdom of God, the Ten Commandments, and the Two Great Commandments are not all identified with God's providence in history.

5. J. P. Moreland, *Christianity and the Nature of Science: A Philosophical Investigation* (Grand Rapids: Baker, 1989). Inductive thinking, which is the process of the scientific method, can never determine truth because it cannot examine every person, place, or thing in the universe.

John Calvin: A Diseased Body with a
Regenerated Mind, Powerfully Gifted

John Calvin's medical problems have been thoroughly addressed elsewhere.[6] These included gout of several joints, kidney stones (including local and systemic infections that resulted from these), pulmonary tuberculosis (sometimes coughing up blood and having severe chest pain), intestinal parasites, hemorrhoids, spastic bowel, and migraine headaches. These were particularly severe the last ten years of his life. He suffered greatly. Even so, as we all know, his scholarly output was prodigious. Modern medicine could have ameliorated his diseases, even cured in some instances. Thus, his production may have been even greater. But God's providence, a cornerstone of Calvin's theology, placed Calvin when and where he willed. Calvin rested in this truth. In 1546, he wrote Monsieur de Falais, who had been suffering from a severe illness.

> For although laid powerless upon a bed, we are by no means useless to him, if we testify our obedience by resigning ourselves to his good pleasure, if we give proof of our faith by resisting temptation, if we take advantage of the consolation which he gives us in order to overcome the troubles of the flesh. It is in sickness, especially when prolonged, that patience is most needful; but most of all in death. Nevertheless, as I have said, I confide in this good God, that after having exercised you by sickness he will still employ your health to some good purpose. Meanwhile, we must beseech him that he would uphold us in steadfast courage, never permitting us to fall away because of lengthy waiting.[7]

There is solid historical evidence, as well as reasonable association, that modern science would not have developed as it did without the Reformation.[8] As the major theologian of the Reformation, this legacy would be centrally that of Calvin.

6. Charles L. Cooke, "Calvin's Illnesses and Their Relation to Christian Vocation," in Timothy George, ed., *John Calvin and the Church* (Louisville: Westminster John Knox Press, 1990), 59–70.

7. Ibid., 68.

8. Charles B. Thaxton, "A Dialogue with 'Prof' on Christianity and Science," in D. A. Carson and John D. Woodbridge, eds., *God and Culture: Essays in Honor of Carl F. H. Henry* (Grand Rapids: Eerdmans, 1993), 275–300.

The sheer act of faith that the universe possessed order and could be interpreted by rational minds . . . . The philosophy of experimental science . . . began its discoveries and made use of its method in the faith, not the knowledge that it was dealing with a rational universe controlled by a Creator who did not act upon whim nor interfere with the forces He had set in operation. The experimental method succeeded beyond man's wildest dreams but the faith that brought it into being owes something to the Christian conception of the nature of God. It is surely one of the curious paradoxes of history that science, which professionally has little to do with faith, owes its origins to an act of faith that the universe can be rationally interpreted and that science today is sustained by the assumption.[9]

Elsewhere in this book the legacy of science and Calvin is more fully developed.

Medicine is a laggard to the rest of modern science. Compared with the physical laws of the universe, the complexity of living cells, tissues, organs, and bodies is logarithmically complex. There are almost too many variables to control in experimentation. Also, there is the spiritual dimension of a man, making him a psychosomatic entity. So, not only are there variable processes within the body, there are also the choices that men make that determine their health or sickness. For example, alcoholism and drug addiction are choices that have severe complications of illness and injury. Immoral sexual behaviors have resulted in epidemics of sexually transmitted diseases such as HIV/AIDS, syphilis, gonorrhea, and herpes, type II.

Medicine is also a laggard because its complexity requires great technical advances that have not been available until relatively recently. The germ theory of disease was not generally agreed upon until the late nineteenth century. Public health departments developed in the early twentieth century. Immunizations that began to be crudely investigated in the eighteenth century became more refined with widespread application during the mid-twentieth century. Effective antibiotics came some twenty years later. Technical analysis for laboratory values developed at approximately the

9. Loren Eisley, *Darwin's Century: Evolution and the Men Who Discovered It* (Garden City, NY: Anchor, 1961), 62.

same time. The mapping of the human genome was not completed until the twenty-first century. Stem cell research is in its infancy.

But for all these great advances, the psychosomatic unity of modern medicine reflects a pagan philosophy manifested particularly in abortion, euthanasia, sexual promiscuity (homosexual and heterosexual), and addiction. Simply, modern medicine must be governed by rules of behavior, for it is as much a science of disease and death as it is one of health and life. We moderns face the same decisions that Moses offered to the Israelites just before his death: to choose God's ways or our own. These laws were summarized in the Ten Commandments, which we will explore relative to modern medicine. Calvin himself points the way to those ethical absolutes. My own conclusion is that modern medicine often does more harm than good because of its philosophical materialism. The proof of my position may be found in the scientific medical literature.[10] This observation should not be surprising to Calvin's children because "the wages of sin is death" (Rom. 6:23), and, "All those who hate me love death" (Prov. 8:36).[11]

Two Giants of Calvin's Legacy in Medicine

Cotton Mather: Theologian and Physician

One of the most notable, and perhaps the first and largest figure in the Calvinist tradition in medicine, was Cotton Mather (1663–1728). He has been recognized as "the first significant figure in American medicine."[12] Mather was first and foremost a theologian and pastor. However, during the time that he lived, it was common for learned men to be well-read in many scholarly disciplines and even to practice them, including medicine.

---

10. Leonard A. Sagan, *The Health of Nations: True Causes of Sickness and Well-Being* (New York: Basic Books, 1987); Nortin M. Hadler, *Worried Sick: A Prescription for Health in an Overtreated America* (Chapel Hill, NC: The University of North Carolina Press, 2008). Various articles may be found on the Biblical Medical Ethics, Inc. Web site at http://www .bmei.org by typing in "efficacy" in the search feature.

11. Biblical quotations are from the New King James Version unless otherwise noted.

12. Otho T. Beall Jr. and Richard H. Shryock, *Cotton Mather: First Significant Figure in American Medicine* (Baltimore: The Johns Hopkins Press, 1954). His father was Increase Mather and his son was Samuel Mather. The Mathers were likely the strongest and longest line of Reformed preachers of their time in America.

He was truly a "Renaissance man" with the exception that many of those recognized as such were not notably Christian. Mather was also perhaps the leading theologian of his time and a staunch Calvinist. In addition to medicine, he has been recognized by later scholars for valuable contributions to astronomy, genetics, and other areas of natural science.[13] He was one of the first native-born Americans to be accepted into the Royal Society, the academy of sciences of Great Britain, founded in 1660.[14] For those familiar with the antipathy of England and the Continent toward those fledgling Americans, the invitation was a major recognition of Mather's work.

Mather never practiced medicine in the ordinary sense. Yet, he occasionally prescribed for his friends and family—to say nothing of himself.[15] "Medicine was more than an avocation or 'side-line' for this clergyman. It was rather a second vocation, to which he at one time intended to devote himself primarily and to which he returned with renewed enthusiasm at various times throughout his career."[16]

In 1720, Mather began writing a book on his "cumulative medical lore," which he titled *The Angel of Bethesda: An Essay Upon the Common Maladies of Mankind*.[17] Although he finished the book in 1724, to his great disappointment it was never published. However, it was preserved by the family, and copies are available today. Of course, remedies in that day were crude and rarely corresponded to the nature of diseases that we understand today. In my opinion, the most important recognition by Mather was the relationship of body and soul in a fallen universe. He noted:

> If we enquire after the Origin of Diseases, we shall not enquire wisely after this Matter, if we do not find our Sin against the Holy and Blessed One, to be the Root of Bitterness, from whence they all have arisen. . . . Hence, under Sickness we should make a solemn Enquiry after Sin. . . . We should be more concerned about for being saved from Sin than from

13. Ibid., 5.
14. Ibid., 42.
15. Ibid., 14.
16. Ibid., 6.
17. Ibid., 53.

Sickness. . . . In fine; The Sickness that enfeebles us, must make us fly more vigorously than ever unto the expiatory Sacrifice of our Lord Jesus Christ, for the Forgiveness of our Sins.[18]

This understanding of disease directly relates to the statement in the first paragraph of Calvin's *Institutes* that the knowledge of man begins with the knowledge of God. This knowledge of both is from special revelation. And, now almost 500 years after Calvin and 300 years after Mather, even most Christians writing on medicine in general, and psychiatry in particular, fail to discern between the regenerate and the unregenerate, as both theologians and the Bible do.

The Angel of Bethesda, however, is mostly a book on medicine. "Of the 66 original chapters, only three are centered on sin and spiritual healing, three on mental illness, and two on the occult."[19]

Mather had a major role in the public discussions and acceptance of a vaccine for smallpox, a disease that was epidemic periodically throughout the world. Americans came to learn of other societies in the world where the intentional inoculation of material from a smallpox victim into a healthy person would protect that person in later epidemics. (This method was prior to Jenner's use of cowpox, a safer method because the subsequent disease in humans was much milder.) There was considerable opposition to the procedure, as stated at the time: "First, the process was dangerous. Second, it was irreligious to interfere with God's 'Providence' in such matters. And, third, it was doubtless criminal from the viewpoint of public law."[20]

As to the first objection, the death rate from the live virus in inoculation was 2.5 percent, or 25 people per 1,000 inoculated versus 15 percent, or 150 people per 1,000 people who acquired the disease naturally. As to the second objection, six prominent ministers, including Cotton and his father, Increase, signed a statement that this procedure was indeed "righteous." The third objection was more difficult to overcome, but eventually the procedure was allowed to be used publically under control of the authorities.[21]

18. Ibid., 131–34, selected.
19. Ibid., 80.
20. Ibid., 104.
21. Ibid., 104–13.

This battle for medical progress has three principles that can be traced directly or indirectly to Calvin. (1) What is the role of the clergy and laymen in using biblical principles to affect the direction of science and medicine? (2) What is the relationship of church and state in governing the practice of medicine?[22] (3) What is the role of the state in public health?[23] We have not space to discuss these issues now, but refer readers to what follows and other sources.

A whole chapter could be written on Mather's *Angel of Bethesda* in regard to physical and spiritual issues, as well as other medical issues that surrounded him. Certainly in his knowledge of medicine he stands out as no other descendant of Calvin in the field of medicine. His achievements were such that they have been acknowledged and honored by secular historians and medical scientists as well.

Abraham Kuyper: Theologian and Encyclopedist

I discuss Abraham Kuyper (1837–1920) because of his recognition of medicine as central to a biblical worldview. He did not pursue medicine as Cotton Mather did, but perhaps more importantly he pursued the lordship of Jesus Christ over every area of human endeavor. In his encyclopedic endeavor, he identifies five faculties[24] that grew out of "the demands of practical need" from the "division given (to them) historically."[25] These faculties are theological, philological, medical, juridical, and natural philosophy. The content and description of these faculties is considerably intertwined with the genre and methods of Kuyper's day. Thus, we cannot develop those here, but refer readers to his *Principles of Sacred Theology* for what I believe is the most comprehensive grasp of the nature of the biblical worldview and the relationship and dependence of its component parts.

22. Herbert W. Titus, "Medical Licensure: Rendering to Caesar What Is God's?" *Journal of Biblical Ethics in Medicine* 9, no. 1; available online at http://www.biblicalworldview21 .org/bmei/jbem/volume9/num1/titus_medical_licensure.html.

23. Hilton P. Terrell, "Ethical Issues in Medical Insurance," *Journal of Biblical Ethics in Medicine* 1, no. 4; available online at http://www.biblicalworldview21.org/bmei/jbem /volume1/num4/terrell_ethical_issues_in_medical_insurance.html.

24. "Faculty" here means an area of academic study.

25. Abraham Kuyper, *Principles of Sacred Theology*, trans. by J. Hendrik De Vries (Grand Rapids: Baker, 1980), 185.

My emphasis here is to highlight the inclusion of the medical as one of those five faculties. There is a two-edged sword here. Medicine is among the central concerns of human endeavors. But it is not the only concern. Kuyper, in his few pages that discuss the role of medicine, states principles that moderns have minimized or even ignored for the governance of medical practice. I list three below.

(1) "The confession of our general condition is neither sound nor normal, but is in conflict with a destructive force, against which help from a saving power must be sought and can be found."[26] Kuyper is saying that an understanding of the human condition must be governed by the "theological" (i.e., biblical truth). The Bible explains that the medical faculty is only necessary because of the fall, the cause of man's injuries and disease. (Note this common theme with Mather above.) The Bible explains the problem of sin and guilt, which neither Freud nor any psychologists or psychiatrists have been able to expiate, even with their Pandora's box of theories. Is this discussion not reminiscent of Calvin's, that the knowledge of man begins with the knowledge of God? Today, modern medicine is positivistic[27] and defensive in its materialism, humanism, and atheism.

(2) "The boundary should be guarded which divides the somatic life of man from his psychical life."[28] Modern medicine only sees man as a biochemical complex. Thus, all answers are to be found in medications or medical procedures. Today millions of children have psychiatric diagnoses that limit their "treatments" to psychologists and psychiatrists. The answers to the stresses of life to which every human is subject, patients are told, do not lie in pursuit of righteousness (that is, the Ten Commandments), but will be found among the materialist "professionals." The degree to which Christians have accepted this materialism may be seen in referrals to these "professionals" for most or all counseling problems, and the faculty presence of these same professionals at biblically conservative seminaries. Kuyper recognized this beginning tendency in his time.

26. Ibid., 197.

27. The first principle of positivism is that any worthwhile knowledge must come from empirical verification and inductive reasoning. Many Christians, including those Reformed, have unwittingly adopted this form of thinking, which is inconsistent with the Bible as absolute truth.

28. Kuyper, *Principles of Sacred Theology*, 198.

(3) "(The medical) demands . . . that public authority shall unconditionally adopt the results from medical and hygienic domains into civil ordinances, and shall execute what it prescribes. This absolute demand should be declined . . . because these results lack an absolute, and sometimes even a constant character."[29]

Today the practice of medicine has infiltrated virtually every area of society. Schools and employers demand "sick excuses," transferring responsibility that should exist only between the contracted parties. Capital crimes and punishment are excused as or ameliorated by "mental illness." The American Academy of Pediatrics takes an official position against spanking. Some states have even enacted legislation to make spanking a crime. Support of gun control laws is sought from and received from various medical organizations. Immunizations are demanded for school entrance, employment, overseas travel, and other endeavors. Wages are garnisheed by law to support Medicare, Medicaid, and other government welfare agencies. And, with these mentions, we only scratch the surface. Contrary to Kuyper's admonition, modern medicine has become an arm of Big Government.

Much more could be ferreted from these few pages, but these will suffice to demonstrate that Kuyper understood far better than most Christians inside and outside medicine today that it cannot be practiced without an understanding that grows from the twofold starting point: the Word of God and a regenerated mind (*palingenesis*) that is scientific (systematic) and consistently Reformed. Kuyperianism is Calvinism advanced, having been Reformed and still reforming.

The Ten Commandments and Medical Ethics

Philosopher Gordon Clark once observed: "One of the excellencies of Calvinism is that Calvin emphasized [the Ten Commandments] more than any theologian before him."[30] In that continuing theme, one of the crown jewels of the Westminster Standards is the Larger Catechism on the Ten Commandments, Questions and Answers 91–153. These comprise almost one-third of the Larger Catechism! Many books with major

29. Ibid., 199.
30. Gordon H. Clark, *Sanctification* (Jefferson, MD: The Trinity Foundation, 1992), 95.

themes and applications of this summary of the law have been written by modern Reformers such as John Frame and Rousas J. Rushdoony.[31]

Continuing this theme of Calvin and subsequent Reformers, I will make a brief application of the Ten Commandments to the crucial worldview area of modern medicine. Indeed, as I went about this process, it was apparent that a whole book could be written from this perspective. I will mostly use Calvin's exposition of the Ten Commandments in his *Institutes* and the answers in the Larger Catechism of the Westminster Standards.

The First Commandment

"You shall have no other gods before me" (Ex. 20:3). Similarly, the Jewish *Shema* states in Deuteronomy 6:4, "Hear, O Israel: The LORD our God, the LORD *is* one!" It is the unity of God, and God as the only idea that "unifies" the "uni-verse." That is, his Person ties together the universe and all that is in it. "All things are upheld by the word of his power" (Heb. 1:3), and "in him we live and move and have our being" (Acts 17:28). No other philosophy or religion has any basis to provide for the unity of all that exists. Philosophers through the centuries have tried to reconcile how man's mind corresponds to the mathematics and physics that govern the functioning of the universe. Indeed, it was the Reformation that "discovered" this unity in God's providence and his immutability, allowing for the development of what we call "modern science" (see above). As Cornelius Van Til, Greg Bahnsen, Gordon Clark, and other Reformed apologists have posited, man can neither speak nor investigate without assuming Reformed theism.

Man was thus created as a unity of body and soul (Gen. 2:7). This "very good" unity did not last very long. Through the fall of Adam and Eve came disease and death of both body and soul (Gen. 3). It is here in this brokenness that medicine finds its place. Both Mather and Kuyper recognized this link as central to any understanding of medicine. Thus, *medicine can neither be understood nor practiced correctly*

---

31. John Frame, *Doctrine of the Christian Life* (Phillipsburg, NJ: P&R Publishing, 2008); Rousas J. Rushdoony, *The Institutes of Biblical Law* (Nutley, NJ: Presbyterian and Reformed, 1973).

without a clearly biblical understanding of these truths. Reformed theology, as refined Calvinism, best clarifies this understanding. However, many modern physicians, even those who claim to be Reformed, have lost their way.

Philosophical materialism, as scientific realism and other designations, often rules the day—even if unintentionally. As a society, we have committed the first sin forbidden by this commandment, atheism (WLC Q.105). Ask this question to any Christian, Reformed or not: "What is the most healthful, disease-preventing (and sometimes curing) endeavor of any person on planet earth today?" If he does not answer, regeneration and biblical obedience, he does not understand medicine within a biblical worldview! As we progress through the Ten Commandments, we will see more particular applications of this truth. But here in this First Commandment is the starting point.

First, health and healing have to be defined relative to both body and soul.[32] Thus, an unregenerate soul cannot be considered healthy. It is still under God's curse and will be condemned to an eternity of torment. Some reader might challenge that such claim is overly simplistic. Let me notwithstanding offer you this challenge. Look at book after book written by Christians about the practice of medicine. You will rarely find a discussion of the fact that the health and healing of Christians and non-Christians differ. This omission is especially true in the area of psychiatry.[33]

Second, health and healing must be prescribed within biblical parameters. "Trust and obey for there is no other way to be happy" . . . and healthy. Do you not think that "love, joy, peace, patience, kindness, goodness, gentleness, faithfulness, and self-control" (the fruit of the Spirit, Gal. 5:22–23) have healthful benefits?

Elsewhere, I have posited that the second greatest sin of modern medicine is its worship of the body.[34] Perhaps abortion should be consid-

32. Dichotomy is the biblical understanding of man's composition, as the Westminster Standards reflect the biblical position that Jesus took "to himself a true body and a reasonable [rational] soul." Spirit, heart, and mind are merely different facets of the immaterial component of man. WSC Q.22 22.

33. By association, this statement includes psychology, as well.

34. Franklin E. (Ed) Payne, "Medical Ethics: Building on John Frame and His Work," in *Speaking the Truth in Love: The Theology of John M. Frame*, John J. Hughes, ed. (Phillipsburg, NJ: P&R Publishing, 2009) 808.

ered as the greatest sin within the realm of medicine, but it comes under the Sixth Commandment. At 16 percent of the GDP, the expenditures for medical care in the United States are more than the tithe that God requires of his people and more than five times the charitable giving in this country. Surely, medical care has become a great idol. But philosophically and religiously, would not the worship of the body be consistent with materialism: the worship of what is seen and felt as the only "real" objects in the universe?

Thus, the First Commandment is the foundation for a biblical understanding of medicine. Early in Calvin's *Institutes* he states that the knowledge of man begins with the knowledge of God. Modern medicine could be greatly advanced with this understanding, but it operates under the religion of materialism.

Few Christians inside or outside the practice of medicine understand this divergence. When we add the particulars of healthy practices both for the body and for society in the second table of the law, the healthful influence of the Ten Commandments will be seen to be quite substantial. The answer to the first question of the Shorter Catechism denotes this benefit as we are "to glorify God and enjoy him [his healthful and healing benefits] forever."

The Second Commandment

"You shall not make for yourself a carved image—any likeness *of anything* that *is* in heaven above, or that *is* in the earth beneath, or that *is* in the water under the earth; you shall not bow down to them nor serve them. For I, the LORD your God, *am* a jealous God, visiting the iniquity of the fathers upon the children to the third and fourth *generations* of those who hate me, but showing mercy to thousands, to those who love me and keep my commandments" (Ex. 20:4–6).

Calvin begins his discussion of the Second Commandment with, "As in the First Commandment, the Lord declares that besides him no gods must be either worshipped or imagined."[35] Even today, the majority of beliefs throughout the world do not involve worship of the Triune God. What may be overlooked in our common abbreviation of this commandment as

35. *Institutes*, 2.8.16.

"You shall make no graven image," are the sanctions attached to this commandment. *Without the proper worship of God, the health of a people will be damaged, not only in the present population, but in generations to come.*

The fullest degree of health and medical care is not possible in a nation that worships other gods and makes images of them. In India, for example, the sacredness of cows prevents their being used for food. Worse, the Indian religion is one without hope or direction in this life. Health has come to India only as regeneration and application of biblical laws in private life and public health have occurred. Many Third World nations continue in their high infant and child mortality rates, as they continue to worship spirits and gods of their cultures. In the United States, the HIV/AIDS epidemic was spawned in a population that openly defied God and his commandments for sexual health. The epidemic of abortion sharply reduces life expectancy as measured from the moment of conception.

The Third Commandment

"You shall not take the name of the LORD your God in vain, for the LORD will not hold *him* guiltless who takes his name in vain" (Ex. 20:7). This commandment is violated in a particularly demonstrable manner by Nigel M. De S. Cameron, Harold O. J. Brown, Allen Verhey, Charles Colson, C. Everett Koop, and other notable Christians who have placed their hope for medical ethics in a revival of the Hippocratic Oath.[36] Cameron says, "We must reassert the transcendent, covenantal character of Hippocratism as the *only* ground of humane, philanthropic medical practice".[37] In my opinion, this statement borders on, or is, blasphemy. Does not his statement sound much like *sola Hippocratism?* Transcendent? Covenantal (by a Scot, no less!)? Only?

If you read Cameron's book, you will see that I am not exaggerating. I know that being winsome is a major rule of the day among certain evangelicals.[38] But how does one call something blasphemy and remain

36. Nigel M. de S. Cameron, *The New Medicine: Life and Death After Hippocrates* (Wheaton, IL: Crossway, 1991). The others cited give endorsements on the book cover.
37. Ibid., 167.(emphasis mine).
38. This is not an isolated claim. I can give many examples. One wonders what would have happened to the Reformation if Luther, Calvin, and others had chosen above all else to

winsome at the same time? How can one be winsome when a person calls on some hope outside of Jesus Christ and his Word?

The Fourth Commandment

"Remember the Sabbath day, to keep it holy. Six days you shall labor and do all your work, but the seventh day *is* the Sabbath of the LORD your God. *In it* you shall do no work: you, nor your son, nor your daughter, nor your male servant, nor your female servant, nor your cattle, nor your stranger who *is* within your gates. For *in* six days the LORD made the heavens and the earth, the sea, and all that *is* in them, and rested the seventh day. Therefore the LORD blessed the Sabbath day and hallowed it" (Ex. 20:8–11).

Calvin comments, "The principal thing delineated (is) . . . the mystery of perpetual resting from our works."[39] The duties of the Sabbath in worship are well recognized, but perhaps not consistently or sufficiently practiced. Much has been written on this subject, so I will primarily leave it to others. I want to focus on rest, the lack of which is surely one of the besetting sins of modern Christians. Jesus said, "Come to Me, all *you* who labor and are heavy laden, and I will give you rest. Take my yoke upon you and learn from me, for I am gentle and lowly in heart, and you will find rest for your souls. For my yoke *is* easy and my burden is light" (Matt. 11:28–30).

I find that few Christians today are truly able to rest. Their days are go-go-go. Their "schedules" are poorly organized. Families do not sit down at meals together. Men and women work late and are often out of the home in the evenings. They cannot even arrive for worship services with time to settle down and meditate. As Henry Thoreau said, most people have "lives of quiet desperation."

Physical and spiritual health suffers, as well as relationships. Devotional times and personal prayer are done on the fly, if at all. Serious Bible study is rare. But there seems to be time for surfing the net, texting, television, organized sports for children and adults, and a myriad of other

---

be "winsome." What about Oliver Cromwell in his battle for English freedoms? What about the American Revolutionaries? This issue is indeed serious and central for our day.

39. *Institutes*, 2.8.31.

activities that seem mandated in our culture, virtually a reversal of the Creation Mandate.

I often wonder what the church and America might look like if the time spent in these trivial pursuits were directed to serious Bible study, prayer, and good works. Indeed, we might just have considerably better health, fewer divorces, and a true continuance of the Reformation.

The Fifth Commandment

"Honor your father and your mother, that your days may be long upon the land which the LORD your God is giving you" (Ex. 20:12). Calvin emphasizes the blessing of life, rather than its longevity. "Honour thy father and thy mother, that thou mayest be able, during the course of a long life, to enjoy the possession of the land which is to be given thee in testimony of my favour."[40] On the negative of this commandment, Calvin states "that an inevitable curse is impending over the rebellious and disobedient."[41]

We can summarize this blessing and cursing in this way. The psychosomatic unity of a person is again in view. Spiritual actions (obedience to the law) have a bodily effect. While there is not always a blessing-curse for every action (John 9:3), both positives (blessings) and negatives (cursings) in response to the law are clearly manifested throughout Scripture. A more complete description of blessings and cursings is given in Moses' farewell address in Deuteronomy 29–31, summarized by, "See, I have set before you today life and prosperity, and death and adversity" (Deut. 30:15, NASB). In the New Testament, Paul cites the promise of "wellness" and "long life" from this commandment (Eph. 6:2–3). Modern Christians may not perceive this link between obedience and health, and disobedience and injury and sickness, but it clearly exists. Calvin negates a direct correlation in that health and long life are "an ordinary symbol of the divine favor," but still one who is obedient in this commandment may be "cut off before mature age" according to God's own will.[42]

40. Ibid., 2.8.37.
41. Ibid., 2.8.38.
42. Ibid., 2.8.37.

This commandment also has considerable relevance for the care of parents in their age of decline and disability, a responsibility which moderns have relegated mostly to the state through Social Security, Medicare, and other programs. But Scripture has numerous and often detailed descriptions of the responsibilities of families and the church in this area (for example, 1 Tim. 5:3–16).[43]

The Sixth Commandment and Being "Pro-life"

"You shall not murder" (Ex. 20:13). The Larger Catechism Question 136 asks: "Q. *What are the sins forbidden in the sixth commandment?* A. The sins forbidden in the sixth commandment are, all taking away the life of ourselves, or of others, except in case of public justice, lawful war, or necessary defense; the neglecting or withdrawing the lawful and necessary means of preservation of life; sinful anger, hatred, envy, desire of revenge; all excessive passions, distracting cares; immoderate use of meat, drink, labor, and recreations; provoking words, oppression, quarreling, striking, wounding, and whatsoever else tends to the destruction of the life of any."

In my estimation, this section of the Larger Catechism justifies my assertion that it is the overlooked jewel of the Westminster Standards. The power and insight can be seen in its summary declaration that answers the difficulties some "pro-lifers"[44] have had trying to be "pro-life" against abortion and "pro-life" relative to capital punishment and just war. The Larger Catechism on the Sixth Commandment gives the biblical position on these four issues: abortion (forbidding "all taking away the life of . . . others"), capital punishment ("except in case of public justice"), just ("lawful") war, and self-defense ("necessary defense"). How powerful is this statement in its brevity!—something that Calvin targeted.

Every position Christians take that improperly represents biblical teaching demeans and diminishes the good they are trying to accomplish.

---

43. While I have not cited the Larger Catechism on the Fifth Commandment, readers would profit greatly to read Questions and Answers 123–33, which expand and develop it in a full and somewhat surprising manner.

44. I use "pro-lifers" with the highest respect. Some may use it derogatorily, but I use it only as a helpful label.

This inconsistency has hurt the pro-life movement because participating Christians have equivocated for or even stood against capital punishment, just war, and taking the life of another in self-defense. This inconsistency has a tradition in church history with the passivity of the Anabaptists, Quakers, Mennonites, and others. One wonders what Western history would look like without people such as Oliver Cromwell and the American revolutionaries, who understood the balanced biblical position of the Sixth Commandment.

"The neglecting or withdrawing the lawful and necessary means of preservation of life" has direct application to euthanasia. I define euthanasia as "any action or inaction that *intends* the death of a person." Sin is always two-sided: "neglecting" (omitting, being passive, failing to act) or "withdrawing" (a subjective action). What may be overlooked here is the "lawful . . . means." "Lawful" in this case means the moral law or biblical law, as all the relative commands of Scripture. These particulars, as biblical prescription and "laws," in their breadth, are common to those who are Reformed, but uncommon to the remainder of Christendom.

Again, there is particular application here that is commonly overlooked or neglected, even by the Reformed. "Lawful" recognizes pertinent principles of economics. In today's climate of end-of-life complexities, many of these would be eliminated simply by the application of biblical economic principles. For example, who pays for this expensive care? Private funds and medical insurance are "lawful," but government provision by funds or payment of care indirectly is not. Now, quickly, before readers start screaming, "You cannot factor economics when we are discussing the preservation of life." Oh? You should simply consider this illustration: "Is it lawful to steal from your neighbor in order to feed your starving family?" You see, part of the law is also the Eighth Commandment which provides for private property (all that a person or family possesses), which may not be "stolen" *for any reason*. Yes, "render unto Caesar what is Caesar's," but he can only tax by lawful (biblical) principles of "rewarding good and punishing evil." The provision of medical care itself is not lawful by Caesar, and neither is a plan of redistribution to take from one person to provide for the medical care of another.

A recent fruit of the continuing history of Calvinism in this area is the adoption by the 16th General Assembly of the PCA of its Heroic Measures Committee Report.[45] This report takes into consideration a more comprehensive balance of biblical principle than is usually found on these issues.

The Seventh Commandment

"You shall not commit adultery" (Ex. 20:14). In the United States there is an epidemic of sexually transmitted diseases. Not only are the longstanding diseases of syphilis and gonorrhea still prevalent, but in the last forty years new ones have developed: herpes simplex-Type II, cervical cancer, hepatitis B and C, and the deadly HIV/AIDS. Perhaps there is no better illustration of the link between spiritual commands and bodily diseases. And, *all sexually transmitted diseases could be wiped out in one generation by a society committed to sexual fidelity as this commandment requires.*

The Eighth Commandment

"You shall not steal" (Ex. 20:15). Perhaps the most serious violation of this commandment is the confusion among Christians concerning government welfare and charity. The establishment of hospitals, orphanages, and other charitable institutions can be traced back to Christians having compassion and acting on that conviction. But modern Christians, for the most part, have relegated such institutions to the government, other organizations, and businesses. I have already mentioned that Medicaid, the federal and state program to provide medical services to poor children and others, is now the largest item in some state budgets.

Other than some limited role in public health, the state has no biblical role in providing medical care. If you search the Scriptures diligently for the government's responsibility to provide welfare in any form, including medical, you will not find it. By definition, charity (not the KJV term for *agape*) is voluntary. Forced taxation is not. Forced taxation is theft,

---

45. See the report online at http://www.pcahistory.org/pca/2-378.pdf.

money transferred for unbiblical reasons.[46] Now, the problem is not so much that we are to obey the government—Calvin is very strong on this responsibility—as that Christians do not understand the difference between charity and government welfare. Thus, not knowing biblical law, they cannot work to that end when they are in situations (jobs, government positions, advisory capacities, etc.) where they could affect social or legal policy. Those who are Reformed should be careful in their use of civil authorities as "nursing fathers."

The Ninth Commandment

"You shall not bear false witness against your neighbor" (Ex. 20:16). Calvin remarks, "To this prohibition corresponds the command, that we must faithfully assist every one, as far as in us lies, in asserting the truth, for the maintenance of his good name and estate."[47] Three applications in medicine come to mind.

(1) Heath-care workers and family sometimes state that "in the best interest of the patient, he should not know . . . that he has cancer . . . that is he is dying . . . that he will not recover." In *these situations, the patient needs to know.* It is not the responsibility of others, including family, to make that decision. Estates need to be planned. Reconciliation may need to be sought. Restitution and amends may be needed. Most importantly, a person's eternal destiny needs to be confronted. Fortunately, I believe that this practice has changed for the better over the last twenty years, as we have recognized that it fails practically, as any unbiblical practice will.

(2) In all fifty states, any minor child may legally have an abortion, treatment for a sexually transmitted disease, and a form of birth control without parental consent. Physicians may lose their state licenses for for failing to report not only likely child abuse but also any suspicion of child abuse. And the legal and liberal practices named above are only the tip of the iceberg. While these practices might better fit under the Fifth Commandment, the positive side of the Ninth Commandment is for those who have responsibility for others to have a right to

---

46. This statement does not preclude there being legitimate forms of taxation.
47. *Institutes*, 2.8.47.

the knowledge (truth) they need to make the best decisions for those under their care.

(3) Physicians often do not give enough information for patients to make decisions. Much of medical care has only marginal benefit, if any. Some is statistically deleterious. Patients and their families should be given the best information available at the time of decision-making. Hadler's book, already mentioned, has examples (see note 10 above).

The Tenth Commandment

"You shall not covet your neighbor's house; you shall not covet your neighbor's wife, nor his male servant, nor his female servant, nor his ox, nor his donkey, nor anything that *is* your neighbor's" (Ex. 20:17). As our society worships health, it also worships youth and beauty. The number of plastic surgery procedures in the United States is staggering: breast implants, "tummy tucks," facial restructuring, botox treatments, unwanted hair removal, gastric bypasses, and myriads of other procedures. The reasons for these include envy, poor self-image, desire to look young and beautiful, desire to cover the effects of aging, desire to attract sexual partners. Some plastic surgeries are necessary for truly disfiguring and dysfunctional problems, such as scars from burns or surgery, nasal obstructions, severely crippling injuries, etc., but too many of these are done because of vanity, and many are done by Christians.

A Summary

John Calvin's legacy is that of systematized theology that is also pastoral. We would wish that the Reformation he started had continued to this day in its scholarship and vibrancy. *Sola Scriptura* is still being compromised among those who most staunchly defend it. Cotton Mather and Abraham Kuyper are spotlights who demonstrate advancement that is truly Reformed. While the Ten Commandments were given to the kingdom of Israel, their fullness was shown by the Lord Jesus Christ, the apostle Paul, and their descendants within the Reformed community. These commandments have relevance to modern medicine in many ways that may not be readily apparent. Readers are encouraged to apply them further in their own study, but we hope the inclusion of medicine as part of a Christian worldview, especially when it consumes 16 percent of the GDP, will call Calvin's descendents to "test everything. Hold on to the good. And avoid every kind of evil" (1 Thess. 5:21–22).

12

CALVIN AS JOURNALIST

WARREN COLE SMITH

John Calvin's achievements as churchman and theologian are so monumental that they reasonably occupy first and second positions in any assessment of his life. It is therefore easy to forget that Calvin's achievements in both of these arenas depend heavily, even indispensably, on Calvin the man of letters, Calvin the journalist.

It is hardly a stretch of the truth to say that modern journalism and the Protestant Reformation that John Calvin helped to birth are blood brothers—one depended on the other, and each made the other possible. While this may not stretch the truth, neither is this assertion self-evident. There is a straight and heavy line that connects Calvin to, for example, the forms of church governance and discipline used by many denominations today. But the line between Calvin and modern journalism is not quite so firmly etched. It requires the connecting of dots, both historically and intellectually. In this essay, we attempt to identify and connect a few of these dots.

The History of Journalism

Journalism did not begin, of course, with Calvin. Marvin Olasky convincingly argues that journalism predates Calvin and the Reformation by at least 1500 years. Olasky identifies the *Acta Diurna*, or "Daily Acts," as the best-known among several examples of early journalism.[1] The *Acta Diurna* was a daily gazette of official acts of the Roman Republic, carved in stone or inscribed in metal and posted in public places. Scribes then copied these official accounts and distributed them throughout the empire. The first known copies of the *Acta Diurna* date from about 131 B.C.

However, the *Acta Diurna* or any of its successors for the next millennium and a half could hardly be called examples of the independent journalism we know today. These accounts promoted what Olasky calls the "official story": the interpretation of events preferred and distributed by those in power. The idea that journalism should serve as a balance to the official story was one still awaiting conception. That is why it is fair to skip forward to the Reformation, where the next major innovations in journalism appear.

The first, most obvious, and most frequently acknowledged of these innovations is the role the printing press had for both the Reformation and the rise of modern, independent journalism. Indeed, so profound was the effect of the printing press on all aspects of culture and civilization that it is often cited as one of the most significant inventions of all time.[2]

When the German metalsmith Johannes Gutenburg (a near-contemporary and countryman to that other great Reformer, Martin Luther) produced the first printed Bible, in 1455—a mere half-century before Calvin's birth—he unleashed a mighty river of words and ideas that, intentionally or not, began an inexorable erosion of the foundations of the Roman Catholic Church as well as the unchallenged authority of

---

1. Marvin Olasky, *Central Ideas in the Development of American Journalism: A Narrative History* (Hillsdale, NJ: Lawrence Erlbaum Associates, Publishers, 1991), 5. Olasky also noted that the *Acta Diurna* included results of Roman sporting events, as well as public notices that today we might call classified ads.

2. In 2000, a number of publications, including *TIME* magazine, published lists of the most significant events of the past thousand years, and most of them cited the invention of the printing press in the top ten.

kings and rulers everywhere. Modern journalist Thomas Friedman has argued that "the world is flat," meaning that the world of the twenty-first century is one in which almost all fields of human endeavor have become leveled, democratized. If this is true, it was not suddenly true; the process began in 1455.

The historical record shows that the Roman church understood the threat. Sociologist Rodney Stark notes that the Catholic Church regarded the translation and dissemination of the Bible into "languages that could be understood by the people . . . as heretical per se."[3] Pope Innocent III wrote in 1215 that "the secret mysteries of the faith ought not . . . to be explained to all men in all places. . . . For such is the depth of divine scripture, that not only the simple and illiterate but even the prudent and learned are not fully sufficient to understand it." The pope's statement is, in an important sense, true enough: No person, no matter how learned and wise, can plumb the depths of Scripture.

But it is also clear that Scripture commands us to study it. And, of course, Pope Innocent and all absolute rulers should grasp either explicitly or intuitively that a literate and educated people are a threat to centralized power of all kinds—religious and otherwise.

The printing press enabled just such an explosion in literacy and education, especially in Northern Europe, where the Reformation began. When the first Bible was printed in 1455, no more than a few thousand Germans could read. By 1500, Rodney Stark estimates, "at least three percent of Germans, about 400,000 people, could read."[4] And what did they read? For the first 100 years after the invention of the printing press, the vast majority of the material being printed was religious in nature, and much of it specifically related to Protestantism. The posting of Luther's Niney-five Theses on the door of the church in Wittenberg in 1517 is often cited as the moment that began the Protestant Reformation. But that posting of the Niney-five Theses on this or any other door had little impact compared with the fact that between 1517 and 1520 at least 300,000 copies of the Niney-five Theses and Luther's other tracts were sold.

3. Rodney Stark, *For the Glory of God: How Monotheism Led to Reformations, Science, Witch-Hunts, and the End of Slavery* (Princeton and Oxford: Princeton University Press, 2003), 74.
4. Ibid.

So the printing press was the indispensable technology of the Reformation, and the printers in such cities as Geneva, Basl, Zurich, Wittenberg, and, later, London and beyond were its unsung heroes.

This is not to say they worked for free, nor was their heroism completely unsung. Indeed, huge industries often emerged in cities where the Protestant Reformers had a stronghold. Robert Kingdon writes, "It is easy to believe that this propaganda industry absorbed in some way the attention of much of the population of Geneva."[5] Printers, papermakers, chemists who mixed inks, editors, and proofreaders—all of them made money. Some of them made fortunes.

But these fortunes could be easily lost. Throughout the sixteenth century, the major cities of Europe fell into and out of Roman Catholic hands. The stories of the major Reformers—Calvin, Luther, Zwingli, and others—are punctuated by periods of exodus and pilgrimage. This was an age when those considered heretics to the Roman faith (and, later, the Protestant faith) often paid with their lives; moreover, the ability to flee a city quickly was an indispensible qualification for the Reformer. A printer, on the other hand, was someone who could not or would not easily run from his press, which may have represented his life's savings and capital accumulation. One notable example is John Day, an English printer best known for producing *Foxe's Book of Martyrs*, a key document in the English Reformation. However, when the English Reformation was turned back and the Catholic Queen Mary I took the throne in 1553, Day continued printing Protestant material. He was imprisoned in 1554 and remained confined until Elizabeth I became queen in 1558.

Thus printers and activities that might be called journalistic, or at least proto-journalistic, were vital to the Reformation. As A. G. Dickens put it: "For the first time in human history a great reading public judged the validity of revolutionary ideas through a mass-medium which used the vernacular languages together with the arts of the journalist and the cartoonist."[6] Twentieth-century journalist Paul Johnson put it more colorfully: "The smell of printer's ink was the incense of the Reformation."[7]

5. Robert M. Kingdon, *Geneva and the Coming of the Wars of Religion in France, 1555–1563* (Geneva: Librairie Droz, 1956), 94.

6. A. G. Dickens, *Reformation and Society in Sixteenth-Century Europe* (New York: Harcourt, Brace & World, 1966) 51.

7. Paul Johnson, *A History of Christianity* (New York: Atheneum Macmillan, 1976), 271.

It is important to note that Calvin's legal training, especially as it related to church governance, and his notions of covenantal theology significantly bolstered secular law in the century that followed. Contract law, private property rights, and the rule of law generally were upheld by Calvin's writing on church governance and the role of the civil magistrate. These writings helped not just printers, but all who endeavored in what today we might call the vocation of entrepreneurship.[8]

However, Calvin's legacy in the legal arena took a century or more to manifest itself. All of which is to say that printers had more than technological skill. To persist as they did as the great enablers of the Reformers, they had conviction and courage.

Indeed, Olasky exhorts us not to give technology more than its share of the credit. "Material developments were useful," Olasky writes, "but beliefs and bravery carried the day and led to a new era."[9]

Calvin as Man Of Letters

In this regard—the shoring up of beliefs—John Calvin was no bystander in this emerging dynamic; he was a central figure. His earliest theological writings, the *Institutes* in particular, made it plain that standing against the beliefs of the Roman church was not a trivial matter. Calvin did no less than call the Roman church idolatrous; he also implied that standing against it was a matter of survival for a biblical Christian faith.

That said, Calvin's first encounter with the printing press proved less than propitious in several respects: First, Calvin's initial published work was not religious per se but a commentary on *De clementia* ("on clemency"), by the Roman Stoic philosopher Seneca, who lived during the time of Christ. Secondly, the printing nearly bankrupted Calvin, who was 23

8. We cannot give Calvin or Calvinism full credit for the rise of capitalism, however. In the fifteenth and sixteenth centuries, the Dutch were among the great trading powers of the world, and because Calvinism took hold in the Netherlands, some historians equate the two. Rodney Stark, however, calls any such association "nonsense," writing that capitalism "far predated the Reformation" in the Netherlands. Rodney Stark, *The Victory of Reason: How Christianity Led to Freedom, Capitalism, and Western Success* (New York: Random House, 2005), 175.

9. Olasky, *Development of American Journalism*, 15.

when the book was published in 1532. He had to sell his patrimony and take out a loan to make the final payments to the printer.

But the book put the young Calvin on the intellectual map and paved the way for the first edition of his *Institutes*, which was first published in 1536 when Calvin was just 27 and which the Reformer revised throughout his life. The first daily newspaper did not debut until 1605, in Strasbourg, an event that is often described as the beginning of the modern era of journalism. Nonetheless, by temperament, training, and work habit, Calvin had more in common with the journalists who would follow than the theologians who had gone before. Calvin's youth, the fact that he had only recently embraced the study of theology after training in the law, his lively writing style, and his penchant for speaking directly to the issues of his day all exhibit Calvin as a proto-journalist, a public intellectual.

Even the Calvin of the *Institutes*—we might even say especially the Calvin of the *Institutes*—shows us a writer who was journalistic in style and argumentation. Indeed, the *Institutes* often drew praise, even in Calvin's day, for a lively and readable style. As Bruce Gordon put it: "A young man who had never formally studied theology presented to the world writings that dazzled his contemporaries. A brilliant writer had emerged."[10]

With the success of the *Institutes*, Calvin became a public figure and was much in demand as a speaker and writer. However, his life during this era was more that of an independent man of letters than a clergyman. Gordon reports that Calvin probably did not begin preaching with any regularity until at least 1537, and Calvin was never ordained.[11]

Nonetheless, as we suggested above, the production and dissemination of Calvin's writings became a major industry for Geneva. Although Luther predated Calvin by a generation or more, it is Calvin to whom modern journalism owes a greater debt, especially in the development of a journalism that is independent of government control, which (as we shall soon see) is the hallmark of modern journalism. To understand this essential contribution of Calvin to journalism, it is important to understand that, as Rodney Stark writes, "in many places Lutheranism

10. Bruce Gordon, *Calvin* (New Haven and London: Yale University Press, 2009), 55.
11. Ibid., 71.

was from early days a 'state church,' in that it was adopted by kings and princes as the new, official faith with little regard for what the 'people' may have preferred. It was Calvin's 'Reformed' brand of Protestantism that rapidly gained several million individual French, Dutch, and German adherents, and a significant number in Italy as well. These converts were not produced by royal edict but were the result of personal enthusiasm, usually in defiance of the state."[12]

Speaking Truth to Power

In this particular, Calvin built the foundation for modern journalism, for modern journalism is not merely recording the "official story" as one might have found in the *Acta Diurna*. Neither is modern journalism a simple accounting of those "Publick Occurrences both Forreign and Domestick," as the first newspaper in the Americas, published in Boston in 1690, described its mission.

No, deeply rooted in the ethos of modern journalism is the notion of the reporter as prophet, as one who speaks truth to power.

Again, Olasky is helpful to us on our journey through the history of journalism. Olasky contrasts the "official story" that typified journalism from the *Acta Diurna* until the fifteenth century with a different kind of story, the "corruption story." The corruption story is one that is helpful to the public discourse engaged by the Reformers of the sixteenth and seventeenth centuries. Olasky explains the corruption story this way:

> Reformation leaders believed that people would seek the good news of mercy only after they became fully aware of the bad news of sin. This was the basis of the corruption story: Man needs to become aware of his own corruption in order to change through God's grace, and writers who help make readers aware of sin are doing them a service.[13]

The corruption story is not fully an innovation of the Reformation, of course. The story of the fall of mankind in Genesis is the archetype

12. Stark, *For the Glory of God*, 95.
13. Olasky, *Development of American Journalism*, 9.

of the form, and both *The Iliad* and the plays of Aeschylus provide examples of the corruption story. But these stories might be thought of as "corruption-story-as-official-story." Such stories, although they pointed to the tragic flaw of heroes, nonetheless extolled the hero. Such stories were not attempts to topple the prevailing powers—whether the prevailing power be God or some existing social order—but had as their purpose to perpetuate it against those (from Adam to Achilles) whose hubris drove them to overreach. The order of the universe was set; man's responsibility was to know his place. So the innovation of the Reformation is not the corruption story per se so much as it is the willingness to say that not just individual humans are corrupt (although Calvin and other Reformers willingly and often said so), but also that the dominant institutions, both religious and governmental, were corrupt.

While no one can refute the seminal and courageous nature of Luther's example, it must be admitted that even where Lutheranism was the strongest—in Luther's own Germany—just a year after Luther's death in 1546, much of Germany was once again a Roman Catholic nation, having fallen to the forces of Charles V.

Calvin, on the other hand, devoted his life not only to speaking truth to power but also to giving language and opportunity to millions of others who could and did speak truth to power. Stark summarizes Calvin's genius: "John Calvin was not only one of the greatest and most prolific Christian theologians and a superb preacher; he was a master strategist of subversive activities, having trained and directed an international network of 'secret' missionary-agents who very successfully built a massive 'Reformed' underground."[14]

It is probably no coincidence that the first calls for freedom of the press began in the 1500s and that by the 1700s, most European countries had laws protecting press freedom and defining libel and slander. John Milton's *Areopagitica*, the treatise condemning government censorship that has become one of the founding documents for free speech advocates, was not published until 1644 and undoubtedly sprang from Milton's broadly Protestant, though not specifically Calvinistic, worldview.

14. Stark, *For the Glory of God*, 93–94.

The Peculiar Curiosity of the Journalist

So a Reformation understanding of the depravity of man unleashed the corruption story. Another Reformation idea—the sovereignty of God—unleashed human curiosity, perhaps to a degree the Reformers would rue today.

Theologically speaking, Calvin's view of God's sovereignty is manifest in the doctrine of election—the belief that God chooses who will be saved and who will not. Said simply, if God is sovereign, then what we do or fail to do has no ability to save, nor any impact on God's ability to save. He saves whom he will.

But the idea that God is sovereign has implications beyond the strictly theological, or soteriological, realm. This doctrine, filtered through Calvin's worldview lens, declared to Calvin's contemporaries with unprecedented clarity that the whole of creation, the universe in both its expanse and its particulars, belongs to God. Such a worldview gave rise to Abraham Kuyper's comment, applying Calvin's doctrine of the sovereignty of God: "There is not one square inch of this universe about which Jesus does not say, 'It is mine!'" It is also from Kuyper that we find support for the notion that Calvin, not Luther, is the true father of many of the principles and institutions we attribute to the Reformation:

> Luther's starting-point was the . . . principle of justifying faith; while Calvin's . . . lay in the general cosmological principle of the sovereignty of God. . . . [Hence] Lutheranism restricted itself to an exclusively ecclesiastical and theological character, while Calvinism put its impress in and outside the Church upon every department of human life.[15]

Therefore, all of creation, especially ourselves and the mysteries of our hearts, are worthy objects of study for the Christian. Indeed, Calvin's first revisions of the *Institutes*, completed in 1538, included much new

---

15. Abraham Kuyper, *Lectures on Calvinism: The Stone Lectures* (Princeton: Princeton University, 1898), Lecture 1.

material that was by no means theological, including lengthy sections on the proper role of the civil magistrate.[16]

In Calvin's view, God was sovereign over all, and we humans, the stewards over his earthly realm, need not apologize for any exploration of God's universe. So it is not without reason that Christians in all fields of inquiry—from pure and applied science to the fine arts—have turned to Calvin or Calvin's ideas (sometimes not knowing they originated with Calvin, or were at least enlivened by Calvin) for their *raison d'etre.*

But students of journalism know that the curiosity of the journalist is a peculiar one. Modern journalists claim to adhere to a set of ethics that place limits on prurient curiosity. In this, too, journalism owes an intellectual debt to Calvin, who was likewise mindful of the limits of man's inquisitiveness, his curiosity. Consider this passage from Calvin's commentary on Romans, which was addressed to the doctrine of predestination but which might be seen as a warning to all who engage in inquiry without placing moral and ethical limits on the imagination:

> So unreasonable is the curiosity of man, however, that the more perilous the examination of a subject is, the more boldly he proceeds, so that when predestination is discussed he cannot restrain himself within due limits, thus he immediately through his rashness plunges himself, as it were, into the depth of the sea.[17]

It is easy to see how the curiosity of the journalist, or perhaps the willingness of the journalist to satisfy the prurient curiosity of readers, leads us to excess. One needs only walk into the nearest newsstand to find in full view gratuitous examples of sexuality and violence, and as current curiosities are satisfied, yet more gratuitous examples attempt to satisfy yet more exotic curiosities. This sex and violence is no longer limited to those publications or media that specialize in such fare, so-called "men's magazines" or violent movies.

A slight digression provides a telling, even emblematic modern example of Calvin's concern: During the very year of Calvin's five hundredth birthday the tension that exists between man's God-given curiosity about the

16. Gordon, *Calvin*, 91.
17. Cited in Ibid., 115.

world and man's tendency to overreach—to "become as God"—presented itself in the form of an Associated Press (AP) photo. Associated Press is the backbone and bedrock of the journalistic world. It is an association of more than 1,700 newspapers—most of the major newspapers in the world. These papers join the AP to put reporters in the field around the world, and to serve as a kind of cooperative for member papers to have wider distribution of their stories. In addition, the *AP Style Book*, revised annually, essentially defines the basic parameters of news writing in the United States and, indirectly, around the world. Because AP has more than 4,100 employees and member newspapers in 120 countries, it is fair to say that as AP goes, so goes the entire journalistic world.

So when AP decided to publish a photo of mortally wounded Lance Corporal Joshua Bernard immediately after he was hit by a rocket-propelled grenade, outrage and public debate ensued. Secretary of Defense Robert Gates called the decision "appalling." Bernard's family appealed directly to AP not to release the photo. But AP officials said it was their duty to publish the photo to show the "reality of war." In one of the many ironies of this story, government sources became the promoters of a moral standard against the monolithic power of AP when the government-controlled Voice of America wrote: "It's a shame that morality or ethics didn't come in to play when they made this decision."[18]

So modern practitioners of journalism continue to struggle with this tension between curiosity and discernment. However, because most modern journalists, who both reflect and shape the culture they cover, reject such intellectual and theological principles as the sovereignty of God and the sinfulness of man, their struggles to resist their baser instincts have been more or less unsuccessful.

This tension between a belief in God's sovereignty and mankind's sinfulness finds its theological resolution, as we said above, in God's grace.

But how do we resolve this tension between our God-given right, even our duty, to be stewards over all of God's creation, and that curiosity? Even if the curiosity is God-given, we must also confess that it has a tendency to

18. Ryan Christopher DeVault, "Associated Press Distributes Photo of Soldier Mortally Wounded," *VOA News* (September 15, 2009).

be misused. It has a tendency to be, as Calvin said, "unreasonable." It helps to return to theological first principles: Christianity is a "revealed" religion. A God who is transcendent, beyond the reach of human understanding, nonetheless chooses to reveal himself to us—in creation, through Scripture, and in the incarnation. Our duty, Calvin tells us, is to observe and study deeply and thoroughly what God chooses in his sovereignty to reveal to us, but to let our curiosity be satisfied with that. When our curiosity asserts that we should explore those areas that God in his sovereignty and for whatever reason has declared off limits, we then are seeking to exert our will over God's.

Gordon describes Calvin's love-hate relationship with curiosity this way: "The path of wisdom requires one to tread between two evils: ignorance and excessive curiosity. The wise person possesses discernment, a word crucial for Calvin, and knows both what is appropriate and the boundaries beyond which it is forbidden to pass."[19]

So Calvin speaks specifically to the notion of human curiosity, and he thereby speaks directly to the modern journalist, for curiosity has rightly been called the indispensable characteristic of the journalist. Both in Calvin's own life—one typified by a voracious curiosity about mankind and all of God's creation—and in his teachings, we find liberty to exercise our curiosity. But we also find in Calvin ample reason to put limits on that curiosity.

These notions—what Olasky calls the "corruption story" and what I call the "peculiar curiosity" of the journalist—informed journalism for hundreds of years after Calvin's death. When Henry Raymond, a "Bible-believing Presbyterian" who stood firmly in Calvin's shadow, founded *The New York Times* in 1851, the paper immediately became known for its accurate reporting and its exposure of fraud, corruption, and deceit. *The Times* helped expose the politically corrupt "Tweed Ring." But *The Times* also sent an undercover reporter into abortion facilities, and he reported graphically what he saw. Even here, though, we find limits. Consider these closing lines from an 1871 report by Augustus St. Clair on New York City's abortionists:

19. Gordon, *Calvin*, 118.

The facts herein set forth are but a fraction of a greater mass that cannot be published with propriety. Certainly enough is here given to arouse the general public sentiment to the necessity of taking some decided and effectual action.[20]

So some facts were "set forth," but only a "fraction." The "greater mass" could not be published "with propriety." Given that sentiment, it is hard to imagine *The New York Times* of 1871 making the decision to publish the Associated Press photo of Lance Corporal Bernard. Even *The New York Times* of today refused to do so.

Despite the limitations imposed by Augustus St. Clair's "propriety," the public's right to know was apparently not compromised much, because as a direct result of St. Clair's reporting, the public did indeed take decided action, and by the 1880s, abortion had been virtually eradicated from the back alleys of New York City—more than three centuries after Calvin's death, but as a direct consequence of his ideas.[21]

The Rise of the Fourth Estate

But how should that tension between curiosity and discernment, transparency and propriety, be resolved, or at least accommodated, in matters of human behavior and human institutions? Individuals, at least those who hold to a Judeo-Christian or even a vaguely theistic worldview, can possess some greater or lesser degree of wisdom and discernment, that notion so vital to Calvin's understanding. But can institutions?

This question is one of the great themes of Calvin's life and career. The general answer to the question is that checks and balances can and must constantly be placed on human behavior, for we have a tendency toward

20. This discussion is about Calvin's impact on the development of journalism and not his views on issues covered by journalists, but it is perhaps instructive to note Calvin's own words on abortion. He said that the unborn child, "though enclosed in the womb of its mother, is already a human being," and should not be "rob[bed] of the life which it has not yet begun to enjoy." *Calvin's Commentaries* (Grand Rapids: Baker, 1981), 3.42, as cited by Marvin Olasky in *The Press and Abortion, 1838–1988* (Hillsdale, NJ: Lawrence Erlbaum Associates Inc., Publishers, 1988).

21. Marvin Olasky, *Prodigal Press: The Anti-Christian Bias of the American News Media* (Wheaton, IL: Crossway Books, 1988), 20.

evil. The more powerful our institutions, be they church or government, the more robust must be these checks and balances.

Calvin and the other Reformers saw that tendency toward evil most plainly manifest in the Roman Catholic Church. Throughout Calvin's career, as he often railed against the corruption and hubris of the institutional church, he nonetheless turned respectfully to the work of Roman Catholic theologians.

Calvin's legal training and his general temperament led him to be in the forefront of establishing emerging institutions. Perhaps the best known of the institutions that Calvin had a direct role in shaping was the Consistory. The Consistory performed a number of functions, but it is most easily described as a court made of church elders that tried cases involving members of the church. In general, these cases were violations of church order, but violations of church law were often, especially in the early modern era, violations of civil law as well. Serious cases were sometimes adjudicated by the Consistory, but sentencing was left to civil authorities.

But we need go no further than Calvin's own Consistory to see how man's institutions inevitably tend to overreach. Robert Kingdon says that as Calvin grew older and his authority became more absolute in Geneva, the Consistory became increasingly intrusive. He estimates that as many as 7 percent of Genevans appeared before the Consistory each year.[22] The Consistory ultimately became a cause of resentment for the people of Geneva.

Of course, the notion that power leads to corruption is not a new one. Lord Acton's expression of the notion is perhaps the most succinct: "Power tends to corrupt, and absolute power corrupts absolutely." However, the overreaching of the powerful is one of the recurring themes of human existence. The story of the Tower of Babel, from early in Genesis, is perhaps man's first attempt to use his institutional power to become "as gods."

So one of the ironies of Calvin's life is that while he "spoke truth to power," his own power and influence ultimately made him one of the powers to whom others needed to speak truth.

To Calvin's credit, he recognized this "will to power" even in himself, and one of the great contributions of Calvin to church governance is the

22. Kingdon, *Wars of Religion in France*, 180–81.

presbyterian system, which distributes power rather than centralizes it, and which tends to prevent any one man from wielding too much authority. This presbyterian system found its secular expression in the federal system of government that became the basis of the American experiment in liberty: a system of checks and balances, with the three branches of government exercising power but being limited by both constitutional (contractual) limits, and by the power of the other branches. The promise of a free press, embedded in the First Amendment to the Constitution, might therefore be thought of as a direct descendant of Calvin's paternity.

Ideas and the Consequences

John Calvin certainly did not invent or practice journalism. Some of us who practice the vocation of journalism look not ultimately to Calvin, but to Scripture itself, for the earliest models of ethical journalism. When God tells Adam to "name the animals" in Genesis 2, we find a description of what the ethical journalist does every day: he looks deeply into the nature of things and tries to say what he sees. At the other end of the Bible, in Revelation, we hear Jesus' instructions to John: "Write down what you see." A newspaper editor cannot read that line without smiling; how many times have they given their own reporters the same instruction?

So while Calvin may not have been the first modern journalist, his ideas and the institutions that came into being as a result of his ideas made modern journalism possible. Calvin sought to reform the church, and he and the other Reformers did so to greater and lesser degrees. But more than reforming the institutional church, Calvin unleashed the Church Militant, the holy catholic (small c) church, the Body of Christ. By doing so, Calvin was not only instrumental in a particular historical period we call the Reformation, but he was also instrumental in establishing ideas and institutions that would, or at least could, allow for ongoing and continual reformation of both the church and the culture in which it is called to be salt and light.

We come, therefore, to this conclusion: that in the consequences of Calvin's ideas the biblical promise that "we shall know the truth and the truth shall set us free" comes to its practical, cultural application.

Calvin said it this way in the opening line of the *Institutes*: "Nearly the whole of sacred doctrine consists in these two parts: knowledge of God and of ourselves."

This twin pursuit—the knowledge of God and of ourselves—was for centuries the hope of modern journalism. Many working journalists operated unconsciously in that milieu, although some, like Henry Raymond in his founding of *The New York Times*, were explicit about this very Calvinistic mission. The fact that journalists of the past century have abandoned that mission, or at least half of that mission, and care more about "ourselves" and less about God, is a topic for another day, except to say this: One could easily trace a straight line from the abandonment of the "knowledge of God" as a pursuit of journalism both to the coarsening of culture and to the current low estate of the credibility and economic viability of many journalistic outlets, including *The New York Times* itself.

However, as I said, tracing that line is a topic for another day. On this day, we must be content to leave the subject with this: Calvin's great pursuit—"the knowledge of God and of ourselves"—was the energizing principle that made modern journalism one of the most powerful and positive forces in history. Calvin's ideas made modern journalism if not inevitable at least possible. The truly great journalism of the past five hundred years has passionately pursued knowledge of both God and man. The extent that journalism can recover these twin pursuits clearly put before us by Calvin is the extent to which journalism can be great again.

13

THE FUTURE OF CALVINISM AS A WORLDVIEW

DAVID W. HALL

To provide a type of conclusion for our Calvin 500 celebrations and this published series, as well as to proffer a concluding unscientific apology for this final volume, I shall attempt to speak to two remaining questions:

- Did Calvin intend to project a unified worldview, comprehending many of the liberal arts subjects discussed in this volume? Or would he distance himself from a comprehensive worldview?
- Does Calvinism as a worldview have a future? And, if so, what contours might it take?

Frequently, essays and sermons from our Calvin Quincentenary commenced with a comment to the effect that, were John Calvin alive today, he would be red-faced or scandalized by the attention being paid to him and his life's work in 2009. What can one make of this common cognitive

dissonance between the descendants of Calvin who seek to applaud him
and Calvin's own sincere humility? Either Calvin's children are besmirching
his reputation by adding fame to one who did not seek it, or the worthiness
of the many tributes may be an unintended consequence of a well-lived
life that has merited such commemorations.

At the conclusion of this commemorative cycle, if I may be so bold,
I should like to argue with a vengeance for the latter interpretation. To
predict the conclusion: it is most likely that the reason Calvin is still
remembered as a worldview shaper a half millennium after his birth—and
likely will continue to be, and rightly so—is that, despite his constitutional
avoidance of the limelight, his character, ideas, and the institutions that
flowed from his sincerely and promptly offered heart not only have altered
dramatically the landscape of the past five hundred years but will probably
do so for the next five hundred.

And all without Calvin seeking notoriety.

Yes, Calvinism has generated a worldview, large and lasting institutions, and a tradition that is growing, rather than heading toward extinc-
tion. It may even be that a corollary of our commemoration is that to the
extent that individuals and communions seek to appreciate and embrace
authentic Calvinism, they are fueled; to the degree that one is ashamed of
his Calvinistic genealogy and seeks to distance himself from it, one may
unwittingly be on the downward slide. The future will prove or disprove
that axiom.

What follows on the second query is also a shameless takeoff on the
title of a 1976 paper by Ford Lewis Battles, who is both a better scholar
and more perceptive than most of us. Nonetheless, since no one else in our
volumes has targeted this exact subject, I am happy for the opportunity
to gather my thoughts and share them below.

First, it must be noted that the properly infrequent celebration
of great historical events makes it difficult to denerate a pattern or
operational folder to follow or by which to evaluate various centenaries. Each commemoration will, of necessity, be somewhat different.
Furthermore, if patterns are not readily available, there are also few
templates for the kind of assessment of Calvin and his life that we have
intended to provide in this year and through this series, since so few

movements thrive and survive for five hundred years. One can easily list movements and worldviews that have endured for a few decades, only to be tossed in the rubbish bin of yesterday's faddism, or some that have lasted for a century—think for example of how permanent the Cold War era thought communism to be, but its Soviet brand fell short of lasting a century (1917–89)—or of a few (mostly religion-based) that have lasted for multiple centuries. Discarded ideas, fads, and movements will continue to depend on historians or encyclopedias for any reference, especially if collective memories continue to manifest amnesia. Notwithstanding, few even of the strongest of intellectual currents have avoided a killing drought for a period of five centuries or more. Calvinism is one of the very few and should be recognized as such, even with its strengths and weaknesses admitted.

So how do we measure the incline or decline of Calvinism over five centuries? It certainly spread rapidly from 1536 (Calvin's first arrival in Geneva) to 1776, becoming the popular choice of many in the democratic West. Perhaps it even reached a zenith in Europe in the 1640s and later in America in the 1770s, only to begin a steep descent. Calvinism's ups and downs are further seen in its swift demise and unconditional surrender to the paper tiger of Unitarianism in the mid-1700s in Europe, and to Enlightenment dilution in the late 1700s and early 1800s in Britain and America, its erstwhile strongholds. By the mid-twentieth century, Calvinism was either an embarrassment or viewed as on its way toward certain obsolescence, likely before it would ever mark the five hundredth anniversary of Calvin's birth.

However, echoing the sentiments of Mark Twain, the early reports of Calvinism's demise may have been overtrumpeted. It may, in fact, now be headed for the largest expansion and rooting that it has witnessed since the 1550s. A short contrast for a mere half-century stretch begins to set the stage for this ensuing discussion.

In 1959,[1] we found:

---

1. Fred Kaplan's recent social history, *1959: The Year Everything Changed*, traces the great cultural distance between 1959 and 2009. However, I think that distance is even greater if applied to Calvinism in particular. Fred Kaplan, *1959: The Year Everything Changed* (Hoboken, NJ: John Wiley and Sons, 2009).

+ Only black-and-white TVs, and at most one in each home.
+ No PCs or Internet.
+ No modern English translations of the *Institutes* available.
+ Research holdings of Calvinalia were rare and mainly European.

In contrast, today:

+ Most American homes have two or three TVs, each with a stunning array of sizes, pixilation, and channel selection.
+ PCs are more affordable and common than ever, and the Internet—started by a Swiss lab and further developed by the U.S. Defense Department—is truly worldwide and within arm's reach of most people.
+ Since the publication of Ford Lewis Battles's translation of Calvin's magnum opus in 1960, dozens of versions of the *Institutes* have been published, along with thousands of scholarly and practical commentaries on Calvin and his work.
+ Multiple study centers and research centers exist on every continent, except Antarctica. Moreover, with the spread of technology and the sharing of resources, each of these probably surpasses the data of all but four or five such centers in 1959.

What changes might we expect over the next fifty years?

+ Extension of life spans into the 90s will mean an expansion of productivity by Calvinist scholars. When the Beatles asked rhetorically in the mid-1960s, "Will you still need me, will you still feed me, when I'm 64?" that ripe old age was viewed as a normal upper extremity; today, the majority of healthy individuals live into their 80s. If one might have been expected to publish until 60 or 65 in 1959, consider Robert Kingdon's, J. I. Packer's, and Richard Muller's final *vitae* (which all may yet be exceeded by those of Herman Selderhuis, John Witte, and Joel Beeke). Ligon Duncan, Michael Horton, or Philip Ryken might well preach at Calvin 550.
+ All the *Corpus Reformatorum* will be on a handheld device in one's pocket or on a Kindle device, yielding instant access to a

catholic database of Calvin's writings and analyses by others. A servant-spirited Calvinism will use the technology for long-term projects. Scholars who care about productivity, innovation, and original contributions will accomplish much, as long as they are less intent on receiving credit for some aspect of Calvin research. A democratization of the database of Calvinism will aid progress in many areas.

+ Language barriers, either in print or dialogue, can be overcome instantly: Google translation, for example, and other software programs will allow students and scholars to leap over the Tower of Babel for constructive Calvin dialogue.

+ Calvinism could well become based outside the West, with far more adherents in the global East or South than the West. Some of today's finest centers—such as Seoul, Brazil, Ukraine, Nairobi, or Australia—could replace Edinburgh, Geneva, Princeton, or Grand Rapids as centers of Calvinism. Think of "Phillip Jensen meets John Calvin," along with the impact among millions in developing nations that will surely catch the technical capabilities of others.

+ A "canon of received results" that is less ideological and faddish will undoubtedly arise. Over time, as long as dissent and critique are allowed to redress, a professional guild will balance the findings of Calvinism (think of the recent social history by Phillip Benedict, for example). Over time, certain urban legends, inaccuracies, myths, and old wives' tales may be retired as Web sites such as Snopes. Calvin.com or CalvinSmokinggun.com may be created to put out the fires of half-truth and bias. Once it is no longer necessary to squander time extinguishing those fires, Calvin scholarship can be even more productive, more heuristic.

+ Instant publishing will accelerate all research. Rather than waiting months or years for the latest study, these can become almost instantaneous, dramatically hastening the speed in which corrections and refinements are made.

Future decades may show that a long cycle of decline has bottomed, and Calvinism is on the way back! A couple of young British authors have a book on the *New York Times* best-seller list that is titled: *God is Back!* Could that be a hint of the future of Calvinism? If, as we think, it is a genuinely superior system of doctrine, then once irrational factors are muted, it should regain ground. We may be witnessing that cyclical revival, following two centuries of loathing by hostile critics.

Such assessment is one reason periodic renewals and commemorations are important! If such gatherings are used to call us back to God and his ways, then they are positive.

Notwithstanding, since none of us are endowed with predictive prophetic gifts, maybe it would be helpful to review highlights of success and failure. These might protect us and keep us on track as we face the future.

What worked and what didn't for Calvinism over the last half a millennium?[2]

Five Large Success Stories

Receiving Immigrants while Persuading and Assimilating Them

Calvin's Geneva doubled in population during his lifetime, and he welcomed Italian, Polish, French, and English exiles. He was probably not strategic enough to consider how they would return to their countries of origin and radiate the truths they learned in Geneva. More likely, he was simply doing his Christian duty, but he did not insist on ethnic homogeneity. Calvin discipled all *ethnoi*, knowing that being in *imago dei*, each could be an ambassador of God.

Spreading Calvinism through Educational Centers

Calvin's Academy, which was modeled on those in Lausanne and Strasbourg, taught thousands and trained the next generation of leaders. Over time, wherever Calvinist ministers planted churches (Nyon, Neuchatel, Lyon, etc.), academies popped up. Calvin sensed early on that ideas had consequences, and he sought to cultivate those in the most positive way.

2. This outline for successes and failures was used in a sermon, "Reformation, Calvinism, and Lessons Learned," David W. Hall, ed., *Sermons Commemorating John Calvin* (Phillipsburg, NJ: P&R Publishing, 2010), but is expanded here and tailored to this context.

Implanting Calvinists in Civil Leadership Sectors

Many of the refugees to Geneva were from the nobility in their countries. Accordingly, Calvinism spawned more disciples in the ruling classes than most other branches of the Reformation. Leaders such as Admiral Coligny and readers such as the king of Poland were impressed with Calvin's reforms. Seeking strategic leaders is one of the successes of the early Calvinists. Whether fully intentional or not, Calvinism's spread was aided by the sympathies of leaders, nobles, and rulers.

Fueling Calvinism by Infusing Economies

Calvinism virtually transformed the commerce and business of the day. Modern market-based economies finally were liberated and found their buttresses in the Calvinistic work ethic, in the tendency to invest, and through the business leaders of Reformed churches. Calvinism likely would not have spread without this favorable economic climate, which it used optimally. Certain business connections may still be rapid transfer agents of Calvinism.

Codifying Truth via Catechisms, Classic Works, and Regular Preaching

Calvinists were quite successful in crystallizing the faith. They drafted catechisms and adopted creeds wherever they went. As such, their influence quickly became multigenerational, all very logo-centric, and preaching became the news of the day, good or otherwise. The practice of setting down consensual truth permits less retrogression than if each generation or community has to discover all truth by itself.

Such were some of the Calvinist methods that succeeded and that will probably guide us for the future. However, there were and are glaring errors as well.

Notorious Calvinist Failures

Pettiness, Censoriousness

From the earliest disagreement with Luther (perhaps not so much Calvin's fault as from the stridency of Dr. Luther), Calvinists have, regrettably, been notorious for splitting hairs and communion with each other. Often there is more concern about a leader's status and recognition, and it is not uncommon to have a judgmental demeanor that hardly attracts converts. Focusing mainly on one's agenda has been a large Calvinist failure.

Racial Discrimination

In certain geographical areas, some of God's children were viewed as second- (or third-) class citizens by certain aristocratic Calvinists. Calvin himself, of course, did not succumb to this, but some disciples crafted ingenious and self-serving rationales to discriminate against races. Future Calvinism, if it is to succeed, must avoid this mistake.

Class Orientation as if Only Upper Classes Could Benefit from Calvinism

Similarly, because many of the original Calvinists were wealthy or from the nobility or aristocracy, it was an easy confusion to think that Calvinism only came to full blossom among privileged elites. To the degree that Calvinists become mono-classists, they will lose people to the socialism of the day or some other popular movement.

Affair with Unitarianism and Socinianism

Calvinism, perhaps because of its emphasis on the mind, became easy prey to new rationalistic movements. Socinius and his children, the Unitarians, quickly recovered much territory that Calvin's disciples had won—and it never returned to the Calvinist column. While we wish to harness the intellect, both compromise with the world and arrogance from educational successes can lead future Calvinism astray.

Attempting to Rule by Force

Calvinists must recall that "though the wrong seems oft so strong, God is the ruler yet," and that we cannot force human consciences to agree with or submit to our particular faith. Often the zeal that accompanies Reformation movements becomes quite regrettable down the road. Mature statesmen and wise counselors must call those back from the brink if they move into behaving as if they may conquer by political or external might.

Another very difficult thing to resist is the altering of the ancient faith in the attempt to make it relevant for the future. It is difficult to make the case that Calvinists have been very good at this. All too often the church or its leaders have been seduced by the sirens of contemporaneity. How tempting to be conformed to the patterns of this world. Perhaps this five hundredth celebration will remind us to use care in translating the faith in the future: for something precious can be lost in the translation. However, it must be translated.

The future translations of faith that echo the name of Calvin might be tested by these hallmarks that we have observed repeatedly in our own quincentenary:

1. It downplays the grandeur of unredeemed man. Sin, in other words, must always be preached.
2. It champions the power of God (not an institution or self) to change our world. Calvinism does not depend on technique but on spiritual power.
3. It opposes wrong schemes of earthly power (hierarchicalism), and espouses dispersed power.
4. It calls us to take our living faith into the marketplace of ideas.
5. It is Trinitarian, calling us to carry the cross and to trust the Spirit.

A Final Question

Based on this, *will future success deviate from past patterns of success?* Probably not, or at least there is little reason to think so. The faith that will win cultures and triumph over human evil will most likely:

1. Hold to God's truth from age to age. It will be confident enough in scriptural truth that the tendency to compromise diminishes in comparison with the greatness of God. The awareness that the church, our lives, and Scripture are enduring inspires perseverance even when times are tough.

2. Target education.
3. Seek to translate into the vernacular, without neutering the content. As G. K. Chesterton advised, we do not retain originality by letting things sit but by repainting fenceposts their original color, again and again.
4. Use strong local churches to keep the flame burning. Calvin knew there was no substitute for the local church. Despite the grandest of schools, organizations, or institutions, the church will remain vital.
5. Include missions and colonizing as regular parts of people's lives

The Spread of Calvinism and Why It Doesn't Die

This year I wondered: Do you think John Calvin might be surprised five centuries after his birth to find three men of African descent in his pulpit for Calvin 500? Or to find more Calvinists in the Southern Baptist Convention than in the Presbyterian Church in America? It was sheer joy to note the participation by the many brothers and sisters below in our Genevan celebration.

- At least one of the "guardians" (deaconal assistants) at Geneva's St. Pierre Cathedral was a Turkish Kurd, having come to the faith.
- Koreans and Chinese populated Geneva and may be the leading visitors to this area.
- The largest seating capacity for a sanctuary of any Reformed Church (5,000) is in downtown Jakarta, Indonesia, a church pastored by a Chinese Calvinist, Dr. Stephen Tong.
- Chinese Calvinism is growing and may prove to be one of the most exciting stories of our century.
- Africans blessed us with the sermon by a most humble Archbishop (of Uganda) Henry Orombi, and with his assistant, Onesimus Asiimwe. On another occasion, the Rev. Dr. Setri Nyomi (of Ghana), president of the World Alliance of Reformed Churches, welcomed us as brothers and sisters.

+ Our church supports a strong Calvinist in Haiti, the Rev. Jean Paul with Reformation Hope International. He knows that the hope for Haiti is the Reformed faith.
+ We met Vimaal, originally from Northern Ireland, but who is leading a German Gypsy ministry in Fribourg im Breisgau.
+ Sebastian Heck, from our presbytery and a former intern at Grace Presbyterian in Douglasville, Georgia, is replanting a Reformed denomination in Heidelberg, Germany.

Conferences on Calvin this year were held in such unlikely places as:

Rome
St. Petersburg, Russia
Prague
South Africa
Toronto
Boston
Holland
France
New Zealand
Australia
South Carolina
California

Dr. Michael Milton of Reformed Theological Seminary (Charlotte) calls this "Global Calvinism" because it is catholic/biblical Calvinism. And that Calvinism is spreading.

How Living Calvinism is Expanding Today

Who would have imagined the following news stories before the first half of this year:

+ The number three potent idea in a *CNN/Time* poll in April 2009 was "New Calvinism."

- More books have been published on Calvin this year than in any previous year. For example, Calvin500.com has released a CD that contains 97 volumes of Calvin materials.
- University campuses, especially in the East, are cropping up with independent young scholars who dare to question tradition, and in so doing find that Calvinism is one of the few ideological platforms that is both stable and capable of transforming dated structures.
- The *New York Times*, *Washington Post*, and *USA Today*, over the birthday week of Calvin, each featured a piece on the significance of Calvinism, even if begrudgingly. Later, in its September issue, *Christianity Today* would call Calvin "the Comeback Kid."
- National Public Radio did a story on "Calvinmania" sweeping Europe, while CBN carried a feature on Calvin's anniversary.
- A thousand people gathered in Boston over the July Fourth weekend to recall the virtues and energy of the Reformation.
- Vibrant, local churches celebrated in their own ways, and many tours visited historical sites of the Reformation.

Calvinists of all stripes surely view this year's memorial not as a terminating eulogy but as another launching pad.

Finally, *will Calvinism last because of Calvin?*

Calvinism carried a burden with it: to prove the superiority of God's ways over the transient ways of man and earthly society. Fully believing that they had lasting truth, Calvinists bravely launched forth into new worlds, into hostile civic environments, and into new fields. Original Calvinists were unafraid to challenge centuries-long usury standards, and thus opened up marketplaces. Early children of Calvin boldly confronted the Roman authority structure and have, since the death of Calvin, provided the world with a strong bias toward democracy.

Why will Calvinism last? Not because of John Calvin, but because of how close he drew to the truths God gave us. Should any of Calvin's followers wish, then, to make enduring contributions, adherence to eternal truths must be the perennial target and measurement.

Ford Lewis Battles in his 1976 "The Future of Calviniana" asked whether Calvinism could survive in the modern world. Even more so, that query is legitimate now. His astute answer then was only if "first, it is known; secondly, believed, and thirdly, practiced."[3] That sage advice sums up the goals of this work and our Calvin Quincentenary. Even if many of the surviving oil paintings of Calvin show no upturned smile on the lips of the Reformer, we believe the Father of Calvinism might involuntarily grin at these prospects.

---

3. Ford Lewis Battles, "The Future of Calviniana," in *Renaissance, Reformation, and Resurgence: Papers and Responses Presented at the Colloquium on Calvin and Calvin Studies,* ed. Peter De Klerk (Grand Rapids: Calvin Theological Seminary, 1976).

INDEX OF SCRIPTURE

Index of Subjects and Names

311

CONTRIBUTORS

Richard C. Chewning is emeritus professor of business at Baylor University in Waco, Texas.

William C. Davis is professor of philosophy at Covenant College in Lookout Mountain, Georgia.

William Edgar is professor of apologetics at Westminster Theological Seminary in Philadelphia.

John M. Frame is J. D. Trimble Chair of Systematic Theology and Philosophy at Reformed Theological Seminary, Orlando.

David W. Hall is senior pastor of Midway Presbyterian Church in Powder Springs, Georgia.

Darryl G. Hart is visiting professor of church history at Westminster Seminary in California.

Paul S. Jones is organist and music director at Tenth Presbyterian Church in Philadelphia.

Paul Marshall is senior fellow at the Hudson Institute in Washington, DC.

Marvin Padgett is Vice President-Editorial for P&R Publishing.

Franklin E. (Ed) Payne is associate professor of family medicine, retired, at the Medical College of Georgia in Augusta.

Don Petcher is professor of science at Covenant College in Lookout Mountain, Georgia.

Leland Ryken is Clyde S. Kilby Professor of English at Wheaton College in Wheaton, Illinois.

Warren Cole Smith is associate publisher of *World* Magazine.

Timothy D. Terrell is associate professor of economics at Wofford College in Spartanburg, South Carolina.

John Witte Jr. is Director of the Center for the Study of the Law and Religion and Jonas Robitscher Professor of Law at Emory University Law School in Atlanta.